DeFOREST KELLEY:

A HARVEST OF MEMORIES

My Life and Times with a Remarkable Gentleman Actor

by

Kristine M. Smith

ISBN: 0-75965-308-9

This book is printed on acid free paper.

Illustrations by DeForest Kelley. DeForest Kelley's poetry reprinted by permission of Carolyn Kelley. Photographs by Bill Dow, Sue Keenan, Carolyn Kelley, Dorothea Smith and the author. Front cover photo by Bill Dow.

"For Once In My Life" lyrics by Ron Miller, Music by Orlando Murden

1stBooks - rev. 10/19/01

DEDICATION

Dedicated to the memory of my beloved "serval son," Deaken,

because DeForest Kelley believed Deaken richly deserved a book dedication.

FOREWORD

"The evil that men do live after them;
the good is oft interred with their bones." Shakespeare

If the above is true – as sadly, it usually is – this book wouldn't have been written, couldn't have been written. DeForest Kelley was never a bad guy, except in movies and in hundreds of television series episodes. At his memorial service on June 22, 1999, on the verge of tears, I stated, "In my opinion, DeForest Kelley was the kind of man God had in mind when He created Adam. If this sad old world could boast a much larger population of DeForest Kelley types, it would indeed be the paradise we all wish it was."

DeForest Kelley – the person, not the actor – became (without trying) such a monumental part of my personal architecture that I'd crumble without his spirit and legacy to support me. I'm not built, or even retrofitted, to withstand a 10.0 magnitude fracture to my superstructure. "De" was a mentor, a guardian, and a devoted friend. I respected him, treasured him, and honored him. His goodness continues.

After reading this book, you will understand all this. He was a decent, gentle, kind human being. He was all of these things, nearly all of the time, which comes close to qualifying him for sainthood in my judgment. You will also understand, I think, why De laughed so heartily all those times I tried to cajole him into writing his own autobiography "before it's too late." I joked once, "You know, De, if YOU don't write it, and *I* end up writing, it may inadvertently launch a new world religion!"

All this might lead you to wonder if he was perhaps too kind for his own good — so kind as to be ineffective when toughness or tenacity mattered. Not so. He was effective and he was tough in the ways that matter in life. I learned a lot watching and listening to him. I sincerely hope some of it rubbed off…

The last 90 days of De's life, I became his personal assistant and caregiver, in the hospital and out and about. Carolyn, his beloved wife, best friend and ally for nearly 60 years, was herself confined to a hospital and to a bed, walker or wheelchair so through De's last days I was their companion, caregiver and advocate. With no children of their own the Kelleys were accustomed to and happiest when taking care of each other. Nonetheless, the time came when De needed extra help to tie up loose ends. He needed efficient, reliable transportation between the hospital and his home, doctor, bank and attorney. He wanted a trusted ally to take in and then recall all that was said at the different meetings with these professionals. Once in a while he just needed to see his own home, look out at his garden, take a shower in his own shower stall, and have a nap in his own bed. These few, cherished outings to his home, lasting just a few hours each, never failed to refresh his spirit and they definitely promoted a peaceful, optimistic outlook within him. He'd forget, for several hours at a stretch, just how desperately ill he was.

Oddly enough, I probably spent more "up close and personal" time with De the first month after I was called in to assist him in the hospital than I had in the entire 32 year span I'd known him up until that point. It wasn't necessary to spend a lot of time with De Kelley in order to discover how special he was. The innate GOODNESS he revealed – even during crisis, tragedy or adversity – shined through, in the many hues of a rainbow: brilliantly and vibrantly. He was truly "good people."

When I got the call about De on March 14th, 1999, it devastated me. There had been no forewarning. My mind and body weren't prepared. I nearly lost consciousness from the shock and sadness I felt, which came in waves for hours afterward. The Kelleys, two years previously, confided to me the fact that De had undergone some surgery, but in order to protect me from worthless worry and anxiety, they had told a little white lie and said the tumor the doctors found was benign, and that all was well. They were upbeat; De began to feel better; he appeared at several conventions; we chatted on the phone hundreds of times, and I went merrily on, blissfully unaware, believing that fate had dealt the Kelleys a lucky hand…

I don't know how many of you have participated in a course of care and treatment for a terminally ill loved one. Based on my experience, it is one of the most unsettling and at the same time one of the most rewarding experiences a person can have. It is knowing, going in, that – short of a medical or God-given miracle – the individual you are helping is NOT going to recover. In fact, they are going to deteriorate progressively until there are times you feel like running from the room and crying your eyes out – but you can't! It is knowing that DESPITE your dedication and devotion, despite all those hours and those truly Herculean efforts, your loved one is going to lose the battle and perish – and more than likely, you are going to be right there when they do, at their bedside, holding their hand. People fearful of death or of the possibility of physical or emotional suffering experienced by the dying often cannot endure it. Usually it's a job left to medical people, or to folks with an ability to transcend their fear and loathing during a tragic situation who have the grit and the spirituality necessary to be able to step up to the plate and say, "Let me help."

Certainly, it came as a big shock to get the call. De was in the terminal stages of cancer and was in an intensive care unit in a local hospital. Could I lend a hand? Could I?! OF COURSE! I could certainly lend a hand, and my ONLY liver and a kidney, if that would help, as well! "I'm your girl!"

What follows are my own personal "life and times" with DeForest Kelley, from the first time I met him as a teenager in Washington State in May, 1968, until his last day on earth, June 11, 1999. While this narrative is mostly upbeat, fun, poignant, funny, and heartwarming – which is what 98% of being in De's presence was all about — the final days may disturb you in some places. It is quite likely that you LOVED DeForest Kelley wholeheartedly, whether as a personal friend, business associate, or from afar, in the outermost reaches of fandom. I have been honest throughout. I have also taken great care to be sensitive to your needs as fans and readers so that I would not unduly upset you when delving into "end stage" events. I know you want the truth. The truth is he was magnificent.

De and I discussed, numerous times, the possibility of my writing his biography. De wanted to be involved in any such recounting of his life and times – with which I heartily concurred. Toward the end, with more pressing concerns occupying our time and minds, we eventually understood and accepted the fact that he'd never be able to concentrate on the monumental task of reflecting publicly and extensively on his life. He then gave me permission to go ahead and write about him; a huge and marvelous gift. Fortunately, following his passing, most of his long-time personal friends and business associates filled in a lot of the blanks, and enough information was assembled for my collaborator, Terry Lee Rioux, to write a remarkable, affecting and thorough tome about De's life and career. It will be available in the near future.

This particular effort is my public salute to De, the man I knew and loved through the best of times and the worst of times. De showed us how to live, and he showed us how to die. He did both with grace, humor, hope and endlessly enduring love.

The world is a better place because he trod here — mindfully and with the indwelling gentleness of a true spiritual champion.

Kris Smith
North Hollywood, CA
September 8, 2001

ACKNOWLEDGMENTS

When it comes to bringing a manuscript to life, it often seems the loneliest of tasks, until one realizes that standing behind each belabored draft are dozens of faith-filled associates and friends who are expecting nothing less than Something Fantastic. There are, additionally, family members who wonder, fretfully, whether lightning will strike and turn their relative into the talk of the town – or into the laughingstock of the planet.

It's always a crapshoot, for the writer as well as for those in the peanut gallery, wondering what will come of the seemingly-endless hours in enforced, intense isolation. I'm sure at least a few worried, "Has she died? Why hasn't she phoned or answered my e-mail?"

This is the place to acknowledge all the people I abandoned during the two months I was giving birth to this book. I'm sure they understood the intense concentration it took to create something that would hang together from first page to last. I think they also understood that this book was — for me — an extended de-briefing and therapy session, during which I again acknowledged my most grievous losses and counted my many, many blessings. Each and every time I chuckled, laughed, giggled, guffawed or roared while recounting many happy instances of my life and times with DeForest Kelley, I ended up crying for several minutes, as well. That's what happens when the rug is pulled out from under you and there is no way to get back to the place where your life was everything you ever wanted it to be.

My friends are almost too numerous to mention, but a few actually helped save my sanity while I navigated the territory we will cover in the last part of this memoir. I want to acknowledge them first. At Warner Bros., my bosses, co-workers, and associates in Technical Support had to hold me together without even knowing what was up until the very end. Dan Kronstadt, my boss and supervisor, is the only person who knew what was happening from Day One (March 14th, 1999). Al Foitag, Dan Alpern and Dorothy Gelhar, my other bosses, had to largely intuit that Something Was Terribly Amiss and that I was in the throes of some sort of personal crisis. Without questioning me, they gave me the leeway I needed to "be there" for De during the three months prior to his death on June 11th, which meant that they had to do without my services a great deal. They knew I wasn't normally a flake, and that's ALL they knew – and that's what they relied on. I thank them for having that kind of faith in me. I couldn't have done what I did for De without this rock-solid foundation of unquestioning support.

Kim Ann Lieberman, Greg Heimbigner, Maria Thompson, Carol Ranken and others at Warner Bros. were also kept in the dark as to exactly what was transpiring until days before I took my Leave of Absence on May 4th. Nevertheless, they became "guardian angels" during my travails. They stayed close, creating an atmosphere of love and comfort that I don't think I could have been without, without cracking up.

Office of Emergency Services people at Warner Bros. – specifically, Mario Guerra, Norma Ruiz de Maldonado and Nancy Mathews – held me together a time or two – literally. Their comforting, encouraging words and hugs kept returning my nervous system to "functional" from "frantic." They know their stuff. I'm living proof. Additionally, their incomparable training sessions helped me to save my nephew's life. How can I possibly thank them enough for that?

At home, compassionate and concerned neighbors Mario and Amada Abelleira, Harriet Rempel, Nayna Patel and Alice Sandkamp became my frequent walking partners during three mile treks designed to keep me from "stressing out." I lied and told them the walk was for physical fitness; it was actually for mental health. So they became physically fit and I remained 99% sane. In the bargain, I made friends that will endure in my heart forever. Special thanks to Alice Sandkamp, who – during the course of writing this manuscript — would call or pop her head in the window once or twice a day to ask, "Are you remembering to eat?" On days when I had to confess, "No," she would prepare me a delicious, delightful meal! I imagine the Sandkamp grocery bill escalated a bit as a result. Thanks, Alice and George (Alice's honey of a husband)!

Other friends in deed (especially while in need) were Nancy Graf in Carmichael, California, Reggie Holloway in Turlock, California, Sandy Zier-Teitler of Elkridge, Maryland, Melody Adams in Tacoma, Washington and of course my collaborator, Terry Lee Rioux, historian and the author of an upcoming biography of De. Their love, support and steadfast faith buoyed me up and never let me fall. I love all of you beyond expression.

This manuscript first went to two women in the Data Center at Warner Bros. – Tasnim Fernandez and Deanna Patellis – and to the aforementioned Terry Lee Rioux and Sandy Zier-Teitler. They read the longest, unedited, most convoluted version of this saga and helped me edit it into a document worthy of being called a manuscript. All they could expect to get out of it was eye-strain and a complimentary copy of the published version. And now this acknowledgment. It is nowhere near enough. Thank you, from the bottom of my heart!

At 1stBooks, John Glasscock and Paul Crawl, technical services gurus, helped format, illustrate and web-able this book so it would please you, the reader. I thank them profusely for making it look so good! (Had I done this part myself, you would KNOW how much their contribution means! "Damn it, Jim, I'm a writer, not a publisher!") The publicity department at 1stBooks shouldered the responsibility of making sure you could find and buy this book. Thanks for the spotlight, Gregory Ryhal, Emily Burson and gang!

I want to acknowledge, as well, my late, great mother Dorothea, who you will also love once you get to know a little about her. My father, Jack, passed away just six months after De, and two months before I started this manuscript. For all the grief Dad and I caused the other through the years, there was never any doubt that we were crazy about each other. I only wish they were here now to read this. (Somehow I think they are.)

Another late and great must be mentioned. My junior high school English and creative writing teacher, Alpha Rossetti, believed in my talent long before anyone else did. She was the one responsible for my first two-year subscription to THE WRITER all those years ago when all I had to hang my hopes on was a high-falutin' dream that seemed impossible for a kid to achieve.

And to Mr. Walter Dobbs, my high school writing teacher and drama coach, I say not only thank you, but WHERE ARE YOU?! If not for you, NONE of this part of my life would have happened at all. It was YOU who insisted that I send that first letter and article to "Mr. Kelley." I owe you one, Mister! Get in touch with me, will you?

My sisters, Jackie Mullens and Laurel Smith, must be mentioned. They comprise the remaining embodiments of my nuclear family, and are beyond dear to me. We've been through a lot together the past three and a half years, and it has brought us far closer than ever before. Although they are far away in distance, they are as close as my next breath in spirit.

Evelyn "Tod" Fremault, my aunt, was there for me, as well, via frequent phone calls and cards, reminding me that God never gives us more than He knows we can handle. (There were a few times when I came close to forgetting that.) Sage advice from a lady who has had more than her fair share of trials and tribulations.

There are a number of Kelley friends to thank: neighbor Don especially, followed by mail carrier Tony Kirk, Grace Griffin, Joe Laden, John Stecko, lawn care maestro Ted Naruo, handiest of handymen Allen Knighton, Tereza and Bill Campbell, Harve Bennett, Nichelle Nichols, aviatrix and barnstormer Aileen Pickering, Anne Jolly, Florene Collard, and godson Tony LaFatta. A residual bonus to assisting the Kelleys is that it afforded me the opportunity to meet and glom onto their incomparable friends. What a treat!

I also want to acknowledge my dear friend Sue Keenan. I don't think I've ever had more fun – or ever will again — than I did with Sue all those years ago when we first collided and became DE-mented (crazy around De) as a "creative endeavor."

Thanks, also, to Carolyn (Mrs. DeForest) Kelley. It is with profound gratitude that I acknowledge your contribution to my life and well-being. I want to thank you, mostly, for being the kind of wife De wouldn't even fantasize about leaving, not in a gazillion years. Earth-based wedding vows may state, 'Till death do us part," but I'm sure De intended his vow to last BEYOND your lifetimes here on earth. Know that he is awaiting you in the celestial realm just beyond our present reach. Keep smiling.

First, last and always, I want to thank Almighty God, whose many blessings are showcased within these pages. I acknowledge Jesus Christ as my Savior and the Holy Spirit as my Guide and Protector.

Kristine M. Smith
North Hollywood, California
September 8, 2001

****

PART ONE

FLASHBACK! Wenatchee, Washington, May 4, 1968.

Wenatchee, Washington, May 4, 1968.

DISCOVERING DeFOREST KELLEY 1968-1993

September 8, 1966. STAR TREK, the first televised space travel series to take itself seriously, debuted. On the bridge of the Starship USS ENTERPRISE were Captain James T. Kirk, First Officer Mr. Spock (a Vulcan), and a cadre of others who would become as well-known to us (perhaps better known, in fact) and as well-loved as our own families and dearest friends.

I was fifteen. I first noticed STAR TREK because my Dad and my twelve year old cousin, Tim, were absolutely crazy about it. When the theme song came on, the order went out to "SHUT THE HELL UP!" It seemed certain that anyone who dared utter a word (except during commercials) would be banished from the house, disinherited, drawn and quartered, and made to suffer in countless other hideous ways, if even a single word of dialogue was obscured by "mindless babble" — or even a sneeze.

So I had two options – shut up and watch, or find something else more interesting to do. I never found anything more interesting than watching the episodes, waiting for the commercials, and then jibing Dad for "being in love with the green man with pointed ears." Dad and I didn't get along in those years; STAR TREK was pretty much all we had in common, and even that was simply because it gave me a chance to make him miserable four times an hour. He usually had the upper hand in making misery.

Then I began to WATCH the show. The fellow I felt most drawn to was the doctor – Leonard "Bones" McCoy, partly because he was such an asset to his shipmates and to his profession, and partly because I felt he was nearly always right. But, sadly, he was even less adept at "winning" arguments with his "nemesis," Spock, than I was with the irritants in my life! Someone else always seemed to be getting the last word!

Mostly I loved McCoy's innate decency and his obvious compassion. He looked as though he belonged on a gentleman's farm in rural Georgia, and he seemed to FEEL that way, too. When confronted by some new alien race, he reacted the way a person could be expected to react, rather than as if this was "business as usual". It was all new to HIM! You could see it, feel it, go with it. You knew you could rely on him to be honest – even when it wasn't particularly wise or logical. His heart – his humanity — usually led the way. Spock could rattle his cage on occasion, turning him into an irascible curmudgeon, but good friends have a way of doing that to each other when they're in a low mood, so that seemed to fit, too.

Just as soon as I began ENJOYING the show, the tables were turned and Dad began jibing ME about my passion for the series. I began to write Enterprise-based stories as creative writing assignments for English class; I began to portray various crew members in Drama class. I began to actually believe in the dream Gene Roddenberry and his cast had created, as it seemed a much nicer place to "play" than our own planet (with its racism, barbarism and paranoia about differences.)

On the 2nd day of May in 1968 I was thrilled to learn that DeForest Kelley – my beloved "Bones" – would be appearing in the Wenatchee Apple Blossom Festival on May 4th. I raced to Mom and Dad, imploring them to drive me there from Cle Elum (two hours away) to see him. They told me that was impossible, as they had to plant the field. "But if you want to go, you have your driver's license now, and you can take the car."

Take the car?! I was a novice driver! I had never driven in a town larger than Cle Elum (population 1600) without Mom or Dad at my side. Wenatchee was a BIG CITY! "If you want to go, you have to drive yourself." Lord God Almighty… It was the scariest thing I had ever considered doing in my life! I quickly called my best friend, Corean Scott, and asked her if she would be willing to accompany me to Wenatchee to see the Wenatchee Apple Blossom Parade and DeForest. She could tell I was petrified and that I needed moral support. She quickly asked her mom and got permission. We spent the next day whipping up some placards with DeForest's photo on them. One said, "HI, BONES! WE LOVE YA!" We bought autograph books, too, "just in case." Neither of us thought we'd actually get near enough to MEET him, but as "eternal optimists" we decided to prepare for EVERY possibility.

The next morning we headed over the pass at 6:30 a.m. It was dark and the road was still slippery in places with black ice. Nervous Nellie that I was, I wasn't as concerned about the pass as I was about driving in heavy traffic on four lane boulevards!! When we got to Wenatchee, a full two hours ahead of the scheduled parade kick-off, I found the first parking lot available, parked the car, and released a huge sigh of relief. As "luck" (fate) (God) would have it, we were all of two blocks from the parade route. Not only were we close, we were also ON THE VERY BLOCK where the limousine for Mr. and Mrs. DeFOREST KELLEY was parked! Corean and I spotted it and looked at each other, stunned. I finally said, "You know, if we play our cards right, we MIGHT get a chance to actually MEET DeForest, not just watch him go by!" I told her, "Here's Mom's movie camera. I'm going back to the car for the autograph books. If anything happens while I'm gone, be sure and FILM IT!"

I raced back to the car, grabbed the placards and the autograph books, and raced back. Luckily, I hadn't missed anything. We loitered shamelessly; pretending occasionally to window shop. Suddenly, I heard Corean gasp, and then she said, "Oh, my gosh, there he is!" I followed her gaze and just about fell over.

I had never (until this moment) been overly impressed with DeForest's looks. Not that I thought he was unattractive; I just had never really considered him "drool material," and neither had Corky. We were both unutterably stunned to see how extraordinarily HANDSOME he was in the flesh. And he was smiling, even grinning! THIS was NOT what we had expected in "our" Dr. McCoy! I said, "Geez, Cork, he's ADORABLE!" She asked, "What do they do on STAR TREK to make him look so…plain?" I shrugged my shoulders and said, "I don't know… but they should stop it! He's GORGEOUS!"

The Kelleys got into the limo. Surprisingly, the driver didn't start the engine and take off right away. A few other passing fans spotted their vehicle and approached it. We stayed back for a good ten minutes, watching. I was a little apprehensive that I might find that he was disinterested in his fans, but it quickly became apparent that such was not the case. He was genuinely appreciative of their attention, and he spoke easily with each of them, thanking them for their interest in and support of STAR TREK. Butterflies inhabited my innards. I wanted to go to the car and greet him, but was afraid I'd make a fool of myself if I attempted it. I held back and hemmed and hawed so long that finally Corean elbowed me and said, "Go on over and get his autograph. I'll film it." I took a big breath and said, "Ho-kay. If I survive it, it'll be a miracle!"

I stepped up to the car. Mrs. Kelley spotted me first – I was closest to her – looked up at me and said, "Hi!" with a big grin. I muttered, "Hello…" and took a step back to recover.

"De," Carolyn said, "over here."

DeForest looked over at me, grinned, and said, "Well, hello, there!"

"H-hi," I managed to stutter. "May I have your autograph?"

"Certainly," he responded.

I handed him my autograph book and the pen I had. He began to uncap the pen, but it was a kind with which he was not familiar, and I watched him start to uncap it the wrong way. The last thing I wanted to do was correct him — so I just watched as he fumbled with it. I was embarrassed for me and for him. He asked me, "What's your name?" still trying to find the way into the pen! I said, "Uh… Kristine. With a K." He finally got the pen figured out, and then asked, "Kristy?" "No, Kristine." I spelled it. He said, "That's one of my favorite names." I blushed. He signed the book and handed it and the perplexing pen back to me. "Thank you," I said. "You're very welcome."

My trial over, I stepped back to the sidewalk. Corean was thrilled. She had captured the entire thing on film. It was then that the driver started the car and pulled away from the curb to get into line for the parade.

Corean and I discussed how nice he seemed. I was on cloud nine. I had not expected him to be quite this amazing as a human being. He had class and charisma and an elegance about him that was just – well, breathtaking. I had never met anyone as classically "Southern gentleman" before. It was as though he respected me enormously, as scared witless as I was!

Not long after, the parade began, and as it proceeded down the street toward us, I grabbed the camera and handed the placard to Corean and said, "They're going so slow, you can take this out to his car and show it to him. Perhaps he'll sign it for you. Go on!"

Corean carried the placard out to the car, which was SURROUNDED with young, fresh-faced Kelley fans. He was signing as fast as he could. When he spotted the placard Corean had, he grabbed it, held it up for the TV cameras, grinned, and then told Corean, "This is terrific! Thank you!" She said, "Thank you! Would you mind signing it for us?" He said, "Not at all," and signed his name to it.

Corean came back to the sidewalk, grinning ear to ear, sighing, "He is SO NICE! Gosh, I just love him!" We watched the parade until our own Cle Elum Marching Band went by, and then got into the car and headed for home. I no longer worried about driving, or anything else. We drove home in a cocoon of affection for the man — expressing over and over how nice he was, how well mannered, how appreciative… how handsome.

That night, I wrote an essay entitled "The REAL McCoy," and submitted it to my English teacher on Monday. Mr. Dobbs was impressed, with a capital I. He had me read it in class, and then, after the session, suggested that I send the essay to Mr. Kelley. I paled and balked. I sputtered, "Oh, no. No way! I don't write to movie stars!" He said, "Look, if you impressed someone as obviously as he impressed you, wouldn't you want to know?" "Sure," I replied, "— but he's an ACTOR. He probably hears stuff like this ten times a day." Mr. Dobbs practically ordered, "Send him a copy." Since he was my teacher, and had a say in what my citizenship grade would be, I agreed. Besides, I told myself, Kelley's secretary would see the essay, and she would probably toss it long before he ever laid eyes on it… so I figured I really had nothing to fear…

School let out shortly thereafter for the summer and I promptly forgot all about the letter and essay to DeForest, what with the assassinations of Dr. Martin Luther King Jr. (in April) and Robert F Kennedy (in June) holding center stage and my heart that summer. One day in August, an envelope arrived from PARAMOUNT. "Oh, my gosh…" My heart climbed into my throat as I opened it. Inside was a brief letter – one that would change my self-image and my life forever. It read:

> Dear Kristine,
>
> I was so impressed with your letter and story that I turned it over to Teresa Victor, Leonard Nimoy's Girl Friday with a suggestion that it might make a good magazine piece. She in turn contacted Pat Langdon of TV STAR PARADE who is interested in using it for a Holiday story.
>
> Seems you are in for more fame."
>
> Live long and prosper,
> DeForest Kelley.

Needless to say, my parents and sisters had to peel me off the ceiling, several times a week for the next several months as I waited for the "debut" of my first-ever published article, ABOUT my favorite actor, SUBMITTED by my favorite actor! I sent another letter or two thanking DeForest for thinking enough of the article to submit it for publication with such a well-known New York publisher. I had been writing since age six, but did not have the confidence to actually SUBMIT anything for publication – and here, DeForest had gone ahead and done it FOR me! It was the greatest thing imaginable. I was so happy, felt so lucky – and Mr. Dobbs made sure to let everyone know when school reconvened, via news reports in the local and regional newspapers.

Shortly before the article appeared in the Holiday/January '69 issue of TV STAR PARADE, I again wrote to DeForest thanking him for the "boost" in launching my writing career. He wrote back,

> "Maybe this will be the beginning of something interesting for your future… we hope… and we shall be looking forward to its publication. That should really make you a celebrity in your own right in Cle Elum! Stay happy as you are now – and "live long and prosper"…
> Sincerely, DeForest Kelley.

When the article appeared, the entire school more or less declared a Kris Smith Day and lots of classmates purchased the issue and asked me to personally autograph the cover or the inside story. I was at first mortified by all the attention – yet, I was also enormously proud. NOT ONE WORD of the essay had been deleted or changed by the New York publisher, which I had dreaded might happen. After all, I was just a kid from the sticks. I'd been given encouragement and a two-year subscription to a writing magazine by my seventh and eighth grade English teacher, Mrs. Alpha Rossetti, who believed, - but come on! I NEVER thought I could actually DO anything PUBLISHABLE.

I wrote one more letter to Mr. Kelley, letting him know the outcome of my "adventure in celebrity." I was going to write still another, but both of my parents derailed the plan. Mom explained: "Kris, the man has been very kind to you. DON'T drive him crazy with your incessant letters. Leave the poor fellow alone, now." I figured she was right. I had always gone a little overboard writing letters – which is why I had about 25 pen pals at the time – and it seemed predictable that had I continued to "play pen pal" with Mr. Kelley, I would have worn out my welcome. So I stopped. Cold turkey. Just like that. For seventeen years!

But I never truly let go. My heart and soul knew better, somehow.

After a couple years of college, I "hired on" as a secretary and laborer in my folks' construction company. They had a fifth wheel trailer and were building and remodeling restaurants all across the mid- and southwest, and I thought that would be a wonderful way to see the country (stay 30 to 90 days in each region, meet folks, learn customs and habits and idioms). Of course, during all this time (1971-78) we had no real address; we were "living like turtles," as Mom put it. I was out of the loop with all things TREK and didn't have the slightest indication that it was anything but "dead, Jim."

I continued to write in my journals, but professional writing was impossible during that period of time. After my stint as a construction worker, I began working in the animal welfare field. Animals had always been a passion, and I felt I could contribute to their well-being with my activism and writing abilities, so I studied wild animal behavior and training, worked for a wildcat sanctuary, and later for an international animal welfare agency.

The strangest thing was going on during all these "in between" years. It was so strange that I was hesitant to discuss it with anyone. In fact, up until now, only two others have known about it. I was having dreams – lucid, detailed dreams — recurrent, evolving dreams – about DeForest and Carolyn Kelley!

It seemed strange even then. After all, I had only been with them – what? – perhaps ten minutes in my entire life. I had left STAR TREK behind three years previously – along with any plans about becoming a professional writer — and was now working in endeavors which had NOTHING WHATSOEVER to do with the Kelleys. I was so "out of the loop" I never even turned on a television set for close to ten years! So, I was intrigued and confused by what I considered this "subconscious obsession" with the Kelleys.

Little did I know!

The first dreams always began almost mid-mission. I was plopped down in a strange Southern California neighborhood and I had a message in my hand from DeForest that I was to give to Carolyn. The problem was I didn't have the address to the Kelley's house. The only thing I knew about it was that in the back yard there was a desert tortoise (Myrtle). So, throughout the dream, I was walking up and down sidewalks, looking over fences and block walls, trying to spot Myrtle! After several recurrences of this dream, with no outcome, I began to dream that no matter where I was, no matter where I went in my dreams – to a lake, to a fair, to a farm — Myrtle would be there! So, now my dreams had evolved to the point where I had found the TURTLE, but alas — no De or Carolyn! This dream continued for some time. I would wake up, scratch my head, wonder and wonder, but my intuition offered NOTHING in the way of clarification. It was just one blasted Mystery to me why I should be "obsessing" over things Kelley!

Then a dream appeared that persisted for YEARS. In it, I was in a familiar living room (mine or another) chatting with the Kelleys as if we were FAMILY. Chatting to them about my writing, De's work, the state of the world, and even about the most mundane things imaginable – the way we often do with trusted family members. It was as if we had been together our entire lives. I loved this dream. The many years of "searching" dreams were over, and never came again. In these new dreams, I had located the Kelleys at long last, and we were as comfortable as three bugs in a rug. There was talk, and laughter, some hugging, and the most pervasive and relaxing feeling of "peace" I had ever known, in the dream state OR awake.

I wanted life to be like this. Of course, then I would wake up, the dream would vanish, and I would be plopped back into the real world – where I had NO contact with the Kelleys. Still, I felt I did. My dreams kept it all alive for me.

Between 1972 and 1985, whenever I wasn't working in construction, I worked in animal welfare. I worked with a veterinarian; spoke at rallies against unnecessary animal research (advising doctors and researchers of alternative, non-animal methods of research), "babysat" cougars and leopards, and wrote about crises facing wild and domestic animals (among them puppy mills, leg-hold traps, seal-clubbing and the like). In 1979, I adopted a week-old, weak-boned serval kitten. His name was Deaken (nickname DeDe or just plain De, at that time). He eventually lost a rear leg due to weak bone syndrome, after which I sometimes wryly referred to him as Tri-pawed.

My animal welfare articles appeared in dozens of newspapers and magazines between 1981 and 1985. They were a source of enormous pride to me, because I felt that they would help to foster a new awareness of each animal's intrinsic importance to this planet. I was using my skill as a writer for a very great cause, and felt that if I accomplished NOTHING else as a writer, this would be quite enough. I also felt I was finally "paying back" folks for their faith in my ability to string words together!

In 1986, after five years of living in the Sacramento area, I returned to Washington State and began living in a guest house at my parents' place in Eatonville. Out the front window was the most gorgeous view of Mt. Rainier that ever existed. I could hardly stand to drag myself away from home: it was in a rural area, surrounded by woodlands and populated by deer, raccoons, elk, squirrel… the whole repertoire of Pacific Northwest wildlife. We could easily visit the magnificent wildlife park called Northwest Trek. After five years of living in a big city, this was more like home, and it felt just right… except that I was almost dead broke, had a job that paid next to nothing, and had bills from Sacramento which threatened to bankrupt me. So I was in a paradise, yet living under a great deal of stress! Dad and I had converted an outlying garage into a very nice unit for me — and for my "serval son," Deaken, who was now six years old and the apple of my eye. I began to write again, in order to try to supplement my income in a last-ditch effort to get the damnable bills paid off and still eat and pay my parents at least SOMETHING for putting up with me again.

In early August, I learned that there would be a twentieth anniversary STAR TREK convention in Spokane. Spokane was at the extreme end of the state from Eatonville, and I had never been to a convention. In fact, after seeing news coverage on television regarding TREK cons, I never wanted to go to one. Based on media coverage, I was under the impression that only "Trekkies" populated these events, pretending they just beamed down from some starship. In short, I thought only show-offs or psychotics went to STAR TREK conventions. I thought long and hard about driving all the way across the state for a "Trekkie" gathering, let me tell you! It seemed a rather terrifying prospect!

BUT! WAIT! HOLD IT NOW! I couldn't get it out of my mind: DeForest Kelley was appearing at this convention – the man who had been appearing regularly in my night-time dreams for seventeen years! I was awfully sure that, with his integrity, he'd NEVER agree to attend any event at which he had to address a roomful of nutcases. Plus, Gene Roddenberry would be there, as would many other essential STAR TREK people. So I felt rather "safe." Hey, I thought, it might even end up being a relatively "profound" experience.

So I wrote Mr. Kelley a brief note, a jovial note, telling him that I would be in Spokane because "I owe you a long overdue hug for launching my writing career." I reported to him that I had since become a freelance writer and that I had numerous articles to my credit. I also enclosed a copy of the first article to refresh his memory, along with a couple of photos of my folks' chalet, and of Deaken and my other domestic kitties. I signed off with, "If not for you, I would probably NEVER have considered myself 'good enough' to call myself a writer."

The moment I mailed that note, I again panicked, just as I had the time I sent THE REAL McCOY to him. I crucified myself with such pleasing comments as, "You LUNATIC! He's an ICON these days! A HOUSEHOLD NAME! You're 35 years old! You sounded like a 17 year old! 'I owe you a long over-due hug'! Fer gosh sakes, have you lost every marble you ever HAD! Jesus, Joseph and Mary! Get a grip!" Plus, I was broke. What was I doing, driving across the state – using gas, paying convention fees – when I didn't even have enough money to buy groceries at times?! I was being the most thoughtless, selfish, stupidest woman the planet had ever known! I jumped all over myself, in the worst ways possible. In fact, I actually talked myself out of going! But Mom and Dad – noting my depression over bills, thought the convention might be something that would pick me up a bit. They encouraged me to go. They offered me their truck, so

I could carry camping equipment in it and stay at a campground when I got to Spokane. Still, I hesitated.

Then the envelope arrived.

I knew it was from DeForest the moment I saw the writing on the envelope. It had been seventeen years, but I recognized his distinctive handwriting. Inside, the note read,

> "Dear Kristine,
>
> Enjoyed the photos of your pretty house and pets –
> Wishing you continued happiness.
>
> DeForest Kelley"

What did it MEAN?! Was he looking forward to seeing me in Spokane? NO promises there. Just a polite, sweet note of thanks for the communication. So I felt I was "off the hook" if I really didn't want to go. Still, I said I'd be there… to give him a silly hug… and… just suppose he looked for me, and I didn't show up? Yes, I realized I was probably fantasizing! I was trying to make something out of a note; trying to write some "between the lines" statement. He WANTED to see me again.

No. That was ME, wanting to see HIM again.

No, it was HIM. That's what he had "meant."

No, Idiot, it ISN'T what he meant. In fact, since he didn't mention the convention at all, he doesn't have any desire whatsoever to see you again. You're making it all up, and if you go, and he doesn't say hello, you'll be even more depressed than you are NOW! So, save yourself additional heartache, and FORGET IT GIRL!

But what if —?

I went back and forth like this for DAYS. I backed out a dozen times.

The convention was three days away. I needed to make a decision!

Aw, what the hey, just go. See what happens. Life is already ruined. Just go and try to have a good time. I called my sister Jackie and asked if she would "loan" me her eleven year old son, Philip. Philip was my "Trek buddy" – he loved STAR TREK as much as I had. I needed a "decoy": a reason to go to a convention with Klingons and Andorians and Starfleet Academy cadets. (I figured I could tell folks I was escorting my little nephew…)

Jackie agreed, Philip was ecstatic… so now I COULDN'T back out. I'd disappoint my beloved nephew!

We drove over Thursday afternoon and checked into a KOA Campground and pitched the tent. The convention would begin the next day. Philip and I toasted wieners and ate marshmallows and chatted about what the next three days might bring. He had more hopes than I did. I tried to keep a lid on his expectations, since NOTHING was truly likely to happen, but his enthusiasm kindled my own hopes, and I don't think I slept more than two hours all night long.

We got up, took showers, dressed, and drove to the convention hotel. I had an original copy of THE REAL McCOY along, "just in case" I actually got a moment with Mr. Kelley; perhaps I could have it signed…

When we walked into the teeming lobby, TREK fans were EVERYWHERE — and, amazingly (to me), MOST were dressed just like I was. There were very few "aliens" or Starfleet officers there. In fact, until I finally saw a Trek fan in a costume, I worried that perhaps we were in the wrong hotel!

I went to the hotel front desk. I had prepared a note for DeForest, and asked a desk clerk if he could deliver the note to Mr. Kelley. The look he gave withered me. "Not another one," he seemed to exude. "No, ma'am, I can't. I have no idea where Mr. Kelley is or what hotel he's staying at. There's NO WAY I can deliver any notes to ANY of the STAR TREK stars." He'd said it a million times already, and I knew there was no way an appeal at this point would do one whit of good. I sighed, said, "Thank you. I understand" —which I did. Philip and I left the desk.

Philip looked up at me, and said, "What now?"

I said, "Let's go find some fun to get into."

We walked down the hallway, signed in and volunteered for some convention duties. There was really nothing I wanted to do there except hear DeForest's presentation, and the program indicated that he wouldn't be speaking until Sunday. I figured we'd volunteer to help the convention managers, earn a SPOKANE STAR TREK T-shirt in the process, and pass the days until DeForest would appear.

Unbeknownst to me, the Kelleys were trying to locate ME! They called around, trying to find my room at the convention hotel. When that failed, they called other hotels in the area in an attempt to track me down. When nothing came of their efforts, they decided I had probably been unable to make it, and dropped the idea of meeting with me.

Phil was placed at the book-selling, book-signing table with David Gerrold, the author of THE TROUBLE WITH TRIBBLES. As luck would have it, Gene Roddenberry's son, Rod Jr. was also assigned to the book table. Both kids were 11 years old, so they hit it off like gangbusters and enjoyed Friday and Saturday together. I was assigned nearby. I don't recall what my tasks were. I know I earned my twelve hours, as did Phil, and we both received convention T-shirts as a reward. I told one of the convention managers that we wouldn't be able to volunteer during DeForest's appearance, because that was the entire reason we had come to the convention. She nodded her understanding and said, "That's no problem. When De speaks, no one will be buying anyway! We'll ALL be in there!"

While wandering around, looking at dealer's tables, I spotted a flyer for the *DeForest Kelley Fan Communique*, a fan club based in California, run by Sue Keenan. I picked it up, folded it, and tucked it into my satchel. "Just in case I decide to join a club," I told myself silently.

Friday and Saturday proceeded swiftly enough. I met Sammie Portman, a computer programmer from Seattle who was a big DeForest Kelley fan. She was fascinating. I didn't have a computer but I listened to all she had to say about the subject. I just knew someday I'd be as enamored of my PC as she was of hers!

On "De Day" we arrived early and got seats as close as we could to the stage. We were back a good fourteen rows, but it was within view of the podium and on the center aisle, so I considered us pretty lucky.

De was almost the final speaker of the day. As the time approached for his appearance, I noticed that the aisle was beginning to fill with fans, so I told Phil, "Let's get up there and sit in the aisle, to get as close as we can." Phil seemed uncomfortable doing that, and said, "No, I'll stay here and keep our seats. If the fans in the aisle get sent back, you will still have a place to sit that's close." I said, "Are you sure?" He said, "Yes." I said, "That's really good thinking, Flip!"

I walked to within about fifteen feet of the stage and then sat down in the aisle. The Fire Marshall didn't object, so that's where I stayed.

Just before DeForest's name was announced, my heart was beating so hard and so loudly that I was embarrassed that someone sitting next to me might hear it. The thunderous applause and the standing ovation he received didn't make me feel much better. I was truly in the midst of a throng which quite obviously adored DeForest Kelley. His talk was interesting, fun, poignant, sweet…it mesmerized me. Then he opened up the appearance for questions or comments from the audience. A thousand hands went up. Mine was not one of them. I had wanted to thank him, yes, but not in front of two thousand TREK fans! I was too shy and too overcome by the tremendous response he was receiving. I had no "right" to slow things down with a personal comment that would be mean nothing to anyone but me – and possibly him. It would look like grandstanding.

He continued to choose hands, and to answer questions. After about 15 or twenty minutes of that, I saw him looking at his watch, so I knew his time was coming to an end, and I squirmed uncomfortably inside my own skin. Okay, Kris, it's now or never. It'll only take five seconds. Do it, or you'll lose the chance forever.

I raised my hand into the sea of outstretched hands and (call it a miracle!) DeForest PICKED IT! I could NOT believe it! He looked at me and said, "Yes? You." I rapidly stated, "I just wanted to thank you for launching my writing career."

De looked at me and asked, "Are you Kris?" I just about fell over. "Yeah," I muttered.

"Well, I've been lookin' all over for you!"

I just about fell over AGAIN. Oh, God…

De continued with the audience, "Well, I want to tell you… This young lady wrote me a letter a long, long time ago… (To me) What year was that?"

"Uh… '68."

"'68 it was. And you presented me with a story. I was so impressed with it that I sent it to a movie magazine, and they published it for her. (To me) Would you stand up?' Under my breath I muttered, "Oh, Lord." I stood up. The audience began to applaud. De then joked, "She was about this high at the time." He indicated waist high. Then he said to me, "And thank you for the beautiful photos you sent me of your home here in Washington. That's beautiful." At this point, a convention manager with a microphone came to me and thrust the instrument in my face, expecting me to react in some way to De's nice comments. I was speechless and my cheeks were flushed with embarrassment. I DIDN'T know what to say, and I CERTAINLY didn't want to say in public what issued from my lips, so I kind of 'whispered' it: "May I give you a hug?" De said, "You certainly may! Come on up here!" I stepped forward – the fans ahead of me parted so I could get through – and I leaped onto the stage. There was pleased laughter from the crowd, and flashbulbs were going off, blinding De (my back was to the audience). I gave him a long, heartfelt hug… then another… then patted his back… then scratched his back, saying, "Thank you so much." He said, "We're proud of you. Keep up the good work." I said, "I will. Thank you again, so much!"

I left the stage and walked back to my seat to join Philip, who looked awe-struck. De was saying, "There! Now we have a writer to our credit." De went on to another fan. Philip looked up into my eyes and asked me, "Did you cry?" "No," I said. "Almost, though!" I waited a second or two and then asked him, "Were you embarrassed when I asked him for a hug?' "No!" he said resolutely. "I was PROUD!"

A few minutes later, De's appearance ended. I told Phil, "If we're fast, maybe we can get over to the exit door from the stage and have a picture taken with him!" Phil nodded, "Okay!" and we flew out the rear of the auditorium, took a sharp right, and headed to the stage area exit door. Sure enough, DeForest came out. He spotted me and grinned, and I said, "Hello, Mr. Kelley. I don't want to impose or slow you down—" "Oh, no, not at all, Kris." I said, "Would it be possible to get a picture with you?" He said, "Certainly." I gave my camera to Philip. He fiddled with it a little bit, trying to put it into focus. He was nervous, and so was I, standing there arm in arm with De. A fellow fan, about thirty, offered to take the camera from Philip and do the honors, so Philip gratefully relinquished it. The picture was taken.

I shook De's hand and he said, "Stay in touch." I said, "Okay."

Philip and I wandered around for awhile, then prepared to leave. Then Philip tapped me and said, "Aunt Kris, DeForest is sitting with Gene Roddenberry in the restaurant!" I looked, and sure enough, there he was, with wife Carolyn, Gene's wife Majel, Nichelle Nichols, George Takei, and others. I said, "Oh, dear…"

Philip said, "I'd like to get his autograph." I said, "I know, sweetie, but I don't think we should interrupt their dinners. That would be rude." He said, "I know it."

We hung around a little bit longer. DeForest stood up and headed into the men's room. Phil brightened considerably. I countered with, "No way. You can't go into the bathroom to get his autograph." He said, "I wasn't thinking of that! I could go stand outside the door and ask when he comes out." I sweated. Finally I said, "Okay… but I'm going around the corner and hiding. I don't want him thinking this was MY idea!" I figured DeForest would accept this ambush from a little boy and let Philip go ahead. I fled around the corner and waited. And waited. And waited. Finally, Philip came back, beaming, showing me his paper. "I got it!" Then he announced proudly, "He wrote Phil on it!" I said, "OK, Phil, we're BOTH happy now. Let's get out of here!"

As we walked down the hallway, he confessed to me, "When DeForest came out, I made a mistake. I told him, 'Hi, I'm Kris's aunt!'" I laughed and then said, "And what did HE say?" Phil reported, "He said, 'You ARE?!'" Then I said "I mean, Kris is MY aunt," and he said, 'That's what I thought you meant.' And then, after he signed his autograph, he asked where you were. I told him you were hiding around the corner!" I said, "Oh, great going, kidlet!"

Philip and I spent the last night at the KOA and then, on the way out of town, we decided to stop one last time at the convention hotel. We'd had such a good time that we weren't quite ready to consign it to memory. I parked the truck and we started to walk in. Mark Lenard, who played Sarek (Spock's father) was standing outside, and we spoke with him for a few minutes. He seemed very shy and a little bit haunted, but he was very, very nice. Then we went inside and I spotted my new computer programmer friend, Sammie, from Seattle. She, of course, had seen De's appearance and was very happy for me, and even shed a few tears while remembering it.

The three of us were off in a corner, chatting in the hotel lobby, when suddenly the whole crowd seemed to have a communal intake of breath; then I heard exclamations of, "There he is!" We glanced across the crowd in the direction of everyone's gaze. DeForest and Carolyn Kelley were entering the lobby, on their way to the limousine which would carry them to the airport! We were as far away from the Kelleys as it was possible to get, which I was plenty happy about, since Philip had divulged the fact that I was "hiding around the corner" when De was accosted for yet another autograph request the night before! I held back, thinking that now it was time for other fans to have their special moments to see and speak with De. De lingered for a few moments, and then glanced across the lobby and spotted ME. He called out, "KRIS! Good morning!" I waved a "Good morning!" wave and smiled. De grabbed Carolyn's hand and started through the throng in my direction. I about had a heart attack. I could not BELIEVE he was coming over yet again to see me! Stunned, but recognizing my responsibility, I started across the lobby toward THEM, so it wouldn't be such a trek for them.

We met in the middle of the throng, which was respectful and didn't crowd us much. De said to me, "Do you remember Carolyn [from 1968]?" I said, "I sure do! Hello!" and reached out to shake her hand. But she took BOTH my hands in hers and said, "Kris, it's so nice to see you again! We always wondered whatever happened to the little girl who wrote so well!" I muttered and sputtered, deciding NOT to tell them the truth. [How would they have reacted to a 35 year old telling them that "Mom and Dad told me to leave you alone; not to drive you nuts anymore"?] Instead, I told a slightly more convoluted, but equally true story: "My folks and I spent a lot of years building and remodeling restaurants all over the country. We really didn't have an address, to speak of. So I lost touch with EVERYBODY, not just YOU." De said, "Well, we're glad you're back in touch." Carolyn added, "Yes. Now, don't be a stranger. Send us some of the articles you've had published!" I said, "Okay!" Carolyn repeated, for emphasis, "We mean it! Stay in touch!" I said, "Okay," yet again, then, "Thanks!" and we parted.

I still had money problems, and I still had a pitifully paying job, but I was re-born. My spirits lifted, I saw a light at the end of the tunnel. Once again, I had some faith in myself. The long nightmare was finally ending. I was out of the self-pity business entirely.

When I got home from the convention, I took charge and re-invented myself. I mailed off the flyer to Sue Keenan and signed up for a year of the *DeForest Kelley Fan Communique*. The first thing I did was write a report of the convention and submit it to her for her newsletter. Then I got silly and started writing other humor pieces about the "adorable" De Kelley, ALL of which she published. I had by now sent the Kelleys copies of many of my articles which had been published, and since most of the articles related to animal welfare, I was delighted to find that the Kelleys were big animal lovers, too. In fact, De's official charity was the North Shore Animal League!

Since the subject matter of my non-fiction, animal welfare articles was pretty heavy and dealt with unhappy topics, I made sure that the LETTERS accompanying them were as wild, wacky and as funny as I could possibly make them. I certainly didn't want them thinking that I was an always-serious, over-zealous, ever-crusading ANIMAL SAVIOR every moment of my waking life. In fact, I had already distanced myself from much of that endeavor, since I realized the intense involvement was actually contributing to a tendency toward depression. I was "burned out" (at least temporarily) on trying to save the animal world, and I wanted them to be GLAD when they got letters from me!

De's next convention would take place in Dearborn, Michigan. I made arrangements with a pen pal, Jeannie Armstrong, to stay with her, and then I had a T-shirt especially made to wear for the occasion. After that, I informed my boss when I would be using my vacation time, and for what reason. Yikes! Unfortunately, our store was having its annual Tent Sale – the biggest sales event of the year – and so he refused to let me get away. Heartbroken, I called Jeannie and told her that I wouldn't be able to attend, but said I'd send the T-shirt, and SHE could wear it to the convention. The T-shirt read: "NO BONES ABOUT IT: I'm a DeForest Kelley Fan!" and had "DeForest" and "Carolyn" written down each sleeve, with hearts where the O's belonged. It was one cool-looking shirt! Then I wrote to tell the Kelleys to be looking for the lady with the most terrific Kelley shirt on the planet!

Amazingly enough, De did look for the T-shirt, had Jeannie model it, and then explained how he had met me twenty years earlier! At that point, he got nostalgic or tickled or something and said, "I get a lot of wonderful mail, and I read it all – I want you to know that – but it is impossible for me to become a pen pal." Everyone laughed at that, of course understanding. Then he said, "If there's anyone I SHOULD write to, it should be Kris… and I HAVE, on occasion…" Then he half-laughed, "I've HAD TO answer her a couple of times! But it's impossible, even with her – even those we have some kind of personal situation for…" and he trailed off without finishing the thought. Well, Jeannie sent me a videotape of that appearance, and when I watched it I was SO touched! Then I suddenly felt GUILTY, thinking he really MIGHT be "sitting up nights" feeling badly that he wasn't writing as often as I was (although Carolyn was certainly doing her best to keep up with me all along!) So, I took out a pen and I wrote a heartfelt letter telling De that he didn't owe me a THING – that it was ME who owed him.

Well, enter "Krazy Kris". For some reason, the day I KNEW the note had to have reached him, the mischievous side of me got INSPIRED! (Thank You, God!) I started to giggle, and I started to type. (Or, rather, Krazy Kris did.) I pictured him at home, reading this heartfelt, "don't feel guilty" letter, while Krazy Kris was writing:

> "Dear Penpal,
>
> Why haven't you written?! I've been sitting here looking forlorn for almost a year now. (Okay, so it's only been seven months. Time FLIES when one is forlorn.)
>
> "I'm NOT one to notice these things, and I KNOW how busy you are, but… WHERE'S MY autographed photo? (I had never even ASKED for an autographed photo!) I AM INCENSED! I have an empty spot on my wall – there's only ONE small empty spot left – that's JUST the right size for a photo of – who? But, of course, I suppose I COULD put a photo of SPOCK there – but it wouldn't go with the rest of my De-cor, if you get my drift…
>
> So… if you want to stay in my good graces (and good gracious, of course you DO!) SEND ME A PICTURE! And sign it something short and sweet like "To My Dear Penpal

(who BELONGS in a pen!) with warmest regards and hugs and kisses and Saurian brandy, Bones." (And don't worry if you can't see the picture afterwards. I have plenty of pictures, but no signed ones!)

Grin! It looks great on you!
XOXOXO

Krazy Kris

P.S. I lock HER up when I see you. Aren't you GLAD???

Within days, I received a teensy weensy, smaller-than-wallet size photo of De with a bouquet of roses. The note that came with it read,

"Dear Kris, Maybe this will shut you up until I send you a big one for your wall de-cor. DeForest.
P.S. Stick it in your wall-et."

I roared. A major breakthrough! GONE were the social amenities. And gone was the "Kelley" from his name! I interpreted this as a near-miraculous leap forward. Needless to say, Sane Kris SELDOM wrote after that, except to Carolyn on business regarding articles I was writing on De for publication.

THE ADVENTURE CONTINUES….

The next convention that featured De was in Los Angeles in October '87, so that became my next goal. I called Sue Keenan, De's fan club president, and asked if I could stay with her, to cut down on expenses. She wrote back and said, "Sure!"

When I arrived in Los Angeles, Sue expected a wacky broad, I'm sure. She got one.

So there we were in L.A. We were so EXCITED to see De again that we didn't eat and seldom slept. We just sat up most of every night laughing and philosophizing and kidding and laughing some more. Finally, when we were completely and utterly exhausted, with our sides aching beyond endurance, we retired.

Carolyn wasn't at the convention because Fancy (the Kelleys' Lhasa Apso) was ill and she was at home with her. I behaved myself in the auditorium during De's appearance. DE didn't, but I did. On Saturday, De introduced me as "Krazy Kris" for the first time, and it stuck in DKFC members' minds. And THAT'S when I decided that, at some point in the future, I would "get even" with MISTER Kelley publicly for "DE-faming" me.

When I got home from the convention, I blasted him with a pseudo-outraged letter regarding his "impertinence." A sticker at the top "hinted" at what might follow. It read: "CAUTION: Contains material that may be offensive to persons lacking a sense of humor."

The letter went like this:

> JACKSON DeFOREST KELLEY! (The sound of thunder or growling goes here.)
>
> (ooh— doesn't that just make the hair on the back of your neck rise? Why, whenever I heard my full name used in that tone of voice, I knew I was in Big Trouble. I only heard my full name used TWICE in my life – once, when I went inner-tubing in Spanaway Lake before I knew how to swim (unaccompanied), and once — but I digress: This is YOUR chewing out, not mine!!)

JACKSON DeFOREST KELLEY! ("Yes?") You are in Big Trouble! ("I am?") YES! YOU! ("What did I do, pray tell?") Well, if you don't even KNOW, I am OUTRAGED! ("So, clue me in, will you?") YOU CALLED ME KRAZY KRIS in LA and now EVERYBODY is doing it – all these people who used to think of me as sane, sensible, reputable, dependable, intelligent, professional… Stop laughing now! There WERE a few misguided souls who really felt that way!

Krazy Kris was a secret – didn't you know?! No one was supposed to know she existed; I had managed to keep her under wraps for 36 years and then you had to open your big mouth in LA and let the cat out! Well, as you no doubt guessed, the DKFC reporters (your stooges, particularly the Top Stooge, Sue Keenan) picked it right up, and NOW it is INTERNATIONAL news! What am I supposed to tell my Trekkie boss who, up until now, thought I was safe to have around? "It was a case of mistaken identity?!"

YOU BLEW MY COVER!

Okay, two can play this game. Don't expect ME to run interference for you ever again. If I see you sneaking down the street in Spanaway or anywhere else in the world in your movie star "They'll-Never-Recognize-Me-In-This-Get-Up" glasses, will I just nod to you and pass by, keeping it under my hat that I know who you are? Not on your life! I'll shriek at the top of my lungs, "Hey, there's DeFOREST KELLEY!" and while everyone on the block is thinking, "Gee willacres… Where do I know that name from? It seems SO familiar…" I will add, "DR McCOY, you guys! Get with it! MOB HIM!" You'll never have another moment's peace, if I have anything to say about it!

I considered punishing you by not writing at ALL this month – but then I decided, hey, the best punishment of ALL is writing to him! Make him suffer for the indignities he has caused me. The mental anguish… the guffaws of my co-workers, WHO I WAS TRYING TO INSPIRE AND LEAD, for heaven's sake! What you have done is the equivalent of calling Captain Kirk a lunatic in front of the Klingons! It will never be forgotten! I am ruined!

If I need a new job as a result of all this, I hope you will be kind enough to write me a letter of reference, leaving OUT anything you might know about me that would indicate I am not working on all thrusters. (No matter how little that leaves to talk about.)

Sincerely yours, (HAH! More like, "Go milk a duck, Bones!") ("Go milk a duck, De," sounds a bit too harsh… Bones can take it, though!)

The One Who Shall Remain Nameless, Faceless and Incognito in order to protect what's LEFT of her shattered reputation!

HAPPY BIRTHDAY TO ME

Three weeks after my birthday, I wound up in Denver — and was invited (via Sue) to dinner with the Kelleys! That was my first actual, sit-down-and-chat meeting with them, and I was so nervous that before we headed into their suite I pleaded, "Sit right next to me all night long, and if they ask me a question, YOU answer it!"

When you find yourself in an overwhelming situation like this one, you want to be at your best. You want to make a good impression; above all, you do NOT want to come across looking like Garfield's little buddy Odie! On the other hand, you don't want to look as if you're having an audience with the Pope. Something right smack in the middle seems about right… but I was nowhere near certain I could handle a middle-of-the-road approach. So I was nervous.

No. I was petrified.

I followed Sue and a couple other DKFC members – all of whom were cool, calm and collected by all appearances – into the Kelleys hotel suite, where we were to meet, and I managed, for a moment, to present myself as normal. I hugged Mrs. Kelley and said, "Hello." Then I went over and shook hands with De. So far, so good. But…witness how quickly I went downhill from there, inside my nerve-wracked body.

We stepped over to the couches and prepared to sit down. De asked us if he could take our coats. Now, if anyone else on the planet had asked me that question, an easy answer would have been yes or no, right? I mean, he wasn't asking my opinion on whether the U.S. should get out of the United Nations; he was just asking if I cared to give up my coat for a while. I gave it serious thought. I thought, "What does HE want me to say? Should I say yes? Will he be upset if I say no?" Finally it occurred to me that he didn't give a fig whether I said yes or no, just so long as I said something, so he could sit down! So, I said no. That seemed to satisfy him – but not for long. Next he wanted to know if we would like drinks. I don't drink, so naturally I said YES. (Well, I had just told him no on something else. I didn't want him to think I was a bitch.) So, I said yes. Then he wanted to know what I would have! Oh, boy… He had me there! He was pitching these incredibly difficult questions at me and I was unable to field them! "Oh…whatever!" I finally "decided," hoping that would end the interrogation. Mrs. Kelley probably recognized the fact that I had slipped into the much-dreaded Idiocy Mode (a common affliction of fans) and tried to help me out. She suggested that I try a "DeForest Kelley." I looked at her, and I thought, "Gee, that is a very generous offer!" But I realized I wasn't getting the proper picture. She explained to me that a DeForest Kelley was a drink known to all of fandom – except me, obviously. "Oh, fine… I'll have one of those…"

Well, after a couple of DeForest Kelleys (vodka and water with a twist of lemon), I felt calmer. No one had raised any other controversial questions similar to "Can I take your coat?" in quite a while, so I was just sitting back and listening and watching everybody talk and laugh and have a good time….Not much later, we went downstairs for dinner. De sat at the head of the table. To his right sat Sue Keenan, and to her right sat Jackie Edwards. To De's left Carolyn (Mrs. Kelley), then me. There was NOBODY on my left – for a hundred miles. I quickly lost my nervousness sitting next to Carolyn, because she is a doll – so nice, and so much fun. She could calm a jackhammer. I know, because she calmed me, and I'm the greater challenge! We lost ourselves in some conversation about having both been raised in the State of Washington. At one point I was explaining something to her in great detail, and a fold or a crease on my left sleeve popped me with a great deal of force and I stopped in mid-sentence and turned around to my left, fully expecting to find a waiter or someone who had come along to ask me a question. THERE WAS NOBODY THERE! I panicked. I thought, "OK, Kris… How are you going to handle THIS dilemma?" Well, I had two choices. I could turn back to Carolyn and just continue the conversation as if nothing at all had happened – or I could explain what happened. Well, naturally, I opted for the truth – but I forgot to provide a complete explanation. Instead of what I just told you, I turned back to Mrs. Kelley and I said, "Strange! I could have sworn somebody just tapped me on the shoulder!" Carolyn accepted this bizarre information calmly. She looked at Jackie. Jackie looked at her. They both studied their salads for a while and said nothing.

I'm amazed the Kelleys didn't signal someone to bring a butterfly net!

It took me over a month to remember all the stupid things I said and did at dinner that evening. I found it comforting, at a later date, to learn that other fans admitted experiencing similar difficulties the first few times they were faced with actually trying to communicate with the objects of their affection.

After the convention (and my debut as a stand-up comic, where I swooned shamelessly over McCoy) by happy coincidence, I was at the

Denver Airport at the same time the Kelleys were, waiting for flights. I wandered over to the United gate that had a departing LA flight. De was sitting in a corner reading a newspaper, and by the time I got there, Carolyn had returned to sit next to him. Neither saw me until I was upon them, and I barely got out a "Good morning" before Carolyn leaned over and asked me, "How did your comedy routine go?" (She asked far faster than my own parents did when I got back home.) I said it went "okay" except for one part where I completely forgot a vital line and couldn't go on without it. The "pause" had lasted only five seconds, but it seemed like five decades. By the time the audience noticed that I wasn't just taking a dramatic pause, I was off and running again, so it wasn't the major gaffe I felt it was. Carolyn was disappointed that she hadn't been able to see the routine, since it was scheduled so much later in the day than De had been.

HUMOR – A DIFFICULT CONCEPT

After a convention, the mood at home is somewhat "ho-hum" (think of post-holiday blues, and you'll have the general idea), so I generally started imagining the next "event," which was a De con scheduled for August in Oakland. I had seen De in a blue and white striped shirt in photos taken at the cruise and at other cons, and had swooned over how attractive he looked in it. I joked that he'd never better show up wearing it around ME, because I might ravage his body. That led into a couple of tamely ribald skits that led into DKFC history.

I sent the skits to the Kelleys and sat back in anticipation, figuring that these skits would certainly put them on the floor (which was my usual aim in writing to them). So certain was I of their hilarious effect that I decided to share the skits with my parents. They listened to them as I proceeded along. Their faces grew more pale and their eyes grew wider the farther along I got. When I finished, Mom said, "You DIDN'T send these skits to the KELLEYS, did you?!" I said, "Yeah! Sure! Why not?" They looked at each other and intoned, "Oh, my God." Dad said, "I can't believe it. THE KELLEYS WILL NEVER SPEAK TO YOU AGAIN!"

Their horrified reaction and prediction put ice water into my veins like you wouldn't believe. I re-read the skits and decided that maybe ON PAPER they were NOT as funny as they had been in my head. IF the Kelleys took them as a true representation of my attraction for De, I WAS doomed!

Of course, I panicked. I kept telling myself, "Be rational, Kris. Don't let your folks panic you! The Kelleys KNOW that if these skits were a true representation of your feelings, you would NEVER have sent them in the first place! CALM DOWN! The Kelleys are NOT going to assign any validity to those off-the-wall skits!" But my folks' concern kept returning and their words kept reverberating in the corridors of my mind: "THE KELLEYS WILL NEVER SPEAK TO YOU AGAIN!" I began to contemplate the odds of that happening. The Kelleys were of the same generation as Mom and Dad… they grew up under some of the same influences… and OH MY GOD!!! DE WAS A PREACHER'S KID, for God's sake! They WERE going to look upon these skits EXACTLY as Mom and Dad had feared and I would be drummed out of the DKFC and out of the Kelleys lives forever, amen!!!

Mom and Dad were hardly talking to me. (I later learned that Dad was really frightened that the Kelleys MIGHT take the skits wrong and distance themselves from me, which he knew would devastate me. He didn't want me to suffer through something like that.)

Well, I was so torn by this time, I thought, "Well, it won't do me any good to sit here and fall apart. I'll write them a letter of apology – JUST IN CASE the skits were not well received." It was the only thing I could think to do in the event I had overstepped any boundaries and humiliated or angered De or Carolyn.

I don't think that letter of apology even was completely read by Carolyn and De before Carolyn fired back a note to me saying, in part, "Don't worry about the shirt skits you sent. We are glad you can have such a lot of fun with all that nonsense."

The Creation Convention folks had heard that I had done a "great" job in Denver with my comedy routine and so Adam Malin said he'd like to see it presented at his Oakland con… right before DE was to appear on Sunday! All right! This meant that Carolyn would be able to come over a bit early if she really wanted to see it! That excited and scared the stuffing out of me all at once! I kept thinking, "I must do well because if I don't, Carolyn will see it and I will want to shoot myself and if I do that I will never see De OR Carolyn again – so I must not blow it, must not blow it, must not blow it."

I memorized and rehearsed the routine until I knew it better than my own name, better than the Pledge of Allegiance, better than the Lord's Prayer. I practiced it until I was so SICK of it that I couldn't see anything at all funny in it! Then, I decided that perhaps I had over-prepared a bit, and backed off and relaxed and just IMAGINED presenting it in front of (oh, my God) Carolyn Kelley! The other fans were a real concern, too – particularly my friends, who I had promised myself I wouldn't embarrass by falling to pieces on stage! But it was Carolyn who was the Ultimate person I didn't want to disappoint.

On Saturday we were all in the front row in various locations, standing up and applauding like mad when De strode in WEARING THE INFAMOUS BLUE AND WHITE STRIPED SHIRT! I couldn't believe it! I sat down and leaned waaay back in my chair, hoping he wouldn't spot me… because I was hysterical, embarrassed, mortified – all the good stuff. A number of DKFC members knew exactly what was going on with that shirt prank, although no one else did. The club members were all looking at me and laughing hysterically. I don't remember a blasted thing he said that day; I had to see the videotape later to recall that appearance because I was too busy dodging De's glances toward the audience in my direction to pay much attention to details!

The next day just before De's appearance I presented "Husband Hunting on the Enterprise," while seriously quaking in my boots. Carolyn WAS in the audience, so I figured De was probably standing backstage listening — and there I stood, "lusting" after Dr. McCoy! Could Judgment Day be any LESS traumatic during the "life review" part, I pondered briefly. (Thankfully, I had previously sent the text to the Kelleys, and received their approval to present it!)

After I left the stage, two nutty women fans (yours truly included) quickly donned *our* blue and white striped "got'cha" shirts (purchased just that morning in a lobby gift shop!) for DE's impending appearance. De came on… spotted us in those shirts… laughed and shook his head… and then settled down to read his poem, "The Dream Goes On." Sue and I hot-footed it back to where Carolyn sat. Carolyn laughed, delighted, when she saw us in those striped shirts – and told us, "I MADE him wear that shirt yesterday! He didn't want to, but I insisted!" We cracked up! (Since I hadn't attacked him, I reckon I passed her test!) Carolyn got serious then and put her hand on mine. She said (of my appearance a few minutes earlier), "Kris, you looked like you have been doing stand-up for ten years!"

Oh, sigh – Oh, Lord… Oh, Carolyn, THANK YOU!

That afternoon during De's appearance, I raised my hand and he picked me, smiling. I said, "On September 7th you will be celebrating 43 years of marriage." De said happily, "That's right." There was resounding applause and then he added: "43 years in the valley with the very same wife." I continued: "Can you share some of the ingredients of a successful relationship?" De paused only a moment, and then said eloquently, "Well, the first thing you've got to do is pick the right girl. That's number one. And naturally you fall in love, and then, when you fall into life, you've got to sustain the love. And the love has to grow into a deeper thing: it becomes a friendship that is intense and becomes like two people living together and loving each other deeply about it. It's a kind of a thing that nobody can really put into words – and in THIS business, you have got to be awful lucky, too, to STAY married. If you don't go HIDE, they'll KILL you!" He finished with, "Thank you very much for asking. I don't know that I'm the easiest guy in the world to put up with, and I've never asked her…"

That night we heard that De and Carolyn were in the restaurant in OUR hotel, rather than in their own, so Sue decided we should go up and see if we were still "alive" after the prank we had pulled on him during his appearance that day. We were happy to discover that we were NOT disowned. While visiting with them then, De said that it was probably time to "retire" the striped shirt now, since he had worn it so many times recently that "pretty soon people will be asking, 'Doesn't that poor man have anything else to wear?'" I boo hooed and hissed that idea, but then suggested, "If you're serious, why don't you give it to Sue and she can auction it off to benefit the North Shore Animal League?" De laughed at such an outrageous notion, but Sue joined in and said it would earn HUNDREDS of dollars for the dogs and cats at North Shore. De pondered that for a short time, and then said, "Do you really think anyone would bid on it?" I held up MY hand immediately, of course, and said, "Sure! I know for a fact someone would bid on it!" Shaking his head in befuddlement, he said, "Well, okay. We'll get it laundered and send it to Sue."

A mere eleven days after I had returned from the Oakland convention, De underwent surgery for a collapsed colon. I nearly hit a tree when I got to the part in the letter about the unexpected surgery.

> "I've been busy recently, playing nurse to the good doctor. Of course by now you've heard that De had surgery September 1st – and all is well. He is recuperating beautifully – no problems. All's well that ends well. Sue sent him a box of silly fun things that gave us both lots of laughs. She's sum'pin', that Sue. Fancy is staring at me and stomping her feet – it's her dinnertime – so must go. Take care and keep smiling. My patient sends hellos – and of course chin-tickles to handsome Deke. Love, Carolyn."

Luckily, Sue and I had just recently inscribed a hilarious photo to De. Jackie Edwards had taken a great photo of us in our blue-and-white striped sweatshirts – the "got'cha" shirts we wore the day after De wore HIS "sexy" shirt — and each of us had inscribed a humorous little note. My note read: "Somebody asked me what color pants you wore with your striped shirt. Did you wear pants? Kris." Sue inscribed: "Some people like to live dangerously… don't you? Next time I'll join her instead of sitting on her! Love, Sue, Your Semi-Sane Prez." We sent the photo to De – having had NO idea he was in a hospital – and Carolyn had taken it to him on September 7th – their 43rd wedding anniversary.

De got such a kick out of it that Carolyn took a photo of him lying in his hospital bed, grinning broadly, holding the photo in his lap. She sent each of us a 4x6 of the photo, and with mine was a note, in part: "De is doing just beautifully. Hope you like this picture as much as we liked the one of y'all — take care — keep smiling! Love, Carolyn. P.S. Chin tickles for YOUR De."

I was, by this point in my evolution, the manager of a continuing education school for real estate, insurance and securities agents and brokers in Tacoma, Washington. On the wall in my office, I had mounted an 8x10 photo of DeForest, which was a great conversation piece and an immense help in building good will. (It seemed EVERYONE was as crazy about DeForest as I was; they were just more closeted about it). Of course, I also had a photo of Deaken (Little De, or DeDe, or Tri-pawed, but usually just plain "De"), my serval, on my desk. My boss, Eric Schram, came into the office one day, down from Seattle, to see how things were going. He was sitting at my desk, and I was facing away from him, doing some filing. Eric asked me, "How's De?" Presuming he was referring to my serval son – since he was sitting at my desk where the cat's picture was — I responded, "Oh, bless his heart, he's just fine, thanks. But I've had to start putting him in his cage at night, because he won't let me sleep!" There was dead silence from Eric. That was strange! I turned back to him, and his jaw was open. I immediately realized what had gone wrong, and I laughed, "Oh, you mean DeFOREST!" Eric nodded. I laughed, "Oh, my God! He's just fine, too!" Eric said, "This is how rumors get started, you know." We both cracked up.

Several months before filming began on STAR TREK V, the Kelleys' Lhasa Apso, by now fourteen years old, began to fail. She was blind in one eye and her coordination was off. De took her to the vet for a check-up and was told that it was simply old age, and that little could be done. Both De and Carolyn knew that it was only a matter of time before she would become so incapacitated that her life would become a burden to her. She had already had accidents in the house, which seemed to upset her very much. Knowing how terribly attached they were to their pets, I wrote them a letter of consolation, hoping to clarify their choices. Their own serenity and stress levels were being affected by Fancy's declining health and abilities; they weren't sleeping well.

Knowing that, I advised them that perhaps it was time to consider having Fancy put to sleep. I told them that I had worked in a veterinary hospital and assured them that her death would be serene and peaceful, especially if De or Carolyn could bring themselves to be with her until she passed, so she would be with a loved one and feel safe. I told them that if that seemed too difficult a task, I would be willing to take Fancy in for them. I had done it for my sister's pet and for other friends' pets, and I would be willing to do it for them, "IF the time comes and you think it would be too hard on you to do it. Speak with your vet about it and see what she can suggest or offer."

It wasn't long after that when I received a note from De:

> "Dear Kris, Just a note of thanks for your thoughtful letter of 6/5. It was informative as well as heartfelt. We put Fancy down yesterday. I stayed with her and she went peacefully…I felt a deep sense of relief for her. She had lost her hearing and her eyesight and was beginning to lose her dignity. It was time – and we miss her terribly, but we are convinced it was the right thing to do. Our vet agreed. We thank you again for your lovely letter and Carolyn joins me with warm wishes. DeForest"

STAR "WARS" – 1988

When it seemed possible that STAR TREK V might proceed without DeForest, due to a salary dispute, I wrote the following poem to try and convince the studio heads that the picture could not possibly fly without De. I didn't tell the Kelleys I was "causing trouble" at the studio, but word got back to them via Richard Arnold. Richard was so tickled with my poem that he called De (not knowing I was the author) and read it to him. De liked it so much that he called Richard back and had him read it again so Carolyn could hear it; then he asked for two copies of it to be sent to him.

FOR FRANK MANCUSO, WILLIAM SHATNER, HARVE BENNETT AND WHOMEVER ELSE IT MAY CONCERN....

STAR TREK V: DEAD OR ALIVE?

You waited a whole YEAR
So "Spock" could appear.
(You didn't use another actor:
It'd have killed the Success Factor.)

And we know you wouldn't swap Kirks —
We don't believe we're addressing jerks!
So what makes you think you can do without Kelley?
What are you using for brains – sand or jelly?

You want our support and hard-earned money?
You'd better be bringing us DE, then, honey!
You'll ruin our joy and the bottom line
If you don't wake up and pay him to sign.

No one wants STAR TREK to die;
WE ALL want to help it fly,
But we have this God-Awful premonition:
Without DeForest Kelley, who will pay the admission???

This is not an idle threat
If Kelley's out, you can take bets:
The show WILL fold, and the only long lines
Will be irate FORMER fans carrying signs!

■ K.M. Smith

Carolyn dropped me a note that read, in part: "Richard called and read us your poem to the studio… very clever. Give handsome Deaken a chin-tickle – I've about worn out his pics, showing them around. 'Bye for now, Carolyn."

THE MOVIE

Not long after De's release from the hospital, the filming for STAR TREK V began in Yosemite National Forest. I had written them early on, urging De to back out if he wasn't feeling up to the stress and strain of a motion picture. I was very relieved that De's doctor had given him a clean bill of health and had released him to do the work. I was still nervous, though; it seemed awfully soon to be making action-adventure movies!

I remembered how thin De had looked at the Oakland convention only two months previously, and figured he probably wasn't much better off after surviving a stint in a hospital. I took on a campaign to "pack on some pounds," and sent him a huge gift box filled with cheese, candy, and (his favorite) chocolate. He wrote me a note back: "Cheese, candies and chocolates! You sure know how to make a skinny actor gain weight. (Happily!)"

A day or so later I wrote an Rx: "Carolyn, put a HUGE plate of mashed potatoes in front of that boy — and slap him upside the head if he don't eat every bite!"

While the Kelleys were on location in Yosemite and at Ridgecrest, Carolyn conscientiously sent post cards every few days, updating me on De's whereabouts and health. She was reassuring me that he was just fine. "All's well here – De never felt better, since his surgery, I'm happy to say. He's looking better, too. And all's going well with ST V. Hope you and Deaken* are keeping dry. We hear there's rain in the Pacific North-Wet recently. * many, many chin tickles to Deaken!"

When production moved back to Paramount, the letters and notes from Carolyn continued: "De took my collection of Deaken's pictures to the studio this week, to show to a cat-lover there. He nor others who saw them, had not even HEARD of a serval – so they were quite fascinated with his story." "Our mailbox runneth over! I'm only glad you don't expect answers (except every six months)!" "You guessed right about De's weight. He hit 135 this week and feels like a million, I'm happy to say."

HOPES AND DREAMS

I had long wanted to work in the entertainment industry – as a writer or in some other production capacity. I mentioned this to the Kelleys in mid-summer of 1988 and from then on, Carolyn wrote back, sending newspaper articles touting the salaries that entertainment secretaries were getting at that time, along with other material touting the splendors of Southern California life. Compared with Washington State salaries, the sums seemed truly gargantuan. (I hadn't factored in the much higher cost of living in California.) Carolyn encouraged me to try and land a job at Paramount and other studios, feeling that once I had my foot in the door, I could "work up" into a creative position if I had the talent, which she and De both felt I had.

Finally, after much thought and encouragement, in the summer of 1989 I took a deep breath and mailed out six résumés and samples of published articles to all the major studios. De had told me to go ahead and use his name as a personal or professional reference. I waited a couple of weeks, and then made a few phone calls, to be sure the material had been received, and to see if there was any interest. Paramount encouraged me to come down and take their typing and other tests, after reviewing the résumé. I quickly called Sue and asked if I could stay at her place. She agreed.

Just before I flew down to take Paramount's battery of pre-employment tests, Carolyn wrote me a long letter. It began: "Is my year up, yet? I wouldn't want to cause you to fall over in a faint by getting too many letters from me…" It went on at length, chatting about our pets: "I hope Deaken had a wonderful 10th birthday and his fill of lobster. He and we have the same tastes! When we were in Australia [publicizing the last movie] I think we cleaned them out of lobster tails." She continued on about De's busy publicity schedule, and then began to wrap up the two pages: "Kris, we want to wish you much luck on your job-search while here. Know you will have a good time – that seems to be a sure thing for guests of the Keenan Hilton."

I flew to California and Sue drove me to Paramount. I filled out the paperwork, took their battery of tests, and then had a short interview with a personnel representative. By some miracle, I had scored 89 words per minute with ZERO errors, which I never had before – and never will be able to do again! The representative told me that there would be NO problem landing a job there. She explained that there were eleven new television pilots being prepared for the upcoming fall season, and felt certain that I would be able to land a spot on any of them. I was elated! I went back to the car with Sue, giving her the good news. I called Mom and Dad and gave THEM the good news. They were happy for me, but also worried. "Hollywood is a cut-throat, tawdry place. It's unsafe for a single woman."

I dropped the Kelleys a mailgram letting them know about Paramount's interest in me, then flew back home to get READY! Within a few days, I got a note from Carolyn which read, in part, "We are glad to hear your job-hunt was so successful. We feel the one who gets you will be the lucky one! De says thanks for all your mailgrams and letters. We can't keep up with you! 'Bye for now – Carolyn ." She drew a heart next to her name.

Sue Keenan had offered me a place to land when I got there until I scored a job – which I figured would take — oh, maybe a week, tops! That left the Problem of Where to Place Deaken while I landed the job. I called a long-time, fellow animal crusader, Peter Rasmussen, and told him my tale. He said he knew someone who might be able to board Deaken temporarily. He said he'd call her and get back to me. A few days later, Peter called again and said the lady had agreed to board Deaken. Then he told me who the lady was: actress Tippi Hedren! He said, "She has a wonderful preserve called SHAMBALA. Deaken will be VERY happy there until you can get him back with you. I can't imagine a better place in all of California for him." Then he told me Tippi would be calling soon to confirm and get more information from me.

Of course, I knew of Tippi. She had been the star of THE BIRDS and several other notable motion pictures. I was on top of Deaken's 7' high cage removing the roof one afternoon when Mom came out and reported, "You're wanted on the phone." I asked, "Who is it?" Mom said, "It's a lady." I said, "I don't want to have to jump down if it isn't important. Can you find out who it is?" "Sure," she said. Ten seconds later she said, "It's Tippi Hedren!" I LEAPED off that seven foot roof and RAN to the house.

Tippi said she was happy to offer "dear little Deaken" a home until I could land a job and then locate a rental and find a land owner in the San Fernando Valley who would allow me to have Deaken there with me. She cautioned me: "That may take a little while, you know. But Deaken will have a home here as long as he needs us. There's no rush, here." I thanked her profoundly, and then told her I had self-published a book of animal poetry that I would show her. I told her, "If you like it, and think it will sell there at SHAMBALA to benefit the animals, I will give you all the copies I have left and you can sell them there for whatever you feel they're worth." I also promised I'd give her a monthly boarding sum (which was paltry, but all I could truly commit to giving) AND that I'd pay for all of Deaken's food and any veterinary services or inspections he might need. With that verbal agreement, it seemed the way had opened! We could be on our way!

I wrote the Kelleys letting them know about Paramount's reaction, and their assurances that I could get a job when I got there. Within days, a large package arrived for "D. Smith." I mistakenly thought it was for Mom (Dorothea), and tossed it into a corner, since she and Dad had taken a trip to Alaska.

A few days later, I spotted the box again and thought, "Mom never orders ANYTHING. Maybe she ordered some bulbs for her garden. I'd better check it out; perhaps I should open it." That's when I noticed that the return address read Sherman Oaks, California. We knew NO ONE in Sherman Oaks except the Kelleys. Sure enough, it was THEIR address. With a start, I realized that the package was meant for DEAKEN!

I raced to the store and bought some film. I'd made it a habit to document everything about Deaken for the Kelleys. When I got back, I released Deaken from his enclosure and showed him the package. He sniffed it; I took a picture. For some reason, he seemed to realize it was for HIM. Instead of walking away, he began to paw at it; then to drool on the packaging. I documented that. Then I tore off the soggy butcher wrap and pulled the box apart. Inside was something wrapped in tissue paper – something large. I showed Deaken the opened box, and he probed beneath the tissue with a long forepaw, then again rubbed his chin on the gift. I documented that. Finally, I opened the tissue and found it: It was an African-print tote bag. Atop the tote bag was a letter.

> "Dear Kris,
>
> We hope Deaken will enjoy having his very own travel bag to accommodate all his gear on his trip here. We saw this bag the other day and decided it was just made to be Deaken's luggage.
>
> "Sue sent us the tape of your PACIFIC OUTDOORS show [a program on which I had been interviewed during my stint as an animal welfare activist]. We thought you came across just great, very un-self-conscious camera-wise. Are you

sure you don't want to be an actress? I can't remember if I ever told you that we enjoyed the tapes you sent us long ago, with your stand-up routine. Very good! And the shots of Deaken are terrific. Thanks even tho' it's late."

"My days lately are taken up with physical therapy visits, all this month, relative to my hip problems, but all will be well one of these days.

"Between you and me, want to tell you that De called ________ at Paramount and gave you a boost – but told her, truthfully, that you had no knowledge of the call. Maybe it will help…De says hello and don't forget the chin tickles for dear Deaken. 'Bye – love, Carolyn."

THE MOVE

My parents, Jack and Dorothea, helped me drive down. I drove my compact car, towing a small U-HAUL, and Mom and Dad drove their pick-up truck and a larger trailer rig that carried Deaken's spacious dis-assembled pen and all his "Deke-cor." As we drove out of the grapevine down the long hill into the Los Angeles basin, smog and an endless landscape of monolithic buildings dotted the far horizon. Mom said, "Are you absolutely SURE you want to do this, now?" I reflected on the blue skies and on the view from OUR place in Tacoma. It was suddenly a rather tough decision! I didn't wait long to make it though, because I'm convinced that had I taken more than ten seconds, the folks would have taken the next overpass and turned around, headed for the Northwest! I told Mom, "Yeah, I'm sure. Mom, it's all I've ever dreamed of doing." I looked again at the smog, and added, "If it takes more than five years, I'll come back." She said, "Okay. I hope you can hold your breath that long." That's the last we ever spoke of my returning home, until Mom fell ill seven years later.

All the way down from Washington, I had let Deaken out of the car every two or three hours to stretch and relieve himself. Each time, when the rest stop was over, and it was time to put him back into the car, he had balked. He was very, very tired of being confined to a cat carrier for hours on end. He was used to having the complete run of the house. So when we finally reached Shambala, I was as happy as I thought HE would be. Finally, a place he could stay, with others like himself, for the first time in his life. I thought he'd think he'd died and gone to heaven.

I was wrong.

I had raised Deaken from infancy in a HUMAN environment, with domestic house cats. I had socialized him and prepared him for a life with raucous, crazy, unpredictable HUMANS. I had always prided myself on having raised a completely HAPPY, completely NORMAL, remarkably un-neurotic "serval son." So when I opened the car door and carried him out at Shambala, he took one sniff of the air, heard several lions roaring simultaneously, and pulled me back to the car door, where he banged on it feverishly with his front paw, telling me in no uncertain terms to LET HIM GET BACK IN! With a pang, I suddenly realized he probably had no idea he was a CAT, let alone a WILD cat!

I fell apart. I bawled. Talk about "separation anxiety" — I was afraid I had doomed my "baby boy" to a period of distress and anxiety second only to being set loose on the plains of Africa itself! Deaken knew by instinct that those lions were on the lookout for "serval snacks," and he had NO interest whatsoever in remaining within a hundred miles of this place.

When I saw Tippi approaching, I quickly dried my tears and greeted her with a smile. She said, "Hello, Kris. Welcome. And here's that darling little Deaken." He was, after all, the smallest cat on the place at that time. The others were lions, tigers, leopards, cougars and cheetahs! He looked like a "pocket panther" in comparison! I admitted, "Darling little Deaken is scared to death." She said, "Oh, we have a big enclosure for him, blocked off from sight of the other cats. He'll settle in fine." Reassured, I said, "Okay." Tippi took us to the enclosure. She was right. It was six times the size of the one I had brought down, and it was housed mostly inside a shed, with only a few feet of one end sticking out, where Deaken could get a glimpse of the other cats. Tippi said, "When he's all settled in, come up to the house and I'll get his Fish and Game paperwork from you and we'll chat a little bit."

I pulled out his rugs, toys, chairs, and other paraphernalia. I wanted to make the new enclosure as much like his old one as possible, so that HIS scents would reassure him that he was in the right place. Tippi told me to feel free to come up as often as I wanted, days, nights, weekends, to reassure Deaken and to do as much for him as I could. She told me I could take him outside the compound on long walks. She told me I could stay there weekends if I so desired, so Deaken would know he was not abandoned. She reassured me he'd settle in quickly. I said, "I think he already has, pretty much. I put all his familiar stuff in the cage with him. He seems happy now."

Later that day, after I had gone, volunteer Leo Lobsenz went out to see the new serval addition. "Frankly, dear girl," he confessed to me later, "I nearly fell over laughing when I saw his over-stuffed chair, his rug, his mousey… Where were his television set and his refrigerator, I wondered!"

Mom and Dad drove me the rest of the way to LA, fifty miles distant. Sue greeted us. Later that evening, the phone rang. De and Carolyn were on the line, wanting to know how the trip went. I told them it went fine. Then Carolyn asked what Deaken thought of Shambala. I started to tell her of his FIRST reaction to hearing the lions roar: "He slapped the car door, wanting to get the hell out of there as fast as we could!" She burst into tears, crying and crying. I panicked and said, "Oh, but he's okay *now*, Carolyn! He's fine! Please don't worry!" She apologized, "Oh, I'm sorry. I just could imagine, that poor sweet cat – scared to death!" I said, "It made me cry, too, but he's okay now, I can assure you, or I wouldn't have left him there!" (As if I had some other choice!)

PARAMOUNT PROBLEMO

I settled in with Sue and then called the studio to "report" that I had arrived. Ouch! Not one of the eleven pilots had been picked up as a series! The studio had no openings for me!

I'd tell you my reaction after I hung up the receiver, but it's unprintable. Then I got scared.

Sue suggested that I call the temporary employment agencies with whose services the studios contracted. I did so, and made appointments to take their admissions tests. Passing those, I began to get temporary assignments at Disney, MGM, the Disney Channel, Fox, and other places. But the work was not steady. I worked only two or three days most weeks. It was nowhere near enough. My attempts to find a steady job were thwarted. I was temping as much as I could. Jackie Edwards had "willed" me her job on Bay Watch in order to work on Midnight Caller, since it looked as though Bay Watch would be cancelled at the end of the first season [which it was], and she wanted a show on her résumé that would be a step up. I was petrified. I had zero experience in the industry and didn't even know the software they used in their computer systems! She said, "Don't worry about that; I can teach you in one weekend." She recommended me; her bosses interviewed me, and offered me the spot then and there, asking, "What are your salary requirements?" I didn't even know what to say! Jackie said, "What I was getting, of course!" And so it was. I learned XYWRITE and SCRIPTOR over the weekend and started work the following Monday morning, shaking in my boots.

Bay Watch was cancelled a few months later, but not before I had managed to make a good impression on the bosses. Both wrote glowing letters of recommendation, and I walked across the street with the letters and a résumé in hand to apply at Columbia-Tri-Star Pictures (later SONY). I interviewed there at Human Resources. Once again, I made a good impression with the representative and began working shortly thereafter as a "floater." I worked days or weeks at a time in different positions, as the needs arose on the lot for the skills I possessed.

Sue assured me I could stay longer than we had originally agreed upon, which gave me a degree of relief, but my chief anxiety was not simply having a place to stay and steady work. My chief concern was getting Deaken "off the hill" and back with ME, where he belonged! In order to accomplish THAT, I HAD TO have steady work – for a period of time, so I'd know I was secure — so I could begin looking for a place in the valley to live, with a landlord who would allow me to keep a "wild animal" in the back yard! I had all the permits to have him legally, but that was only the first hurdle. Landlords worry about liability — and how many landlords are going to say "Oh, sure!" to a serval cat?

When I wasn't working steadily, I would drive up to Shambala (a 100 mile journey round trip) to see Deaken and to reassure him that he had not been abandoned. Every time I drove into the driveway, he'd hear my little car with those "satellite dish" ears he sported and he'd begin to cry at the top of his considerable lungs! I've heard that human mothers will leak milk when their babies cry with hunger. I nearly leaked tears every time I heard his plaintive wails for my IMMEDIATE attention! I couldn't get from the car to his side fast enough! Tippi told me the only time she ever heard him make a sound at all was when he heard my car coming in. I was happy to know he wasn't crying from the time I left until the next time I came! Whenever I'd leave at the end of the visit, Deaken would cry out to me. THAT'S when I'd cry, having to leave him! After several visits, I figured out that if I fed him just as I left, he'd be busy with his meal as I drove off, and then neither he nor I would experience the pain of separation. It worked, thank God.

We existed in this state of limbo for fourteen months. I spent every weekend driving to and from Shambala, and every night hoping that God's divine plan would very soon include the reunion of my unorthodox "family"! During this time, De and Carolyn continued to console me, encourage me, and tell me that I was just one step away from having it made. Each time I got a job, even a long-term temporary one (lasting a few months) they would send a card or a plant, congratulating me and the new employer on our mutual good luck. Without their encouragement and help, I would probably not have stayed long enough for anything else to happen.

In April of 1990, Carolyn called to tell me that De had spoken with Rick Berman, executive producer of STAR TREK: THE NEXT GENERATION, and had told him about my skills and that I was a friend of his and was looking for a job at Paramount. "Rick told De to have you call him sometime this week and set up an appointment for an interview at TREK!"

I was beside myself with excitement – and trepidation! Nearly unable to speak, I listened as Carolyn coached me: "Be sure you tell Rick you're a FRIEND, not a fan; tell him that you're a friend and that De says you're just the greatest and that you can do everything well!" Then she said to ask for $600 a week! I just about croaked! She said, "If you don't ask, you don't get!"

That weekend, I wrote the Kelleys a note, not totally tongue in cheek, and delivered it into their mailbox. In it, I mentioned that if I repudiated the fact that I was a DeForest Kelley fan, Berman would know I was lying, because "there isn't a person on the planet who isn't a DeForest Kelley fan!" Not long after, Carolyn called me, apologetic, saying, "I just want to tell you not to worry so much about that interview on Monday — and don't pay any attention to what I said about not saying you're a fan of De's. I shouldn't even have mentioned it." I said, "A LOT of people have mentioned the same thing, about not saying I'm a fan. They're kind of leery about fans working there, from what I hear. They're afraid they'll GET ——"

"Flakes?" she offered, laughing, quoting my letter.

"Yeah," I said.

"Well, we all know YOU'RE not flaky!" she said, and laughed.

I said, "Right!"

She said, "So you just go in there and be yourself and tell 'em you're De's biggest fan! It'll be all right. Everybody's a fan of De's!" I finally said, "I'm just more nervous over this interview than is normal. I REALLY want to land this job!" She said, "Then just be yourself. And ask for $600/week!" Then she laughed again. I said, "That all depends on what the job IS. I don't even know THAT, yet!" After covering several more, unrelated topics, she finished with, "Well, I just wanted to call and let you know we have our fingers crossed... We'll be thinkin' of you on Monday. Don't worry about a thing. Just treat it as you have all the others and you'll have good luck." I said, "Thank you so much."

On Monday, I drove to Paramount and entered the STAR TREK offices. Berman was busy – a meeting was running overtime – so the receptionist seated me in the hall and I waited 90 minutes. When at last I was ushered into Berman's office, I was flabbergasted when the first thing out of his mouth was, "De Kelley says you're the greatest thing on earth!" I thought, "Well, so much for trying to sell myself!" I blushed, embarrassed, and finally responded, "Well, allowing for a little hyperbole, I hope to prove him right!"

Rick asked me what I wanted to do and I said I'd had experience as a writer's assistant and as a producer's assistant. He said, "Well, I can't hire for my writers or for my other associates, but I'll let them know you're interested, and if they give you a call, come on in and interview with them." I said, "OK. That sounds good." I left the STAR TREK offices with high hopes. I felt it was "just a matter of time" before I'd be helping in some small way to perpetuate the legacy started by Gene Roddenberry and his cast and crew so many years before. When I did get an offer, the money wasn't adequate to meet my needs.

WALK OF FAME GAMES

In 1989, the Chamber of Commerce had voted to give De a star on the Hollywood Walk of Fame. Paramount Pictures had nominated De for the honor. We were thrilled. Then we waited and waited and waited for what seemed to be an eternity, and STILL no announcement as to when the star would be presented.

During this interminable waiting period, De became a little concerned that perhaps Paramount or the Chamber had dropped the ball! One time on the phone he asked me, "Do you think they have forgotten about me?" He sounded serious, so I assured him that couldn't be the case, and called Paramount to find out what the hold-up was. That's when I learned that Paramount was planning to present De's star when the next STAR TREK motion picture came out – to help publicize the movie's release! So I called De back and let him know the scoop. He said, with gallows humor, "I hope I LIVE that long!"

Sue and I were in Hollywood one day and found a store that would put any name on a look-alike Walk of Fame star in their shop and then take a photo of it. We shelled out the money for a DeForest Kelley star and then bought several prints of it. We mailed one in an envelope to De, c/o Carolyn with a note to Carolyn that read, "You'd better stand behind De when he opens the envelope, in case he faints!"

De opened the envelope, saw the star, and then the attached note: "WE WERE THERE. WHERE WERE YOU?!"

De called us and asked us how we managed the illusion. We explained what we had done. De guffawed!

I sent De and Carolyn star paperweights. One had "Carolyn" on it; the other had "DeForest." Carolyn opened hers early and then wouldn't allow De to open his until Thanksgiving. When he saw it, he called to thank me and then said, "Good! Now that I have THIS star, I don't have to worry about that f——n' star in Hollywood!" It was the first time he had ever "talked dirty" within earshot of me and I laughed!

HOUSE HUNTING – KELLEY STYLE

As a temporary, I was gaining recognition and a good reputation and feeling that almost any time now I could consider myself "permanently employed" and start looking for an understanding, wildlife-loving landlord who would allow me to move in with an African serval cat! As soon as I reported to the Kelleys that I was feeling "pretty secure" and that I'd be able to get a rental now and bring Deaken home off the hill, they pitched in! They reviewed classified ads, and called me often to report on places they had found that looked like good candidates. They suggested areas of the valley to search. They even called a realtor friend and asked her to lend a hand.

Before long, another call came in from Carolyn. She just "had to" tell me a story: De had found a place where I could have Deaken! She told me that he had been driving around and had spotted this nice house not far from them. She continued, "So he stopped in there. The landlord happened to be there at the time, painting, so De stopped in. The landlord recognized De right away, and De told him he had a lady friend who needed to rent a home with a nice, high wall fence, and this place seemed to be a good candidate. So then De told him, 'The only problem is that she has a cat.' The fellow said, 'Oh, Mr. Kelley, a cat is fine; a cat is no problem.' So then De said, 'Well, it's a rather LARGE cat,' and the fellow joked to him, 'As long as it's no bigger than a LION, I have no problem with it,' and De said, 'Oh, no! It's no bigger than a lion!' So here's the address; you go on over there and introduce yourself and tell him that you're the girl De told him about." She gave me the address and then I asked what the rental price was. She said, "$1350 a month." I just about had a heart attack! I said, "Oh, Lord! That's WAY out of my league, Carolyn!" She said, "It is?" I said, "Heavens, yes." She said, "What do you want to spend?" I said, "Gosh… $550-600 a month, unless I find a co-renter."

That didn't end their search. Not at all. I'd be sitting at work and the phone would ring, and it would be Carolyn: "We drove around a little bit this afternoon, looking at rentals in your price range." (I was speechless!) "My hip is hurting me, so I couldn't get out of the car, but De knocked on a few doors and we have a few addresses we think you should look at!" I could just imagine the looks on the faces of the people who had OPENED the doors after hearing De's knock! I wondered if any of them had passed out!

I confessed to the Kelleys that I felt I should wait until I had such an established record in the industry that there was NO WAY I would ever lose my job. De advised me, "The entertainment industry is probably the most insecure place there is to work. You'll never be able to count on it absolutely. You just have to proceed on faith. And we want you to get Deaken back home where he belongs." So did I. So did I.

I found three possible roommate candidates, but one by one, they didn't pan out… I was becoming morose. I was feeling like a rotten Mom-cat. I was even considering giving up the dream and returning home to Washington, but the Kelleys wouldn't hear of that. They just "knew" I'd be a big success as soon as I'd had my "break."

But waiting for my break was breaking my heart…

THE KELLEYS MEET DEAKEN

After seven months of waiting for me to get Deaken off the hill and into THEIR valley, without success, the Kelleys could wait no more. Carolyn called and said she and De would like to take a drive up to Shambala and meet Deaken. She asked if Sue and I would drive them there. I said, "Certainly!" She said, "Oh, good!" We decided on a day. Then Carolyn said, "So, we'll see you here at the house at – oh, how about 9:30?" I said, "Sure. You'll have to give us directions." She was astonished by that. "You have our address!" she exclaimed. "Yes, I know," I said, "But neither of us have ever been by there." She said, "You're joking!" I said, "No, I'm not." She couldn't believe that we hadn't driven by to "sneak a peek" at their home. I said, "We're NOT voyeurs, Carolyn!" She said, "Oh!"

Excited and a bit rattled, Sue and I wondered which car to use. To us, my ten year old compact car didn't seem adequate for the occasion, while Sue was concerned that her larger, classic beauty might not have the gumption to get up the mountain. Sue called Jackie Edwards and asked if we could use her new Hyundai for the occasion. Jackie was more than happy to oblige.

So, on the Big Day, Sue and I drove to the Kelley's house. We had no sooner pulled up than De and Carolyn came out the door, grinning, looking like two kids on their way to a candy store! Sue was in the driver's seat, and I figured De would join her in the front seat, and that Carolyn would join me in the back. I was wrong. De suggested that Carolyn ride "up front" with Sue, which she did. De climbed in the back with me. MY FAVORITE ACTOR in the rear seat with me, in a rather small vehicle. We put our seat belts on, and Sue started to back out of the driveway. De surprised me by grabbing my knee and grinning, "Hi, Kris! How ya doin'?!" I darn near jumped out of my skin – and he could tell! I was SOOO embarrassed – and so was he! I stuttered, "Aw… FINE! I guess! Thanks!"

Almost as soon as we got on the freeway, an inattentive driver came over into our lane without looking and just about wiped us out. Carolyn and I both saw the impending crash. Carolyn raised one leg to cushion the impact and I yelled, "Oh, God! Look out!" Fortunately, Sue quickly got us out of harm's way, with only inches to spare! The driver continued on, blithely unaware that he had come *this close* to taking out one of the Big Three of STAR TREK! No sooner had Sue avoided the collision, when De commended her, saying, "Great driving, Sue! Sure am glad we didn't dent Jackie's new car!" Of course, the thought running through OUR minds (Sue's and mine) was, "Thank God the world wouldn't be reading about a VERY tragic accident on the highway!"

The rest of the trip was happy. De told me about revisiting his boyhood home in Conyers, Georgia about twenty years previously, trying to locate a black woman whose son he had grown up with. "He was one of my closest chums," he told us. "I found the family's home – they had lived on a street, I'll never forget it: the street name was Needmore Street, and was it aptly named. These people were so poor. I found the home, and knocked on the door, and an old woman came out. I asked her if she had any idea where Emma Banks might be. She told me, 'I saw her only a few years ago.... Three or four, I think. She was very old, was in a rollin' chair...'" De said he had done several interviews in the area at the time, touting STAR TREK. At the conclusion of each interview he had asked anyone with a knowledge of Emma Banks' whereabouts to call the radio or television station and provide an address or a phone number where he could reach her. "Unfortunately, nothing came of it. I would have liked to do a little something for her." What a thoughtful man.

When we arrived at Shambala, we got out of the car and De noticed the back of my DeForest Kelley Hollywood Walk of Fame jacket, which I planned to wear at his star ceremony. De noticed the jacket – it was his first opportunity to see it since I had received it from a fellow Kelley fan. De queried humorously, "Who's that handsome fellow on your back?" I said, "Oh, some guy... I forget his name."

I directed everyone to remain very quiet outside Deaken's enclosure while I went inside to greet him, so they could see how we responded to each other without his being aware there would soon be other people entering his domain. I stepped inside the cage and greeted him, leaving the cage door open. He was sitting high atop his 5' tall den box, and when I hopped up to sit beside him, he greeted me with the customary mew and purrs and enthusiastic head rubs, then started watching the cage door, knowing that something was up. He continued to purr and head-rub, so I invited Carolyn in first. (She was halfway in already: I thought that to delay her long-awaited meeting any longer might be detrimental to her health!)

Carolyn came in, grinning ear to ear, and approached him. I told Deke, "This is Car'wyn, sweetness... the lady who sends you all those chin-tickles." I'm sure Deaken didn't understand a word, but he instinctively understood the LOVE she was telegraphing to him, and the fearlessness with which she approached him. He continued to purr and she came right up to him. He kissed her hand several times, then rubbed his chin on the back of her fingers. She was in seventh heaven! I jumped down from the den box and had Carolyn stand next to him so I could get a few photos of them together. After the photos, Deaken started looking outside the open door for other visitors, and saw Sue and De standing there. A little growl rose in his throat, but nothing outrageous, and he continued to purr in between little growls. Carolyn and I patted him and tickled him some more, and then Carolyn said, "De, come on in and meet him." Deaken let De come near, but hissed and mumbled, so De stepped back and said, "He's nervous, and I don't want to push him to do anything he doesn't want to do." I said, "Let me carry him out of his own territory, so he won't be so protective of it." I wasn't sure that was the problem. I leashed Deaken and walked him outside the compound gates, to areas where we often "played," turning him loose in the elephant straw pile. He immediately settled in to roll and play in the stuff, which everyone enjoyed witnessing. He still wasn't amenable to having so many people near him all at once (one of whom was male, tall, and undoubtedly "a veterinarian with a big needle" in Deke's mind), so we just watched him play for a time from a relative distance.

After a while, I positioned everyone near Deaken and took a few group shots of the occasion. Deaken kept facing away from the camera, so occasionally I'd call, "De!" in a high-pitched, serval-like chirp, which was my way of getting his attention. Well, it surprised me when DeForest stopped watching Deaken and looked in my direction! I laughed heartily and then clarified, "When I chirp 'De', that's for Deaken. When I say (and here I assumed as masculine a voice as I could) 'De', that's YOUR cue." De grinned and nodded – but forgot the next time I chirped, "De!" De said, "OK, I'll try to forget that I'VE always been De, too!" I said, "It should be easier for you than for a cat!" It wasn't.

I was delighted that Deaken was being civil and loving to the Kelley who most wanted to meet him "up close and purrsonal" – Carolyn – or this entire first visit would have been a fiasco. Deaken just wasn't into being a "celebrity" that day. But he did cope.

After the photo session in the straw pile, I put Deke away and said I'd take the gang on a trip through the compound. I directed Sue to drive to the first compound gate. ""I'll be the gatekeeper all the way through," I told her. "Any time we come to a gate, I'll jump out and open it." Sue behaved and drove to the first gate – but as soon as I opened it, she drove through AND KEPT GOING! I called out, "Hey! Wait for ME!" and ran after it and thumped on the trunk to get Sue to brake, so I could get back into the car. I opened the back door to get in; De was grinning ear to ear and Sue said, "It was HIS idea. He TOLD me to drive away and leave you wondering!" I threw a scowl at him. We proceeded to the next gate, and it happened again! De thought it was great sport. Now I knew why Rory Calhoun called him "a little shit" – what a prankster!

We finally got a complete tour – although I was by now quite out of breath from chasing the car down that was supposed to be transporting all of us! I told them I'd go get Deaken again and we could sit by the lake for a spell and relax. I walked to Deaken's cage and picked him up, then carried him back to the lake area. When De saw me packing a 35 pound serval over my shoulder, he joked, "Is that how Deke gets his exercise?! No wonder he's having a tough time losing weight!" I explained to De that he didn't enjoy walking around in "lion country," as the king of beasts viewed servals as snacks, "and Deaken knows that full well."

Carolyn was completely enamored of Deke and stayed right near him while Sue and De walked around to view the lions, tigers, and cougars. She couldn't keep her eyes off him.

Shortly after we settled at the lake to take some photos of De with Deaken, Tippi came out to greet us. I introduced everyone, and they had a pleasant conversation. Tippi invited them back on a Shambala weekend (a weekend that would be open to the public). When the morning was over, I put Deaken away and we headed back to Los Angeles. As Sue drove back, De said he and Carolyn would take us to Hamburger Hamlet in Van Nuys for lunch..

The meal was wonderful. I was famished, after having chased the car and carried big boy, three-legged Deaken around half of the morning. I'm embarrassed to say I wolfed down the food in such short order that I was finished almost before the rest of the party had buttered their toast! Carolyn looked over and spotted my empty plate and exclaimed, in true amazement, "Goodness!" De noticed too, grinned, and then joked, "Well, carryin' around a serval cat all morning makes a girl hungry!" Since I couldn't melt and fall underneath the table, I just turned red and endured the razzing.

De said he'd like us to meet Myrtle, the Kelleys' octogenarian desert tortoise, when we got back to their house. Sue and I were tickled pink to be invited to do that.

As we got out of the car at their home, De – behaving like a gentleman (*I* thought) picked up my jacket AND Sue's purse (hidden within the jacket) from the back seat. Sue headed to the rear seat to fetch her purse. NO

PURSE. I opened my mouth to reassure Sue, "De has your purse," but De gave me a look that could kill which indicated, "Keep your mouth shut." I hated to do that – knowing what a trauma it is for a lady to lose her purse – but complied. Sue looked on the back seat, then on the floorboards – I was agonizing for her – while De looked on, OH SO sympathetically. Sue began to get a little nervous, then stepped backward and noticed that De had my jacket in his hand. She regarded his face for a moment; he was innocent as a lamb, and concerned for her loss. Finally, Sue looked at me. I wasn't concealing the "joke" very well, I'm afraid, so she figured it out and grabbed at De's handful of goods, saying, "You tacky actor!" The gig was up—he was busted – but delighted that he had pulled one over on Sue.

We went inside the house and then out to the back yard. De found Myrtle in the shrubbery and carried her back to a spot on the lawn; Carolyn arrived with an already-prepared "Waldorf" for Myrtle. Sue and I got on the ground to meet Myrtle "face to face" and to watch her eat. De decided to join us on the ground, so I quickly grabbed my camera and took some shots of Myrtle, Sue and De. When Sue saw what I was doing, she muttered, "I hate having my picture taken." De dead-panned, "So do I." I laughed and got Sue's reaction shot; it became one of her favorites.

Carolyn gave us a tour of the house and then Sue and I took turns having our pictures taken with De and Carolyn. Sue wasn't certain how to operate my camera, so I gave her a little instruction while tucked arm-in-arm with De. I held up a forefinger vertically and told Sue, "Just focus on my finger. When it looks like a clear shot, WE'LL be clear, too." She focused and then said, "I think I'm ready." Then I said, "Oh, what am I SAYING?! Don't focus on THIS [my finger], focus on THIS!" – and I pointed to DE! De grinned at me with such love and pleasure that Sue said, "I snapped the shot. I wasn't going to lose that look on his face!" The photo turned out beautifully.

De then said he wanted to pick a "few" lemons from their lemon tree for us, so he proceeded to do that. He picked an entire large grocery sack full and then said he'd carry it to the car for us. Good thing! It could have given Sue a hernia! It weighed in at nearly twice Deaken's weight!

Carolyn was radiant at visit's end. She had been the one "drooled over" by Deaken that day and I'm not sure I ever saw her as overjoyed again in all the years I knew her after that — except when she was with Deaken on a few more occasions.

SEATTLE CONVENTION - 1990

In September 1990, I flew back to Seattle for a visit with some of my family and a few friends, whom I hadn't seen in nearly a year, and De Kelley was scheduled to appear at a convention there. I contacted my friends and family and let them know I'd be arriving – and said I hoped they'd all want to take advantage of this opportunity to see De on stage. My sister, Jackie, and her son, "little" Philip, now age 15, 6' tall and nearly 200 pounds jumped at the chance; Mom and Dad were out of the area on their way down to Southern California to see ME at the tail-end of their trip, and couldn't be there. Melody Adams, with whom I'd worked in Tacoma at the continuing education school, and her daughter and son-in-law, Johnni and Gerald White, were also eager to see me and to see De. All three were big TREK fans and had never seen De in person before. Also in attendance was Edward Smith (no relation), with whom I had worked at a wildcat sanctuary several years before. He shared his life with a lion so we were still in touch and exchanging "lion son/serval son adventures," the way two doting parents often do.

Just about the first thing out of De's mouth when he got on stage the first day of the convention was the story about how he had met me in Wenatchee. He said that since that day I had become a successful freelance writer and that I had recently moved from Tacoma to Hollywood "with all the animals" to see if I could carry my writing career even farther. The audience applauded and roared their approval. Then he motioned to me to come onto the stage. I was speechless and became almost weak-kneed! I gave him a kiss and wrapped my arm around him, mostly to keep myself upright in front of all those fans, who continued to clap and make a big to-do over someone most didn't even know. As the crowd quieted, De asked me, "You were just in Los Angeles a few weeks ago at a con I was at, weren't you?" I nodded my head. "And now you're HERE." I nodded again. The crowd started to clap and cheer again, so I said to De quietly, "I'm STILL following you around [meaning 'since 1968']." When the crowd was quiet again, De repeated, "She's STILL following me around! I can't shake her!" Then he joked, "She has something on me; that's why I have to introduce her." My mouth flew wide open with shock and surprise as he uttered this spectacular verbal intrigue (because it was such utter nonsense) and he grinned broadly. I knew I had the perfect opportunity to say something nice about De to the people gathered there, but I was profoundly speechless and couldn't say a blasted thing. It was a thrilling moment for me, but also embarrassing.

While he read one of his TREK poems that day, I went to the back of the room to sit with Carolyn. She said, "I want you to know we called Deaken just before we left there and he said to tell you it was all right for you to be up here this weekend, instead of with him." That was so sweet, because they knew I was feeling real guilt over being away from him for eight straight days, which was unheard of and Unforgivable in my own personal Book of Sins. I told her, "Thank you. I'm sure glad *you* asked him. If *I* had been the one to ask, he would have told me NO!"

Carolyn noticed that the convention's owners and promoters were hanging out at the registration table, and asked if I knew them. I said I knew them a LITTLE – knew them by sight, mainly. So Carolyn introduced me to the woman first, asking her if she knew me. The woman smiled and said that she'd seen me at a few of their conventions – any convention DE was at! Then Carolyn asked the fellow if HE knew me, and he said, "Oh, YES! Of course I know Kris! I've known her for years!" That was news to me! Either I was known in fandom before I was aware of it, or exaggeration ran rampant for that moment. I'm not sure which!

Carolyn asked when Sue and I would be flying home after OktoberTrek, the next convention, and I told her. I also told her that Kerstin Dartsch, from the former East Germany, would be coming to LA with us from the Oktobertrek function. Kerstin had been writing to the Kelleys for about six years, and since the Berlin Wall had finally come down, this was her first opportunity to see De in the flesh, and she was looking forward to it. Carolyn was happy to hear that Kerstin would be able to get to the Baltimore convention and then to LA afterwards.

At that point, De was finishing his poem, so Carolyn turned to head back to her seat. She said, "Let's get back in there and sit down," indicating that she expected me to go in and sit with her. I stopped and said, "Uh…Carolyn?" She turned back. I said, "I think I'd better go back up and sit with my friends and family from here – if that's okay with you." She looked disappointed but she understood.

The next day when I got to the con, the convention owner came over and said, "Carolyn told me to take good care of you." I joked, "What does she mean by THAT?! Hire a hit man?!" VERY sincerely, the woman responded, "Oh, no! The Kelleys are very fond of you. Don't you know that?" I didn't know how to respond to that, so said nothing. She added,

"We had dinner with them last night and we all talked about you. The Kelleys think you're going to be famous." I flushed bright red and said, "Well…wow… I hope I don't disappoint them!" And she said, "Oh, you won't. WE feel the same way." I was shaken by her information – in a good way, of course, but still… it seemed a leap of faith to truly believe she had heard all of that from the Kelleys! I wondered how I had become so lucky.

After a while, Carolyn came up and stood in the doorway until I spotted her, which didn't take long! She motioned to me to come over. As I reached her, she was responding to a question I had not heard, from a young fan. She was saying, "I married him BEFORE he became a movie star." She looked at me after answering the fan and as he walked off, I just shrugged and gave her a BIG hug. Then she hugged me and said, "OK, now skedaddle back to your seat!" She could tell I was amidst LOTS of friends and family that day. I said, "I love you!" She said, "I love you, too, Kris."

OKTOBERTREK SHENANIGANS

OktoberTrek in 1990 was long anticipated. Anticipated with a certain degree of trepidation, it's true, because Sue Keenan (and Sandy Zier, too!) had conspired with the Kelleys over Something Evil. I didn't know just WHAT it was; all I knew was that it had arrived in a box from De and Carolyn to Sue. And Sue had told me "it" was alive. There were holes in the little box. It was for me, I was told, but was to be kept carefully secured by Sue "until OktoberTrek". She would let me *gently* shake and rattle the box (because it was "alive"), but not a word slipped from her lips as to what IT was. Sue was "getting even for all the "grief" my shenanigans had caused her in the past. (By this time, during several conventions, I had short-sheeted Sue, watered down her wine, De standee'd her bathroom, and embarrassed her publicly with a campaign to bring her back for "four more years" as our President. Being the shy, retiring type who didn't like a fuss made over her, she had decided to retaliate.) Sue's and Sandy's conspiracy involved not only the noble and virtuous Boy Scout himself (De) but also the hotel staff, and I was certain I was in for first-class trouble.

Upon arriving at the Hunt Marriot Valley Inn convention hotel, I got up to the room and found that Sandy and Sue had DE-corated (more like DE-stroyed) the room with more than 700 balloons and "Disaster Area" streamers. I was in shock!

After I "sorta" cleaned up the room (shoved all the balloons into one corner so I could find the bed), I went to Sue's room and found her hiding beside her bed. She thought I had already seen "it" (the long-anticipated "got'cha"). No, the balloons and the streamers were NOT "it." There was MORE, she assured me. I decided I'd better go back and have another look.

Short-sheeted? No.

MORE balloons in the CLOSET? No

Cellophaned toilet? No.

What I eventually found was "Bones" (an inflatable Halloween-type skeleton) luxuriating in a bathtub that was more than half-filled with SHAVING CREAM! (30+ cans of shaving cream!)

The shaving cream was the "it" on which Sue and De had done their "research." She had written him of her plans for my bathtub, but had said that she didn't know how long shaving cream would last after it was out of the can, so De had taken it upon himself to TEST its durability in a dish near his bathroom sink at home. THAT'S why he kept reporting to her that "it" was still alive," and what I had been scratching my head over for 3 ½ months! The box Carolyn had sent to Sue was actually a decoy: It was EMPTY except for some excelsior shavings; she had sent it just to add additional mystery and intrigue to Sue's plan.

Well! Friends took MANY photos of "Bones" enjoying his bath – and many MORE photos of me enjoying "Bones" — and I had the photos developed the next day at a mall across the street. While I waited for the photos, I took a walk in the mall and (Thank You, God!) discovered an insulation display with two, two-foot-tall mounds of what looked exactly like SHAVING CREAM! I WANTED them, needless to say, for a "get even" got'cha in response to Sue's got'cha. I called the insulation firm (since no one was manning the booth) and explained why I needed the cone insulation so desperately. The owner of the firm chuckled and gave me permission to take them!

I took ONE of them to Sue's room in a black plastic garbage bag. Jackie Edwards (Sue's roommate for the weekend) gave me the key to the room after I cleared the joke with her, so I "broke" in – only to find SUE sitting there! YIKES! Sue looked at the large garbage bag and asked, "What's that? And HOW DID YOU GET IN HERE?" "Oh, THIS?!" I said, lifting the bag. "It's nothing, really. Just a little token of my affection for you. See you later!" I turned to leave, bag still in hand.

"GET BACK IN HERE!"

"Yes, ma'am," I said, and returned. Finally, miraculously, after a few moments of sweetness and light discussion, I convinced Sue to await my surprise from the confines of the hotel bathroom. I closed the bathroom door and put the "shaving cream" insulation cone near it, then made a sound as if I was spraying something out of a can. I sprayed and sprayed for a good thirty seconds. Sue could hear me. "Kris? Kris! What are you doing?! Is that silly string?! You'd better not be doing anything to the room that will damage it!" I continued to "spray." Finally, she couldn't stand it any longer and burst out of the bathroom. The look on her face indicated that she was — LIVID. If looks could kill….

She looked at the pile of "shaving cream," and hissed, "I HOPE you put something underneath that."

"No," I said breezily. "Shaving cream can't hurt the rug – can it?"

I could SEE her thinking, "She's REALLY done it this time. She has damaged hotel property. She has gone over the edge and betrayed good sense and common courtesy." She was speechless, but it was evident that I had "crossed the line" as far as SHE was concerned.

I couldn't take it anymore. I smiled and said, "Sue – relax." I leaned over and lightly kicked the cone of insulation; it moved over about two inches. Sue cracked up. The relief on her face was evident. She LOVED it! She said, "I should've known it was fake! It would've taken three or four cans of shaving cream to make that big a mess!" Her thumb STILL hurt from filling my tub with the stuff.

I hugged her and left, then went to my room with Reggie Holloway from Turlock, California and began to prepare for my next got'cha for De and Carolyn. We prepared a "ransom note" by cutting out words from a newspaper. We took one of the "Bones-the-inflatable-skeleton in Bed with Kris" photos (from Sue's got'cha in the bathtub) and attached it to the ransom note which read, "SEND US $50,000 IN UNMARKED BILLS OR THESE INCRIMINATING PHOTOS WILL BE TURNED OVER TO THE NATIONAL ENQUIRER!" Other photos showed "Bones" dancing with me, sitting on a table near the balloon pile, etc. We put 'em all in a manila envelope and asked Sandy to deliver them to the Kelleys the next time she drove over to their hotel.

She also had our "Pachyderm Poo Plaque" to deliver. I had made TWO shellacked plaques – one for Sue, one for the Kelleys (whom I considered "partners in crime" over the 3 ½ month long "nervous mystery"). BOTH had an enormous elephant dropping on them, borrowed from the dung pile up at Shambala, and BOTH had an engraved brass metal plate, as well, which read, "THANK YOU FOR PUTTING UP WITH ALL OUR SHIT." Atop the pachyderm poo I cemented two little love bugs, and they had little placards, containing songs:

De's and Carolyn's Song
I love you, D&C
Oh yes I "doo"
I don't love anyone
As much as you
Sometimes it's hard to tell
That's true –
But D&C I love you!

Sue's Song
I love you Sue Keenan

Oh yes I "doo"
I try so hard to prove
This fact to you
But I am sure you know
It's true
Oh Sue Keenan I love you!
UNDERNEATH the plaque, I affixed a "contents" label:
Contents: 100% Pure Pachyderm Poop
Compliments of Shambala Preserve(d)

Sue received HER "award" Thursday night. The Kelleys' was delivered to them on Friday. The "ransom note" and photos were delivered on Saturday.

Friday night I presented my comedy routine once again. It was passable. Just barely. I jotted a note to myself: "NEVER present a comedy routine to people who have just eaten a big meal. They smile and chuckle. They do NOT laugh. You die."

We spent Saturday waiting all day for De to appear on stage at 5:30 P.M. We did a lot of laughing and visiting with DKFC members and friends and also visited the Dealer's Room. By this time, we had met Kerstin Dartsch, from former East Germany, and a few other De aficionados, so we were all hanging out together in front row seats: Kerstin, Reggie, Marcia Coates and Sally Scheef. We had earned the front row seats by lining up for them as early as 3:30 A.M.

As the time approached for De's appearance, those members who had not seen De live before were fit to be tied. Kerstin was beside herself with anticipation. Another giddy, giggling fan had a chocolate cowboy that she wanted to present to him, and wasn't sure she'd have the guts.

De came on-stage to thunderous applause and a standing ovation – which was typical of his fans' reaction. He was in a fantastic mood – for some reason, even more fantastic than usual. (That should have tipped me off, but I was naïve.) He didn't seem at all nervous as he razzed me unmercifully from the stage.

His "introduction" of me actually started out very sweetly – but quickly DE-evolved. A fan raised her hand and told De, "I have something for you." De responded: "You have something for me? Come on up here." As she delivered the wrapped package into his hands, he smiled at her and said, "Thank you very much. I'll open it later, if that's all right with you?" The girl nodded her consent.

Then De went on: "I hope your gift is as interesting as what a couple of people that really deserve mention... Kris Smith... and another one is Sue Keenan, my fan club president... They have been contributing to their fan book that comes out periodically... and Kris presented me with a lovely gift this afternoon before I came. Kris has a very beautiful animal that she keeps at Shambala, which is a lion preserve. She has a beautiful serval and we were out there to see Deke... that's the serval's name. And animals are strange. Deke loves to roll in elephant dung. I know there is some joking going on in this group, and I opened this present today and here was a petrified pile, elephant dung, mounted on a lovely plaque with two weird shellacked love bugs, and it said, 'I love you... I doo doo doo.' Thanks, Kris! I really appreciated it!"

De brought Kerstin Dartsch up on the stage and introduced her as his little East German friend who had recently "been set free from her cage." Kerstin received a rousing ovation and lots of cheering. De told her he enjoyed her letters and the pictures of her pets. He asked her a question, but she was so stunned by the focus on her, and so afraid to try to speak the English she had taught herself that she wasn't able to say much, beyond, "Thank you so much!"

Later the same day, there was a bit of confusion about the sound system speaker that had been placed on the stage in order that the entire audience could hear the questions that were being asked of De before he uttered his response. De took full advantage of the weird set-up by pretending he didn't know what the heck was going on LONG after he had figured it out. (He pretended he didn't know where the questioner was standing, and kept talking to the sound system speaker.) As it got crazier and funnier, De turned in mock exasperation and said, "Boy, this is a crazy bunch. Kris, you certainly have found the right crowd!" After De's Saturday appearance, it was my pleasure to escort two happily tearful fans back to their respective rooms. It was wonderful.

Following that, the DKFC auction began, with all proceeds to benefit De's favorite charity, the North Shore Animal League. We were into the 15th or 16th item up for bid when Sandy opened the door and asked Sue, "Is it all right if I bring two members with me who aren't pre-registered?" Sue said, "Sure..." and in walked De and Carolyn! Everybody gasped and stood up, but out of respect, no one stepped forward. They just all applauded and then sat down again. Two DKFC members relinquished their chairs to the Kelleys and sat on the floor at their feet. De said he wanted to stop by for a moment to thank Sue and everyone for their support and love all through the years.

After a short time, De suggested that all of the members introduce themselves and say from whence they came. The members did so, and if De had been in their areas of the country or world, he remembered and mentioned the specifics. He had a great memory for detail, as everyone found out, even recalling who had asked which questions during his appearance earlier in the evening.

After the Kelleys left, folks swooned for a while, saying how nice the Kelleys were. Then the auction resumed, and $2,500 was raised for North Shore. The party lasted to the wee hours of the morning, so I got only two hours of sleep.

During the party, Sandy left to take De and Carolyn back to their hotel. THEN (unbeknownst to me) she got back into my room and "trashed" it again! She put a little "Bones" on the bed wrapped around a shaving cream can and left "shaving cream footprints" leading from the bathtub to the bed. In the bathtub, she had sprayed the words "IT WAS HERE." She put more streamers – and toilet paper – all over the room. I invited the party guests in to see the OLD trashed room, and we walked in on the NEW trashed room! Sue and Sandy were hysterical over that!

The next day De appeared at 4:30 PM and once again had to bring up the pachyderm poop plaques! I was afraid some "reverent" Trekker might take me out behind the hotel and lynch me afterward, so I really wished he hadn't brought THAT particular "got'cha" to public attention!

A number of us carried huge yellow fans to the convention, which were designed to read DE KELLEY FAN when opened. When De saw those fans, he got a big kick out of them and had us turn around to show the rest of the audience what was on them. THEN he said, "That's some bunch of fans I've got. You all see that? That's the same smart-ass group that presented me with that petrified… I told you about that yesterday. Elephant dung. It's an inside joke, but now that it's outside, I was thinking about it and I know why they did that. THEY know the story. A number of years ago I was doing a Western with Rory Calhoun, and Rory is a prankster. He's always doing devilish things like pretending to sneeze behind your back while dipping his fingers in a cup of coffee and then flinging it on the back of your neck… that sort of thing. So one day we were sitting outside and it was very cold. It was in the winter. We were shooting on location and we all had these little canvas dressing rooms that they had thrown up… put electric heaters in all of them for us. But, I was sitting outside on my chair, and Rory is walking by with Chill Wills… so he feigns tripping over my legs and spills coffee all over me 'accidentally.' I thought I'd had just about enough of that, and I noticed that one of the men, who took care of the horses, was walking around cleaning up the horse manure. So I asked him if he would do me a favor and take a shovel of that fresh manure and put it in Rory's dressing room. So he did – and I went with him, of course, you know... He put it in Rory's dressing room and I had him place it inside this little bitty closet. I turned the electric heater on it. True story!" The audience was in stitches by now. "Rory had to appear that night on the ART LINKLETTER SHOW and had this beautiful sport coat and flannel slacks hanging in that closet. So, I checked first with the Assistant Director, and asked him, "Am I still getting off early this afternoon?" He said, "Yes," so I left!

"The next morning I was doing a fight scene in a corral and Rory came in. He was a big strapping guy, ya know? He came in and he jumped over that corral and he grabbed me... and he shook me, and he said, 'You little shit!' But he never played another trick on me! So I KNOW the reason for that little joke you played on me!"

Later during De's appearance, a fan asked him to describe a typical week in his life, and he said, "Well, the first thing every single morning is I sit down and read my DAILY LETTER from one of my fans sitting here in this room..." He indicated me. I blushed over his "slight" exaggeration!

Following De's appearance, I was invited up to Sue's room for drinks and conversation with De and Carolyn and Sandy. Sandy's dog, Radar, was in attendance and we all had a great time petting him and having our pictures taken with the Kelleys and Radar. We talked for what seemed like an hour and then Kerstin, from Germany, came in to thank Sue for such a wonderful weekend. She was stunned to find the Kelleys there, and apologized for her intrusion, then attempted to leave. De and Carolyn both said, "No! Don't go!" The Kelleys discussed with Kerstin the positive changes in life she would experience now that the Berlin Wall was down and Germany was reunited once more. It was poignant.

Not long after, the entire gang went to my room to show the Kelleys the balloon corner. On the way down the hall to the room, De mentioned that now that I was back in the motion picture industry [working at Columbia Tri-Star, later renamed Sony Pictures Entertainment] and "on my way," there would be a lot of changes. "In a few years, Kris will probably be the head of a studio." I turned around: "Oh, right!" Unfortunately, De looked very serious about that! I again noticed how his dreams for me were much grander than MINE were for myself!

MORE HOUSE-HUNTING – KELLEY-STYLE

After having met Deaken and seeing the relationship he and I had – which was wonderful and trusting beyond belief – the Kelleys decided that he and I just HAD TO get back together under the same roof as soon as possible. I had by this time established a good reputation at the motion picture and television studio, but I did not by any means feel completely secure in it. It was again in a position as a "floater," and I didn't work steadily. I was getting great "reviews" from every person I worked for, though, and the Kelleys felt certain that I would have a job at that studio just as long as I wanted it.

They again began to look for places to rent. They found one in the newspaper in Encino, drove by it, and then called to tell me about it. I checked it out and fell instantly in love with it. It was PERFECT! I met with the landlord, and miracle of miracles: he even knew what a serval cat WAS, having seen one on a camera safari in Africa there a few years previously. The landlord was happy to allow me to have Deaken there! I was on Cloud 9. I had located a roommate – presently living in Pennsylvania, but planning to move to the San Fernando Valley — and proceeded to let Fish and Game and the City Animal Regulation Department know the address and the other particulars, so they could inspect the area and okay the permits for Deaken. It was only a matter of a few weeks, now, I thought…

Two days before the move-in fees and security deposit were due, my friend in Pennsylvania called to back out on the deal, saying she couldn't leave her mother, who was in failing health. I was BEYOND devastated. If I didn't get those fees to the landlord right away, not only would I lose my earnest deposit, I'd have to start all over again, from scratch, with permits and landlords.

I called the Kelleys from work, nearly in tears, and told them what had happened. They were easily as upset by the news as I was. Then Carolyn said, "Kris, will you let us help?" I said, "Oh, Carolyn, I can't. I can't get this place without a roommate. The monthly rent is $925 plus utilities. There is NO WAY I can afford it by myself." She said, "Suppose a little fairy helps with the rent." I said, "No way. Never. Thanks, but I could never live with myself if I did that." She said, "OK, then, let us loan you the money for the move-in fees and the security deposit. You can pay us back whenever you can." I repeated, "I can't afford that place by myself. I HAVE TO find a roommate." She said, "You will. Now, you get that house and worry about a roommate later. It won't take long." De got on the phone and said, "Get that house. Don't worry about it." I moaned, "This is scaring the s— out of me." I had never spoken in "colorful metaphors" like that to them, ever. He said, "I know it does – but do it anyway."

Carolyn got on the phone with me again and said, "De will get in the car right now and go get a certified check for the security deposit and the move-in fees. What's your new landlord's address? I'll have him drive it over to him right now for you." I gave her the landlord's address and then I started to cry, "Oh, Carolyn! You guys are so good to me! I'm crying!" She said, "So am I! See you later!"

I hung up the phone and called the landlord's wife to tell her that someone would be coming by to deliver the move-in fees and the security deposit. She was happy. Then I felt obliged to forewarn her, "Uh, don't faint when he gets there." She asked, "Why would I faint?" I said, "Well, did you ever watch the original STAR TREK?" She said, hesitantly, "Yes." I said, "Well, the fellow who's bringing the money is DeForest Kelley." She said, "Which one was he?" I said, "Dr. McCoy." She said, "Oh, my God!" I said, "He'll be by real soon." She said, "OK."

Later, she told me that she felt great trepidation waiting for De. She was under the impression that HE would be as irascible and quick tempered as McCoy was in his tiffs with Spock. Then she said, "But, Kris, when he walked in the door, he was just the sweetest, gentlest man I have ever MET! And do you know what? He is your BIGGEST FAN! He says you are going to be famous some day!" I thought, "From De's mouth to God's ears!"

So, the place was MINE, at long last. On December 22nd of 1990, I moved in. I was certain that it would be a matter of days before my "serval son" would join me there. I couldn't wait! But there was a glitch. Although the inspections for Deke's facility had been made and approved, and the permits had been issued and were tacked on the facility door, the Fish and

Game inspector hadn't been by for the "final" inspection. I called two or three times, but did not receive a call back. Finally, I called and said I'd HOLD until someone could speak to me and let me know how soon I could expect the final inspection. A lady came on after a while and reported that the final inspection wouldn't take place for another "six weeks or so." I just about flipped. I begged, I cajoled, I told the long, long story of how long Deaken had already been up at Shambala, waiting to re-join me. It fell on deaf ears.

Deflated, dejected, and utterly beaten, I hung up and cried.

I finally recovered and called the Kelleys, who had told me to call them the MOMENT Deaken got home with me. I told them the sad story, and De again offered his help; he said he would call Sacramento for me. "No," I said. "Thanks, De, but I don't think even you can perform a miracle with a state agency. You can't fight City Hall. If what I told them didn't work, nothing will." De consoled me with, "Well, I know it's hard to wait, but six weeks is certainly better than six months." I agreed.

Then I hung up and cried again.

In early January, Desert Storm broke out. The newspapers reported that, depending on the length of the war, gas rationing might become necessary. I was living 35 miles away from Shambala! "If we get gas rationing," I told the Kelleys, "Deaken may as well be in SIBERIA! We'll only be rationed enough gas to get to work and back." A day or so later, the Sacramento-based Fish and Game agent called me and said, "With Desert Storm underway, you'd better get up to Shambala right away and bring your cat home. I'll take the responsibility for any flack you get when our inspector finally gets there." I thanked her, and Deaken was underneath my new roof within four hours.

I will never know if De made the phone call to Fish and Game, but it is not outside the realm of possibility that he DID "fight City Hall" and win yet another battle for Deke and me. I suspect this, because not long after Deke came home, I got a very nice letter from Fish and Game apologizing for any inconvenience or extra trauma their delays may have caused me or my loved ones. How many times does a state agency write such a letter?

Within days, the Kelleys arrived for a tour of my new digs and to see how well (and how immediately) Deaken had settled in. I found a roommate, and all was family bliss again.

MICHAEL LANDON'S BATTLE WITH CANCER

I was working at the Columbia Tri-Star switchboard during the time word was released that actor Michael Landon had been diagnosed with terminal cancer. Like everyone else who had grown up watching BONANZA, LITTLE HOUSE ON THE PRAIRIE, HIGHWAY TO HEAVEN and various other productions in which he starred, I was enormously saddened to learn the news. Landon was a Columbia Tri-Star man at the time, and a huge gray cloud descended across the lot.

Sitting at the switchboard, I was one of six others. Our supervisor let us know that the switchboard would likely be inundated with calls from thousands of people, seeking to speak to Michael and to fax him cures, clinical trials, prayers, and anything else they thought might help. "Now, I want you to remember – as hard as it will be to do it — we are not working for Michael Landon here. I want you to spend no longer than 30 seconds on each call that comes in for him." I understood the supervisor's concern that the six operators could easily become tied up with tearful or insistent fans, doctors, and the like. On the other hand, I realized the public's immense feeling for Michael.

When the calls started coming in, it was truly in a flood. It seemed that eight or nine of every ten calls were for or about Michael. His voicemail capacity soon reached its limit; there was nowhere else to route the callers. Tearful, long-time devotees of the man poured out their hearts to me and to the others. We had to "cut them off at the pass" in as short a time as possible, although it broke our hearts to do it. I devised a short statement for myself, sharing the caller's sorrow and hope for his recovery, thanks for prayers, and I gave out his fax number to any doctor or researcher who seemed to have anything of significant value to offer him. I was on THEIR side; I wanted what every caller wanted: reassurance that Michael would learn (in case he didn't already know) how much he was loved, and that prayers and hopes and medical information would be sure and get to him. Grown men were sobbing on the phone; doctors from Russia were INSISTING that they had a treatment that would cure him. It was a trying time for everyone, and we were Michael's ears, trying to decide who to allow through and who to handle personally, briefly, compassionately ourselves.

After a couple weeks of this, I realized that callers were personally asking me to do what they couldn't do: REACH HIM with their love. This was one thing I COULD do: to let him know that the calls he was receiving were only the tip of the iceberg and that many callers were leaving it to the switchboard operators to let him know the depth of their love and devotion to him. So, I bought a hopeful, humorous little card, and enclosed a brief note letting Michael know how many thousands of people had been calling that we at the switchboard HADN'T put through. (This was to protect his remaining time and to allow him to use it in the ways he needed to use it), and then I enclosed a few photographs. One of them was a photograph of DeForest and myself. On the back of this photo, I had inscribed, "I'm the girl in this picture. You know who the fellow is: You doubled for him in an A.C. Lyles movie during your BONANZA days!" I drew a smiley face next to the inscription, put it into an interoffice routing envelope, addressed it to him, and sent it off.

It was after Michael passed away that I received a sweet, thoughtful response from his personal secretary telling me how deeply moved Michael was by my reaching out to him with love and hope. She especially mentioned that the photo of DeForest had brought back many happy memories. Needless to say, I was thrilled to know that something I had instigated had touched Michael so deeply and had given him smiles during what was surely the toughest time in his life. Yet little did I know, until De's star ceremony reception at Paramount years later, how truly impressed Michael had been.

Not long after Michael Landon passed away, the studio began cutting back the hours of temporary secretaries and floaters (I fit both categories). I went from being requested 40 or more hours a week to fewer than twelve to fifteen hours.

SECURITY GUARDS AND MISTAKEN NOTIONS

At the end of March I called Carolyn to see if she and De would be attending the annual Equestrian Celebrity Horse Show's STAR TREK NIGHT, hosted by William Shatner. Carolyn told me that she wouldn't be attending, but that De would. Her bunions were killing her and she was going to stay home and soak her feet. Then she said, "But you go ahead and look for De. You can give him a hug!"

I drove to the horse show with a friend and we wandered around, star-gazing, until the event began. It seemed that every star from the original series was in attendance, as were several of the stars from The Next Generation including Brent Spiner and Marina Sirtis. My friend and I walked over to the area where the TREK stars were all sequestered in celebrity boxes. I had purchased a stuffed bunny and had written a little note on it for Carolyn. The note read, "Some bunny loves you and missed you tonight at the horse show – ME!" I was planning to give it to De when I saw him, so he could transport it home to Carolyn.

Problem was, I was unaware that where Shatner and Nimoy are, there is something known as HEAVY SECURITY. I was wearing my Walk of Fame DeForest Kelley jacket, so I was immediately a SUSPECT. Not knowing this, I approached the celebrity box, and four or five security guards, men and women, blocked my way. I said hello and asked them if I could say a word to Mr. Kelley. "No." I then asked if they would give him a note from me, or if they'd relieve me of the bunny and deliver it to Mr. Kelley for me. "No." I was getting nowhere, fast. Worst of all, it was FREEZING in the arena that year. My feet were frozen, my nose was cold, and I was not looking forward to staying around for very much longer. Still, Carolyn had said to go say hello to De, and I had the bunny... so I stuck around a bit longer.

At various times, I could see De twisting around in his seat, looking for someone. I figured it might be ME, so I'd lean in his direction, but always there would be a MAXIMUM SECURITY guard watching my every move, and whenever I'd lean to catch De's eye, HE or SHE would lean to cut me off! I contemplated pitching the bunny rabbit in a high-flying arch, hoping the trajectory would put it somewhere near De in the celebrity box. But then I thought, "If I do something that outrageous, the security guards will take me out of here, for sure." So I waited some more. And then some more. My feet felt like ice cubes. I began to think that perhaps it wasn't worth it; I could MAIL the bunny to Carolyn...

That's when De decided it was time to leave the celebrity box for a break. As he stood up, "my" security guards crowded together in a tight configuration, right in front of me. They had my number, and I was NOT getting anywhere NEAR Mr. Kelley. Knowing I was defeated, I signaled my "surrender" and stepped BACK. At that moment, De spotted me as he climbed the steps toward me. His face lit up in a big grin and he called out, "Kris! There you are! I've been looking for you!"

You should have seen the look on the faces of those security guards. Like the parting of the Red Sea, they stepped aside so I could approach De. He gave me a big hug and quick kiss and I handed him the rabbit. We walked to a safe area and visited for a short time before he excused himself to use the bathroom. I went home and saved my feet from frostbite!

SO CLOSE…AND YET SO FAR…

Then the phone rang one day and I picked it up with a cheery, "Hello! This is Kris!" and the voice on the other end responded with an equally cheery, "Hello! This is DeForest!" I laughed, delighted, and said, "Hi, De!" He joked, "Are you fired yet?" I said, "Fired?!" Then I realized he was pulling my leg and said, "Nope. Not yet. Wednesday is my last day on this temp job." He said, "Well, I have some news for you. I was at the studio today for some fittings, and as I was leaving, I ran into Martin Hornstein, who is the Production Manager for STAR TREK VI. He asked me, 'Is there anything I can do for you, De?' and I said, 'No...' and then I got back to my car and thought about you, and I turned back to him and said, 'Yes... there is.' And Marty said, 'Anything.' So I said, 'I want to tell you about this girl I know...' and I told him about you, and he said, 'Gee, I wish I'd known about her three weeks ago. I'd have her working right now! We're pretty well staffed, but have her give me a call and if anyone drops out or I can think of another job, I'll give her a call.'" I was struck dumb. I finally managed to say, "De... thanks!" He said, "Now, it's nothing at all certain. He said he doesn't have any openings, and that it's a matter of someone dropping out... but it's a start anyway."

I called Mr. Hornstein and he gave me an appointment to meet with him the following week. I quickly mailed off my résumé and a few letters of recommendation, along with a brief cover letter stating, "I'm the race horse DeForest Kelley is backing." I thought that was kind of cute – and who knew, perhaps Mr. Hornstein was a racetrack aficionado! I decided "it couldn't hoit" to be a little avant garde!

On the day of the appointment I walked into Mr. Hornstein's office and he greeted me warmly with, "Well, you must be Kris Smith, the race horse De Kelley is backing!" I smiled, acknowledging that he had received my résumé package. He pointed to a memo on his bulletin board. "As you can see, I already have issued a memo stating that if there are any drop-outs in the production, I want to be notified. That way, if it's anything you're qualified to do, YOU will get it." There was no way to respond to that verbally. I looked at the floor, and said, "Gee, I feel... overwhelmed by all this! Thank you." He said, "If I had known about you a month ago, you'd be here now. I don't even have a spot for you on camera in a scene." I just about dropped dead! "We like to do that with good fans of the show, to show our appreciation." I shook my head and said, "That's okay. Just knowing I'm under consideration to work with you is fantastic." He didn't say anything more, and I realized he was busy, so I excused myself and floated out of there...It didn't even matter that I hadn't landed A Job. I had landed something far greater: a sense of adequacy, of belonging, of validation.

It seemed I was in a strike-out pattern with all things TREK! I had to call and let the Kelleys know about it. They were supportive and said that things usually happen for the best, and that perhaps something better was coming along, and that's why this hadn't panned out. I hoped they were right.

SURPRISING SUE

On April 23rd Carolyn called. I had written them a letter in which I'd mentioned that Sue would be over on Saturday afternoon for a visit. I had told Carolyn that I'd cook some burgers and we'd kick back and yak. Carolyn called to ask if it would be all right for her and De to come by during that time to surprise her. I said, "OF COURSE! That would be WONDERFUL!" She asked, "Are you sure? It won't inconvenience you in any way or wreck your plans?" I said, "Are you kidding? Of course not!" Then she asked if I'd be able to keep it a secret from Sue. I said, "Certainly. I can keep my mouth shut." So, we planned out the surprise: I was to call the Kelleys as soon as Sue arrived at my place, since I wasn't exactly sure when Sue would arrive.

The following Saturday, Sue arrived at about 4:45 P.M. I got her a drink and a chair and sent her to the back yard to smoke. Then I quickly dialed the Kelleys and told Carolyn, "She's here!" Carolyn said, "We'll be along shortly!" I had previously directed the Kelleys to just walk in; not to knock upon arrival, to delay the surprise for as long as possible. They agreed to that. When they arrived (silently), I escorted them through the house to the back door. I greeted Carolyn with a big hug and kiss and whispered, "I love it when a plan comes together!" I stepped over to greet De and noticed that he was packing a pie box. MY voice rose significantly (too significantly, I soon found out)!

"What's this?!"

"Our contribution to the picnic."

It was a variety mousse pie – different flavors. I put it in the fridge. Carolyn said, "I sent him for a carrot cake, and he came back with THAT!" By now we were talking in normal, non-hushed tones.

By this time Sue (who was lounging in the back yard) had heard the commotion and had recognized De's and Carolyn's voices, so she came into the kitchen. They greeted each other with smiles and hugs.

We left the kitchen for the back yard. Carolyn was clutching a small white tissue-wrapped package; "Deaken" was written on it in her beautiful calligraphy. I told her we'd go see Deke as soon as I got everyone settled with drinks. I asked if De wanted a DeForest Kelley (vodka and water with a twist of lemon) and he said, "Sure." I asked Carolyn what she wanted, and she selected a wine cooler.

We went out to see Deaken, who was lying in the back yard on the grass for the occasion. Deke was very happy (and relaxed) to see them again and he began to drool copiously on De's outstretched hand. Carolyn exclaimed, "I want him to do it to me!" As De was petting Deke, I noticed a huge bruise on his right hand. I asked, "What happened to you?!" He said, "Oh, yes. A stunt man kicked me." After a few minutes with De, Deke did go to Carolyn, and he also accepted her gift: a little white teddy bear hugging a red heart. I joked, asking them if they had doused themselves with Purex before coming over (because they knew that Deaken was a push-over for bleach), and De joked back, "We thought about it, but didn't do it." I explained to Carolyn all about Deke's moment-by-moment attitudes and body language, explaining what the head, feet and tail positions and movements indicated. She was fascinated.

After fraternizing with Deke for about twenty minutes, we stepped away and I started to cook the hamburgers and chicken. I asked everyone how they liked theirs done. Carolyn said, "Rare to medium rare." De said, "Medium." Sue said, "Cremated." Everyone got theirs cremated, because I ain't no cook and never claimed to be one. No one complained and everyone complimented "the cook." There were great liars in the back yard that day.

Deke decided HE might like to join the line at the food table, so I knelt down in front of him, blocking his further approach, and said, "No, sweetie. You have to go lie down and wait until we're finished." Deke, responding to the blocking position of my body language, did an immediate about face and went back out into the yard, where he lay down as "directed." I stood up to find Carolyn looking at me with total incredulity. "Did he UNDERSTAND that?!" she asked me, awed. "Yes," I said. "Really?!" She looked at Sue for confirmation and got it.

After we ate, I brought Prissy (my pet chinchilla) out for them to meet. Prissy sat atop their shoulders and looked adorable. At several points, chinchilla poop (inoffensive as can be) rolled off their shoulders and onto the porch. When it happened on De's shoulder, I joked, "Ain't it great to be a big movie star to a chinchilla?!" De laughed and said, "Yeah." While De held Prissy, Carolyn mentioned the exquisite softness of the animal's fur, and at the same time Sue was mentioning the exquisite softness of De's beard in TREK V during the campfire scene. As Carolyn mentioned stroking Prissy's "whoop-tee-do" (tail), I was stroking De's beard, to confirm Sue's claim to its softness. So the conversation went something like this:

Carolyn: Stroking Prissy's whoop-tee-do is really something!
De: They're not stroking Prissy's whoop-tee-do; they're stroking MY whoop-tee-do!

I jumped right in and joked, "Carolyn, I'm INNOCENT! I'm NOWHERE NEAR De's whoop-tee-do!"

After we put Prissy back into her cage, we yakked about Gates McFadden, LeVar Burton and other "new" cast members, whom Carolyn had met the week before at Leonard Nimoy's get-together. Carolyn said, "They're very nice people." Then she grinned and added, "We didn't watch the first series, either!"

Carolyn began to speak of a favorite model of hers, Iman, whose career she had been following for years. Iman would be appearing in the next film with De, and Carolyn related that De worked until 11 P.M. with Iman one night – "or so he SAYS he was working!" De lifted up his eyeglasses at that point, arched his eyebrows and winked dramatically, joking, "I've got to keep these old engines primed, you know!" Sue tried to pry more information out of De about TREK VI but had no success. His lips were sealed.

Carolyn asked what day we could visit the STAR TREK set – which surprised us. We decided on a day and she said she'd make the arrangements.

We walked out to the car, their famous 68 Thunderbird (still in showroom condition), and oohed and aahed over it. Then I asked Carolyn if she wanted to see MY car, which had been bashed in on one side by an out-of-control sedan weeks earlier, and she said, "Oh, yes!" so we headed over there. De, still a bit out of the loop, inquired of Sue, "Where are they going?" and Sue said, "To see the accordion." Over at my car, Carolyn pointed out the bumper sticker to De: "Lifestyles of the Poor and Unknown," and they both laughed about that. Then De looked at the undamaged side of the car and said, "Gee, this side doesn't look bad at all!" Shortly thereafter, they drove away, after we had hugged again and thanked each other for a wonderful time.

FATHER'S DAY

I had been sending De "Like a Father" Father's Day cards, and Carolyn "Like a Mother" Mother's Day cards ever since moving to California in 1989, because they always seemed so interested and had been so helpful in any way they possibly could – just like real parents who support and encourage their children's dreams and goals! Most of the cards and gifts were sentimental and poignant, but in 1991 on Father's Day, I found a shaving kit in a Hallmark shop that I felt would put De right on the floor. (I was right.) The kit was imprinted with primitive drawings of a toothpaste tube, a hairbrush, dental floss and other similar items. The inscription on the face of the kit proclaimed, "Stuff that I don't want touching my underwear."

VISIT TO THE SET OF STAR TREK VI

Sue and I drove to Paramount to watch a bit of TREK VI being filmed.

We got onto the Paramount lot and eventually made our way to one of the stages where TREK VI was filming. Producer Ralph Winter's secretary had said we should plan to stay no longer than about 40 minutes; I nodded my agreement, and we went over and entered. Jimmy Doohan (Scotty) and Walter Koenig (Chekov) were standing around shooting the breeze. De was nowhere to be found at the moment, so we struck up a conversation with the other actors, exchanging jokes and other comments. After a short time, Shatner and Nimoy entered the sound stage, but passed us by and went to a corner where they could run their lines. Still no De, so Doohan and Koenig and we girls continued to chat.

After about fifty minutes, De ambled into the sound stage. He was dressed in a Starfleet uniform that was draped with deer hide and his feet were covered with animal skins as well. His blue eyes shone so brilliantly, even from thirty feet away, and he looked so handsome that I caught myself nearly gasping. I had never seen him in person as McCoy before, and it almost took my breath away! At the time, I was sitting in De's director's chair, and before he could come over and claim it, I asked Jimmy Doohan "to act like you've known me for decades." Taking up the little improvisation, Jimmy got behind me and draped his arms and hands over the top of my shoulders, ALMOST grabbing my breasts! I quickly vetoed his assertion regarding THAT much knowledge of me! He snuggled his face next to mine and looked to be crooning into my ear.

De came around, spotted us, and – perplexed — asked, "Do you two know each other?" I said, "No! We've just met!" De said, "I see!" I peeled Jimmy off me and asked De, "Do you want your chair back?" De said, "No. I've been sitting all morning." So I stayed put for a time. But then I got up, again noticing his deerskin wrap, and accosted him. "Mr. Kelley – I guess you KNOW what DEAKEN will think when I tell him Uncle De was dressed up in animal skins!" De's eyes became real wide, and he said, sounding slightly panicked, "Don't tell him! I'm not responsible! It's what they gave me in wardrobe!" I laughed then and said, "Okay, then. I won't tell him. It's OUR secret."

Soon thereafter, the director, Nicholas Meyer, came into the sound stage and De introduced him to us. De said, "I'd like you to meet Sue Keenan, my fan club president." They shook hands. Then De said, "And this is Kris Smith, who's working on becoming a screenplay writer." We shook hands.

Not long after that, Meyer called "Action!" to the cast, and we watched while the actors exited a turbo-lift and headed down a corridor of "the Enterprise" talking about assassins. We had been there a good hour and a half, and I knew we had vastly overstayed the time alotted us to be there, so I reluctantly tapped Sue, and we left. De called later that night to ask me, "Why did you leave? The next scene was MINE!" I apologized and told him we didn't KNOW what to expect, and that we had already overstayed our time limit by more than an hour. "I didn't want to have the crew thinking you had fans who didn't follow instructions." He agreed that I was right in leaving, but we were BOTH sorry that we had missed his scene.

CAPTURING A HALF-CENTURY OF LOVE ON FILM

Although De had been photographed from every angle thousands of times during his career, I wondered if he and Carolyn had ever sat down for a photo session TOGETHER – so I asked them. They had never had it done, they said, because they had no children and didn't know of anyone else who would want anything like that. I quickly assured them that all of their friends and a number of relatives would undoubtedly LOVE a photo of them together. They had been married 46 years by this time and I felt that a photo session was LONG overdue. I told them I knew a professional photographer, Bill Dow, who would photograph them for FREE, at my house in my back yard, even with Deaken if they wanted. Carolyn said, "Let me think about it." A few days later, she called back and said they would like to take us up on the offer. I called Bill Dow and decided on a date and time, and then let the Kelleys know.

Bill hadn't met the Kelleys before, so there were a few minutes of chatting and getting to know each other before the photo session began. They chatted while Bill erected the umbrellas, lighting and other paraphernalia. De gave me his crew cap from STAR TREK VI, which I immediately planted on my head for a moment.

While Bill finished setting up, De and Carolyn went out into the yard to visit with Deaken, who was again friendly, but not overly so. He was on steroids for an ear problem, and so after a little while he "checked out," closing his eyes – his way of indicating, while he still appreciated their petting, he didn't want to have to react personably! He wanted to relax and enjoy it without reciprocating in any way. The perfect guests, they understood and didn't force the issue.

When it was time to shoot the photos, Bill got several of De and Carolyn together, and while they sat for those, we chatted and laughed – a lot! At one point, Bill apologized to them, saying that he was more accustomed to photographing wild animals up at Shambala or dogs and cats – at which time De assured him, "Oh, that's all right!" and he began to bark! Carolyn jumped right in and began to meow! I took my cue from their silliness and grabbed a few squeaky toys and began to squeak them and call to "doggie" De and to "kitty" Carolyn, in the way a pet photographer would in order to get an animal's proper attention for the camera! De and Carolyn cracked up; so did Bill and I, and Bill caught the hilarity in a couple of photos. Bill then asked Carolyn if she'd like a few photos alone with the newly-acquired Poppy (a black and white kitten, whom Deaken had promptly adopted). Deaken was still in the yard, not amenable to having HIS nap spoiled by the goings on beneath the patio roof. Carolyn said yes, eagerly, so Bill took several photos of her with Poppy. Then Bill asked De if he'd like to sit for a few pictures. When De said he would, Bill asked him, "Which is your good side?"

(knowing that some actors have a preference). De responded, "I don't HAVE a good side!" I objected, telling Bill, "De doesn't have a BAD side!"

Just as the photo session appeared to be over, De motioned to me and said, "Get over here, Kris. We want our picture taken with you." I was flabbergasted! I sputtered, "But, I'm dressed for DEAKEN. I'm not dressed for a photo session!" (I looked real frumpy!) De wouldn't take no for an answer. "Well, go CHANGE, then!" I said, "Good heavens! *Why?!* Are you SERIOUS?!" He was. Then Carolyn directed me, "Go get changed!" I quickly bolted inside the house, threw on a blue turtleneck shirt, and then returned. Bill sat me on a chair between De and Carolyn, and one of my favorite photos of all time was snapped at that moment. I'll always be grateful De thought of that, and insisted!

After the photo session under the eaves of the patio, we sat in the back yard HOPING Deaken would eventually decide to have his picture taken with the Kelleys against the lovely background Bill had provided. It was not to be. Deke just wasn't in the mood that day to have his serenity botched by flashing cameras. I cajoled, begged, and petitioned mightily, carrying Deke into position for the photos, but he got grumpy, growled unhappily and slapped me with a forepaw. De said, "Don't force him. We'll do it another time." I suggested that they could just sit with Deaken on the lawn, under his OWN terms, and have their pictures taken with him there. They smiled and agreed with that.

As the afternoon wore down, we visited more, talking about many different topics. They spoke of long time friends of theirs, cinematographer William Daniels and his wife Betty, who used to live in Palm Springs, and of all the good times they'd had there. De mentioned that security on the set of TREK VI was so tight that "You'd think we had something to do with National Security! It's to the point where they almost ask to look in your trunk as you exit the lot!" De told me he got everyone to sign his script so that Sue could auction it off and get the best possible price for it to benefit the North Shore Animal League. De again impressed upon me, with great intensity, the fact that I was the only one who got a TREK VI production crew cap who DIDN'T work on the movie. It made me feel really special!

After De sat with Deaken on the lawn for a few photos of just him and me with Deke, I explained how a cat on steroids is more unpredictable than a cat with all its senses intact. De put his arm around me and hugged me playfully, then SHOVED ME AWAY (equally playfully) and then said, "NOW you tell me! Now that I've put my LIFE in jeopardy with a DRUGGED CAT!" I responded, "THAT'S why I was sitting so close to you and watching Deke's every move – so I could INTERVENE if he decided to do anything uncivilized!" De said, "I know. I'm just joking. I didn't really feel in any danger!" Bill intoned, "The serene confidence of sheer ignorance." They both laughed.

As we parted company that day, De and Carolyn spotted Bill's car, which had a bumper sticker attached that proclaimed, "ONLY ELEPHANTS SHOULD WEAR IVORY." De agreed with the sentiment and mentioned that it was hard for him to watch circuses on television because of the exploitation of the animals.

STAR TREK CEREMONIES — 1991

Sue had surreptitiously asked her club members to send De cards and notes of congratulations for his upcoming star ceremony on the Walk of Fame scheduled for December 18 that year, so she could send them to him and Carolyn as part of the year's anniversary package. Carolyn called to tell me how "choked up" De was by the sentiments expressed therein, from all the fans who had responded to Sue's request.

The card that I had sent De read: "Great men may be among us… but none compare to you." I had taped a few small photos of De, De and me, and De and Carolyn inside the card and then written, "Congratulations on your STAR and for remaining the wonderful person you are! Love, Kris." On the empty, inside facing page, I had quoted the trailer from TREK VI: "They have been our guides, our protectors, and our friends." Beneath that, I had written, "How *very* fortunate I feel! Most fans have had only the reel McCoy as their guide, protector and friend – and are grateful. I have had DeForest Kelley as 'all of the above.' Your caring has transformed me into someone worthy of being cared about. Thank you. God Bless you. I love you." For the accompanying letter, I created a special letterhead on my PC. The heading was respectfully engraved, "YOU DESERVE ALL OF LIFE'S GOOD THINGS. YOU ARE ONE OF LIFE'S GOOD THINGS."

The letter read:

> Dear, dear De,
>
> Where do I begin?
>
> Your star ceremony affords me the opportunity to get *really serious* (for once) and to pour out to you all the love, pride and respect you're engendered – seemingly FOREVER.
>
> So where are the proper words to adequately express any of it?! **sigh** I'll try…
>
> Your skill as an actor is exceeded only by your skill as a wonderful human being. In a way, I wish I had met you FIRST in the way that I met Tippi – without knowing much, or caring much, about "who" you were as an artist. Why? Because it took me so long to get OVER seeing you

primarily/chiefly as "my FAVORITE actor" – with all the accompanying jitters and shyness and paranoia that that "awesome" perspective entails. It took a LONG time before I could genuinely RELAX in your presence and appreciate you as a real, flesh and blood human being who is special DESPITE what you do for a living (instead of BECAUSE of it).

That's what I first responded to in Wenatchee in '68 upon scrutinizing you from the sidewalk (before introducing myself): your genuine NICENESS. I stood fidgeting on the sidewalk, gauging whether or not you were going to DISAPPOINT me if I approached you for an autograph and a smile. (My initial fear was, "Do I really want to RISK being turned off by an actor I'd really LOVE to keep on LIKING?" It had happened before!)

Well! After studying the situation for several long minutes, it became abundantly apparent that you and Carolyn were *very nice people*. So THAT'S when I gathered the courage to step forward and open my mouth – and hope that my heart wouldn't leap out of it and land on the floorboard of your convertible!

You DESERVE the star – and I mean this in the "old-fashioned" way: You deserve the honor to the degree for which stars were ORIGINALLY bestowed, NOT in the way they are too-often awarded nowadays (as a publicity gimmick). Your career has spanned (don't say "Ouch!") nearly five decades. You're genuinely one of Hollywood's *decent, honorable* guys (there might be four or five others, but their names escape me at the moment ☺). You do good deeds (quietly, which makes them even "gooder," 'cause they're not done for the sake of publicity). You're a GENTLEMAN star (who's an accomplished and convincing "bad ass" ONLY in the movies). You meet, exceed and ANNIHILATE the criteria for being awarded an "old-fashioned" star. In fact, I can easily envision you being named MAN OF THE YEAR, no problem… no exaggeration… no stretch of the imagination. I think the Creator (the REAL "Big Bird of the Galaxy") delights in you and sees you in the same way He sees Yosemite or a healthy new bud on a rose bush: as a damn' fine piece of workmanship, if He does say so Himself…

I don't know what else to say… how else to express how proud I am of you… how lucky I feel to have "fallen" for you… how blessed I am to know you well enough to know I'm RIGHT about all of the above!

You are an inspiration to me. "When I grow up" — I want to be just like you!

I love you, De. Kris

There was one other important ceremony that year, thirteen days before De's star ceremony. On December 5th (which, coincidentally, was De's mother's and Sue Keenan's natal day), Mann's Chinese Theatre in Hollywood honored the entire original STAR TREK cast by having them place their signatures and handprints in the forecourt of that world-renowned place. Hundreds of fans gathered hours ahead of time, and we were of course among them, to get good spots from which to observe the proceedings. We arrived at around seven a.m., and we were among the first, so we were positioned against the restraining rope. It wasn't long before the entire boulevard was crowded with fans from all over the world. Bleachers were erected across the street to accommodate as many as possible; crowds of fans also extended down the boulevard for a block or more in each direction. Fortunately, microphones were set up so that those in attendance farthest away could still hear the event, if they couldn't actually see it. At about 11 o'clock, a local band approached Mann's from the east, playing the STAR TREK theme. Behind them, in three separate cars, was the cast. The crowd went wild.

Before the ceremony took place, there was a "photo op" for the media. The cast came very near where we were standing. This gave me the chance to see what De was wearing. He had selected the black wool and leather sweater I had given him for his birthday that year! I was tickled pink. But, just in case I hadn't noticed, when De spotted me, he waved, grinned, and then pulled the hem of the sweater outward, pointing at it, and mouthing the words, "Do you see what I'm wearing?" I nodded "Yes," and then mouthed back, "Thank you."

The cast gathered on the sidewalk and milled around as the cement was prepared for their signatures and prints. While there, they engaged in some private banter that no one else was privy to. There were lots of smiles; there were also some somber faces. De looked ready to cry a time or two as he apparently considered the honor that would soon be bestowed on the cast. When the time came to write their names in cement, Shatner and Nimoy went first. Their names appear side by side at the top of the large cement slab. Then it was De's turn. The space provided to him was immense, as he was writing alone, so he took advantage of it and signed his name twice as large as the other two had. During the signing, a photographer called out to him, "DeForest, look up here! Look up and wave!" so De obliged him, then went back to his signature – but left the 's" out of DeForest! The emcee for the event, Johnny Grant, who had previously mentioned that sometimes people were so nervous that they misspelled their names, jumped right on the situation, and announced, "I told you! It has happened again! DeForest Kelley has misspelled his name!" De, still on his knees, assumed his gruff McCoy persona, then threw his hands outward in mock exasperation, and groused, "Damn it, Jim, I'm a doctor, not a bricklayer!" Everyone cracked up; De quickly added "s" to his name, and then stood up, laughing and shaking his head. Following the cement-signing, someone on the stage asked Shatner if the rumor was true that STAR TREK VI would be the last feature film for the cast. Boos emanated from the crowd the moment the question was posed. Shatner responded, "STAR TREK VI, without question, is the last of the STAR TREK movies." Boos and catcalls met his comment. He continued, "The heads of Paramount, who are wise men, told us this was so, and we never go against the heads of studios."

Shatner handed the microphone to Leonard, who confessed, to many laughs, that he was "emotional." He mentioned that Gene Roddenberry had been the first writer honored with a star on the Walk of Fame. Then he thanked the many craftspeople responsible for the show. He said the cast was receiving an honor which could not have happened were it not for the thousands of writers, directors, producers and other behind-the-scenes folks who had made it all possible. He handed the microphone off to De, who at first joked, "Damn it, Jim, you didn't say it was gonna be BIG!" Then he thanked the late Gene Roddenberry for his creation and vision, and then he thanked Mann's Chinese Theater for the honor; and then the audience. "If it wasn't for you, the fans, none of us would be standing here today!" The crowd cheered wildly. De handed the mike to Jimmy Doohan, who disagreed vehemently that this would be the last STAR TREK.

Walter Koenig respectfully and sincerely thanked the behind-the-scenes folks (especially the writers) who made STAR TREK possible. Then regaling the crowd with a humorous account of the LAST time he had played in wet cement: "I was a 9 year old boy in New York, and what I wrote in wet cement at that time is unprintable in a family newspaper." He then handed off to the ebullient Nichelle Nichols, who looked heavenward and said, "Mom, daddy said I'd be here someday, and here I am!" George Takei said, "On the future of STAR TREK: I agree with Bill Shatner. We do go by what our bosses tell us, and I think our bosses don't reside in the executive corridors of Paramount. MY bosses are all out there!" – indicating the fans – "and frankly, I think we will keep on Trekking!"

Just a few days before De's star ceremony, I knew he was probably extremely nervous, so I dropped him a brief note telling him that I had written his acceptance speech for him and so he didn't have to worry about a thing. "Here it is," I wrote. "I hope you like it. Don't change a word or I'll be mad."

My acceptance speech read,

> How lucky and how grateful I are
> To have my very own f——n' star!"

I knew it would give him a big laugh, and a little comic relief, as it would refresh his memory of the time I had given him a star paperweight and he had said, "Good. Now I don't have to worry about that f——'star in Hollywood!"

On December 18th, hundreds of fans gathered again to honor De when he received his star on the Hollywood Walk of Fame, only a block and a half west of Mann's Chinese Theater. Once again, Sue and I were there, along with Sandy Zier (later Zier-Teitler) from Maryland, Ann Johnson from Texas, the Gerald Whites and their new-born daughter Amber from Washington State, and many others.

It was a glorious morning, perfect for a star ceremony. Some of us silently thanked God or Gene Roddenberry, up in heaven, for the weather, as a terrible storm had been forecast, and here it was, sunny and warm!

Sue, Sandy and I were "honored guests" of De's, and were afforded the opportunity to stand with the celebrities during the ceremony. After consideration, we elected to stay with the crowd for two strategic reasons. The celebrities and honored guests were positioned BEHIND De and the podium, which would have prevented us from seeing De's reactions to what was being said. Also, I had planned to document the event on a still camera, so I could give the Kelleys an album of photos afterward with which to remember the day.

The event began in a spectacular manner. De's star is located at 7021 Hollywood Boulevard, directly in front of the Galaxy Theater, a two-story complex with two escalators leading up to the theater. The powers that be had decided De should make his entrance down the west end escalator, so Johnny Grant announced, after a few preliminaries, "Today we have the pleasure of honoring the man who brings to mind the qualities of a self-confident, mature actor who has honed his skills with deliberate care and success. Today in front of the Hollywood Galaxy, we honor DeForest Kelley… And now… I know that you all know the characters, I know that you all know the stories better than I do, but I must tell you a little more about this gentleman. I want to remind you this morning and the historians who will be looking at these tapes years and years from now. As you know, DeForest is known worldwide for his popular role as Dr. Leonard "Bones" McCoy, Chief Medical Officer of the USS Enterprise in the highly successful STAR TREK television and motion picture series. DeForest was born and raised in Atlanta, where he first used his talents in the church choir. Later, a radio performance on stage at WSB earned him an engagement with Lew Forbes and his orchestra at the Atlanta Paramount Theater. After moving to California, he joined the Long Beach Theater Group. During WW II, a Paramount talent scout noticed him in a Navy training film. This resulted in a screen test and a contract. DeForest remained with Paramount for 2 ½ years, making his motion picture debut in Fear In the Night. Let me tell you just a few of the other films he has appeared in: Gunfight at the OK Corral, Raintree County, Warlock, Where Love Has Gone, The Law and Jake Wade, and a myriad of television appearances include Schlitz Theatre, Playhouse 90, Zane Grey Theater, Rawhide, Bonanza. DeForest made his debut in the STAR TREK television series in 1966, and needless to say, the rest is history. DeForest has given freely of his time and talents to many humanitarian efforts, including his many hospital visits to children and veterans. DeForest is currently reprising his role as Dr. McCoy in STAR TREK VI: The Undiscovered Country, which I have a feeling all of you have seen at least six times." (Cheers.) "Ladies and gentlemen, please join me in welcoming DeForest Kelley as he receives his star on the Hollywood Walk of Fame! And here he is, beaming down from the Enterprise – DeForest Kelley!"

De suddenly appeared at the top of the Galaxy escalator, as the STAR TREK theme played. He stepped onto the escalator and rode it down to the thunderous cheers and applause of the crowd gathered there. De told me later that it was the longest escalator ride he had ever taken! "I felt like a

Ziegfeld Girl! After I threw the Vulcan salute, I didn't know what else to do!" To the crowd assembled there, he looked calm, collected and radiant.

Upon reaching the elevated staging area, at least two feet above the level of the sidewalk, De vaulted right up next to Grant, who marveled, "My God, you're nimble!" De shook Grant's hand, then stepped back while Grant introduced the many celebrities and other guests who had come to say a few words about De. Grant first welcomed and introduced legendary Paramount producer A.C. Lyles, a long-time friend of De's, who spoke of his affection for De and of their long association. A.C. bounded up on the stage and joked, indicating De's entrance on the escalator, "We at Paramount love DeForest Kelley so much that we spared no expense; we built him this escalator just for this occasion!"" The crowd and De laughed, and AC added, "If that isn't an entrance, I don't know what is! As Johnny Grant mentioned, I have been with Paramount 54 years, and De has been with us 45 years, but the best thing is that Carolyn, here, has been with De for 46 years." There were cheers and applause. "And I tell you, I look over there and I see some of De's fans, like Kris Smith and Sue Keenan, and I know that when they say STAR TREK, the word STAR means DeForest Kelley." More applause, as other fans agreed with the statement. "And now De has his name and his prints at Mann's Chinese Theater, and he's going to have his name here on Hollywood Boulevard – but the main thing is that DeForest Kelley has his name in all of our hearts." De was overcome by A.C.'s statement, and lifted his glasses to wipe away some tears. The fans whistled and cheered and applauded. "Our arms are around him, our hearts are with him, and we at Paramount love De as much as he loves us. Thank you." Then A.C. said, "You will see all the stars of STAR TREK here today to honor De, but Bill Shatner couldn't be here, so he sent me a letter to read for him. It says: 'DeForest Kelley has long deserved a star on the Hollywood Walk of Fame. I'm just a little apprehensive that all this excitement might be too much for him, so everybody put your arms around him and make sure he knows he's loved. I'm very sorry I can't be there with you, but I'm in the tropics trying to get you a coconut! Love, Bill." A.C stepped down and Grant introduced Leonard Nimoy.

Nimoy jumped onto the stage, shook hands with and hugged De, and then grinned into the microphone, "I wouldn't miss this for anything. This is really great. I hope that one time, during this ceremony, we will hear him say one more time, 'He's dead, Jim.'"

Then he got serious. "In the great tradition of people like Gary Cooper, this is the man who stands there beside you and says the lines, and plays the drama when it's drama and gets the laughs when it's funny – and don't turn your back on him, because he really knows what he's doing. He is great. He's a friend, he's a colleague; he is a rock on which much of STAR TREK stands. De, may you live very, very long and prosper. God bless you."

Next Johnny Grant introduced George Takei. George was eloquent. "This is a very, very happy day for all of us. It's great sharing this wonderful day with De. Two weeks ago, we shared another happy day, just a block down, at Mann's Chinese Theater, and De announced that he was a doctor, not a bricklayer. After he finished, he didn't have to tell us that; we knew. But one thing that doesn't need to be said, he is most definitely an actor, and he certainly most appropriately belongs right here in the Galaxy – Dr. McCoy right here in front of the Galaxy... It's appropriate that he be here, because he has friends all over the galaxy. He's beloved by everyone, and De... it's wonderful to be able to say, Friend – we're really happy to be here to share this happy day with you."

Walter Koenig stepped up next. After hugging De, Walter recounted a tale. "Several years ago, DeForest was at Madison Square Garden as part of a celebration honoring Dr. J, and they asked various doctors – fictional and factual – to come down during half time and to be saluted by the crowd. When DeForest was introduced as Dr. McCoy, there resulted an unprecedented eight-minute standing ovation, which no one else was accorded. Dr. Ruth was there, and she asked DeForest, "What is it? What do you do?!" Dr. Ruth was not only the only person in Madison Square Garden, but in the entire world, who doesn't know that DeForest Kelley is Dr. McCoy."

Producer Harve Bennett bounded to the podium with great enthusiasm, after hugging De, and said, "Well, I didn't expect to say anything, but since I'm here... I'll tell you a short story about the only time I've ever seen De Kelley thrown for a loop...It's my first picture, it's my first – and almost last – STAR TREK convention, in Houston. It's come to be known, in STAR TREK annals, as The Con of Wrath. And the story simply is, I'm fresh off the airplane, I walk into the hotel, and Dr. Bones McCoy – ACTION! – greets me and says, 'A thousand people are in the streets! Nobody has rooms! YOU'VE got to do something!' We did something, and in the bargain, became friends for what I know is life. This is a really great guy."

Nichelle Nichols was last. She said, "I am so thrilled and excited to be here. It is also an honor. It's an honor because DeForest Kelley is such a special, special kind of guy. He is always exactly who he is. He is so down to earth." Then she recited a poem she had written especially for the occasion.

"I love you, De, and you deserve every moment of people walking all over you!" Johnny Grant then brought his part of the ceremony to a close by reading a proclamation from the LA Board of Supervisors, which congratulated De on his honor. The document also proclaimed December 18, 1991 as DeForest Kelley Day in Hollywood!

At that point, De stepped up to the podium to accept the document and to speak a few words. "I want to thank all of you wonderful people for coming out here and helping me celebrate this very special, special day. I am particularly proud that Paramount Pictures happens to be sponsoring my star, because in 1946, as AC Lyles pointed out, as a young man, I started my career at Paramount. There are so many people to thank – from Bill Meikeljohn all the way through to Gene Roddenberry. My career has also encompassed a great number of people who perhaps you never heard about – but there are the directors Don McDougall, Bill Witney, the guys that make fast and hot television shows; and there's AC Lyles, who kept bringing me back to Paramount, and eventually John Sturgis brought me back for Gunfight at OK Corral; and then Eddie Dmytryk, who finally got me out of those bad guy roles by bringing me back to Paramount again to do a picture called Where Love Has Gone. So, all of those people and too many more to name here — the people who have worked so hard on this event, Allison Jackson and Hank Ehrlich – all of these people that have worked to bring me to this position that I'm finally going to be in. I'm particularly proud that all of my roommates (indicating the STAR TREK cast) are still here, and I'm proud that I can look at Leonard, and that I don't have to say, 'He's dead, Jim.' This has been a very exciting year for us, as you know. Everyone has mentioned dates — December 5th at Mann's Chinese Theater; December the 18th for this event; September the 8th, which was the celebration of our 25th year of STAR TREK. A very important date just preceded that. September 7th, when I celebrated my 46th wedding anniversary with this lady sitting here. And speaking of support, I can assure you I would never be here without her. I have often said, and I say it again, I make the living, but she makes the living worthwhile."

STAR CEREMONY RECEPTION AT PARAMOUNT

After the media-driven "grip-and-grin" photo opportunity pictures were finished at the site, three ecstatic women (Sue, Sandy and I) headed for our cars in the Galaxy garage for the trip to Paramount, where a reception for De was scheduled in the studio commissary. In the garage, we crossed paths with De, Carolyn and AC Lyles, who were traveling to the reception together in a studio limousine. We hugged them. De was all grins, and said, "It's times like these when I need to remind myself that I still have to go home and take out the trash!" We laughed, knowing that the "humble" De was still alive and well.

I got into my humble, "Lifestyles of the Poor and Unknown" car – the "accordion" – and drove to the main gate at Paramount. As I pulled up at the guard station, I couldn't help feeling embarrassed and out-of-place. Here I was at a fancy function, and my "chariot" looked like something that belonged in a wrecking yard — (well, to me, it did). Just then, the white limo carrying the Kelleys and AC pulled up beside me on its way through the employee gate. The driver honked – which is what alerted me to their presence. I looked over my right shoulder and melted when I saw that the rear limo window had been lowered a little – just enough for De's fingers to reach out and give a wave! I thought, "What a guy! MOST actors in this situation would drive by and not even ACKNOWLEDGE they KNEW anyone in a car like this!"

I walked to the commissary, reconnected with Sue and Sandy, and chose a table near the door, just inside the commissary. The Kelleys, AC and a few others were seated across the room from us.

Lunch was delivered and we ate while chatting happily. Afterwards, a few people stood and offered toasts, and then AC stood and said some very kind and true words about the honoree. "On the logo here at Paramount, as you know, there are a series of stars spanning across above the mountain. DeForest Kelley is definitely one of the stars represented in that logo. He means so much to us here, as he does to fans around the world. Not long before Michael Landon died, I called him in the hospital. I think most of you know that Michael doubled for De in a fight scene here on the lot when BONANZA was being filmed and De was doing a movie here for me. Well, when I called Michael shortly before he died, I told him, 'Michael! You don't sound sick at all!' and he said, 'AC, it isn't my voice that's sick.' Anyway, we chatted for a short time and then he told me, "You know, AC, I just have one concern left.' I asked him, 'What's that, Michael?' and he joked, "I don't know who's going to double for DeForest Kelley now!'" The audience chuckled. I just about fell out of my chair! The remembrance of my note to Landon at De's reception felt like a miracle!

AC continued: "But I want to tell you something. Michael Landon may have been able to double for De in a western, but nobody – NOBODY – can double for De in real life. De, you are unrepeatable. Our arms are around you and we are so proud to be able to claim you as our own. Congratulations, you rascal!"

After people finished eating and the plates were cleared, De stood and made his way slowly around the room. As he got very near, breathing at our table became shallow and hearts beat faster. I could tell by the gaze of my friends that De was practically behind me, but I didn't know his EXACT location until two warm, friendly hands caught both of my shoulders, and rubbed them, then patted them. They felt like the hands a dad would put on the shoulders of a daughter sitting at home in familiar surroundings – so comfortable and unabashed. I grinned and looked up into his eyes. He grinned back and patted me on one shoulder one more time. Then he proceeded to kiss one of the hands of each of my tablemates. We felt blessed.

Not long after De finished making the rounds of the tables, people began to leave. We waited until De and Carolyn were heading out the door, then approached them, thanking them for inviting us. He turned to me last. I smiled and whispered VERY discreetly into his ear, "Thank you so much for inviting me to your f——n" star ceremony!" His head came up, and he grinned like a Cheshire cat. Then he said, quite seriously, "You know, Kris – when you're in a situation like I was [at the star ceremony], everything just goes right out of your head. I'm sorry. I was going to READ that little ditty you prepared for me while I was up there! And thank YOU for it!" He said it so dead-pan, I wasn't sure whether or not he was serious. "You're KIDDING! You wouldn't have said that at your star ceremony, would you?!" He reiterated, "Yes!" I said, "Thank God you forgot, then!" He chuckled and gave me a hug.

A few days later De and Carolyn called to thank me for the photo album and the video of the star ceremony. De told me he finally spotted me in the star ceremony crowd. "I was looking for you, but I mistakenly thought you were a newswoman for the longest time, because you were all dressed up!" I joked, "I clean up real nice, don't I?" He said, "You sure do!" De said he had been going over in his mind about the ceremony… what was said, stuff he should have said that he didn't. Carolyn interjected, "There are TWO dizzy people here right now!" I assured De it was a wonderful ceremony and couldn't have been better. "It was just perfect." I told them about Sue's Rowdy Cowboy Celebration at the Holiday Inn in Hollywood the night De got his star. I mentioned that I had created what looked like a HORSE DUNG centerpiece for Sue's table, with fake flies buzzing around it, while everyone else got nicer ones. I added, "Before the centerpieces were put out, Richard Arnold showed up and announced that he wanted to sit at Sue's table! I tried to discourage him, but he insisted, so he got to sit at the horse dung table, too!" They both laughed and De commiserated, "Poor Sue." I continued, "Then I had a game where we tried to guess the title of De movies by pictorial clues. They were pretty decadent. The only two I'll tell YOU about are these: I took a map of the US and over the top I pinned a pair of under shorts. Know which motion picture that represented, De?" Total silence greeted my question, so I solved the puzzle: "The movie was 'The Undies-Covered Country'! No one else got it, either, De, so don't worry. They got Apache Uprising, though! That drawing showed an Indian with his loincloth sticking out at about a 45 degree angle!" Carolyn howled and De guffawed!

STEADY WORK AT LAST!

On November 6th 1992 I was given word that I would be hired on permanently at WARNER BROS. I called Carolyn right away to give her the good news. She WEPT! I joked to her, "For heaven's sake! I'm going to have to stop telling you good news! You can't handle it!" She said she knew how hard I had worked for this and how long I had waited. "I'm just THRILLED for you!" Then she asked, "Have you called your parents and told them?" I said, "No, I just found out, thirty seconds ago! My BOSS doesn't even know, yet!" She said, "I'm the FIRST person you called?" I said, "Yes." She continued crying. "Carolyn, get a grip!" She repeated, "I'm just so happy for you!"

Murphy's Law. A week later, the producer of BAY WATCH called. He said his wife had started a new production company "up there in the San Fernando Valley" and that he had recommended me to be her assistant! I was flattered, and I was torn. I had just accepted full-time work at WB, the studio I had felt intuitively drawn to for a number of years!

I called Carolyn and De, and explained the situation. De was the voice of reason. "You have the option of WB, which is settled, stable and permanent – and you have this other option, which is a start-up concern with no real history." I said, "Yeah, but the new one is working in PRODUCTION, where the action is!" He said, "Production is the least stable area in the industry, unless the show is already a hit – and *then* it's staffed."

I sighed and then said, "I know." I paused again, thinking, and then said, "It's nice to have a steady, permanent position." Carolyn appended, "In a company that's going to be here for another thousand years." De said, "I realize the other offer is flattering as hell, and you TAKE it, if that's what your heart says to do. We're not directing you. You will be a success in WHICHEVER direction you choose. These are just our thoughts." I said, "That's why I called, and why I asked! You're more level-headed than I am when it comes to stuff like this. I'm just glad you confirmed what I've been thinking." Carolyn said, "I think you're smart to stay at WARNER BROS. You can be there forever as long as you don't 'screw it up,' as they say!" I assured her, "Oh, I don't INTEND to 'screw it up', as they say!" She then said quietly, "That's NOT what they say, you know! They don't say 'screw it up'!" I whispered back, "Yes, I know. But WE won't say what the men folk say, will we?! We are ladies, we are!" She laughed and said, "Yes, we are, Kristine Marie!"

THANKSGIVING 1992

Mom and Dad drove down from Washington State to spend Thanksgiving with me. I was very excited about that, because Thanksgiving without family members can be a truly pathetic time. Mom and Dad had never met De and Carolyn, and because they hadn't, they were under the mistaken impression that I was over the edge about this mythical couple. In a word, Dad particularly thought I was nuts. That was kind of okay with me, because I thought he was pretty nuts, too! I dropped a note to the Kelleys inviting them to share Thanksgiving dinner with us that year. I knew they probably wouldn't, or couldn't, but… it couldn't hurt to ask. I'd be giving special thanks for them at the table.

So it was a big surprise – and a relief, and a scare – when the Kelleys called. Carolyn said that although they couldn't partake of the dinner since they had other plans with another couple, they would like to drive over for an hour or so early in the day to meet Mom and Dad! I hung up the phone and Mom and Dad looked a little like deer caught in headlights. I got goose bumps. This was going to be Really Something: the moment of truth. Mom and Dad were going to be able to proclaim, at the conclusion of this visit, whether or not I was bonkers.

On Thanksgiving Day, Mom and Dad dressed up a little more than usual and Dad jabbed me with the caustic comment, "We'd better dress up for these GODS who are visiting with us today!" I could tell he was ready to pronounce me insane well in advance of the event. Needless to say, I was a basket of nerves when the doorbell rang! I went to the door and opened it. De had a lovely little plant in his arms for me. I said, "Thanks!" and hugged him and Carolyn. I made the introductions and we all sat down. I sat as far away from everyone as I could get, hoping they'd settle into couches and chairs close to each other. Much to my relief, they did.

I poured everyone coffee, and they began to chat. Before long, Dad and De were chatting up a storm, and Mom and Carolyn were conversing. Then it became a kind of free-for-all. This occurred rather quickly, the moment the Kelleys decided my folks were comfortable with them and not at all intimidated by the circumstance. They got into a sort of gabfest about me – because initially that was their common frame of reference. Instead of Dad's usual caustic remarks, I heard him saying some of the sweetest things about me! Then I thought that he was probably just following the Kelleys' lead, since they were being so complimentary! Then I decided, no…. I guess Dad really DID think I was worth claiming as a kid – he just had an uncommonly weird way of showing it. Acutely embarrassed by their comments, I finally directed, "Okay, you guys. Knock it off." Carolyn grinned, "Just stick your toe in the rug and take it, like a good little celebrity." I laughed. So did De!

Dad told De a bald-faced lie: "I never *did* like STAR TREK much (hah!) but I enjoyed the hell out of your westerns." That was music to De's ears. He enjoyed nothing better than having people recall and recognize his non-TREK roles. Dad said, "I tell you, now that I've met you, and see for myself the kind of guy you really are, I think you deserve an OSCAR for those sons-of-bitches you played in westerns! Sitting here, you don't look like you could act at all!" De threw his head back and laughed. That was Dad. He had a way of complimenting people that just never came out quite right! When De laughed, Dad realized he had said something a little amiss and made a course correction. He amended, "What I mean is, you are such a gentleman, such a nice, quiet, reserved man. Your roles in westerns – I just don't see how you managed to DO that so convincingly. You don't look like the kind of guy who could find something that alien to his own nature. I mean, even your *good* guy, McCOY, is crabbier than YOU are!"

De got the point, and was touched by it. "Well, thank you very much. That's a very great compliment." Dad zeroed in finally and sincerely with, "You deserve an Oscar!" I agreed, "Yes, he does!" Carolyn nodded, "Yes, he does!" Mom said, "It's unanimous!"

When the door shut and the Kelleys were gone, I was pretty well convinced that the visit had been a whopping success. Dad turned to me, sighed, then said, "Kris, I apologize. I THOUGHT YOU WERE OUT OF YOUR MIND! I really did. I was AFRAID for you! But now I see… You were absolutely right about those two." Mom said, "They're precious. You're very lucky to have them in your life."

It was then that I said, "And I'm lucky to have YOU in my life —" and then I joked, "and *on my side* after all these years!" Dad shot back, "We've ALWAYS been on your side!" I hugged him and said, "I know." After that, I couldn't even JOKE about the Kelleys without Mom or Dad coming straight to their defense! NOW who was "over the edge," I mused, smiling!

One morning, De called. He started out by saying that a LA TIMES columnist had retired, and that he thought I should apply for the opening and write a daily or weekly column. We discussed that for several minutes. I told him what a tough job it would be to come up with stuff anyone would want to read on a daily or weekly basis. He said, "Well, you manage to do it for us on a daily basis, so I know you can do it for others, too." He said the reports of my trips to Builder's Emporium and everywhere else I went were always very funny, and that the newspaper would probably jump at the chance to sign me up and write for them. He said he didn't know how to go about getting something like that started. I said I did. He said, "Then do it!" I said, "Yes, BOSS!" But I never did follow up on his suggestion.

On January 20, 1993 De called just as ENTERTAINMENT TONIGHT was in the process of announcing his 73rd birthday. I picked up the phone when it rang, a bit feverishly, because I didn't know it was De and I was going to instruct the caller to "hold on for just a second while I record De's birthday announcement!" Then I found out it was HIM! "Are you there?" he asked. "Yes, but, De — I'm just about to record your birthday announcement. Here it comes! ... There! Got it! Hello!" He said, "Well, I'd just as soon forget those birthdays." I said, "You go ahead and forget them. I'LL remember."

De said, "I want to thank you for everything…" He listed every single item I had given him and ended with, "and those photos of Deke with the balloons really put us on the floor. He looked like he'd really had it by the time he got to the paper sack. I got a bunch of balloons today. Would you like to come by tomorrow evening after work and pick them up for Deke to pop?" I said, "Sure." Then De said, "No more birthdays. I'm gonna go stick my head in the stove." I said, "No, De…Your birthday will be over at midnight. Relax."

I asked if he had been sung to enough already today. He said, "No, I believe I could stand another one." I said, "Oh, I guess I shoulda practiced then!" I sang HAPPY BIRTHDAY. De said, "Well, thank you. That was wonderful. You sound just like one of the Andrews Sisters." I laughed and facetiously intoned, "Right!" He said, "Well, thanks again for everything." I told him I loved him and hung up.

CREATION CONVENTION PASADENA CALIFORNIA 4/4/93

Reported by Krazy Kris Smith

DeForest Kelley was an honored guest on the final day's roster of events, so of course I had to be there to droo —— I mean, to watch De cast his spell over the entire audience.

Paramount producer AC Lyles was asked by Creation to introduce De (as a surprise), and AC cast his own spell briefly over the proceedings with his glowing words regarding De. He said of his long-time friendship: "I've known and worked with just about every producer, director, actor and executive on the Paramount lot over the past 55 years, and nobody is more well loved at Paramount than DeForest Kelley. He is so well loved that Kris Smith goes down to Hollywood Boulevard every Sunday morning to polish his star on the Hollywood Walk of Fame. I have a star, too, in front of the El Capitan, and because I'm a friend of De's, Kris polishes MY star, too!" (Reporter's note: This is malarkey. If I polished all the stars of people who are friends or fans of De's, I'd never get OFF the Hollywood Walk of Fame!) There was warm humility in AC's voice. He continued: "De is everything a Boy Scout is. He is respectful, reverent, kind, all of that. And there's something else he is, too." (Someone yelled, "SEXY!" and AC chuckled at that.) "I'D add LAZY. It takes him five minutes to smile! I've seen some laid-back people on that lot – Perry Como, Bing Crosby, Hank Fonda, Dean Martin — but De is so laid back he makes these people look like Robin Williams!

"My three favorite people in this industry are James Cagney, Ronald Reagan and DeForest Kelley. I don't know which one I love best, but today I love De best. My arms will always be around him and his wonderful wife, Carolyn, who is just as sweet and wonderful as he is. (Applause.) He is the sweetest, nicest guy in the whole wide world. I want to give him a big hug and welcome him: DeFOREST KELLEY!"

De came out and was greeted by a two minute standing ovation and thunderous applause, screams and whistles. He thanked the audience when it quieted and sat down and then said of AC, "AC says what a sweet guy I am. I'm gonna tell you what a sweet guy he is. I very seldom made it through one of his westerns alive! (Laughter.) One time he tied me to a wagon wheel and shot an arrow into my chest and turned on the rain birds, and then had the Assistant Director call, 'Lunch!' — and left me there tied to the wagon wheel! So that's what kind of guy AC Lyles is!

"But really… I feel as if I've passed away already! I know I'm lazy, but I'm not THAT lazy! Any time AC has called me out of my rose garden to go to Arizona or somewhere to do a movie, I've always packed my bags and run to him. I hope I can live up to the nice things AC said about me."

He mentioned the recent torrential rains and said he was glad they finally called off the drought before everyone drowned. He asked how many people in the crowd were from far away, and the responses included England, Germany, Texas, Georgia – and Vulcan. He said this was the biggest crowd he had seen since the 25th anniversary at the Shrine Auditorium. Then he told the story of what happened at the Shrine when he "got even" with Shatner for stealing his English muffin during the filming of STAR TREK VI. THEN he explained how Shatner got even for getting even, right there on the spot at the Shrine… and then how he almost got Shatner with a stage hook… and how Shatner got even when De left the stage hurriedly, thinking he'd be murdered otherwise by the Cap'n. It was hysterical.

De then told the stories revolving around the filming of WARLOCK with Henry Fonda and Edward Dmytryk, much to everyone's delight.

He asked me to stand up so he could spot me, and thanked me for polishing his star. Then he got me into trouble by asking if my boss, Michelle Sucillon, had come along. When I said, "Yes," he asked HER to stand up and immediately proclaimed her "beautiful." I went over to where she was sitting and she immediately told me I was fired. I assured her I had NOTHING to do with it. She laughed and assured me she was just joking. (She had never seen De before and had never been a STAR TREK fan nor visited a convention of TREK fans, so she was astonished to see how beloved he is. "He's an ICON!")

After De was finished raking me over the coals, he said he was told by a fan (who had attended one of Shatner's and Nimoy's conventions) that Bill and Leonard couldn't figure out why De was given the most space to sign his name at Mann's Chinese Theater. With a big smile, joking, De said he had told the fan to tell them, next time he saw them, that "They finally figured out who the real star of STAR TREK is!" The crowd went nuts applauding and whistling and agreeing with him.

He added: "But I tell ya, when I saw that huge space for my name, I thought, 'Boy, that's sum'pin'... and the emcee had said that some stars got so nervous that they misspelled their names. Well, I was down there spelling mine, and photographers kept tellin' me to look up and smile and wave, which I did, and then I crossed the T but forgot the S! Boy, Shatner and Nimoy got a big kick out of THAT!"

At that point, De opened up the floor to questions and one of the fans mentioned that Walter Koenig had said that De saw a flying saucer. De repeated the question: "Walter Koenig says that I saw a flying saucer." Several people laughed at that, and De, in mock exasperation, said, "Well, YOU'RE a hell of a crowd to be laughing at THAT!" The whole place came unglued with uproarious laughter. De then described what he saw on that night in the early 1950's and said that other people reported seeing similar sightings that night to the newspapers, so he and Carolyn and their friend weren't the only eyewitnesses to the strange craft. He finished with, "That's all I know. I know what I saw."

A woman told him that he had a great influence on her life and that she had recently become a doctor. He thanked her for telling him that and said that it is always heartwarming for an actor to find that they will be leaving something significant like that as a legacy. He said he had heard from many, many medical people who had been influenced by McCoy, and hopes to hear from many more. "I wish I had kept more of those letters." Someone asked if he really drinks mint juleps. He said that he has had them, but that his favorite drink is vodka and water with a twist of lemon in it. "I call it the Kelley julep." Another fan asked how he liked being an Admiral, and he said, "I loved it, but the minute I got home I was immediately stripped of my rank!" Everyone laughed. "But I have my little insignia in the bedroom."

Another question involved whether De knew that STAR TREK would be the big hit and legend it has become, and he said, "No idea in the world, until about 1972 after it went into syndication. I was at a convention in New York where 500 fans were expected and 10,000 showed up. I went home and told Carolyn, 'I don't know what's going to happen with STAR TREK, or when it's going to happen, but something big IS going to happen.' I knew then, but not any earlier. YOU are the people responsible for the success of STAR TREK, and I want to thank you right now." There was much applause.

One of the final questions involved whether we will be seeing De in any more movies. De said, "I really don't know. That depends on AC Lyles. (Laughter.) STAR TREK really took charge of my life after 1966. Before then, I was doing something that was very unusual in this business. I was crossing over between movies and television, which was rare at that time, but then STAR TREK grabbed hold of us and I became so identified with this role…" At that point, he queried the audience: "Incidentally, just out of curiosity, how many of you would like to see a STAR TREK VII with the original cast?" The house came down with roaring, stomping, cheering, whistling and other ear-splitting jubilation. De said, "The reason I ask that is, I don't think Paramount even knows the amount of mail we receive regarding this, and I know there are some Paramount people here today. We, who DO see you so often, know what the feeling is…" He turned back to the original question and continued: "I will have to sit down with my agent and decide, OK, this is where I want to go, or where I don't want to go. I have to re-align my life."

Someone asked about the episode FOR THE WORLD IS HOLLOW AND I HAVE TOUCHED THE SKY (the love story between McCoy and Natira) and De said, "Oh, yes! That was the episode where they gave Shatner a break from the broads… but it almost killed him!" (Laughter.)

At that point, De read his most recent poem, THE DREAM GOES ON AND ON AND ON, and the audience loved it. Then he thanked everyone for coming and received another standing ovation as he left the stage.

He was DE-lightful, as always.

VISITS AND CALLS AND SUCH, OH MY!

On May 16th, 1993, Deaken's 14th birthday, he received a card from Carolyn and De. The inside was hand-printed in exquisite calligraphy by Carolyn. She called that afternoon to ask how Deaken was enjoying his birthday. I said, "Great, except that he just about ATE your card!" I thanked her for sending me a newspaper article re dress codes in different industries and joked, "It's reassuring to learn that I haven't violated the entertainment industry dress code yet, which is NO BARE CHESTS." She laughed.

On July 10 1993 I had a wonderful visit with the Kelleys at my home in Encino. As De and Carolyn got out of the car, they headed for the trunk, so I went to the screen door and peeked out to see what the deal was. Carolyn spotted me and motioned for me to come out. De was pulling boxes of stuff out– I could see they were treasures still in their original packages. Also inside the trunk was a small sack of miscellaneous goodies. De loaded me to the gills with all the trunk stash I could possibly pack. He picked up the remaining sack of oranges and held them out to me, grinning, "Here are some oranges, too!" I joked, "Put 'em in my back pocket. I think they'll just fit."

We headed indoors and sat the goodies on the dining room table. Then everyone met my newest addition, R.C. (Rowdy Catboy), Deaken's newest playmate, an eight week old black and white kitten. De and Carolyn petted him while he remained snuggled in my arms. Carolyn showed me pictures of Fancy, Cheers and Maggie, her dearly departed pets (two dogs and a cat). Then she showed me the card and x-ray she has to show to Security at airports to prove she has an artificial hip so they would let her through the metal detectors at the check points. She said that De always wore cowboy boots with metal in the heels "and is always detained and practically asked to undress to get through security."

After a while, I opened one of the boxes they had brought. Inside was a Tholian web globe. Carolyn said, "If you look right here, you will see what happens." I looked and looked and nothing happened. She shook it a little bit and exclaimed, "There it goes!" I looked again and noticed little stars floating in it, but that was all. I said, "That's neat." De said, "Turn it on." I tried. Carolyn said, "There it goes!" and I watched and watched… but could see absolutely NOTHING different at all. De asked me, "What's happening?" and I confessed, "I don't know. NOTHING, that I can see." He said, "Maybe you should check to see if it has batteries in it!" I looked at Carolyn, "YOU'VE been seeing things, and I was trying to see them, too!"

Carolyn asked if I was ready and eager to go back to work, and I said, "Oh, yes!" I told her I got some new duds, and they asked to see them. I went into the closet and pulled them out on hangers. De said he liked the Indian one best. "It must be my Cherokee blood." I queried, "Cherokee blood, did you say?" He said, "Yes." I said, "I have a little Cherokee blood in me, too! Oh, God! Maybe we're related! Palefaces weren't exactly on friendly terms with Cherokees, we're they?" De said, "Apparently *somebody* was on friendly terms with them!" We all laughed.

I brought Deaken into the house and they watched him groom RC for a while. As he did that, De mentioned that watching Deke do that was as relaxing as watching an aquarium. I agreed.

De told me he was doing an infomercial the following week regarding the 25th Anniversary STAR TREK GAME. Then he said, "It looks like a tough game." I asked if they had seen the MCI commercial he had just finished, and neither had yet. Deke suddenly became intensely interested in some noise in the next room somewhere, and seemed to be staring right through the wall, so I asked him, "What is it, Baby?" De mused sarcastically, "I'll bet he hears another ant." I looked at him and scowled. Carolyn said, "He's not going to let you forget that, Kris – EVER!" I said, "I guess not! But damn it, it's a TRUE story!" De grinned.

The true story was this. I had told De and Carolyn in a letter (years earlier, while still living in Washington, before the Kelleys knew me all that well) that when Deaken was a kitten, he and I had been wrestling boisterously in my living room at least sixteen feet across the room from a wood stove. Deaken had suddenly broken off playing when something attracted his attention that was located behind the wood stove, hidden from view. He chirped a little greeting or exclamation. I thought perhaps he had heard Ivanhoe, my German shepherd, walking around on gravel outside the building, but then Deaken got up and went over behind the stove to investigate. Then he started chirping even more excitedly and started to paw at his discovery. Thinking he had perhaps discovered an errant mouse, I went over to investigate and to remove the little critter before it came to grief. When I got there and could see Deke's "prey," I was utterly amazed to find that he had heard and responded to an ANT that was walking on the brick floor behind the stove! Flabbergasted, I had written to the Kelleys: "I knew servals had good ears, since the encyclopedia says they can hear rodents burrowing three feet underground, but GOOD GRIEF! Can you BELIEVE this?! *I* wouldn't, if I hadn't seen it myself!" Apparently, De found it impossible to believe. Several years later, after Deke had been at Shambala, De had drawn a sketch indicating what HE had decided Deaken had heard lurking outside my cabin in the Pacific Northwest. I just about fell out of the chair laughing! He never missed an opportunity thereafter to jibe me for making up ridiculous stories about my marvelous cat!

Carolyn was amazed at how large Poppy had grown, and mentioned the photo she had taken of her a year earlier when she was a kitten. She said it was the best photo she had ever taken, and I agreed, saying it was good enough for a magazine and that I had it on my refrigerator door, and always would. We sat outside and watched Deaken for a while. De noticed Deke's weight loss and said he was looking good.

Poppy in Tree   photo by Carolyn Kelley

De asked how long it took me to get to work, and I said, "About 35 minutes. It's twelve miles." Carolyn said, "De goes to Beverly Hills for a haircut, and THAT'S too far, anymore, with this terrible traffic."

Very soon thereafter, Carolyn looked at her watch and exclaimed, "It's 4 o'clock. We've got to go!" and De agreed. Carolyn added, "We have to get to the market," and joked, "They're waiting for us!"

I escorted them back to their car and noticed the sunroof on their '91 Lexus for the first time. De joked that he'd only had it open once. "It almost sucked me out, so I haven't had it open since!" We chatted for a few more minutes. I told De, "You don't have to bring me goodies every time you come over, you know." He said, "We'll do that sometime – neglect you!"

TV GUIDE ANTICS

The July 24, 1993 issue of TV Guide carried a large section in it about STAR TREK. In a sidebar, "What's Kirk's Crew Up To?" the cast was profiled and interviewed briefly. The paragraph regarding De read,

> "DeForest Kelley – the star's who's been most reluctant to milk TREK for all it's worth – is still waffling about his autobiography prospects. "I'd want it to be richer, more encompassing, and maybe more novelistic than just the 'I…I…I' thing," says Kelley, whose pre-TV career included such movie hits as *Gunfight at the OK Corral.* So what's the holdup? "It would involve a tremendous amount of digging and research," sighs 73-year old Kelley. "And I'd have to go out in the garage…"
>
> (Reprinted with permission from *TV Guide*, 1993 TV Guide Magazine Group, Inc., volume 41, No.30)

On July 23rd, Carolyn called. I asked if she had seen the new TV GUIDE yet, and she exclaimed, "Oh, yes! We just got it yesterday!" I directed her, "You tell De to go out into the garage and pull something out and go 'I-I-I' or 'we-we-we' but to DO IT!" Carolyn turned to De right then and there and told him, "De, Kris says you're supposed to go out into the garage, pull something out, and go wee wee!" She cackled loudly and I nearly deafened her, protesting loudly, "That is NOT what I said!" hoping De would hear me. I said, "Carolyn! You straighten him out right now! Tell him I didn't say that! Carolyn! Please tell him I didn't say that!'" I was mortified; Carolyn thought it was hysterical.

After we had settled down, she mentioned that a noted STAR TREK chronicler had called De sometime recently to try to get an okay to write a biography on him, or to help him write his autobiography, and De had thanked him but said no, he wasn't going to do one. I protested, "I wish he would. Can't you just get him to turn on a tape recorder when he feels like reminiscing?" She said, "Oh, he'd clam up right away if I did that." I said, "It's important!" She didn't respond to that. She said she wanted to give Sue and me some STAR TREK cachets. I queried, "Those smell-pretty things?" She said, "No, those are sachets. These are postal service envelopes celebrating STAR TREK." She described them to me. She said they had four of them left and wanted to give two of them to Sue and me. I said, "That's wonderful. Thank you." She asked if I wanted De to inscribe them to us individually, or just to sign his name. "They'll be worth more as collector's items if he just signs his name — in case you want to sell them somewhere down the line." I said, "Oh, Carolyn, I would never sell anything you or De gave me. Of course have him inscribe it to me!" I said, "I can't speak for Sue. I'm afraid you'll have to ask her individually." I told her about a young collector I had met in an autograph line once. I told her I had come awfully close to offering to break his neck for him, because of some of the things he had said about how valuable his collection would be after the original cast croaked. She laughed and said, "Yes, we're aware of why an awful lot of these requests come in here."

On August 25th, 1993 Carolyn called to ask how I felt. I had been under the weather, so I quickly reassured her that I was fine again. I asked how she was and she said, "Oh, I'm fine, but De has a cold. He was dyin' yesterday, but he's better today!" I heard De, in the background, joking, "Don't tell her I'm dyin'!" (Perhaps he thought I might report it in a newsletter!) She said, "De caught the cold in Detroit last weekend after he got out of the shower in his shorts and stood watching television under air conditioning for a few minutes." Commenting on her sentence structure, I joked, "He got out of the shower IN HIS SHORTS?!" She laughed and said, "No, that wasn't how it happened." I said, "Oh, that's good! I was a little concerned for a minute, there!"

On a fall afternoon I visited with Carolyn at her home. After about an hour, De wandered in. I didn't see or hear him until he was in the room next to me, offering his hand. I stood up and said, "Howdy! Er, How! De!" Indian-like, referring to our Cherokee heritage. He pulled up a chair and sat on it. The chair gave out a large cracking sound, and he jumped up quickly, then sat down on it again. Carolyn told me, "It's just settling." I said, "I'm glad. I was going to offer to trade chairs with you, De, but you weigh less than I do, so you just stay right there!" He laughed and nodded, "I will!"

I managed to diagnose the problem of a "chirpless" mechanical bird for Carolyn (dead batteries) and left briefly to facilitate its rehabilitation. De and Carolyn were very pleased with my veterinary services. We visited for an hour or more and discussed a lot of topics, some serious and poignant, others humorous. At one point, we were discussing Underground Atlanta and Underground Seattle. Carolyn exclaimed, "I didn't even know there was an Underground Seattle until after I left there. It's down there near where the

Space Needle is now, isn't it? Near Yesler?" I said, "I think so." She said, "Well, when I lived there, Yesler was the red light district, and good girls like me didn't go down there." De joked, "Yesler, That's My Baby!" I scowled at him and then laughed. Then I said, "I suppose THOSE ladies were familiar with Underground Seattle!" and De chimed in, "It isn't too likely they'd be 'entertaining' right there on the street, I don't suppose!"

A day later I called Carolyn to be sure they would be home to accept a delivery the morning before their anniversary (September 6th). Carolyn told me they would be home that morning but then had to fly to a QVC station in Pennsylvania in the afternoon. Then she said, "De was just trying to call you, but your line was busy." I said, "I was arranging for tomorrow's delivery to you." She said, "Oh!" I said, "So! What did De want?" She said, "Here. He can tell you." De got on the line and sounded very sincere (momentarily). He said, "Kris?" I replied, "Yes, sir?" He said, mock-sincerely, "I can't think of a nicer anniversary present than the one you've already given us… Nothing will ever top it… so don't even try. You have given us THE BIRD!" I laughed real hard! Then he said, "Here's Carolyn again." Carolyn got back on the line and said (of the bird) "You know, it's really a silly little thing, this little bird, but we got used to sitting here and having it chirp at us, and it means a lot to have it chirping again." I said, "I know. I KNOW how much that little bird means to you!" She said, "They say, if you need something done, ask a busy person to do it!!! Thank you very much, Kris." I said, "My pleasure. Any time."

SURPRISE TRIP TO VALLEY FORGE

The next day when Carolyn and De called to thank me for the anniversary basket, I was expecting just that – a brief call of gratitude. But the conversation took an unexpected turn almost immediately. "Kris, the hot air balloon just arrived. It's sitting right here on the floor of my office. De just carried it in." At that point, De got on the line and joked, "We've cancelled our flight for Tuesday and are going to ride to Pennsylvania on THIS!" Then he handed the phone back to Carolyn and she said, "It is just MAGNIFICENT! You're spending all your money on us again!" I protested, "No, I'm not!" I added, "Did you read the card?" She said, "No. It just got here. De just now carried it in to me. De, get the card!" De handed her the card. She read it aloud (choking up as the meaning sank in) "For two people who know how to stay high on love. Kris and Furballs."

At that point, she dropped the bomb: "Listen. We've made arrangements this morning for you to go to the [upcoming] Valley Forge convention, unless you don't want to go." My mouth fell open. I was just speechless. I managed to say, "Oh, Carolyn!" then just went silent! She said, "I've got flight schedules here and I want to know when you want to fly." She gave me a couple of options. I was SO hesitant, knowing I couldn't afford ANY of the trip, not just the flight, but didn't want to admit THAT was what was troubling me. Finally, though, the truth had to come out. (Lying to the Kelleys had never been an option with me.) "It isn't just a matter of the flight. I can't afford the hotel or the shuttle or anything. That's why I decided a month ago that it was impossible." Carolyn asked, "Well, how much are the rooms?" I said, "$80 something a night, I think. But maybe I could stay with Sue and Sandy one night – they told me I could – and get down to only having to pay for one night. I could handle that."

About an hour later, she called again. "Kris, I got you a Weekender's Special at the convention hotel for $82.00 night for Saturday and Sunday nights in a special suite with two TVs, a coffee pot, a whirlpool bath, and including a free breakfast…" Oh, man... I thanked her and then reported, "Then in that case, I can afford the con tickets," and she said, "No, I'm going to arrange for THOSE, too." She started to repeat the amazing room amenities. After listening through the lengthy list again I laughed and said,

"Gee, I hope I can drag myself away from the ROOM long enough to see De's appearance!" Carolyn howled.

During the QVC show the next day, I was astonished and tickled pink to hear De relate the story about the day I got batteries for their "phony little" bird! The next time Carolyn called, she asked me, "Did you catch the show?" I said, "I sure did. It was great!" "Did you collapse when De mentioned your name?" I said, "God, Carolyn! I just about DID! I couldn't believe it!" She said, "I was sitting back stage in the green room, and when I heard him start to tell that story, and then when he said your name, I thought, 'Kris must be losin' her mind!'"

A few days later I went to the Kelley home to pick up the tickets. I got to the house and walked to the porch. The front door was wide open, but the screen door was shut, so I rang the doorbell. After about 20 seconds, De peeked around the corner from the hallway. He smiled and opened the door, saying, "Come on in." I hugged him. He motioned me toward the living room. De sat down on one of the love seats, and I sat in the other one, across the room from him and presently Carolyn joined us. I asked if they had seen Myrtle yet that day and De said, "Yes. She was circling the wagons out there about an hour ago. She'll be back at around five looking for dinner. She goes over by the garbage cans and rattles things there when she wants our attention, and then I go out and feed her." Carolyn said, "Well! I guess we'd better dig out the tickets for you now!" She got them, handed them to me, and said, "Now, don't lose these!" I said, "LOSE them?! NEVER!" She said, "Go ahead and look at them. Make sure everything's there." I looked inside and joked, "Mom said to check and make sure they're ROUND TRIP TICKETS!" Carolyn assured me, "They are!" De (playing on Mom's comment) exclaimed, "They ARE?!" feigning surprise and dismay. I looked at him and scowled. I asked if I could take them to dinner one night at Valley Forge as a thank you, and she said, "No! Merry KrisSmith EARLY!"

We talked for a while. I asked if they dream in color. Both said yes. Carolyn said to De, "But you didn't always. I remember when you started dreaming in color. You were astounded and told me about it when it first started happening." I said, "I remember having my first Technicolor dream. I was about ten. It was just after I'd seen THE MUSIC MAN for about the tenth time. Robert Preston came to my ranch home in his band uniform and danced around on the green grass!" They laughed. I theorized, "We still had a black and white TV at that time, but that's about the time that motion pictures started coming out ROUTINELY in color." De said, "Perhaps that's about the time I started dreaming in color, too, for the same reason." I joked, "Because you loved Robert Preston?" He shot me a look and said, "No." I said, "Maybe our brains switched over as soon as movies showed us that color was an option!" He said that was very likely. She asked what year I was born and I told her, "1951." She said, "We were living in New York when Kristine Marie came into the world." I said, "Yes. You were working at Warner Bros. just a short walk from your home." She said, "Yes! You know all about us by now!"

She asked if I had seen the orchid in the bathroom, and I said no. She said, "Oh, come on – let's go back! You have to see it. It's what's left from the anniversary basket Sue and the club gave us!" We went in and I said I had never seen an orchid that looked like it before. She said, "I hadn't, either, but it's the longest lasting one we've ever had, and the loveliest." Then she added, "I love orchids. They last so long."

We returned to the kitchen and she handed me a sack of six home grown tomatoes. Knowing that I didn't relish tomatoes, De joked, "We only give my tomatoes to people who don't LIKE them, so they don't ask for any more!"

On September 29th I got another call from Carolyn telling me they had received more studio samples and she asked if I'd like to drive over and pick out what I wanted of it. While visiting with them Carolyn mentioned having lost four pounds recently during her cold and the many weeks she spent coughing. I said, "Coughing is hard work! It's no wonder you lost four pounds." She said, "Especially the way I cough! I don't cough like a lady; I cough like a lumberjack!" I told her, "I do, too. I also blow my nose like a fog horn. It's real embarrassing, because without thinking, I'll do it at work and people will just stop everything to marvel at it!" De threw his head back and laughed. He told a hilarious story about a loud belly flop Carolyn essayed at the Riverside Hotel many years ago. "We laughed about that for DAYS afterwards!" Carolyn said, "We're STILL laughing about it, as you can see, fifty years later!" I straightened up and asked, "So! You swim?" and she joked back, "Not as well as I DIVE!" and we all cracked up again. We talked about exercise. I said I'd walk, but don't feel secure doing it alone. De said, "It's getting to be a scary world, isn't it? Twenty years ago I wouldn't have thought twice about going for a walk, but I do now." I told them that my Arrest, Search and Seizure class (to become a Humane Officer) trained us how to avoid looking like victims or easy targets.

De pulled the TREK box over to me and I went through it, piece by piece, to see what I wanted to keep. De had a set of Starfleet insignias in a case and asked if I would deliver it to Sue some time. I said, "Sure! You bet."

He added: "No hurry. Just the next time you see her." We watched their backyard critters and I was able to spot a mutant ground squirrel they had been telling me about. I said it looked as though it was put together by a committee!

De told me about a tall tree that used to be in their back yard. It had a jay living in it that grew fond of De and Carolyn and would even land on their shoulders. The jay raised a family. One of the little jays fell out of the nest and De rescued it and put it in a cage and then sat it near the air conditioning unit next to the house. "The mama jay would fly over and feed it through the bars. We thought it was such a phenomenal thing that we called the LA TIMES and a photographer came out to do a pictorial on the situation. Because the photographer was a stranger, the bird wouldn't come back in and feed the baby. So I had the photographer hide, and I went down by the cage. The mama jay came back in right away. The photographer got some fantastic shots. Sometime I'll dig 'em out and show them to you."

On October 5th (her birthday) Carolyn underwent surgery to try and alleviate severe pain she had long endured in her lower back. She called two days earlier than the surgery date to let me know what was happening, but made it clear that she didn't want any visitors in the hospital or any flowers. She said De would call me following the surgery to let me know how everything went "if he can ever get off the line long enough to do it!" He'd have a lot of people to inform that day.

De called at about 4:30 the afternoon of surgery and said, "Hello, Kris. This is DeForest." I said, "Hi!" He said, "How are you?" I said, "How am I? I'm on the ninth fudgsicle of the day, waiting to hear how Carolyn is!" He apologized, "Oh, sorry…Well, she came through the surgery just beautifully. She has a young doctor from the east coast who really knows his stuff and loves his work, and he told me she lost only 22 cc's of blood during the whole thing." I asked, "How long did the surgery take?" He said, "FOUR HOURS!" I said, "Good Lord!" He said the incision site was heavily bandaged and that her legs were in a leather-like get-up to help with circulation. He added, "She has a little pain medication bulb that she can squeeze whenever she feels any pain, but she hasn't needed to at all, and seems to feel fine during her periods of wakefulness." He said the flowers from Sue's club were delivered to her at the hospital, and when I said I wanted to send some too, but Carolyn had told me no earlier, De said, "Oh, please don't. There's no room for them there, and your cards are all she wants or needs. Don't strap yourself. Just call her tomorrow evening and keep those cards and letters coming!" I said, "Not to worry. I'm on top of

THAT!" He gave me Carolyn's phone number at the hospital. I asked how long she'd be there, and he said, "Four days." I said, "Good. Back home on the weekend!" He said, "Yes," sounding relieved. I asked if he was tired, and he responded, "Oh, yes! We didn't sleep at all the night before, and then – as Carolyn told you – we had to be there at 5 a.m. for the preparations…"

I called Carolyn every day. She reported that the doctor was very pleased with her progress. She said she had NO pain in her legs at all when she walked. "It's my best birthday present ever!"

But her stay lasted a couple days longer than anticipated. On the 8th she called and, after visiting on the phone for a while, reported, "I wanted to tell you that I won't be going to the Valley Forge convention." Heartbroken, I said, "Oh, CAROLYN!" She said, "Well, you probably had it figured out anyway, didn't you?" I said, "Well, I was HOPING you'd be able to make it." She said, "No. It would be too much, this soon after surgery, with that long flight and the long drive at both ends." I sighed, very disappointed, but of course understanding. Then I offered, "Can I stay here and help you, then, while De's gone?" She said, "No! You have tickets! I arranged the trip for you! You have to go!"

I called De a few minutes later and offered, "I'll be happy to go shopping or do other errands for you to free you up to be with her, or just to rest." He said, "That's very thoughtful, but I shopped just before she went in, and I'm in like a bear." I said, "Well, I'm serious…. so, if there's anything I can do to help out, you let me know, okay?" He said, "Okay. Thank you very much, honey. Thanks a lot."

VALLEY FORGE

On October 20, 1993 Carolyn called to wish me a happy trip. Then she asked me, "You *will* write me every day while you're gone, right?" I said, "Oh, sure!" She laughed and said she was just kidding. I told her that Mom had called to wish me a happy trip, too, and that I had told her, "Oh, Carolyn has seen to THAT!" She giggled.

At the Valley Forge convention, De introduced me as his star polisher on both days. On the second day, he said to the crowd something along the lines of, "You really know who LOVES you, when a fan will do something like THAT!" He said it very sincerely, and the audience accepted it as such. Afterwards, several fans came over to me to talk about their love and respect for De, and one of them said, "If I lived close enough to his star, I would be honored to polish it, too." Then she thanked me for keeping De's star the shiniest star on the Walk of Fame.

At one point, De was talking about Pennsylvania's gorgeous autumn leaves, and then he said, "We Angelinos are happy just to be able to see a TREE, let alone one that changes colors for us!" That got a laugh. Then he said, "Carolyn and I do have one magnificent tree – an oak or a maple, I guess – out over our back fence that changes color in the fall." At that point, he turned back toward me, sitting in the audience, and asked, "YOU know the tree I'm talking about, Kris? YOU'VE seen it." I nodded, confirming to him that I had seen it. "Well, it's a beauty, and we love it." Following that statement, a fan came up to me following De's appearance and said, "You KNOW him! You REALLY, REALLY KNOW HIM! You've been to his house and everything!" I nodded and let her know that De was every bit as sweet as she felt he was, which made her day.

De relied on me a couple of times to relay questions from fans in the rear of the auditorium, since the acoustics in the place weren't entirely adequate.

De got downright philosophical and spiritual for a short period of time each day. At one point, an Ohio man told De, "Our children think it's wonderful that YOU are the son of a minister, too." De responded, "Oh? Are YOU a minister?" When the man nodded, De cautioned him, "Go easy on your children. They have a rough row to hoe. It isn't easy growing up perfect, you know. It's ONE of the reasons I moved to Hollywood from

Georgia and became an actor!" Then the minister's wife chimed in: "Our daughter wants to be an actress, too!" De said, "See? There you go!"

The next day, De said, "I guess it's not possible to kick all the religion out of a preacher's kid. I wrote a couple little poems. Hope I can remember 'em. There's a Catholic Church not far from us, over our side fence, and most of the time I can go out into the back yard and see the cross that's on the roof there. But not long ago, a tree that stands between us and the church sent branches out that obscured my view of the cross, and I couldn't see it any more, so I wrote a little thing... let's see if I can remember it... just a minute, now....

A branch has blocked my view of the cross
I always thought God was boss
Then again He must be
For only God can make a tree!"

The audience applauded and roared its approval. Then he said, "A little while later, I saw that someone had pruned that tree back, so that I was again able to see the cross, so I wrote... I won't get this one exactly right... I wrote something like...

I'm happy again, I'm able to see
The cross that stands above the tree
I know it's silly but I like to think
Someone did that just for me!"

Then De said, "One more." He pulled this one out of a pocket.

Time is really
The blink of an eye
Where do they go
Those who die?
What is below?
What is above?
What is in store
For those we love?
All that's been written

And all that's been said
Still does not answer
What happens to the dead?

The audience was awed and silenced by that briefly, and then they applauded warmly, at which time he promptly changed to a happier subject.

"Hallelujah and amen! What else is on your minds today?"

****

PART TWO 1994-1998

Dedicated To the Memory of Dorothea Hope Smith

Kris and Dorothea Smith with A.C. Lyles on the Hollywood Walk of Fame in Nov. '95, seven months before Mom's troubles began…

NORTHRIDGE EARTHQUAKE 1994

At 4:31 AM on January 17th the entire San Fernando Valley was jolted awake and bounced around for forty five seconds by the strongest quake to hit the area in decades. Measuring 6.6 on the Richter scale and centered in Northridge, it demolished a shopping center and an apartment complex three miles from the Encino house I was renting and seven miles from the Kelley residence in Sherman Oaks.

At my place, the cement block wall came down in the back yard; the external chimney on the patio collapsed; rafter beams were twisted; and nothing in the house was in its usual place: it all lay scattered or broken on the floor throughout the structure. It was truly a nightmare come to life. After digging myself out of the chaotic mess in which I suddenly found myself and going outside into the dark, cold morning, I shut off the water supply to broken pipes in the garage and the gas supply to the place. I somehow managed to accomplish this between aftershocks that rivaled the main event. There was no electricity and no phone. Badly shaken by the temblor, and still shaking like a leaf, I waited until dawn and then climbed into the car to listen to the news. THAT'S when I learned, for the first time, how badly damaged Sherman Oaks had been. I immediately searched the neighborhood and found one house on the block that still had power to their telephone line. I stood in a line and waited my turn. As soon as I had the chance, I tried calling the Kelleys to see how they were. The phone lines were down in Sherman Oaks. The call wasn't going through. I then quickly called my sister in Washington State to report my status. Then I tried the Kelleys again. No luck. Others were waiting to use the only existing live phone, so I relinquished control and went back home.

I considered driving or walking to Sherman Oaks, four miles distant, to ascertain the Kelleys status, but had heard that the National Guard and emergency vehicles had been called to Sherman Oaks. Reports indicated that no one was being allowed into the area who wasn't there as a resident or as a rescue worker. I returned to the neighbor's house to try calling several more times; then that line went out for the rest of the afternoon, and I was "dead in the water." I would have to wait until telephone service was restored or the "all clear" was given so I could drive over.

At about 4:30, phone service between Encino and Sherman Oaks was finally restored, and my call went through. Carolyn picked up the phone and said, "Hello?" I cried out, relieved, "Carolyn!" She said, "Yes! Kris?!" I said, "Are you okay?!" "We're okay," she said, then asked, "Are you okay?" I said, "Scared spitless, but okay!" She said, "Our lines, just this minute, started working again. Our friend from Long Beach just called. She has been trying every twenty minutes all day long." I said, "So have I!" She said, "As soon as we hung up with her, I said to De, 'We've got to call Kris!' and then the phone rang, and it's you!" De came on the line and they both started talking rapidly, asking if I was all right, and what happened to the cats. They said they stayed right in bed and rode the quake out, but that the place was a total wreck – "everything came down and scattered everywhere."

De interrupted at that point and said, "Just a minute: I need to tell you something. There might be a 6.0 aftershock—almost as bad as the main one." I wasn't overjoyed to hear that bit of news. I asked Carolyn if their crystal collection had survived the quake, and she said, "No… and some of my jalapeno jelly broke, too… but it's all replaceable. Of course, it's the sentimental value, not just the replacement. We knew which item came from which fan or friend, and that can't be duplicated by buying copies." Then she added something completely uncharacteristic of her: "It's just the shits!" I agreed, "It sure is."

On the 19th, Carolyn called to see how I was doing. I reported that I was sleeping a little better, "But just as soon as I get to sleep, the phone will ring. People are calling from all over the world, now that they can get through – from Germany, Australia – asking, "Are you okay? Are the Kelleys okay?" Carolyn said, "Yes, that's happening here, too. De's sister-in-law finally got through, just after De had managed to fall asleep…"

De reported their chimney had come down, and their block wall was wobbly and would have to be taken down and replaced. Later that evening I called the Kelleys to tell them goodnight, as they had been calling to wish ME goodnight ever since the earthquake, and I was planning to retire early. De answered and I told him why I was calling. He said, "Just a minute, I'll get Carolyn." Then I told her I'd bring De's birthday presents by in the morning, and she said, "Oh, don't do that. That's silly. You just stay home and stay safe. You can do it when the aftershocks die down." I said, "Well, okay… but I have to get brave and go out sometime!" She reiterated, "Well, not this soon. You just stay safe." I asked her to tell De Happy Birthday for me, in that case, and she said, "Just a minute. You can tell him yourself." She put him on the phone and he said, "OK, let's hear it." I sang him Happy Birthday and then he told me, "I'll take that in the spirit of a celebration."

After a few days I got brave and put De's birthday gifts on the porch and kept on going. That evening De called and identified himself. "This is the birthday boy." He said they worked on the house all day and entirely forgot about the gifts on the porch. "I just got to them." I told him I was busy all day, too, cleaning up my place. He said he loved the vest I got him – "especially the fact it has a tie in the back of it. They usually don't have that anymore." He also said he loved the bolo tie and the scarves from the cats. "It was very nice of the cats to remember me." I said, "Oh, the cats would never forget you!" I told him, "You probably shouldn't wear all that stuff at once, as it doesn't go together!" He joked, "Oh, really?!" I said, "You'd look pretty wild, if you did!" He laughed. He said the cards were great and that he got a lot of laughs out of them, "which I needed after the last few days!" I asked De how long we are supposed to boil water to purify it, and he said, "I heard five minutes, but Carolyn heard 10." I said, "I'm listening to Carolyn! I usually do!"

A few days later, on January 27, Carolyn called me at work at around nine a.m. to ask how I was handling the aftershocks now. I said, "Hey, just fine – especially since (I quoted a recent letter I'd sent them) I found out I could control them just by saying, 'Knock it off, damn it!'" She laughed and said, "De and I got a big laugh out of that when we read it." I said, "I still jump whenever anybody drops a box or crumples up paper around here, though – so I haven't recovered completely yet!" She said, "That happens to all of us for a while after a big one. You'll get over it."

I told her a sad story: "I lost my star ceremony pin here somewhere yesterday!" She commiserated, "You didn't?!" I said, "I did. I've looked everywhere for it. I put up a little sign, so hopefully someone will find it and get it back to me. I feel naked without it."

It wasn't an hour and a half later that a little package arrived on my desk while I was in the restroom. It had been delivered via special courier from the Kelley residence! I tore it open. Inside was a star ceremony pin with a little note attached from Carolyn, written in her exquisite calligraphy. "Let No Day Dawn… without De's star pin!" the note proclaimed.

A few days later, at 3:30 a.m., a 5.0 aftershock hit, and so the phone lines were once again occupied between the Kelleys and the Smith residence as soon as dawn struck. Carolyn reported that she and De fell right back to sleep as soon as the big one stopped rattling around, and didn't even feel the second one. Then she said, "I took my first real shower – of normal length, I mean – since the one on the 17th. De has been taking normal-length showers since a few days after the big one." I said, "My, you *are* brave people! But what really concerns me is that I might be on the pot when one hits!" Carolyn said, "Oh, it happened to me already! It's… quite interesting!" Then Carolyn said, "De and I have been here forever, and WE stay, with all the quakes and aftershocks." After that, Carolyn alluded to having enjoyed speaking with "Kristine Marie, her cheerful little earful."

On February 5th, I thought up a funny out-going message for my answering machine and recorded it: "Thank you for calling [phone number]. Kris is over in Sick Bay pursuing my doctor — I mean, pursuing my DUTIES! If you will call back a little later or leave a message now, you WILL have my un-DE-vided attention. Hailing frequencies are now open."

Thinking Carolyn might enjoy hearing the new message, I dialed the Kelley's number. DE answered. I said, "Oh, great! Hello, sir!" and started giggling with an acute degree of embarrassment. De joked, "Are you sitting over there smoking marijuana, or sum'pin'?" I retorted, "Gawd Awmighty – NO!" and added, "No, sir! I… I just recorded a new out-going message on this answering machine and I was calling to see if Carolyn would call me back and be sure it's working." De said, "Carolyn's busy, but I'll call you back." I said, "Oh… Okay! Thanks!"

I laughed hysterically as the phone rang five times and the out-going message came on. De's response was recorded for all eternity. With his permission, I added it to my out-going message: "Kris is *SICK*, and *that's* the reason she's in Sick Bay!"

Not long after that, a stranger called, having dialed the wrong number, but she had to leave a message after hearing mine. "I've dialed the wrong number, and I'm sorry about that, but I just have to tell you — I'D like to be pursuing that doctor, myself – so I know where you're coming from! Your voice-mail message is very cute. Live long and prosper. Bye!"

TYPEWRITERS AND COMPUTERS AND SOFTWARE OH MY!

Carolyn called and said she had been calling around in the Valley, talking to various dealers about a new typewriter. I exclaimed, "Oh, great! That's fantastic!" She said, "I called one particular gentleman and told him what I wanted, and he said he has them. Then he asked what I have, and so I told him it's a museum piece by now — a 1955 Olympic from Germany. He told me, 'Oh, it's worth its weight in gold! Even if you get a new one, don't get rid of that one!' He told me that in an earthquake, my old one can go sailing across the room and will still work. The new ones won't." I said, "The old one can kill you if you happen to be sitting across the room from it during a quake, sweetie. Keep it, but put it in a closet somewhere. You'll be safer!"

She said, "He was very nice. If I decide to get a typewriter, I will go see him." She added, "Five years ago De and I went to every typewriter store in the Valley, looking for a new one, but we decided to just keep what I have. We came home empty-handed." I could tell, then and there, that prying Carolyn's arthritic hands off that hard-to-manipulate, antique, ponderous museum piece was going to be quite the challenge! But De felt she should get a new typewriter OR a computer, to make her working life easier, so I was determined to sell her on the idea of one or the other.

On February 5th, I went to an electronics store in Sherman Oaks to scout out an electronic typewriter for Carolyn that had italic type and could justify both margins. I found a good one for under $600 and got the flyer that described it and on which there was a photo of the model. I called Carolyn to tell her what I had found. I told her I was at the House of Typewriters and that I had found "her" typewriter – the perfect model – and that I had gathered some information on it that I'd be dropping into her mailbox momentarily that would show her a photo of it and describe its features. She back-pedaled and said she wasn't sure she'd get a new typewriter, but told me to come by and stop in for a few moments with the material. "We're not doing anything – just sitting here." I drove over and knocked on the door. Carolyn answered the knock and I hugged her. We went to the loveseat and sat down. I began my pitch with, "Now, DON'T BE AFRAID when you see the photo of this typewriter!" De came into the room at that point and patted me on the shoulder, laughing at the unique sales pitch that was underway.

I showed the photo to Carolyn and said, "See all these extra buttons? They mean NOTHING! Forget they exist. You DON'T NEED 'EM to type a letter." She asked, "Then why are they ON there?" I said, "Funny you should ask!" De laughed out loud again. I said, "They're there for a reason, but you don't have to know the reason, so you can just forget about them. They're there to make your typing jobs easier and faster." I glanced at De. He was shaking his head and grinning. Carolyn said, "I just want a BASIC typewriter—" I assured her, "This *is* a basic typewriter that justifies margins the way you want!" She joked, "How big a commission are you pulling on this sale?" I joked back, "Oh — 50%!" She said, "Then I'll buy it, but I won't use it!" I whimpered, "CAROLYN!" and she and De laughed like crazy. Then I said, "Fine! Have it your way," as though exasperated, which I wasn't, and they knew it. It was a game, played strictly for fun.

De asked to see the information on it, so I took it over to him. He said it looked great, and agreed that he thought she should get it. She protested to me, "But I just use a typewriter to type De's letters before he signs them at the bottom, and I've stopped doing THAT, even. I just have him sign a photo and send it." I said, "Then you don't need a typewriter. Case dismissed." She looked at the information and said, "It looks like a lot of fun, though." I assured her, "These days, they are. They sure make working life easier." After another twenty minutes or so of conversation, I hugged them both and turned to leave. They thanked me for coming and accompanied me to the door. Then De said, "We'll probably take a close look at that typewriter." I said, "Just call around first and be sure they have that exact model in stock before you wear yourselves out driving around." De said to me, "Whatever you do, don't mention (and he mouthed the word) software." Carolyn wasn't looking at him and asked me, "What did he say?" I said, "Whatever I do, I'm not supposed to mention… software." De shook his head. Carolyn said, "Oh, God, no! Don't mention software. I don't even know what it is!" I said, "Relax, Carolyn. Your typewriter doesn't have any. That's something that goes into computers. Your typewriter is NOT a computer." She said, "I'm glad."

In April that year, during the time I was completing the gathering of an earthquake preparedness stash, subsequent to Northridge, I ran across a nifty, combination emergency radio, spotlight and siren. I picked up two of them and dropped one in the Kelley's mailbox, mentioning in a note that it could be real handy. De thought it was dandy. My line rang at work one morning. When I picked up the receiver, there was a loud siren at the other end. My first comment was, "What the hell—?" Then I figured it out and laughed. De distanced the mechanism from the phone and then raised the receiver to his ear and laughed, "I've been walking up and down the street all morning, waking people up!" I said, "Great! Just remember that little story about the boy who cried, 'Wolf!'" He laughed again and joked, "I think I'll take it out into the back yard now and chase off the contractors with it!" I said, "Your wall will not get rebuilt THAT way!"

Then he said, "It's really great," and thanked me for it. I said, "This way you don't need to leave the house with the flashlight, a radio, and an emergency signal – providing you're able to leave the house at all. The siren is in case you get trapped anywhere and need rescuers to dig you out." Then I said, "But if you GET out, all you need is that gadget, some food bars, a jug of water and you're set." De repeated that to Carolyn, and then added, "Now we're set for the Big One!" He was laughing like hell. Carolyn came on the line. She told me she was going to do the quote in calligraphy that I wanted ("Use the talents you possess. The woods would be very silent if no birds sang there except those that sang best.") We discussed changing "woods" to "forest" so "woods" and "would" weren't juxtaposed, then I got silly and said, "DeForest would be very silent if it weren't for that damned siren!" and she laughed like crazy, and repeated that to De.

On May 15th I stopped at the Kelleys to pick up a video Carolyn said she'd leave out for me. When I opened the mailbox, it was empty — no video — so I figured Carolyn had meant Monday when she said "tomorrow" and I deposited my morning letter and headed back to the car. By the time I started to pull away from the curb, I noticed that De was sauntering out with the videotape, so I backed up and re-parked the car. I got out and walked halfway up the driveway to meet him. He said, "Good morning. We both just fell out of bed." He didn't look a thing like anyone who had just fallen out of bed. He was clean-shaven and looked fantastic.

On May 24th 1994 Carolyn called. All during the early minutes of the conversation, I could tell she was responding in a subdued manner. Finally she came out with it: "I have some bad news. De has had to cancel out of the Spokane convention. He won't be going to it." I said, "Oh… That's too bad, Carolyn. I'm really sorry." She said, "He hasn't been feeling well and he has been having tests. Today's tests came back unreadable, so they re-scheduled him for Friday. That's the day we were planning to fly. So De called Adam and told him. We have NEVER canceled out before – and Adam was so sweet." I said, "Well, sweetie, he LOVES you two! Of course he'd be sweet!"

She said, "This is all confidential, but I thought I'd let you know so you can cancel your flight and reservations, if you don't want to go." I said I would, right away, and thanked her for letting me know, so I could. She said, "We hate to disappoint everyone like this," and I said, "Oh, Carolyn, don't even WORRY about that. It's not even a concern. Be sure and give De a hug for me and let him know I've got my arms and heart and prayers around him." She said she would.

I said, "I could tell from the moment you spoke that something was wrong. Why didn't you tell me right away?" She said, "I was trying to ease into the subject, so it wouldn't be a shock." I said, "Oh. Well, I feel like a fool for making happy talk when I felt all along that something was wrong…" She said, "He's okay. He's just having tests, and one of them didn't come out, so he has to go have it again. He doesn't feel very well and we didn't want him to get up there to Spokane and then possibly have him become sick." I agreed, "Well, of course not!" I asked her to keep me informed of De's status and she said, "Oh, we won't know anything more until Friday, if then." I said, "Okay." I told her to take good care of herself. She said she was.

Several days later, Carolyn called to report that De had diverticulosis. I said, "Oh, God, that's awful. I had that once, and Dad has, too. It can usually be handled just with a change in diet. It's no biggy at all unless it gets worse and becomes diverticulitis."

Handling news (or no news) about a world-renowned celebrity was delicate. Sometimes it was just impossible to know what to do or say, to fans, friends or even to Carolyn. A day later, May 30th, Carolyn called. She laughed and said I might tell people who inquired regarding his cancellation that, "De had a tummy ache and that Carolyn says he's feeling much better now." On June 5th, Carolyn called. After a fun, rollicking conversation, I asked her, "Who drew the picture of Deaken on the plastic bag I picked up this morning at your place?" Carolyn said, "Oh, that was De!" I literally fell off the chair laughing. Carolyn asked, "De wants to know if he got the ears right." I laughed, "Oh, yes! Just right!" Carolyn heard me laughing and started laughing too. I cried, still laughing, "I didn't even see it until I got home, I was so taken by the sign you did in calligraphy on the paper bag, but then I got home and sat down and thought 'What's this?!' and spotted the drawing!" De and Carolyn were both laughing by now. After that attempt, De kept trying 'til he finally got it right!

Carolyn and I talked more, and somehow got on the subject of Deaken's eventual demise. When I mentioned it, Carolyn said, "Oh, no! Not for another ten years!" I said, "No, Carolyn. I don't think it'll be quite that long, somehow!"

In early August, I arrived at the Kelley's close to 6 p.m. and parked across the street, then walked up to the front door and rang the doorbell. Carolyn opened the door. De was standing in the hallway near the living room and I went over and hugged him and said hello. I walked into the living room. We had refreshments. I sat a coaster on a table which was supporting a huge box next to where they had motioned me to sit. De saw where I had placed the coaster and where I planned to sit my cola while opening the box, and said, "Sodder theah." (Meaning "Set her there.)" Then he chuckled and said, "That's what Grandma Casey used to always tell me: 'Sodder theah, F'ost.' She called me F'ost." Then he said, "I really hated that. So one time my mother helped me buy her a scarf — I was eleven years old — and I said, 'Grandma Casey, I have a present for you, but in order to get it, you have to promise me you'll never say, 'Sodder theah' to me ever again.' She promised me. So I gave her the scarf, and she loved it, and then put it on the table and said, 'Sodder theah, F'ost!'" De threw his head back and guffawed at the memory. I laughed too and then said, "Your first real lesson in giving: Don't give anything with any thought of reward in your mind, or you may be disappointed!" He laughed and nodded, and then I fantasized (aloud), portraying him in conversation: "Now, Grandma, let's go ovuh this again! What did we just discuss?" and he laughed and said, "Sodder theah, Kristine Marie.." (Move the coaster to the other table). I looked at Carolyn and she indicated where to put it down, so I did. I said, "Yes, suh."

De said, "Christ! Can you believe it's August already?!" I said, "I cannot. It feels like it should be about APRIL to me." He said, "That's exactly how I feel. I've NEVER had a year travel the way this one has." I said, "I really think that quake had something to do with it." He pointed at a remaining chink in the ceiling, and said, "I'm sure of it!" Then he said, "You know, when you're ten you can't wait to be twenty. You get from twenty to thirty without thinking a thing about it at all, and then — I just don't what happens to the years after that! They just DISAPPEAR! Suddenly I'm near the end of the road — REAL near the end!" He said it with a laugh and with a degree of startled realization that had poignancy in it, but without disappointment, fear or frustration. I paused and didn't say much, and Carolyn said, "Open that box and look what's in there."

I went into the box and began to pull out a bunch of Star Trek paraphernalia. She said, "There isn't very much that's De, but we thought you might like it anyway." I pulled each out piece by piece, commenting on all of it, some with genuine joy and other stuff with humor. I pulled out a Kirk doll. Carolyn said, "I don't know why they send us everybody else's stuff and none of the McCoy stuff." As I pulled out some bookmarks, Carolyn said, "I must confess something here. There were two De bookmarks, but I kept 'em. I want to send one to Ann and I want to keep one." I pulled out helium Enterprises, a puzzle, a medallion, several ties, magazines, a T-shirt, two mugs (of Kirk and Spock). At that point, De said, "I want to call Bill and Leonard and ask 'em, 'Who got my cup!?'" I said, "Do that! Hold theirs hostage until you get YOURS!"

When the Star Trek collector's edition scripts came out, De said he would sign them if I wanted, and I said, "Yeah! That would be great!" He got up to get a pen, and then I remembered, and said, "Oh! Since you're doing THIS, would you also sign a photo to Joe? He's a consultant to my boss and a big Trekkie." De said, "Sure," and headed into the workroom for pens. Carolyn hollered in to him, "Get the big black marker for these scripts!" She opened the cellophane that had been protecting the scripts with a razor blade knife that De brought back, and De said, "Just sign them, right? Or do you even want me to?" I said, "De! YES, I want you to!" He said, "I'm just going to sign my name. They'll be worth something someday — probably already are!" I said, "De!!! Knock that off. I'm NOT selling them EVER." He still just signed his name and said, "You should." I said, "Tough."

Carolyn said, "Oh! We've waited until you got here to feed Myrtle her dinner! Would you like to go out and watch her eat?" I said, "Yes!" We all got up and De headed out the back door to locate her. I called to him, "If she has waited this long, it will probably be real easy to find her. She's probably about ready to knock on your door!"

I followed Carolyn into the kitchen and she took the tortoise salad out of the refrigerator and we went out the side door. Myrtle was at the edge of the lawn. We went onto the lawn and Carolyn gave Myrtle a chin-tickle before setting the salad down. Myrtle liked the chin tickle and I got down on the grass. The creature just cocked her head and looked at me, and didn't eat for the longest time. I said, "Maybe she's nervous because she doesn't know me." De said, "Oh, no.. She's just slow. It always takes her this long to take her first bite. She's gettin' slower, too." Carolyn said, "Yeah, she's slower than her old man, now." I looked up and shook my head and laughed. So did they. I said, "Deke's getting slower, too..." De said, "Well, he's old. But he's happy." I said, "Oh, yes. He is THAT, for sure, still." He said, "That's what matters." Myrtle finally started eating and De asked me if I thought they should scrub the top of Myrtle's head because it looked dry. Carolyn said, "Oh, no. It's a lot better than it was." I looked up at De and said, "She's a wild animal. In the wilds, there'd be no one scrubbing her head. She looks fine to me. Her eyes are clear; her nose is dry. She's got a great appetite! She's fine." Carolyn said that if the tortoise didn't eat everything, the mockingbirds would descend and scarf the rest down.

On August 16th Carolyn called to tell me the essay I had written for a LA TIMES essay contest, "Why I Live in the Valley" was a "sure-fire winner." I said, "Oh, I wish YOU were the judge!" She said, "I'm just sure it's going to be a winner." I asked her to let me know if it appeared, so I could be sure and get a few copies. I told her the expected publication date – "Sept. 6th, the day before your anniversary" – and she said, "Oh, yes, I won't forget THAT!"

Several days later I was informed by the newspaper that my essay had won first place. I called to let the Kelleys know. They were ecstatic, and Carolyn hastened to remind me, "See, I TOLD you it was a winner!" I said, "Yes, you did. Sure am glad I listen to you!" Then I said, "But I have to do something goofy in order to publicize it." The photographer wanted me to wear a fairy godmother costume, hold a wand and make a spectacle of myself on Ventura Boulevard in the middle of the street! I reneged on the costume but agreed to the wand and to the mid-street photo shoot during rush hour, against my better judgment. Somehow the photographer and I survived the ordeal – but not without soiling our reputations as sane human beings, I'm sure.

On September 5th, the day before the article was scheduled to appear, the Kelleys visited me in Encino. Sue was with me. Carolyn mentioned that she hadn't seen Sue in two years, since the last time Sue was in my back yard. We all went outside to see Sue's new car. She was still smarting over having sold "Tony," her classic car. De said, "I know how you feel. I still feel terrible for having sold the Thunderbird. We never should have done it."

We visited for a long time. After about an hour and a half, the Kelleys announced they had to be on their way. I asked if they wanted to say good-bye to Deaken, who had been sleeping on my bed all afternoon, and they said, "Oh, yes, of course." They went in, with De dodging McCoy standees in two places along the route. After the second encounter, he inquired, "Who IS that guy?"

As the visit came to an end, we hugged all around and I said to Carolyn as we hugged, "I love you." She said, very sincerely, "Well, we love you, too – ALL you girls. You know that, don't you?" I smiled at her and said, "Oh, yes. If I'm sure of anything in this world, I'm sure of that!"

The next day "Why I Live in the Valley" appeared in the newspaper. Carolyn called and left a funny message on my answering machine, which I treasure. "This is your press agent calling, and I'm calling to see if you have a suggestion on what we can do for the next – pardon the expression – layout on you." I called her back and she was SO excited! "You won first place AND look at that big, beautiful, color picture, too!" I was less-than-ecstatic that nearly ALL the humorous references had been edited out but she said, "Oh, don't let that bother you at all! It's just wonderful and you should be proud and happy! I've already received a call this morning about it!" Surprised, I said, "You have?!" She said, "Yes! The lady I bought my pantsuit from yesterday called me right up this morning to tell me my husband was mentioned in the newspaper! So I got to tell her about you. And De got some publicity. It's just a wonderful thing and we're real proud of you, and happy!" I said, "Good Lord. Then I'm happy, too! Okay, I'm happy, too!"

The next afternoon, on their 49th wedding anniversary, Carolyn called to thank me for their anniversary gifts. At first, she seemed nearly overcome with emotion and all the love-filled things I had gathered for them and by the sentimental cards I had found to give them. She said, "I just love it all." Then she added, "We don't open our presents until around 4:00 every year, because we were married at 4:20, so I hope you don't think we opened them early and have been ignoring you all day." I assured her that I did NOT think that. Then I joked, "So! You're getting hitched in about ten minutes, huh?" She said, "Yeah…" with a big, nostalgic smile in her voice. "We're gonna drink some wine at the exact moment." I joked, "Aren't you in the least bit nervous? Sure you don't want to back out? Are you absolutely certain you're making the right decision on the love of a lifetime?" She said (I'm sure while looking at De), "Absolutely." I said, "You were married in the Los Angeles County Courthouse, downtown, right?" She said, "Yes. We did it right in the courthouse—" then joked, "real fancy!" I said, "Well, that just goes to show it doesn't have to be fancy to last!" She said, "That's for sure!"

She said, "AC called a little while ago, and since De was outside, I got to talk to him. I told him all about your wonderful article and picture in the newspaper. He said he was going to go in search of a copy this afternoon and see if he could still find one. The Lyles don't get the valley edition, you know." I told her, "I've sent him a copy already." She said, "Oh! I didn't know that. I hope I didn't steal your surprise!" I said, "No, not at all. It wasn't planned as a surprise; I just wanted to be sure he received a copy. I'll call him after I hang up with you and let him know one is on the way, so he won't go nuts looking for a copy." Then she said, "The moment is arriving, so I'll hang up now." "Happy anniversary, you two lovebirds!" I said. She said, "And again, thank you for making this anniversary so memorable! We love you! Good-bye!"

In mid- August, it was discovered that Dad's chronic and increasingly debilitating back problems would require surgery. Carolyn hastened to reassure him that the surgery would be no problem at all and that he would feel immediate relief and would wonder why he waited so long to have it done. I passed along the information, knowing how nervous he must be to have to undergo surgery.

The first week of September, while being put through standard tests prior to his back surgery, it was discovered that he had heart complications, and that before his back could be fixed, his heart had to be repaired. He was at serious risk for a heart attack.

Carolyn called me four days after her anniversary to commiserate over Dad's diagnosis and prognosis. Then she said, "I want to thank you for sending me Dennis Morgan's obituaries from the trades." I said sadly, "You're welcome. I sure thought of you when I heard the sad news on Gregg Hunter's radio show." Dennis Morgan had been Carolyn's favorite actor for over fifty years. She said, "That's when we heard it, too. De and I were in bed, listening to Gregg's program, and when he announced dear Dennis's death, I just froze. I couldn't speak. De reached over and patted my hand. And then I cried." She started crying again. Then she said, "I suppose it's silly, but it was almost as if I'd lost De. I loved Dennis for a very long time…" She cried a little more. I consoled her with, "I know… and it's not silly. Not at all." She quickly changed the subject to regain control of her emotions. "Cutie is outside eating her sunflower seeds." I told her how much Deaken loves cantaloupe, rinds and all, and honeydew melons, and Carolyn said, 'Oh, we love honeydews, too. They're getting toward the end of their season now, so you' better get them now!"

Then it was back to Dennis Morgan. "I received lots of calls about Dennis. Everybody knows how much I love him." She told about the time Bert Marks, an agent, called them at 11 at night. De answered the phone and Bert told De that he had Dennis Morgan at a party and wanted to know if Carolyn wanted to talk to him. De asked Carolyn, and Carolyn said, "FORGET IT!" "I wouldn't talk to him. That was about 1952 or 1954... no... later than that... about 1959."

Carolyn said, "You are going to know everything about me pretty soon!" I said, "Good! Then I can write the Carolyn Kelley story!" Carolyn said, "You might as well. De isn't going to [write an autobiography]." I told her, "I guess you know that if I write it, it will be the inadvertent start of a new world religion!" She laughed like hell at that, and repeated it to De, who also guffawed.

Later on De told us, "I did a TREK retrospective interview recently. It will be on videotape once it has aired, and the video will have more on it than what airs." Then he said, "You get a long interview and imagine it's going to be really sum'pin' when it airs, and then you see the final version, and you wonder what happened! You're on there for only a few seconds, and you were interviewed for hours! I hesitate telling anyone about upcoming things I've done, because sometimes they'll sit through it for an hour – as friends did during the recent BONANZA retrospective – and I'm in it for two seconds at the very end! It's embarrassing!"

In September I accepted a full-time position as an executive secretary in Technical Support (MIS) at Warner Bros, after having worked there for five months as a temporary. My bosses, Dan Kronstadt and Paul McDonald, were such terrific people to work for and with, as were their staffs, that I fell in love with the department. It hadn't been what I was looking for – in fact, I had been terrified of accepting work there even on a temporary basis, as I knew so little about computers and "tech talk" – but the chemistry among the people was so marvelous that I decided to stay.

I called Carolyn on her birthday to sing Happy Birthday and to update her on Dad's upcoming heart surgery on the 11th. She said she and De were in stitches over that morning's letter from me, in which I had regaled them with Dad's recollection of my conception. I said, "Oh, you think it's real FUNNY that I was conceived on a rock in the middle of Lake Cushman, huh?!" Carolyn laughed, "YES! We DO! We think it's WONDERFUL!" I said, "It's now readily apparent why I'm a little rocky, isn't it?!" and she laughed, "Oh, yes!" I added, "My father is Fred Flintstone!"

I flew to Washington for Dad's heart surgery. It went well. De sent a signed photo to him in the hospital. The photo was of De in hospital scrubs and he had inscribed, "Dear Jack, If they give you any trouble, you know who to call! DeForest." Dad pinned it on his wall and the nurses and doctors treated HIM like a celebrity! One of the doctors told Dad, "We'd better take good care of you, if your Primary Care Physician is BONES!"

Several of the physicians and medical technicians asked Dad if he could get signed photos for THEM, so he asked me. When I called the Kelleys with an update on Dad, I asked De if he would mind signing three more photos to Dad's medical team. He said, "Not at all." I joked to De, "I begged him to hide that photo, so you don't get any MORE requests, but he refused!" De chuckled and said, "It's okay. Don't worry about it." Dad was so cheered and encouraged by De's kindness and by the response of his medical team to it that he perked right up, worked hard to recover quickly, and earned the "Best Patient Award"!

Mom wrote the Kelleys a note some time later:

> Dear Carolyn and De,
>
> I apologize for being so late in thanking you for the pictures and good wishes. As you know by now from Kris, De's picture made such a hit with the doctors and nurses. Several nurses even followed him from floor to floor on his many moves to visit and bask in reflected glory!!
>
> Believe me — it sure raised Jack's spirits!
>
> I wish I had the same sort of magic to make Carolyn feel better! Our thoughts are with you.
>
> With love,
> Jack and Dorothea

Anne Richardson, president of a DeForest Kelley fan club in Australia, visited California in October, just shortly after Carolyn had contracted a severe case of shingles. The Kelleys had planned to meet with her while she was in town, but Carolyn was in such sad shape that those plans had to be scuttled. I asked her if De would be able to meet with her, and she said, "Oh, no. He won't do anything like that without me along." She asked if I would call Anne when she got in and say hello. I told her, "I'll be happy to do that. I can go meet her and take her star polishing, if she wants." Carolyn said that would be wonderful. She said, "I'll call her when she arrives to express my regrets and to let her know you'll be calling and getting in touch with her." I said, "Give her my phone number, so in case I miss her, she can contact me." She said, "Okay. Thanks." I said, "I'm happy to do it. I've WANTED to meet her!" She said, "I really wanted to meet her, too, but you can't understand how miserable these [shingles] are."

Anne arrived on October 23rd. I called her and took her star polishing. It was such a terrific day I didn't want to drop her back at her hotel when the day was over. I didn't get her back there until nearly eleven at night!

The next day, De called me at work, asking, "Are you terribly busy right now?" I said, "No." He said, "I wonder if you'd do me a favor." I said, "Certainly!" He said, "I want to get Anne on the Paramount lot sometime this week, if I can find out when she wants to go. Will you call Anne and see what her wishes are? When you find out, give me a call back and I'll call Rick Berman and see if his schedule can accommodate her then." I said I'd be happy to do that.

I called Anne and got the information, then got back to De. "Get a walk-on for Anne, because she says she'll take a cab from her hotel." De said, "I'll do that. Thank you for the help and for taking Anne around the sights last night." I said, "I am, and was, happy to do it." He said, "Well, we sure do appreciate it."

About 20 minutes later he called back to let me know he had arranged a private tour of the Deep Space 9 and Voyager sets with Rick Berman's assistant, and that Anne would be met at the gate by the assistant, who would escort her on the tour. I told him, "I'll let her know. She'll be tickled pink." Then I said, "You'd better get back to your duties now, Nurse" and he half-chuckled, half-guffawed at that and responded, "I'll have to think about that one!"

Carolyn called a little later to thank me and to get a report on all I had done with Anne the day before. I told her, "We went to Hollywood to see and polish De's star; then we went to my place so she could meet Deaken. You'll be happy to know he treated her real special. We went through my De collection. I guess you know THAT took quite a while!" She said, "I'll bet!" She said sadly, "I was so looking forward to meeting her. I shuffled around the house today gathering what I could find to give to Anne: an audio tape De made a long time ago; some photographs. She might like them." I assured her, "She'll LOVE them, Carolyn!" She said, "It's wonderful that Deaken was so sweet to Anne." I said, "I think he must have known she was special to you. He treated her just great, and I was really glad. She loved it." I let her know how high off the ground Anne sounded when I told her that De had procured her a special tour of the TREK sets. Carolyn said she was sorry the next movie wasn't in production yet, as she was sure Anne would have preferred to visit that set. I said, "She's happy with what she has." Then she said, "It's too bad you can't get away to go too, but you work at a studio and all of this stuff is probably old-hat to you." I told her it was, and that I had to stay put and work, as I borrowed vacation days from next year's calendar already in order to fly up and be with dad for his surgery and to go up for Thanksgiving.

Even though she was still battling shingles and a painful hip, Carolyn continued to stay in touch. At work I had been handed a little teddy bear named Amy. Amy wore a knapsack and was attempting to make an around-the-world voyage in one school year. A little girl, Whitnie Sill, had begun the bear on its journey from a school in Battle Mountain, Nevada. I was the little bear's second or third stop. I asked De and Carolyn if they would like a little visit from Amy, the jet-setting bear, and they said, "Oh, yes, we would!" So I dropped it off.

De and Carolyn pulled out the journal in the little bear's knapsack and wrote Whitnie little hand-written notes, letting her know that the bear had visited them.

De wrote:

> 10-14-94
>
> Hello Whitnie,
>
> My name is DeForest Kelley and I play Dr. McCoy on Star Trek. Having had considerable experience with tribbles, I gave Amy a complete physical. She came through with flying colors.
>
> I'm sure she will be able to thoroughly enjoy her future TREK around the world.
>
> Live long and prosper,
> DeForest

Carolyn wrote:

> October 14, 1994
> Hi, Whitnie,
>
> I am married to DeForest. We have had the pleasure of Amy's company overnight in our home. Amy was quite intrigued when I fixed lunch and she shared it with us and our turtle, Myrtle. Myrtle is very old, maybe over 80 years, and has lived with us for 30 years. Amy and Myrtle enjoyed each other, as Amy said she had never met a turtle before – but Myrtle has met several bears before!
>
> We wish Amy "happy travels" and we wish you "happy days."
>
> Carolyn Kelley

The little bear continued its world tour, spending time in several foreign nations before returning to Whitnie. Whitnie wrote to me later, "Amy came back to Battle Mountain, Nevada. These are some of the places Amy has been: Oregon, California, Hawaii, Virginia, and seen DeForest Kelley of Star Trek fame. From there she went to France, Germany, Russia, and Japan. The most interesting place she visited was with DeForest Kelley."

On December 18th Carolyn called to ask if I had gone star-polishing. I of course said, "Yes! The Anniversary Boy's star is shining like gold this morning!" She said, "I can't believe it has been three years already." She then said, "You sound a little tired this afternoon. Are you okay?" I said, "I just got up from a nap. I had another bout with Deaken last night." She said, "Oh, I'm sorry to hear that. What happened?" I said, "He just has what I will describe as power failures. He'll start across the floor, go just a few steps, and then will pant, lie down and almost faint. Pretty soon he comes out of it and acts as though nothing has happened." She said, "Is it old age?" I said, "It's something. I'll take him to the vet as soon as I can get an appointment and have some tests run. He did that once as a kitten and scared the stuffing out of me, but this is the first time he did it as an old guy." She said, "Try not to worry, if it has happened before and he was okay." I said, "I'm trying not to, but it ISN'T normal, and I'm going to find out what's up."

Soon after I returned with Deaken from the vet the phone rang. "De asked me to call and ask you how Deaken's check-up went," Carolyn began.

I gave her the information. "His blood work checked out ten months ago and they expect it to check out again. The lump is probably either fat or an infection in a salivary gland; it's NOT a tumor." She said, "De wonders why he collapsed then." I said, "If everything checks out, it's probably just age and his weight. He wore out and laid down until he got his wind back." Carolyn said, "I don't know how you'll ever get the extra weight off him. He's just like his Aunt Carolyn – can't exercise at all, can he?" After a while I said, "Well, we'll just do all we can for him and he'll live with it for as long as he can happily. Like the rest of us mortals."

Still, I knew that time was running out on my one and only "wild one." I spent a lot of time talking with De and Carolyn about his eventual demise, and we often choked up reminiscing over the many wonderful times we had shared with him through the years. Carolyn and I occasionally even sniffled and cried over the situation. De counseled, "Keep a stiff upper lip." I told him, "I am. Deaken keeps me smiling even through my tears!"

De and I had tummy problems with diverticulosis that month, too. I suggested to De soaking as often as needed in a tub of hot water, saying, "It always gives me such relief that it's impossible to think I hurt so much only moments earlier."

Shortly after the New Year (1995) Carolyn called to check up on me, and to respond to an inquiry, telling me that De did not want a gift from me for his birthday "in any form whatsoever. A card is enough." I said, "Okay. I just wanted to be sure. That's why I asked. 'If De says no, ask Carolyn, and if Carolyn says no, FORGET IT!" She laughed and said, "Carolyn says no and I'll put De on the phone, too, if you want to hear it from him!" I said, "Oh, no! One no is enough!"

She told me that Cutie squirrel was on the screen that morning. "De took her some walnuts. She's the only squirrel we've seen today, so she's the only one that's been fed. But it's raining, so the others are smarter." I said, "Not necessarily! Next she'll be on the screen asking you for a teensy, weensy little raincoat!" Carolyn laughed and said, "And we'd get one for her, and I'd put it on for her!" I joked, "I bet she'd stand still for THAT!" and we both laughed. I said, "My Mom is where I get my sense of humor, can you tell?" She said, "Oh, we can tell!" I said, "She's more sedate about it, though, fortunately. SHE isn't crazy – just funny!"

We talked about Bruce in the meat department at Pavilion's, and about what a great guy he was. "He saw my De shirt and told me, 'DeForest shops in here all the time.' I told him, 'You're not supposed to tell FANS that!' and he ducked as if he was about to be busted for some heinous crime! Then I told him it was all right to tell ME, because MRS. Kelley is the person who turned me on to this place because of your great deals on Ensure!"

De was on the other line and chuckled, "One time I went to another store where we frequently shop, and there was a new checker there. I hadn't seen her before, and she hadn't seen ME before, but I ended up going though her line. I could tell she knew who I was; that was pretty obvious – but she wouldn't say anything; kept lookin' down at the groceries and working. I guess she didn't want to risk how I might react. A lot of stars don't like to be acknowledged when they're shopping, you know, and can be pretty obnoxious if you approach them. Anyway, her subconscious must have been bothering her, because pretty soon she starts humming the STAR TREK theme!" He laughed. "She never said another word; didn't even seem to realize she was doing it!"

On January 20th, De's 75th birthday, he called me, sounding tickled as heck. I soon found out he was EMBARRASSED, not tickled. "I have to tell you… I just got back from the DMV, and … this is so embarrassing: I flunked the written test the first time!" I laughed and said, "You DIDN'T?!" He said, "I DID! Then I talked to another man there and he said he did, too! And the man told me, 'I consider myself a reasonably intelligent human being, but these questions are— '" He paused, and I filled in the blanks: "—worded in such a way that you're not sure what the hell is being asked?" "Exactly!" De agreed. "Plus – on one of them, I just accidentally marked the wrong answer even when I knew the right one. That's the one that put me over the errors limit. It was about parking on a hill; whether to turn the front wheels toward the curb or away from the curb. I marked 'make 'em parallel to the curb!'" He laughed heartily at that and then said, "That way the car can shoot down the hill at full speed unobstructed!"

On January 29th De called me. I had written a "heart piece" earlier in the week for De's and Carolyn's eyes only called "DAMMIT, JIM, HE'S MY HERO, NOT A DOCTOR!" I had shown it to Mom, who said she thought it would be a wonderful magazine article. I said, "I don't think so. It's too personal. I don't think De and Carolyn want very many people knowing this kind of stuff about them." Mom said, "Well, that's a shame. I wish more people DID know this about them, so people know why you're nuts –about them!" I said, "Gee, thanks, Mom!"

I dropped off the article to the Kelleys in a sealed envelope.

De and Carolyn read it, and then De called. "Hello. Kris. It's DeForest." He had on his "business voice." I said, "Well, hello, DeForest" (in my best, albeit much less-believable, business voice). He was very serious and said,

"I've just finished reading your article for TV Guide – and I think it's fine." I inquired, "For TV Guide?" He said, "Yes." I said, "Serious!?" (I'd long since lost my business voice, but he still had his!) He said, "Yes. TV Guide is doing a special on STAR TREK in March and they are interested in me again. I'd get it in right away, and I also suggest that you request to see a copy of the edited version, so that you'll be satisfied with what goes in. Oftentimes, you'll see an interview and think, 'Gee, that isn't what I said or intended at all,' and it can be very frustrating." I was in shock. I asked, "Are you SURE you want this published?" He said, "Well, it's very flattering, of course, but it's also well-written and it's all true." I said, "So, then, you think I should submit it?" He said, "I don't see why not. I have no objection to it." I said, "Wow! I'm surprised. I thought you'd think it too personal." He said, "No. I think it's fine." A day later De called again to say he had re-read the article and thought it was "just wonderful. I think it might even be used as a special article, possibly not even in the STAR TREK issue, but all by itself at some point..." I joked, "From your mouth to God's ears!"

I slapped that puppy into an envelope with a cover letter and mailed it to TV GUIDE within the hour! They didn't publish it – considering it "too fan-nish." I subsequently placed it on the Internet on every DeForest Kelley website that would carry it. Thank God there's more than one way to shout good news from the rooftop!

In mid-April Carolyn called to ask me, "How's dear Deaken these days?" I said, sadly, "He's winding down, I'm afraid. He's very old. He's healthy and happy, but old age doesn't last very long in kitties once they begin to show it, especially in wild ones. They try to stay as hale and hearty looking as they can for as long as they can, because the minute they start to show their age in the wild, some other predator capitalizes on it and enjoys a serval snack." I told her, "He hugs my neck at night with his forepaws, several times each night. He'll even wake me to do it, and then he'll purr and head rub me. I know it's anthropomorphic, but I sometimes wonder if he KNOWS our time together is coming to an end and that's why he's more huggy and kissy than he has been in the past. He has always been sweet and loving, but now he's kind of smothery about it." I started to get a little bit misty, and so did she. "It's making me cry, too." I said, "I'm sorry. I had NO idea this was going to happen when I started this subject. Sometimes I can discuss it totally dry-eyed, and other times I get surprised like this." I told her, "Deaken has been a special pride of mine. Raising a wild cat who is healthy and happy and unstressed in captivity, and well-socialized is something that's rare and beautiful. Domestic animals have been genetically designed over thousands of years to cope with people, but wild ones are genetically engineered for self-sufficiency and autonomy." She said, "I understand completely the attachment and pride you feel in what you've accomplished with Deaken."

On June 13, 1995 I was at work when the phone rang. It was De. Deadpan, he said, "Hello, Kris, this is DeForest. I'm calling to let you know that a package for Father's Day arrived here at the wrong address this afternoon." Thinking he was serious, I hastened to assure him, "No, it didn't, De. It went where it was supposed to – if it's made of chocolate." He said, "Hush up, loudmouth, and listen!" I smiled. "Yes, sir?" De continued: "This MUST have come to the wrong address because I'm not your father – although I'm certainly old enough to be – but I have a proposition." I queried, "Yes?" He said, "Since it came to this address – and happens to be Chocolate Decadence Cake – I thought I would keep it and we'd eat it anyway!" I agreed, "That's a very good plan! Just don't tell my father: he'll be very jealous. HE'S getting a healthy food basket for HIS Father's day!" De chuckled and said, "I won't say a word."

TRANSPORTATION TRAVAILS AND TRANSITIONS

Later in June it became obvious that my car was in its last days. I called Carolyn and told her the story. She said, "I wish you could get a new car so you'd be sure of its reliability…We didn't want to sell the Bird and get a new car, either, but it got a point where we couldn't rely on it. It's a terrible feeling when you don't know whether or not your car will start when you need it." Carolyn asked me, "Guess how many miles we have on our '91 Lexus." I thought about it and guessed, "12,000?" She said, "Cut it in half. We've gone 6,000. The farthest we've gone in it is Long Beach."

Three days later I reported to Carolyn that my bucket of bolts had left me stranded again and that I wouldn't be by with their letter or to go star polishing. Carolyn interrupted me with, "You and that car!" I said, "Have no fear! I was approved for a $5,000 car loan at the credit union and just today my mechanic told me he has knowledge of a tremendous buy for $3,000, so we drove out and looked at it. And I LOVE it, and he's going to go through it – put it up on the rack — and be sure it hasn't been abused and that it will be reliable transportation for me." She got real excited and said, "Tell me about it!" I told her, "It's RED! Boy oh boy, is it RED! But that's okay – I never speed anyway! I've never had this new a car before! I'm excited!"

Then she said, "Listen – why don't you let us loan you the $3,000 to get the car and you can pay us back when you can – in ten years or so!" I just about cried! I misted up and sputtered, "Carolyn! It isn't necessary! First Entertainment gave me a loan." She said, "It's NO INTEREST with us!" That stopped me cold. "Really?!" She said, "No interest. That would save you a pretty penny, and you won't have the worry of having to come up with a payment every month, if you get strapped for some other important reason." I sighed. "Let me think about it." She giggled. "The little business analyst wants a conference." I laughed and said, "No, the little business analyst wants to CRY!" She said, "Cry, then call me back. But first, talk to De." She handed the phone to De, who said, "Congratulations! It sounds as though you've found a new set of wheels, if everything checks out on it okay." I said, "Yeah! I'm excited! It's just the CUTEST little car!" He said, "Well, I hope it checks out for you and is everything you want."

Referring to a book of humor I'd just written about being a floating secretary in the entertainment industry, De said, "I enjoyed it very much." I said, "Carolyn told me you have some suggestions to make it even better." He said, "Now, I've been known to be WRONG a time or two, so these are just my IDEAS…Put one or two of your BEST anecdotes up front. You have plenty of them. That first one brings a smile, but not a guffaw like the later ones do. You have to catch the reader right away, as soon as they open the book, or they won't take it from the shelf and buy it." I agreed with that. He said, "That's IT. That's my only suggestion. I thought it was thoroughly enjoyable. I wish it was longer; that's my only gripe. It was so much fun, I wanted there to be more of it…Well, I hope you get that car, if it's the one you want." He handed the receiver to Carolyn, who said, "We're holding all good thoughts that it checks out all right!" I said, "Thank you again for your sweet offer!" She said, "We'd love to do it for you, Kris. You just let us know. I'll put your book out in the mailbox and you can pick it up whenever you get by again."

A few minutes later, she called me again to say, "De asked me what kind of car it is you're looking at, and I couldn't remember. Tell me again so I can write it down and tell him. He wants to call a friend and see what he has to say about that model." I said, "Okay." I gave her the specifics again and she said, "Okay. I have it all now. Thanks!"

Then she said, "Kris, when you get the car, our check is a gift to you. You don't have a thing to worry about, so stop worrying." I cried, "Oh, Carolyn!" then sighed, silent and overcome.

I called the Kelleys on the 27th to let them know the Mazda had checked out. I told Carolyn everything was ready. Carolyn said, "Let me call the bank and see if I can transfer the funds and write you the check. I'll call you right back." She called back a bit later and reported, "The check is writ." I sighed and said, "I can't tell you how much I appreciate this, Carolyn." She said, "I know you do. We're happy to do it. Just don't copy the check before you cash it." I said, "I won't. I'll be by at about six, so you can put it in the mailbox then." She said, "Oh, no. You come on in when you get here and get it!" I said, "Great! I need a hug!" She said, "I bet you do! See you soon!"

When I got to their house, Carolyn invited me in and I hugged her. She got me a cola and a party napkin with the words "Indulge Thyself" on it. At that moment, De sneaked up behind me and poked me in the ribs. I jumped, startled, and then gave him a hug and a hello.

They invited me into their living room and sat me down on a love seat. There was an envelope on the table near me. Carolyn sat in a rocking chair next to my love seat. De sat across the room in another love seat. De and I talked about growing up on ranches or in the South. We had similar experiences regarding animals – using them for food (subsistence hunting, etc.). He mentioned eating squirrels and opossums and rabbits; I mentioned ducks, pheasants, deer and rabbits. We spoke about veal – the cruelly-raised kind. They wanted to know how to tell which veal had been raised in tight little stalls, so they would avoid buying it in the future. De mentioned how they trapped rabbits and treed 'possums and squirrels and told how they quickly and humanely dispatched the animals with a quick blow to the head. Carolyn interjected, "This was done by a minister, remember!" De said, "We were not a well-to-do family. Often what we caught was all we had to eat. A minister's life is not lucrative."

Not long after, they asked me to open the envelope. I did. Inside was a check for $3,000, made out in Carolyn's exquisite calligraphy. I marveled at it and then said, "You can't KNOW how much I appreciate this…" De said, "You just get that car and I hope it gives you YEARS of fun and good transportation." I assured him, "Oh, it will!" Carolyn again repeated, "Please don't copy the check before you cash it." I reassured her, "I won't. I'll just MEMORIZE it right now!" and sat and stared at it as they laughed. Pretty soon thereafter I looked at my watch, eager with anticipation, and Carolyn said, "Go get your car." I asked, "When do you want to see it?" They discussed that and said, "Tonight, if you can manage it before 7:30 or 8 o'clock." I said, "I can manage it if I leave here right now. I'll be back before 7:30 or let you know otherwise." They said, "Okay." I hugged them both, sighed, and said, "Thanks again. This is just tremendous. I'm NEVER gonna get over this!"

In two shakes I was back at the Kelleys with my new car. I didn't even have to knock. De was out the front door and heading down the sidewalk the moment I pulled up. I asked, "Where's Carolyn?" He said, "She'll be out in a minute. She's getting something. Let's take a look at this little jewel." We walked out to the car, and by the time we reached the hood, Carolyn was walking out, holding her camera at the ready. I walked back to greet her and hug her. I pointed at the car and said, "Isn't it just the COOLEST?!" She admitted that it sure was. I went over and opened the hood so De could peer underneath. He spotted a rubberized cap that was up and not doing its job over the battery cable, so he pushed it back down. By this time Carolyn had positioned herself in the middle of the street with the camera and said, "Look up, you two. I want to get a picture." I wrapped my arm around De – he reciprocated – and we stood still for the photo. The grins were genuine! I asked Carolyn to come over for a picture and she said, "Oh, no. Not now!" and then joked, "I don't have my eyelashes on!"

She positioned me around behind the car and took a few more photos. When we finished with that, they studied the car minutely, inside and out, and agreed that it was quite the deal and that it was in terrific shape. Then De said, "Just don't screw it up with those [DeForest Kelley] window stickers you have on the other one!" I feigned anger and blustered, "Excuse me?!" He laughed. I asked him, "Whose car IS this?!" He said, "Yours." I agreed, "Mine! It's gonna LOOK like my car, too!" I hugged them no fewer than six times each during the course of all of this, and they grinned mightily and kept saying that my joy was all the thanks they needed.

The next morning Carolyn called me at work and asked, "Did your new little car get you to work okay this morning?" I assured her it did. I told her, "I just LOVE it – and it has a new wax shine on it and new floor pads and a new Club and a sun visor and – what else?" She asked, "Did you doll it up with stickers again?" I asked, "Are you kidding?! Do you even have to ASK me that?!" She laughed and asked, "What did you put on [along those lines]?" and I said, "I have my NO BONES ABOUT IT, I'M A DeFOREST KELLEY FAN license plate holder and a MAY DeFOREST BEWITCH

YOU window sticker – and on the rear view mirror I have wooden key chains that say DeForest and Carolyn on them."

The Kelleys asked me to keep mum regarding the car, so at work I had to pretend nothing unusual at all had happened. I managed to do that only by "divorcing" myself almost entirely from the happy event. But after a month passed, and on the day I would have had to make the first car payment, I was in the parking garage at Warner Bros. Placing the key into the lock to unlock it, it hit me that the car was *mine*, then and there, PAID IN FULL, and I started to bawl. I quickly jumped into the car and sat there sobbing, hoping no one would come by and ask me what was wrong. What could I have said?

No phone calls came in from the Kelleys between June 29th and July 5th. I was used to hearing from Carolyn or De no fewer than three days a week, so this was ODD; worry material for my brain. It put me into Mother Hen mode with a vengeance. I wrote and asked them, "Is everybody okay over there?"

Carolyn called on July 5th to tell me, "I felt I should call to let you know not to worry about me." I said, "I DO worry when you make yourself scarce for so many days running like this. It isn't like you. I can't help it." She said, "Well, don't worry about it." I explained, "I LOVE you, lady and gentleman!" She didn't say a WORD, so I added, "So BIG DEAL, right?!" She laughed at that, sounding a bit surprised that she COULD laugh!

The call did nothing to alleviate my concern regarding their uncustomary absence since Thursday. It heightened it.

She called again on July 12th and sounded wonderful. She said, "We have been real busy and I realize we haven't been in touch for a while, but I can't call all the time." I said, "I know that. I'm just happy to hear from you when you CAN. You sound real happy, too!" She said, "I am. De has been having some tummy troubles again—" I said, "Oh, no!!" She said, "He had a test this morning. It came out fine, so we're relieved." I cautioned her, "It's those nuts, Carolyn! Hide those nuts! They're murder on a person susceptible to diverticulosis!"

De called on July 21. I had asked if he would be willing to write either an introduction for FLOATING AROUND HOLLYWOOD or a blurb for the back cover. He thought about that and then called with his response. "Hi, honey. Do you have a minute?" I said, "Sure." He said, "I'm going to back out on writing a foreword for your book." I said, "Okay." He said, "I have a couple of reasons. The first is, you've already written about me in the book.

It wouldn't be politically correct for me to say much more on it." I said, "Okay. And you don't have to give me ANY reasons, De!" He said, "The second reason is, I'm just no good at this type of thing. I'm a poet, not a writer." I joked, "A long time ago, in a state far, far away…" (mimicking his earlier STAR TREK poems). He said, "I WILL try to write a little something for the back of the book, though." I said, "Cool! Super! Thanks!"

He asked if Deaken would be in the book, and I said, "No." He said, "He should be in the book." I asked, "What would he be doing in a book about floating around Hollywood?! He'll get his own book someday, probably." De said, "I'd imagine so. It'll be a good one." Then he said, "Deke could be on the acknowledgments or dedication page." I said, "OK, OK! I'll think about it, De!" Then I got serious and said, "Uncle De loves his nephew — my little serval son — doesn't he?" He said, "We sure do."

Within a week of this conversation, my landlord, pushed over the brink emotionally and financially by the Northridge quake and by the expense of repairing his two rental properties plus his own place – mentioned to me that he and his wife were considering selling out and moving to Florida. The news panicked me. He wanted OUT. I recalled how long it had taken to find a landlord willing to let me have Deaken. Still, with the landlord's pressing concerns and incessant fear, I could well understand his need, so it seemed to me a dead certainty that, before too long, I'd be searching for new digs, the difficulty of such a search be damned.

I considered moving back to Washington. Mom and I both vetoed that idea, with Mom saying, "Much as I'd love to have you move back here, you'd be insane to move back solely for a cat that's about to expire anyway. That just doesn't make good sense at all." So it came as a big relief when the landlord reconsidered and told me I could stay for at least another six months. It would buy enough time for a sane, rational approach to the next housing option – and who knew, perhaps Deaken wouldn't even be a factor in six months, since he was obviously sliding downhill health-wise. Searching for a housing situation sans Deaken would be a picnic in comparison to looking for a place for him and me.

Out of the blue Carolyn phoned one day, "Do you have any plans for tomorrow?" I said, "No." She said, "You sure?" I said, "I'm sure, Carolyn." She said, "Would you enjoy a little visit?" I said, "I'd LOVE it!" She repeated, "You don't have any other plans?" I repeated, "No." She said, "Okay, we'll come by." I said, "Here? Awright!!! When? Morning?" She said, "Not morning. I'm not out of bed in the morning! How about 2:00?" I said, "Okay! You can see Deaken again!" She said, "I'll bring my camera."

They arrived at about 3:30 after phoning earlier to let me know they would be delayed in getting over. Carolyn accidentally hit the car horn when backing into the street parking spot, so I ran out there and joked, "So now you're HONKING AT ME!?"

De got out first, so I went over and gave him a hug, and then went to the driver's side and waited for Carolyn to emerge. I gave her a big hug and we started up the sidewalk to the house. De spotted the Mazda and said, "There's that little red gem." I sighed, "Yeah… Ain't it purty? I called and told Mom I put another coat of wax on it today and she said, 'If you keep doing that, pretty soon it won't fit in one lane of traffic! You'll have to get an Over-sized Load sign and blinking caution lights!'" They laughed.

We went indoors to escape the heat. Deaken was lying on a bunch of strategically-placed pillows in the living room. They immediately started exclaiming, "There's our boy! Hi, Deaken! Hi, sweetie!" Deaken lapped it up and gave De a kiss on his hand. Carolyn said, "Oh, look! He kissed you! Oh!" Carolyn put her hand out to Deaken and he kissed her and started rubbing his chin all over her hand, drooling a little bit, ecstatic. Carolyn exclaimed, "Oh, thank you! Thank you, Deaken!" Deke was pretty laid-back and sleepy, and almost fell asleep with his chin in the palm of Carolyn's hand. She exclaimed, "Oh, his head is HEAVY! He's weighing me down!" She said, "I have to get my camera out. I want pictures." She handed the camera to me with her free hand and said, "Get some pictures of us with him, will you?" I said, "Sure." Deke remained lying in her hand, so I got a photo of that, then additional photos of De and Carolyn with him.

De stepped behind me to get an ashtray and inquired, "Does Deke mind if I smoke?" I said, "Not at all." Carolyn said, "Oh, that's right. I forgot about not wearing perfume. Some smells upset wild animals." I told her, "Whatever you have on, keep it! He obviously LOVES it! I don't know of any scent Deke DOESN'T like." De joked, "Bleach, elephant dung, armpits…" I said, "Those are just his FAVORITES, De. He likes Dioressence and White Linen, too!""

De reached out and Deke enjoyed chin-tickling again, then they straightened up and sat properly on the couch. I got a Gatorade for Carolyn, and De and I shared a diet cola. I gave the Kelleys cups that had their pictures on them. When Carolyn noticed hers, she exclaimed, "Oh, look! This cup has ME all over it! And Fancy! Oh, look, De! Fancy! Oh, it makes me cry!" De looked at his cup and he said, "This one has ME on it, too." They exchanged cups and studied them minutely. I said, "I only use them for special occasions. In fact, I think this is the only time I've ever used them!"

Carolyn said, "Let's go out and take pictures with the car." I asked, "Already? We were just out there. Want to go again so soon?" She said, "Sure, if you want to." I said, "It's fine with me." They stood up, Carolyn grabbed her camera, and we went back out into the hot sunshine.

I backed the car out. De took a couple pictures of Carolyn and me with the Mazda, and then Carolyn took a couple of De and me with it. Then I took a couple of them with the car. After that, we went back indoors. Of course, they greeted Deaken again, petted him, and let him know he was a handsome boy. Carolyn went into my bedroom to study the "Kelley Shrine" on the walls, so De followed her. I did, too. Then De noticed the Indian dream catcher and we commented on the legend behind it. I told them "It works!" Carolyn noticed again the many photos of her with Fancy and she mentioned how much they loved her and how much they missed her.

We went back to the living room, where Carolyn looked lovingly at Deaken again and asked, "How are we going to survive losing Deaken?" I said, "We'll survive it – but it's gonna be a trial! I can't think of it for more than about three seconds these days without falling apart." She said, "It's so hard." De offered, as consolation, "He'll probably out-live all of us." I said, "No way. Who would be here to take care of him and love him the way we do?" De said, "That's right." Then he said of Deaken, "A part of you is in him, isn't it?" I said, "Forever. I'll NEVER be without him, any more than I'll ever be without YOU TWO. It just ain't possible."

On August 31, I was a woman with a mission. When Carolyn called to chat, I wanted to somehow steer the conversation around to find out the call letters of her favorite radio stations. Then I planned to call those stations and let them know that the Kelleys 50th anniversary was coming up, so they'd wish De and Carolyn a happy 50th and play their favorite courting songs in honor of their long union. But FIRST – I had to get the information out of Carolyn without her becoming any the wiser.

I told her, "You know – I feel real dumb – but you have mentioned several times that I ought to tune in to the radio stations you listen to most often, because the music on them is so good… but I can never remember which ones. If I promise to write them down this time, would you tell me one more time?" "Sure!" she said, delighted. "They play all OUR music – music of the 40's, 50's and 60's, sometimes even earlier." She listed four stations; I wrote them down.

Eventually I even found out their theme song from Carolyn. "Our favorite is TWILIGHT TIME. Do you know it?" That information made its way to the radio stations, too.

A few days later I called Carolyn at around noon, shaking like a leaf, after ENTERTAINMENT TONIGHT called me in response to the anniversary date notice I had sent to them. The photo coordinator reported that she didn't have a photo of De and Carolyn together to air during the announcement of their 50th wedding anniversary. I had told the woman, "I have a photo of the Kelleys together that was taken in my back yard" – and she wanted me to bring it to the studio post haste if we owned the copyright. I told her Carolyn owned the copyright, and that I would have to ask her. So I called her, not knowing how she would receive the information. She also wanted a photo of the Kelleys on their wedding day, if one was available.

As soon as Carolyn answered the phone, I cried, "DON'T BE MAD AT ME!" She asked, "Is this Kris?" I said, "Yeah. I told ET about your anniversary, and they called me today and say they need a photo of you and De together that they can show during the announcement of your 50th anniversary. I told them I have one that was taken in my back yard, and they want me to bring it to them, but I want to know if that's all right with you." She said, "De isn't here right now to ask – but — oh, I think it would be all right. Go ahead and do it!" I said, "ET also wants to know if you have a wedding day photo you can provide." She said, "No, we don't." I said, "OK. I'll go with what I have, then. Thanks!" She said, "Thank YOU!" I told her I loved her and we hung up.

Sadly, the photo never aired and the announcement was never made. The lady explained that they had wanted to do something more extensive, and when the photos weren't available to do a larger piece, it fell by the wayside. She did say that the photo might be used as a later date, possibly on Valentine's Day, as part of a larger piece on the few celebrity marriages that have stood the test of time and all the temptations. I told Carolyn that and she said, sarcastically, "They'll probably use it after we're DEAD!"

Mom and Dad arrived on Halloween Day while I was at work and called in to let me know they were at my home. Then they took a nap. Carolyn called at about 2:00 to wish me "Happy Spooks!" I excitedly and enthusiastically reported Mom's and Dad's arrival. Just before we signed off, I told her that a co-worker, Greg Heimbigner, had heard a commercial for the upcoming Pasadena convention with De, Leonard and Bill. "Funny thing is, the announcer said that McCoy AND Bones will be at the convention! Greg told me, 'I guess De is going to be BESIDE HIMSELF at that convention!'" Carolyn laughed at that and added, "Two for the price of one!"

On November 30th, the axe fell. The landlord sent a move-out notice, giving us 90 days to find other digs, as he had made the decision to move out of California and re-locate to Florida. I was beside myself with worry. I was enormously glad that Mom and Dad were in Southern California for the winter and could scout out options while I worked. Carolyn and De called often to tell us of places they'd heard of, and to try to keep my panic at a manageable level. Deaken was the obstacle. And I wasn't about to have Deaken euthanized out of expediency. No way. I'd give up my career and everything I had going for me in Southern California if it came to THAT. The commitment I'd made to Deaken the first time I held him in my arms, at five hours old, was inviolate.

In December, Emese Fisher, my guardian angel Realtor, kicked around the idea that rather than locating a rental, we should go for the purchase of a house or condo. Dad was for it. "You'd OWN the place, you wouldn't be pouring money down a rat hole."

The decision made, I let the Kelleys know of the new direction. Carolyn wanted to know how I would come up with the down payment! I said, "Dad and Mom said they can help with most of it. I just have to be sure and get it back to them by summer." "Why?" "Well… they're both retired and on a limited income." She said, "We could loan you the money. No interest. Up to ten years to pay!" I countered, "Carolyn, I have heard this story before, with the Mazda, and you wouldn't let me pay you back!" She giggled and said, "Oh, have you?" Then she got serious and said, "No, you'll have to pay this one back." "Promise!" "I promise." "Will you please let me pay you interest on the loan?" "No. It's no interest, or no deal… Now you can relax a little bit and find the perfect home for you and Deaken with much less strain and trouble for everyone."

That same week, a producer called and left a voice mail message at home asking if he could interview me at De's star for a segment he was producing for the Popcorn Channel. Mom encouraged me to take a few hours and do it. "It will be good for you. You need to do something fun during this, too." I called him back and asked if his crew could meet me at De's star on Sunday at my usual star polishing time. He said, "Certainly."

On Sunday morning, we did the shoot. It turned out so well that the producer called the next day to proclaim me "a star." He said, "You were just fantastic. We interviewed other polishers, but you have the preponderance of time in the edited version that will air. I think DeForest will be very pleased." I asked if he would provide three copies of the segment. "I want to have two, in case one breaks, and I'd like to give the third to the Kelleys." He said, "Certainly. I'll have a messenger take them to you this afternoon at your studio. Give me your particulars."

I called the Kelleys to let them know the producer was satisfied and that we'd be getting copies to see and keep. Carolyn said, "Oh, we don't need a copy to keep. We'll just look at it and give it back to you. We can't keep everything that's sent to us, you know. We'd have to move out!" I said, "I understand. That's cool. I'm more than happy to have three copies of my two and a half minutes of fame!"

I dropped off a copy on the way home. They didn't look at it until the next morning, but when they DID, it was all I could have imagined. They called to tell me they truly LOVED the segment. Then Carolyn said, "May I retract my earlier comment that we'd return the tape? We want to keep it!" I said, "You certainly may!" She said, "Kris, you looked so comfortable and natural!" I joked, "I did?! Where's my Emmy, in that case!" At that point, De jumped on with a hearty "Congratulations! That is a magnificent piece." I thanked him and told him I was VERY glad, and very relieved, that they liked it. Carolyn got back on and said, "We'll take it to Long Beach to show our friends – if we ever go there again!"

On March 13th 1995 we moved my belongings to the new condo and began unpacking with our remaining, albeit lagging, energy. I'd just recently had Deaken's necessary permits transferred to the new location, but kept quiet about him to the condo association and to my new neighbors. I'd had enough crises for the time being; I certainly intended to avoid any others that were attributable to sharing my life with a geriatric, three-legged, rapidly-failing "wild animal"!

That afternoon, a lovely plant basket arrived at my doorstep. It contained three plants and three flower blossoms. Atop the arrangement was a vinyl balloon which proclaimed, "Best wishes." The attached note read "Happy new home and happy days ahead. De and Carolyn." I called to thank them during one of the rare breaks Dad allowed us to have. Dad knew if we quit for long, we'd collapse!

Carolyn said she had also procured a complimentary seat for me at the upcoming Arizona convention. I protested, "I can afford this now, Carolyn!" and she said, "I know you can, but we wanted to do it anyway. We got you one for Sacramento, too." I said, "Thank you. You two are just too much!"

Carolyn called on the 21st to ask if it would be all right if she and De drove over for a little while on the 24th to "finally" meet my visiting sister Jackie and her fiancé Dennis, along with Mom and Dad, and see my new condo. I was totally thrilled that they wanted to do that, and told her Mom would make lemon meringue pies for the occasion. Carolyn said, "Oh, we won't stay long – maybe just an hour – but we'll eat pie – or take it home with us!" and laughed. I said, "Mom will make you a pie. You can have a piece of ours and then abscond with your own!" She said, "Your mom makes the best pies. I accused her to De of getting them down at this famous little bakery in our neighborhood." I said, "No way! Your famous little bakery can't even COMPARE with MY mom's pies!" She said, "I think you're right. We're not big pie eaters, but we sure do manage to choke down every last morsel of your mother's pies!" We both laughed.

On March 24th, De and Carolyn visited. They met Jackie and Dennis, then took a short tour of the new condo. (Small condo, short tour!) De confessed, "We're surprised you found a nice place for such a great price! We were a little concerned. I must say, we are VERY impressed. It's small, but it's certainly everything you need and it looks just terrific!"

They gave chin tickles to Deaken, who was luxuriating in my bedroom during the get-together. They studied the Guest/Kelley Room briefly, and then returned to the front room to sit and visit with Mom and Dad, Jackie and Dennis, Poppy Cat and me.

At their departure, Carolyn said, "Your mother sat way off in a corner by herself most of the time. Is she all right?" I said, "She says she feels fine, but she has mentioned a stuffy sinus, and she keeps wiggling the upper part of her nose with her fingers, as though trying to dislodge stuffiness. But she's all right, I'm sure. My Mom's the healthiest soul on the planet. She NEVER gets sick." [Famous last words.] The Kelleys got into their car, waved good-bye, and were gone.

Some days later, Carolyn said she really enjoyed talking with everyone on Sunday and then made the observation, "Your mother is the saint in the family." I confirmed, "You have THAT right! We thank God for our mommy day and night, night and day. Dad can be a real human hemorrhoid sometimes – but we love him, anyway!" She guffawed at that: "Human hemorrhoid! That's very funny, Kris." I joked back, "Not when you're living with one, it isn't!"

MEDICAL MALADIES MULTIPLY

On May 16th, Deaken's 17th birthday, Carolyn called. She sounded tired and very subdued. After a brief few sentences, she said, "I want to tell you something, but I want you to keep it entirely confidential. I don't want you to tell anybody. Can you do that – keep a secret?" I said, "I can." She said, "I'm only telling you, because I'm friendly with you, and because De said I could." I said, "Okay…"

She said, "De's in the hospital." I took a deep breath and said, "Okay…" and waited for more information. She could tell I wasn't entirely surprised, and said, "You knew something was up, didn't you?" I said, "Well, it got awfully quiet over in your neck of the woods recently, so I was concerned that something might be up." She said, "He had surgery a couple of days ago." I waited for more information. She said, "They removed a tumor from his colon." I said, "Oh, God." She said, "It's okay. The doctors say he'll live to be 95, as slowly as these things grow, but they wanted that one out of there." I said, "I imagine that's what's been causing him the tummy problems." She said, "Oh, absolutely. He should have had this done years ago." I said, "As long as he'll be okay…" She said, "Oh, yes! He'll be okay. He said I can tell you and one other person – no one else – and that he DOESN'T want flowers or balloons – and please don't send anything to him at the hospital." I said, "Can I send cards THERE (to the house)?" She said, "Absolutely. I'll take them to him whenever I go."

Then she said, "I'm exhausted. I've been there from eight to eight both days. They have a tube down his throat that's giving him fits – and tonight he just told me to get out of there and to come back later in the morning tomorrow. He worries about me being there all the time." I said, "Well, he's probably just sleeping most of the time right now, anyway." She said, "He is, but every time he wakes up, I want him to see I'm there. But he doesn't think it's good for me, so he sent me home. I'm very tired…" I said, "Well, sweetie, my arms are around you." She started to cry a little bit, but caught herself. She said, "I know you want to do something – help me out in some way – but the little gal across the street is doing everything I need to have done. If I need anything else, I WILL let you know." I said, "Okay." I added, "My thoughts and prayers are with you." She said, "I know they are. I'm going to try and get some sleep now. And remember – this is totally confidential." I said, "Oh, Carolyn, I SWEAR – I won't even tell my Mom!" She said, "Good. That's the way we want it." I said, "Thank you for telling ME." She said, "Well, I knew you had to be wondering what was going on." I said, "Yeah, I was." She said, "Well, now you know, and you can stop worrying. All's well that ends well." I told her I loved her and we hung up.

Carolyn called the next day to thank me for the stuffed bunny I sent her and the stuffed wild kitty and the box of goodies I sent De. She said, "Everything's fine here. De hasn't done anything more than smile at his 'serval' and goodies and then go back to sleep, but he'll look at them more closely later on." I told her, "Squeeze the kitty's toe for De. It will roar if you do that." I told her I had a friend staying with me over the weekend, so I wouldn't be stopping by to drop anything more, so she'd feel comfortable coming and going without risking running into us. She thanked me for my thoughtfulness. Then she said, "We very much appreciate all you've done." I told her, "I love you two, Carolyn!"

On May 21st Carolyn called to report that things were going fine. I asked when De would be home, if he wasn't already, and she said, "Maybe tomorrow." I said, "Cool…"

She said, "I don't want you to worry. All is well." She added, "It upsets me when you're upset." I said, "Don't worry about ME. As long as you two are okay, I'M fine." I asked if I could take any of the workload off her, and she said, "No, I have to take care of it all myself." I said, "Okay, but if you need me, I'm here." She thanked me and we hung up.

A few days later we celebrated. Carolyn reported, "De has NO MORE lower extremity pain at all any more, and he's been eating like a horse and walking around the back patio to satisfy the doctor's orders for exercise. He's asleep right now." I said, "He's probably hungry now that he can eat without it hurting afterwards." She said, "That's it exactly!" She sounded relieved and happy. She said, "You can go ahead and tell your folks now."

Finally when De was up to talking, I asked him, "And how are YOU?" He said, "Well, it's a slow process, but I'm doing FINE. I'm hugging my leopard right now that you gave me and I enjoyed all of your cards." I said, "I thought you should have at least two a day from me." He said, "I certainly did — and I appreciate them. Thank you." I asked, "Did you squeeze your little leopard's toe?" He said, "I squeezed him all over." I asked, "Did he roar for you?" He said, "Roar? No." I said, "Then you haven't squeezed his right toe yet. When you do, he'll roar for you." He said, "I'll have to try that."

I was weathering some news about Mom's health on top of worrying about De. On June 9, De called. When I answered the phone, he said, "Well, hello, Santa Claus!" He was in GREAT spirits and thanked me for the large sack of decadent food I dropped on his doorstep that morning, and then quickly added, "Now, STOP THAT!" I giggled and said, "Yes, sir!" He said he had so much food there, sent from well-wishers, that he was thinking about opening his own grocery store! Carolyn motioned for him to give her the phone, so he did and she said, "Hello. I'm still really busy but I want to tell you I hope all goes well for your dear mother." I said, "I'm sure it will." She said, "I'm sure it will, too." I said, "The doctor will probably just tell my Dad to lay off her and let her retire!" She said, "What does he have her do for him?" I said, "Everything! Tote and fetch and shop and carry and wash and clean and build bunk houses and RV trailers — you name it, she does it." She said, "Heavens! I can understand why she might be having problems!" She then asked, "Did I tell you that De quit smoking?" I said, "No! That's GREAT!" She said, "I'm so proud of him. He hasn't had a ciggy since May 11th." I said, "Oh, that's just terrific! I'm gonna cry!" She said, "Don't cry!" I said, "It'll be a happy cry! Give him a big hug for me and tell him I'm proud of him! That MAKES MY DAY!" I told her he would probably automatically gain some weight as a result of having stopped — everyone does — and she said, "Oh, really?" I said, "Yes. Eight to twelve pounds, on average, from what I've read." She said, "That would be wonderful." I said, "It'll happen. Just hang in there." I asked her to be sure and hug De for me for quitting smoking — she said she would — then told her "I love you" and we hung up.

Carolyn called first thing in the morning after reading an updating letter about Mom. "We read your letter and we're so sorry that your dear mother has to have surgery." I started sniffling right away, but managed to keep talking, giving further details and answering whatever questions she asked. She asked how Dad was doing over this thing. I said, "Oh, he's hanging in there. He almost lost it once on the phone, but got it back. I'm sure he's a basket case inside."

She said, "I wish we could wave a magic wand and make your mother's problem just go away!" I said, "I know that, and I can hear you waving one wildly, and that means the world to us. Thank you." She said, "It's awful to want to DO something to help, and to know there isn't a darn thing we can do about it." Then she said, "You take good care of YOURSELF. Try not to worry too much." I said, "Don't worry about ME. I'll handle it." She said, "I know you will. We just wish you didn't have to." I said, "Oh, well. I guess it's my turn."

I told her, "I HOPE it's a sinus infection, because tumors in the head tend to come back often, the doctor said," and she said, "Oh, don't even THINK about that. It may NEVER happen again. Everyone is so different." I said, "Okay. I just DO NOT want my mom in the surgery room every three months. She'd HATE that." Carolyn said, "Just think positive." I said, "I am. I'm just real scared once in a while!" I sniffled when I said that, upset again. She said, "I know. We'll be thinking of you up there constantly, sending all of our good thoughts your way." I sniffled again and said, "Thank you." She said, "You take care. Give your family our best."

On June 19th, 1996 I called the Kelleys from a hospital waiting room in Seattle at about 10 a.m. to give them the bad news about Mom's prognosis. I told them I didn't want to lay the bad news on them right at bedtime the night before, so I had waited. I told them, "The doctor thinks it's a grade 3 or 4 cancerous tumor, and if it is, it will be back in 2-4 months without radiation and chemotherapy, and within a year WITH radiation and chemotherapy." I became upset talking about it again, but managed to control my emotions enough to answer their questions. They gave me their love and good wishes and Carolyn ended by saying, "Take good care of yourself."

In that blur of days the Kelleys made known their loyalty and their love. I told them their flowers gave Mom a big boost and that she went from "probably not leaving the hospital this weekend" to "out of there the next afternoon" following Phil's delivery of them to her. She said, "Oh, it would be nice to think they made that big a difference." I said, "She was VERY happy to get them and you can call it a coincidence if you want, but I think they had a very positive effect on her."

A couple days later, I let the Kelleys know that Mom's liver tests came back normal, so the decision to go ahead with radiation and chemotherapy had been made. "Had that liver test come back showing liver cancer, that would've been all she wrote. The doctors wouldn't have suggested chemo and radiation. Once cancer gets into the liver, I guess that's it – no time left to try anything else. So Mom and Dad are dancing on the table tonight – on the ceiling, too, if they can get to it!" She said, "That's wonderful. Give our love to your mother and father when you see them over the 4th, won't you?" I said, "I sure will."

When I got back from the 4th of July visit, Carolyn wanted to know how it had gone. I told her Mom was doing just great and her spirits were terrific. "She's a case study in centered living. Nothing seems to rattle her. She just keeps on smiling and joking and LIVING!" Carolyn offered, "She's a very special lady." Then she said, "I'm still so proud of De. I was on him for years to quit smoking – and he finally did it!" I asked if he had gained any weight as a result, and she exclaimed, "Oh, yes! He's up to 128! I'd like to see him put on another twenty, but I'll be happy with ten."

DEAKEN'S FINAL DAYS – THE KELLEYS' HELPING WAYS

Soon thereafter, in the middle of the night, Deaken suffered either a stroke or a spinal injury and became unable to right himself or to stand. His obvious distress roused me from sleep. I called his veterinarian, Dr. Chris Cauble, right away. He asked me about his vital signs; I reported them. I told him Deaken was very unhappy and upset by his inability to function and I thought it was coming close to the time when he should be put down. The vet agreed, and said he'd come out the next morning to evaluate the situation and see if euthanasia was the only proper solution.

I dropped off a note letting the Kelleys know what was happening. They called right away after reading it to console me. Carolyn started off with, "We're so sorry to hear about dear Deaken," and De pretty much took over from there, because Carolyn and I both began sniffling and wiping our noses. De told me what a happy, wonderful, long life Deaken had with me. "I understand how difficult it is to make a decision like this one – we had to do it with Fancy – but don't feel guilty about it." I sniffled, "I don't feel guilty. It's for HIM. I want him with me forever – but he will be, whether he's here physically or not. I just don't want him to suffer or to be unhappy."

De asked me, "Are you planning to cremate him?" I said, "Probably. I think so. Yes." De said, "That's best." Carolyn said, "Our thoughts are with you and our hearts go out to you. Give dear Deaken a chin-tickle for us, will you?" I said, "I sure will. You bet. I love you. Thanks."

After the veterinarian evaluated Deaken's condition and recommended a waiting period to see if he would recover without risky medical intervention, I called Mom and Dad to let them know what was happening. I told them my next trip up to see them – scheduled for the middle of the month — would be delayed by a week or two while I awaited the outcome of Deaken's current struggle. Mom reassured me, "That's all right. I'll still be here!" I told her, "I'm beginning to think I inherited your curse, Mom." She asked, "What curse is that?" I said, "Every time a loved one of yours fell ill, TWO or more loved ones fell ill – so you've always been torn as to who to go to!" She said, "It isn't a curse. It's the old adage; "It never rains but it pours!" I said, "Oh, is THAT what it is?" She said, "You're not cursed. You're blessed. And so is Deaken and so am I, to have such a good Mom-cat and daughter in our lives." She said, "You just take good care of my grandson and yourself. Come up and visit when you can. I feel fine and there's absolutely NOTHING to worry about up here right now."

The next few weeks were a roller coaster of emotions – elated at each minuscule (or imagined) improvement that Deaken showed, dejection and fear with each set-back. I tried to keep my reports positive, but not wildly hopeful – and I tried to keep them humorous, as well, difficult as that was. I regaled the Kelleys with reports of midnight butt-dips and bedding changes. At one point, when I could see Deaken wasn't making the comeback we had hoped for, I told Carolyn that I almost wished Deaken was a little more miserable than he was, "because it's going to be hard to put him down when he doesn't seem to be suffering. But of course, he's not suffering ONLY because he's on pain killers." She agreed. "It's a tough call, but it's the right one, Kris. He doesn't have the quality of life now that thrills him, OR one that makes your life easy or happy, being constantly concerned about his comfort and cleanliness. It's time. He has had a wonderful life up until very recently. A wonderful life. You don't want it to end in frustration for him." I sighed and agreed. "No, I don't."

The next day, I called Dr. Cauble and made arrangements to have Deaken euthanized on Cauble's next available date, September 11th. I wrote it on my calendar and then went into the bedroom to snuggle and caress the love of my life, knowing I'd just sentenced him to death. He kissed my wet face and purred.

Carolyn called shortly thereafter, while I was still sniffling. She asked, "De wants to know if you want him to put out some more newspapers for Deaken or do you have enough?" I said sadly, "No… I won't be needing any more, thanks. I've made arrangements to have him put to sleep on the 11th. He's not happy in his present situation and it doesn't look as though he's going to walk again." Carolyn said, "Oh, I'm so sorry, Kris. You're a loving mom-cat to do that for him. I know it's tough, but it's absolutely the right decision." I sniffled, "I know, or I wouldn't be doing it, believe me! It's really a terrible decision to have to make."

On September 8th, De was in Huntsville, Alabama at the 30th Anniversary STAR TREK Weekend. Carolyn stayed home, and of course I was spending my last weekend with Deaken. She called in the afternoon to see how I was doing. When she heard my subdued voice, she asked, "Are you crying?" I said, "Oh – off and on!" Carolyn asked, "Is Deaken having a bad day?" I said, "No, he's having a WONDERFUL day. We've had a lot of fun today – he's been purring and kissing me and hugging me with his front paws. It's just that whenever someone calls to see how I am, or to tell me to hug him for them on Wednesday – as Dad did just a few minutes ago — I tend to fall apart." I laughed through the tears and Carolyn said, "Oh, my!" feeling my angst. Then she said, "De thought of something. We discussed it before he left and again this morning on the phone. We'd like to pay for Deaken's vet bill and his cremation services." I said, "Oh, Carolyn, that's not necessary, but thank you anyway." She said, "I know it isn't, but we'd like to do something, and this is what we've decided to do." I protested, "You've already done so much for me." She said, "You don't have to worry about paying this back. This is our contribution to your commitment to Deaken. We want to do it, and I want you to send me the bills as soon as it's all over and we'll send you a check for the amount." I was sniffling again and said, "All right. Thank you."

Dr. Cauble gave Deaken a sedative to relax him completely prior to the lethal injection. His assistant, Gigi Grossman, and I were at Deaken's side. Deaken was propped mostly in my arms. I rubbed his belly with great aplomb and tickled him the way he loved. He reached over and gave me a little purr and a kiss. Tears were leaking out of my eyes, but I was handling my emotions very well, in a sort of transcendent manner, to keep from transferring my internal anguish to Deaken. Dr. Cauble said, "Well, if this is any consolation to you, I heard from a spiritual friend that the ease with which we leave this life is the ease with which we enter the next phase of our existence in the afterlife. If that's true, you are giving Deaken the best send-off I have ever witnessed. He's going to be very happy very soon." I said, "I hope so. He deserves it – don't you, baby boy? He's the best." Then he said, "Okay, let's do it." He took Deaken's back leg and injected the solution. Within seconds, Deaken relaxed completely, sighed, and passed over to wherever perfect souls go.

For some strange reason, I felt elated. I had managed to handle my emotions in such a way in Deaken's last moments of life that I was certain he had felt only my love and joy regarding the life we'd shared together. I knew he had felt no anxiety or fear or concern at all. I almost couldn't wait for the veterinarian to leave so I could call the Kelleys and report the good news.

Carolyn answered the phone. When she found out it was me and noticed how up and good I sounded, she called De to the other extension so he could hear the full report, too. I told them how it went, and they were thrilled. I told them, 'Now I can say I did absolutely EVERYTHING right for that cat!" De said, "You sure can." I told them about Deaken relaxing and sighing and slipping away right in my arms, and De said, "Fancy went peacefully like that, too – just relaxed and that was it." He started to say something more about what a wonderful life I gave Deaken, but he choked up on it and couldn't continue. Trying to cover for his upset feelings, I assured him, "It was wonderful. This couldn't have gone better. I'm okay, and I want you two to be okay now too." De added, "You'll still have your moments, though. You're probably exhausted right now." I said, "That, I am. Guaranteed." He said, "But you did the right thing for Deke, and he loves you for it." Carolyn said, "He's all better now and in a better place." I said, "I know." Carolyn said, "I wish we could be there for you during the cremation tomorrow, but we can't." She added, "We'll be with you in spirit, just as we were all day today, though." I said, "Oh, I know. I can feel it." She said with great intensity, "We've been thinking about you all day long." I said, "Well, be happy now and don't give me another thought. Relax and have a good night now." I sighed deeply and told them proudly, "I love you!" They both responded, "I love you, Kris."

Within a week, I was able to report that I was having almost nightly dreams about Deaken, and that he was happy and healthy and had four legs again! Carolyn said, "I'll bet he's having sweet dreams about YOU, too!" I said, "I think he, or God, is sending me these dreams, so I know he's all right."

Most of Mom's formerly beautiful, silver mane had fallen out as a result of radiation and chemotherapy treatments she received in an effort to resist the return of the malignant brain tumor. That seemed to be her main regret. Otherwise, she remained vibrant, funny, and emotionally radiant. I flew to Washington for a week not long after Deaken died, then returned to work. One day on the phone I told Carolyn about Poppy, "TWICE now recently, when she was in the throes of wailing at the top of her lungs, I asked her, 'Poppy, what do you want?' and both times she jumped onto a dresser or a night stand and reached up and patted a different photo of DEAKEN." Carolyn said, "Oh, my! Did she really?!" I said, "Yes, and then she jumped down and went over to one of his favorite places on the rug and laid down near it, the way she would when they slept together. It half-killed me." She said, "Oh, that would! It would kill ME!" I said, "So, I have to go out and find her another kitten real fast. I'll go nuts if she keeps this up. She's just inconsolable over the loss of her papa kitty." Carolyn said, "I'll mail you the classified sections for pets from the LA Times and Daily News this afternoon. You should have them tomorrow."

Within two days, I had two little brothers for Poppy. I called right away to describe the new brood to Carolyn.

On my next visit to the Kelleys we talked about Mom and we talked about dear Deaken (what a wonderful life he had). As De was bringing the cola in, I noticed that my shoes still had mud on them from a trip to their garden and told them I ought to go out and get rid of it. Carolyn said, "Oh, no, don't do that. Don't bother. If it hasn't fallen off by now, it won't." I said, "Okay…" A few seconds later a huge clump fell off, then another! I said, "Oh, great," and took my shoes off and started to pick the mud clumps up and put them into my shoe, and Carolyn said, "Oh, don't do that! Don't worry about it. Really! I have a little man who cleans up all those things for me whenever they happen." I glanced over at De. He raised his hand and waved it, indicating that HE was her "little man". I said, "Some little man!" We all laughed. I got up and took the shoes outside, along with the detritus from them that I could pick up by hand, then came back in.

I was gulping cola like mad and De said, "If you keep gulping soda like that, you're gonna belch." I said, "I drink EVERYTHING like this!" He said, "That's what John Carradine used to do in order to let out a big belch when we were doing TOBACCO ROAD on the east coast. Just before the second act, he'd drink an entire cola down, so he could come on and do his line, which included this tremendous belch and the words, 'Damn' turnips!' Carolyn played the impoverished old lady who was always beggin' John for a turnip for her aching tummy. John did that play later with a REAL elderly woman playing the part of the old lady, and he told HER "I had a twenty year old who made a better old lady that YOU do!" Carolyn grinned at that. De said, "The night that play closed, we were playing to a house with about 35 people in it – I'll never forget it – and John came out onto the stage for the curtain call and announced, "You'll be happy to know I'll be back next season in KING RICHARD III!" He guffawed at that, remembering. "Last time I saw John was at Universal a few years ago. He was crippled with arthritis. It was very sad."

We talked about Mom's case and about Dad's problems and anguish. Then De spotted Myrtle out and about. De said, "She was just over getting a blessing from St. Francis, and now she's headed west along the back fence." I spotted her and said, "There she is! I see her now." De said, "Did I tell you how we got that St. Francis statue?" I said, "No." He said, "Bill Shatner bought a new house – the one just before this one he has now. His realtor was a friend of ours, and she invited us to take a look at it after Bill bought it. We spotted the St. Francis statue in the yard—" Carolyn added, "Bill's Jewish, you know." De continued: "…so I went to Bill and said, 'You don't want that St. Francis statue in your back yard, do you?' and he said 'No,' so I told him, "We'd like to have it, if you'll let us," and he gave it to us. I went into the back yard and lifted that heavy piece of concrete all across the yard and into a car and into the back yard. I look at it now and don't know how I did it."

He then told about lifting a massive piece of marble from another back yard, up steps, and showed me the piece. Carolyn told me to go over and try to tip it, let alone lift it! I went over and tried, and about croaked. I was amazed. I said, "It's amazing what you can do when you want something badly enough. 'Forget the crane – I can handle it!'" We all laughed.

Carolyn and I sat down again and I asked how they were doing. They said they were doing fine but that Carolyn would have to have hip surgery eventually – probably sooner than later. I commiserated with her over that. She asked me NOT to spread it around, as she didn't want to be inundated with cards and gifts and flowers from well-wishers, as it would make more work for her (she felt she would have to answer them all). I said, "I won't tell anyone. You just lie in the hospital and be unheralded; no one will be thinking of you at all!" She giggled and I said, "I really won't tell." She said, "No flowers, either. There are always too many flowers to bring home. It's just a waste." I said, "Cards are okay – as long as I don't send seven a day, right?' She smiled and said, "Yes." I said, "Oh, good."

De said, "This has been a bad month for people's cats, hasn't it?" Carolyn said two other friends of theirs lost cats at around the same time I lost Deaken. She took me into their bedroom to show me photos of her/their pets throughout the years: Flossy (her first cat) in her arms when she was about four; Stardust (her dog); and of course Fancy, Cheers and Myrtle. She showed me the first gift I ever sent her (a little dog and cat statue), and said that she just LOVED the plaque I sent them a few years ago. It read, "It doesn't matter where you live, what you do, or how much you have. It's who you have beside you." She showed me a few of De's achievement plaques in the office/study and we gazed at Deaken's photo in there. Carolyn said, "It's my favorite" and I agreed, "It's one of mine, too." She got tears in her eyes.

On October 9th Carolyn called me at work. We talked about the impending surgery for her hip. She asked me, "Did you see the 30th anniversary show Sunday night?" I said, "I sure did." She said, "De got a lot of coverage, didn't he?" I said, "Yes, he did – and you ought to see the stuff on the Internet: 'DeForest Kelley just gets better looking all the time!' The girls are all gasping. Your guy is still DE BEST!" She said, "He is a pretty boy, isn't he?" I said, "Woof woof." She said, "I took a picture of him in his tuxedo." I stupidly asked, "Off the TV?" She was sweet enough NOT to laugh and said, "No… I took it here at home!" I said, "Oh, yeah… YOU can do that, can't you?" and she laughed. She said, "I've never seen him in a tuxedo before." I said, "He sure is handsome – in or out of a tuxedo!" She said, "Well, I took a picture because I don't expect I'll ever catch him in one again!" We both laughed. She was in good spirits. I again wished her the best for tomorrow's surgery, told her I loved her, and we hung up.

The next day De called. "Carolyn is doing well. She got out of surgery at about ten this morning and is doing fine. She told me to call you and let you know so you can relax." I said, "I'm glad. Thanks." He said, "She's a little dingy right now."

A few days later we connected again, and De asked, "Do you have a moment to talk?" I said, "I sure do… How's Carolyn?" He hesitated for an instant – scaring the hell out of me – and said, "Oh, she's doing all right, but this morning when she walked for the first time, she passed out." I said, "Oh, no." He said, "The doctor doesn't consider it anything to worry about… with the fact of how sedentary she normally is, and the fact of her age and what she has just been through. She did this after her back surgery, too." I said, "I remember she did it with her other hip surgery." He said, "Yes… she's pretty susceptible to this sort of thing. To be honest with you, she has passed out a time or two at home with me here. So it's nothing that we need to be overly concerned about." I said, "Oh. Okay. But I know it has to be frustrating for her – and even scary."

He asked how I was doing and especially asked how Mom was doing and what I heard from up there. I told him about the new treatment for her type of cancer and that "the longer she hangs in, in as good shape as she is—" He completed the thought, "—she will likely outlast the cancer, as a treatment or cure will be found." I said, "Exactly!" He said, "Well, we're certainly wishing her all the best here. You be sure and let her know." I said, "I will. Thanks!" I added, "Give Carolyn a hug for me when you see her next, will you?" He said, "I sure will." I said, "Thanks for calling, and take it easy, De." He paused briefly at that and said, "I'm trying!"

The early weeks following Carolyn's surgery were trying for everyone. We all felt relieved as she began to recover her sense of humor and joie de vivre. By the end of November that year, her spirits were again robust and the frequent calls resumed.

On November 23, 1996 Carolyn called. The first thing out of her mouth was a cheery joke: "Are you packed yet?" I said, "No…" She said, feigning incredulity, "You AREN'T?!" I said, "No. If I pack now, the stuff'll get wrinkled! I don't leave for four days!" I was going to be heading north for the Thanksgiving holiday to spend time with my family— especially Mom.

She said, "De got up yesterday morning to find a swimming pool in our kitchen. One of our pipes broke." I said, "Oh, no!" She said, "It was our own fault. Our plumber told us two years ago we should replace that pipe. It was copper on iron, and it should have been copper on copper, but we let it go. He came here yesterday and fixed everything." She said, "This is the first day since I got out of the hospital that we've been by ourselves, and it's just wonderful. We prefer being alone, you know." I told her, "So do I." I asked her if De watched the football game that day, and she said he hadn't: "He was doing odds and ends around here, catching up."

She mentioned the inclement weather in Washington and said that De heard there was snow in Spokane. I said, "That's clear across the state from where I'll be." She said, "I know." I said, "Mom said there were six inches of snow in Tacoma this week sometime, but it's gone now." Carolyn said, "I remember living in Seattle and sledding down Capitol Hill – up by Volunteer Park – when I was a little girl…Well, have a happy trip up and tell your family hello for us. We'll be thinking of y'all on Thanksgiving Day." I said, "We'll be thinking of you, too, you may be sure! … Mom's 75th birthday is tomorrow, but we're saving it until the 30th, because we're going to have a big celebration that day with the family and with friends of hers." She said, "Oh, that sounds terrific." I said, "I'm calling this Mardi Ma week!"

Thanksgiving over and Christmas fast approaching, I arranged to return to Washington once more. On December 15th Carolyn called to tell me she was planning to have De put some camellia blossoms in a plastic bag for me before noon on the day I was flying back to Washington, "the same way I did for you this morning out in the mailbox. Your family can use them as a centerpiece for the holiday dinner. De will also put out some lemons to take to Washington for Jackie and Dennis." I thanked her, and told her I'd get them just after leaving work, before catching a cab to the airport. At one point, she told me, "I gathered those blossoms you got today and washed them off and put them into the bag." I was surprised by that and said, "You did? Can you get around that well already?" She said, "Well, no. I got the Ziploc bag out and handed De the scissors and said, 'Go get some camellia blossoms for Kris.' And HE did THAT part." I said, "That's kinda what I figured. But I will say one thing, Carolyn: YOU'RE A WONDERFUL DIRECTOR!" She laughed and shared that with De: "She says I'm a wonderful director!" He must have nodded, because she told me, "He agrees!" and laughed.

On December 18, 1996 I called the Kelleys to wish De a Happy Anniversary on the 5th anniversary of his star ceremony. Carolyn answered the phone, and I started with, "Now you KNOW I only call for VERY special occasions!" and she said, "Yes, I know you do. What have you done now?" I said, "Nothing!" and she laughed. I said, "I called to say Happy Anniversary." She said, "Anniversary?" I said, "Yes! This is the 5th anniversary of De's star on the Walk of Fame!" She reflected, "Oh… is this December 18th?" I said, "Yes, it is." She said, "I don't even know what day it is anymore." I told her, "I buffed his star again this morning," and she said, "AGAIN?! I didn't think you were THAT crazy, Kris!" She called out, "De… get on the phone. Someone wants to say hello." De got on the other extension and said, "Hello?" I said, "Happy Anniversary!" He queried, "Anniversary?" I said, "Yes! It's the fifth anniversary of your star ceremony!" He said, "It is? Has it been five years already?" I said, "It has. Doesn't seem like it, does it?" He said, "No. It seems about 2 ½ weeks!" I said, "I feel that way too! Pretty scary, isn't it?" He said, "I should be congratulating YOU on the 5th anniversary of that star. You've been doing that job for five years." I said, "It just doesn't seem possible, but the calendar doesn't lie!" I added, "I did it again this morning just before work." He said, "You did?!" I said, "Sure did." He said, "Well, thank you." I said, "I hadda be sure it looked PERFECT on its 5th birthday… and it did, and now it looks even BETTER!" He said, "I have no doubt!"

On December 23rd Carolyn called me at work to thank me for the goodies I sent. I made the mistake of letting her know how swamped I was at work when she asked, tying up loose ends around there before flying away to Washington for the holiday. She said, "I won't keep you on here long. I just — I have a man here pawing at me – pawing at me to give him the phone!" I joked, "Carolyn, when a man paws at you, you're supposed to HANG UP the phone!" She laughed and handed the phone to De. He thanked me for the 5th anniversary letter booklet I created for the occasion with the cooperation of friends and fans at Warner Bros. He sounded filled with emotion – almost overcome – as he described how touched he was by it. A few of the words caught in his throat, so I covered for him by saying, "I'm very glad you enjoyed it." I added: "As soon as I started the ball rolling on the idea, I got a little panicked, 'cause the thought struck me; 'Just what De NEEDS is a bunch more fan letters' – but you don't have to respond to THESE ones!" He very sincerely told me, "Oh, no; this is nothing like that. This is very different. I just loved it. Thank you very much for going to the trouble." Then he joked, "It's so nice to see that HALF of the people at Warner Bros. are fans of mine!"

Just before my departure for Washington I stopped by the Kelleys. Carolyn came out then and I hugged her. She gave me posies and the photos to take home. When I got to my condo, I found a popcorn tin from them, sent from Harry and David's in Oregon, so I called them briefly and thanked them.

On Christmas Day I called the Kelleys from Washington. When Carolyn answered the phone with a "Merry Christmas!", Mom, Jackie, Phil and I sang, "We Wish You A Merry Christmas." Finally Dad got on and asked, "Is this the Rowdy Cowboy?" and De said, "Yes, it is."

Our holidays were brightened by our Kelley connection. I finally had some good news for my California Mom and Pop: "If Mom's MRI comes up clear on Wednesday, she and Dad may fly down for a week to three weeks – depending on how long the doctors will let her out of their care."

The day before De's 76th birthday he called at noon to thank me for the cards – and especially for the Trader Joe's bittersweet candy bars. He said, "I was delighted to receive those candy bars. You couldn't have given me anything better." I protested, "You mean, you OPENED your birthday stuff already?!" He joked back, "Yes, of course I did! I may not BE here tomorrow!" I told him adamantly, "You'll be here!" He asserted, "I certainly INTEND to be!" and chuckled again. He sounded very hoarse. I attributed it to the killer colds that were rampant that winter. But in the ensuing months, calls from them became less frequent and more mechanical in nature. Still, I didn't read anything into the subtle change in their behavior. It was still friendly, just no longer overly forthcoming or candid. But I reassured myself with the fact that we didn't have a lot of wildly positive information to exchange anymore. Mom was dying; Deaken was gone; I was working hard at a "nothing new" kind of job; the ha-ha's had more or less vanished, and there wasn't all that much to share…

But there would be again. My positive spirit insisted on that thought…

VALENTINE'S DAY 1997

I became the happy recipient of a Valentine's Day card from Mom and Dad a few days before Valentine's Day. Mom didn't write often but when she did, it was always a treat.

> Dear Krissy Ree,
>
> I s'pose this will get there a little early – but don't trust the mail to get there on time.
>
> Hope you have a good Valentine's Day – but don't forget – you are *OUR* VALENTINE!
>
> I hope you know how much we appreciate your many letters, even tho' I am lousy at replying!
>
> Vernie sent over a thousand test strips for Pa. SHOULD LAST A WHILE!
>
> So glad you are so happy with your condo. Makes us feel good to think of you in nice surroundings and as safe as can be.
>
> Love you without limit.
> XXXOOO Mom

The birthday card half a month later was sum'pin' special, too, since it was chosen by a mom who didn't know how many more birthdays she would be sending cards. A "credit card" was attached. It looked just like a genuine, plastic credit card except that it had two large hearts on it. Super-imposed over the top of the hearts were the words, "Daughter's Credit Card. This Card is not for material things but is to give you credit for being the greatest in the world and for that you deserve credit." On the back were the words "Authorized By One Who Knows." Mom's name was written there. My two sisters, Jackie and Laurel received them, too, on their special days.

"A COMMMUNION OF SORTS"

On March 27, 1997 Carolyn called to let us know that she and De would like to drive over to my place the following Saturday and visit with my folks and me. "If that's all right." I said, "It certainly is!" and she giggled. I gave her careful directions, as they had only been to my condo once before. Then she said, "Be sure your new kittens are on their best behavior and that they're looking good!" I said, "I can guarantee they'll look good – they always do – but, BEST BEHAVIOR? They're eight months old, Carolyn! They don't HAVE a best behavior unless they're ASLEEP!" She laughed and said, "They'll be fine!"

The Kelleys visited with us for an hour and a half. Mom was wearing a turban on her head to hide the fact that her hair had grown back in mis-matched colors and textures. The hair was still patchy in spots. Instead of the silvery mane she had once enjoyed and been complimented on endless times, she felt she looked "like someone who would make babies cry in the supermarket!" Despite the fact that the turban was warm and itchy, she insisted on wearing it when company was around or when she went out in public. The wig she had bought had long since been cast aside as too hot, too scratchy and too artificial-looking.

I was happy to see how good both De and Carolyn looked. The regimen of walking six blocks daily had given them a look of such robust health that they both appeared radiant. De had gained weight, too.

The Kelleys and Mom and Dad discussed their various health challenges. Carolyn bragged on De for having quit smoking. She said, "We're both real Puritans now." Mom mentioned having developed a sweet tooth following chemotherapy. "I never had it before." Carolyn said, "I've developed a sweet tooth for that bittersweet chocolate De always gets." De leaned over to me and chuckled, "Now you know where it goes!"

De told Dad that he was finished with acting. Dad told De, "You're a helluvan actor. I never knew HOW good until I met you. I thought you'd be a real son of a bitch after seeing those Westerns you did!" Then he added, "Nothing against STAR TREK, but you could hardly get a word in, with SHATNER hogging all the time!" De threw his head back and laughed at that, then clarified for Dad, "In the fourth and fifth years, we were supposed to get our due. Each of our characters was supposed to have episodes spotlighting them – but the fourth and fifth years never came to pass."

They met the kitties. As luck would have it, both of the little rascals had worn themselves out prior to the Kelleys arrival, so Ashley (the shy one!) actually slept on Carolyn's lap while she stroked his long, silky fur and cooed to him. "He's the loveliest cat I have ever seen!" she exclaimed. "His photos are beautiful, but they don't do him justice!"

De and Carolyn mentioned how wonderful Mom looked. She said, "Well, thank you." Then she said, "I miss my hair!" Carolyn said, "Don't worry! It'll be back – better than ever! Maybe even curly!" That's when Mom began her personal contribution to the visit. "I don't normally do this, except around family. It's pretty frightening to the uninitiated. But I feel comfortable with you. Let me SHOW you how my hair is coming in – then you'll KNOW why I wear this turban!"

Slowly – painfully slowly, I thought – she pulled the turban from the top of her head, revealing the multiple colors of her hair and the remaining bare patches. I knew how much courage that took. I held my breath, knowing it might be a difficult moment for the Kelleys, as sensitive as they were.

De stood up at that moment and adopted a McCoy-like stance and authority – but he was still genuinely and authentically De. It wasn't false at all. Then he walked over to where she was sitting and said, "Yes, let's get a good look at you. It's time for your physical!"

Mom stood up. He embraced her and held her for a long moment. Then he gently pushed her out to arm's length, gave her the once-over, head to toe, and proclaimed, "You are a beautiful woman, Dorothea, and you're going to be just fine!"

I never loved DeForest Kelley more than I did at that moment.

Mom melted, hugged him again, and responded gratefully, "I know I'm going to be fine. I wish all you people would stop worrying about me." Then she joked, "I'm going to out-live ALL of you!"

Mom left the turban off a lot more often after that visit. DeForest Kelley had told her she was beautiful and that she was going to be fine, and that was the only prognosis she was prepared to believe. She and Dad drove home to Washington with happier hearts.

By May 6th, the horizon for Mom was becoming ominously dark and cloudy. Carolyn called to say, "De and I were very sorry to hear about your mom." The MRI specialists had noticed "something more" going on in Mom's brain. It was too small to be seen as a recurrence of the deadly tumor, but something was going on at that location. I let them know that Mom was handling the new information just great. "She doesn't seem to be at all afraid and is directing her medical team to wait until they know something more definite. If they wait a month and find out it's coming back, they can go in and take it out and do whatever else needs doing, all in one procedure, instead of opening her head up twice." Carolyn said, "She seems to be the kind of person who has her head on straight about things." I assured her, "She's AMAZING in that way. I asked her if she was scared, and she said she doesn't feel any differently about dying now than she did before this whole thing started. 'It's going to happen someday. I'll live until I die' — very straightforward and with full acceptance. She told me the drugs to keep her comfortable are great and that she didn't suffer a bit with the tumor taking up so much of her forehead or after the surgery, so she really isn't all that concerned about what might happen next. She says she's lucky she has what she has, and not a more painful type. She feels sorry for the little kids who have cancer and the young newlyweds and the young parents with kids who have it. She's just — remarkable, all the way around!" Carolyn listened to this soliloquy and agreed, "Yes, she is." Then she asked me, "How's your dad handling it?" I said, "Okay, for the time being — as well as can be expected for a control freak." She chuckled at that. We discussed how I was emotionally torn between staying in Southern California to live and work and my duty to my mother in Washington State. After a lot of soul-searching, I decided to stay in Los Angeles and fly home whenever possible. Carolyn said, "I'm glad you decided to stay. I think it's smart, but I know it's hard to be so far away from them at a time like this." I said, "Yeah, it is. The rest of the family gets Mom for hopefully another two years. I get her for thirty days, if I'm lucky. That's a TERRIBLE feeling!" She said, "I'll bet it is."

In June, Carolyn called again, in response to a letter I had written them, saying she was sad to hear Mom talking about her own cremation already. I said, "Well, it was a funny conversation, so it was okay. They are going to implant radioactive electrodes in her brain next week sometime – I told you that in the letter — and they said if she dies before a year is up, she can't be cremated, because the process would release radioactive particles into the air. So I told her, 'Oh, good! That means you *can't possibly* die for at least a year, 'cause you said you want to be cremated!' and she thought about that and then said, 'That's right! I'm safe for a whole year!' That's when she told me, 'If there's such a thing as reincarnation, I want to come back as one of YOUR pets!'" Carolyn laughed at that and said, "I know why! I'd like that, too!" I continued, "THAT'S when she got a little serious and said she doesn't care what anyone does with her ashes – but she wants at least PART of them in my bedroom near Deaken's ashes, so she can keep an eye on me and be my guardian angel." Carolyn said, "Could you do that?" I said, "To tell you the truth, at first the idea kind of gave me pause! But now I think, by golly, if that's what she WANTS, she GETS it. And now I even LOVE the idea!" She said, "Well, I hope all this talk of cremation is premature. I think she's going to beat her cancer." I cautioned her, "It's a long shot. It's the longest shot in the field of cancer, I think. But of course we're hopeful, too."

A few days later I had to call the Kelleys and thank them for a signed photo De had sent to Mom prior to her entry into the hospital for the clinical trials procedure. Carolyn answered the phone, so I started to thank her, but she stopped me and said, "Just a minute. Let me get De! DE! It's Kris! She has news about her mother!"

"Dear Dorothea, if they give you any trouble, you know who to call! DeForest"

De got on and I continued, "I wish you could have heard Mom's voice. She was SOOO tickled. Thank you, De. You made her day, and her tomorrow and her weekend, by the sound of her voice! She's taking it to the hospital with her, so she gets the royal treatment!" He chuckled and said, "It works that way sometimes." I said, "I know it does. It did with Dad!" He said, "Well, I'm glad she enjoyed it. Just a minute. Carolyn wants you again."

I told Carolyn Mom's surgery was scheduled for the next day, and she said, "We're holding all good thoughts here for her." I said, "I'm sure it will be fine. She's so positive and gung ho." She said, "She's a great lady." I said, "Yes, she is – and a very HAPPY lady, too, with that photo in her mitt!" She said, "It's nice to know that something that little can make such a big difference." I said, "It does. It's a type of magic, pure and simple!"

Carolyn called the next day to see how the surgery went. I told her it went well and gave her the good news that the surgery could offer her a year or more of the good, status quo quality of life, with other protocols that might also extend her life after the radioactive protocol wore out. She was thrilled to hear about that. Then I told her, "De's photo made such a hit at the hospital and Mom is getting such good treatment as a result that she says she's thinking of becoming a hypochondriac!" Carolyn howled at that!

When De called to thank me for his Father's Day gift on June 15th, his throat was coated WITH the gift – Trader Joe's bittersweet chocolate. I didn't recognize who was calling, as a result, but it was certainly a HAPPY voice. I could tell THAT much!

"Hello," he began.

"Hi." I sounded more noncommittal than I customarily was with him, so he figured out the problem and identified himself. "It's DeForest ... I'm eating your birthday chocolate! Thank you! And – hey! That's wonderful news about your mother! I said, "Yes! Isn't that fantastic? She's 'stuck' with us for at least another year!" De said, "Just terrific. Oh! And congratulations on your upcoming debut on E. [They wanted to interview De's star polisher.] You can do your stand-up routines and become a star!" I laughed and said, "Oh, right! THAT'S what they're after me for – NOT your star!" Then De said, "But my main purpose in calling you today is to thank you for the candy bars – and to ask you to give our love to your mother." I said, "I will! Thanks! And thank you for calling!"

The E! interview was canceled "for at least a month" just a day before I was scheduled to do it. I was glad, because I had fallen ill with a bad cold that suddenly and unexpectedly turned into bronchitis. So, on the morning I had originally agreed to do the interview, I was instead in an emergency room in Burbank at Saint Joseph's Hospital being rehabilitated and sent home with a prescription and doctor's orders for lots of rest and NO activity for several days.

When the E! reporter called to cancel the interview, she let slip some information she shouldn't have. She said the cancellation was due to the fact that "DeForest was planning to come down to the star and surprise you while you were being interviewed by us, but he isn't feeling well just now and we want to wait for his availability."

I hadn't known De was feeling ill again – neither De nor Carolyn had alluded to it in months — so the news startled me in two ways. I was tickled pink that he wanted to surprise me, but I wondered how ill he was feeling and whether or not I should let the Kelleys know that I knew about the upcoming "surprise." I decided to "play dumb," deciding that De or Carolyn would tell me whatever they wanted me to know WHEN they wanted me to know it. After all, the interview was still on; it would just be delayed a month or so. That didn't sound terribly ominous. And I remained giddy because De thought enough of me to want to surprise me in such a public way — on television, in front of millions of viewers! YIKES and eegads!

In a phone call with Carolyn I said, "It's lucky the E! interview was cancelled for a month, because no way would I have been able to show up this morning. When the reporter called yesterday, I didn't feel badly enough at that time to decline. So they would have arrived there this morning, and I wouldn't have been there! THAT would have been a fiasco!" At that point, my concern for De's condition overrode my earlier decision to keep quiet regarding what I'd heard from the reporter, so I said, "I heard De isn't feeling well." That comment seemed to jar Carolyn and she asked me, almost irritably, "Where did you hear that?!" I said, "The reporter from E! told me that De was planning to come down to the star and surprise me, but that he isn't feeling well, and that's why they decided to cancel it for now." Carolyn queried, "Did she—?" I said, "Yes." So there it was. I added, "I didn't think she should have told me about the surprise, but she did. That's how I found out he doesn't feel well." Carolyn said, "Well, he'll be feeling better in time for next month." Then she added, "Now, I want you to stay down, take good care of you. And have a good trip to Washington, if I don't get a chance to call you again before you go." I said, "I love you SO much!" She said, "I love you, too, Kris. Take very good care of yourself."

I made it to Washington, bronchitis and all. We had a wonderful visit, except for two serious health emergencies, which of course I immediately reported in letters to the Kelleys, as humorously as I was able. "Having a wonderful time – GET ME OUT OF HERE! People keep trying to die on me!"

The first incident was when my nephew, Phil, was stung by a bee in Cle Elum on the 4th of July and went into anaphylactic shock. Thanks to first aid/first responder emergency training I had received just weeks before at Warner Bros. in order to become a volunteer Emergency Warden on the studio lot, I recognized the crisis within minutes and insisted that Dad and I drive him the six miles to the emergency room. On the way in, Dad's car stalled and died. Dad got out to try and re-start it. Phil's entire body had become swollen by this time – only two or three minutes into the trip — and he told us he couldn't see or breathe. Thank God, instead of waiting even a moment to see if Dad could fix the car, I advised Phil to relax as much as he was able, and started flagging down passing motorists until one of them agreed to drive Phil the rest of the way to the hospital. Dad and I helped Phil into the small two-seater sports car, and off they set, the driver and Phil, on the final four miles of the journey to the emergency room. I said a prayer skyward that they would make it in time and turned back to see how Dad was doing. I wanted to get going again to be sure Phil had made it to the hospital in time. Dad's car still wouldn't start. Feeling downright frantic, I started to walk back to the campsite, trying to remember to go slowly because I was still compromised with bronchitis. Frustrated after just a few minutes by my slow progress, I hitched a ride with a stranger back to the campsite. I quickly told everyone what had gone wrong and what we had done about it. Then several of us (including Mom and Wendy Rebar, Phil's girlfriend and future wife) got into Phil's car and headed for the hospital, leaving Dad at the roadside, still working on the disabled vehicle.

When we got to the emergency room, the dear woman who had driven Phil in met us at the door, quickly saying, "He made it. He'll be all right." Crying with relief, I hugged her and said, "Thank God." (I was wearing a Touched By An Angel T-shirt and the woman who agreed to help had been on her way to Mass.) Then she told us: "The doctor said we made it here just in time. Two more minutes, and he couldn't have done anything for him." I sat down, hard, on the bench, feeling enormously drained, suddenly. Mom noticed the paleness of my face, and said to someone "Get Kris an orange soda right away." I swallowed it down and recovered soon thereafter.

The next incident happened on the way to Tacoma from Cle Elum, two days later. I noticed that the surgical site on Mom's skull was becoming red and puffy. She insisted that she felt just fine and that it was absolutely nothing to worry about; "probably a little too much sunshine." All the way across the pass, the swelling increased and the redness spread. I suggested we go directly to Seattle to her doctor's emergency room, rather than return to

Tacoma, but Mom didn't want to go and Dad, for once, didn't override her druthers.

By the time we got to Tacoma, I insisted that we at least call the Seattle hospital and report the condition. My sister Jackie did that. The nurse on call advised us to watch for an elevated temperature above 101 degrees and any confusion or clumsiness on Mom's part. By this time it was 8:30 at night and I thought, "We'll all be asleep in an hour or so! How will we be able to tell if Mom's confused or clumsy if she's asleep?!" Within the hour, Mom's temperature was at 101 degrees, and she began to have chills and started to behave a little weird. Jackie called again, and the triage nurse said, "Bring her in."

So we piled into the car once again and headed north to Seattle. Twelve hours later, following a spinal tap and various other tests, it was decided that Mom had an infection at the site of one of her radioactive implants. A course of treatment was followed and she eventually recovered. The doctor later reported that "anecdotal" evidence revealed that people who get brain infections during brain cancer treatments "for some unknown reason" have a longer than normal life span in comparison to patients who DON'T get infections! Dad, who had been blaming himself for the delay in getting Mom to Seattle, was glad to hear that!

When the "vacation" (or, the "disaster prevention period", I should say!) was over, I flew home to Burbank. Carolyn called to welcome me home within an hour of my arrival time. Then she said, "We were sorry to hear that so much of your vacation was filled with emergencies." I said, very sincerely, "Let's just thank God I was up there! I might not have my nephew today if I hadn't been! That Emergency Rescue and First Aid training – that's GOOD STUFF!"

The next comment out of her mouth scared me. "We had some bad news ourselves while you were away." I said, "Oh, no! You did?" and held my breath. "Yes. While you were away, De was in the hospital again." I said, "Oh, nooo!" She said, "They removed more tumors, this time from his intestinal tract." I said, "Oh, God…" I asked, "Is he back home yet?" and she said, "Oh, yes." I asked if there was anything I could do for them and she said, "If I can think of anything, I'll let you know. De says to thank you for the Trader Joe's chocolate." I asked, "Can he still eat that?" She said, "Oh, yes! He has no restrictions on his diet at all. The doctors want him to drink eight, eight-ounce glasses of water every day, but he can't stomach water at all – it's like medicine to him. He just can't drink it at all. He drinks orange juice in the morning and thank God he's still drinking that one beer every night!" I told her, "You're both in my prayers!" She thanked me for that and said, "I'll call you again sometime." I said, "Okay. I love you." She said, "Bye-bye."

Unasked, but feeling an immediate need to do SOMETHING pro-active and helpful, I drove around the valley to various grocery and drug stores and gathered a variety of small bottles of Gatorade and several six packs of various kinds of nutritional supplements. (I made sure the nutritional supplements were CHOCOLATE-flavored.) Then I dropped them into a large grocery bag and deposited them on the front porch of the Kelley home. I didn't ring the doorbell. I knew they'd find the "care package" in the morning. The next morning when I got to work, there was a voice mail message. "This is DeForest, Kris. Will you give me a call when you get a moment? Thank you."

I returned the call. He said, "I'm calling to thank you for all the goodies and to ask if you make round trips." I thought that meant he liked the stuff I found for him to try, and I said enthusiastically, "I sure do!" He said, "I want to thank you so much for the thought and for your efforts, but I'll never drink it. The only thing I can tolerate is orange juice – and my nightly beer." I said, "Well, if those are what you can tolerate, how about drinking more of what you like? I could get you some O'Doul's or Sharps. They're non-alcoholic, so you could drink it all day long!" He joked, "You want to take ALL the fun out of life, don't you?" and chuckled. I clarified my intention with," I mean, you can drink the non-alcohol variety real often during the day without falling on your butt, and THEN drink the usual one at night. See?" He said, "Oh, I see," and chuckled again. Then he said, "But thank you again, VERY much, for thinking of me in that sweet way. I really appreciate all the time and thought and trouble you went to, to do that for me." I said, "It was absolutely no trouble at all. None." He said, "When shall I put this back out for you? Sunday?" I said, "If it isn't too underfoot for that long, that's fine. I'll get it sooner, if it is." He said, "No, Sunday is fine. Thanks again."

The following Sunday, August 3rd, I dropped off a letter, more Trader Joe's chocolate bars, and some other information I had received via the Internet, and then giggled when I saw the note De had placed on the out-going beverage sack.

> Dear Kris,
>
> Thanks for your thoughtfulness. I decided to keep the Sustacal as I am on a high protein routine and too cheap to give it back. De

That same afternoon De called again. I picked up the phone and said, "Hello?" De said, "I thought you'd be out in the pool." I said, "Not me." He said, "You must be with your cats, then?" I said, "Nope. They're in the other room right now." He asked, "Am I interrupting anything?" I said, "Nope." He said, "Thank you for the candy bars." I said, "Gee, you're very welcome." He said, "I just read the Internet thing you delivered here this morning, and I want to respond to it. I want you to know what the facts are, so you won't be so tied up in knots over it. As Carolyn told you, they took a tumor out of my intestinal tract and they zapped a couple of spots on my liver. The throat cancer rumor on the Internet is entirely false. And I'm on a drug that's supposed to take care of it." I sighed happily, relieved. "Oh, God, THAT'S a big relief to hear!" He added, "The information WILL get out. I'm amazed it isn't out already, with the reaction there at the hospital. I don't want you to feel responsible for anything that's said when it does." I said, "Oh, I won't! I haven't told anybody except Mom and Jackie, and they're utterly reliable as far as confidentiality."

"You'll hear every diagnosis and prognosis in the world when the word comes out," De cautioned me. "I'LL tell you – or Carolyn will tell you – the FACTS of my case; everyone ELSE is going to be GUESSING." I said, "OK. I feel a WHOLE lot better!" He said, "That's why I'm calling. Another party called from back east, all upset, saying that Creation had told her I canceled because of throat cancer. I KNEW that couldn't be right, so I called Creation, and they told me they were telling folks I canceled due to illness, and fans have taken it from there." I said, "I see." He said, "So you can STOP worrying about me." I said, "Okay, I will! … I loved your note this morning, by the way." He chuckled, "You did, did you?" I said, "It cracked me up totally." He paraphrased the note: "You can KEEP the cheap stuff; I'll hold on to the rest!" and laughed. I did, too.

Mom and Dad came down for the holidays again in 1997, and while they were here, I got Mom an appointment with a pre-eminent brain cancer surgeon, Dr. Keith Black, at Cedars-Sinai Hospital after reading a wonderful article about him in TIME magazine. Black had been the "cover boy" in an extensive article about new brain cancer treatments, and I thought, "If we can get Mom in to see HIM, it may be just the miracle we need."

Dr. Black agreed to see her. He was friendly and agreed that if the current protocol in Seattle began to fail, and she wanted to move down here for further treatment, he would accept her as a patient. He did tell us, though, that the Seattle program at the University of Washington was one of the best cancer research programs in the nation, and that it was every bit as state-of-the-art as his program. He assured us that her care to date had been excellent, according to the records he had reviewed, and that he probably would have done no differently than the doctors in Seattle had for her. He also made it a point to tell us, "There is no cure for this type of cancer. The best we can do is buy some time and try to retain as much quality of life as possible."

On December 7th De called. I was surprised, because Carolyn most always made the calls. He said, "Hello, Kris. This is DeForest…I'm calling to let your mother know how thrilled I am to hear about her visit to Cedars-Sinai to speak with the physician there." I said, "She's right here. Do you want to speak with her?" He said, "Yes, I would." She got on the line and said, "Hello, good morning, De." He asked if Dad and I were taking good care of her, and she said, "Yes, they're taking good care of me, but they're working me too hard." He chuckled at that – realizing she was joking — and then told her how happy he was to hear of her visit to Cedars Sinai. She said she was happy to know she can relax for a few months: "I'm getting a little tired of being a (clinical trials) guinea pig. But if it helps someone else down the line, I guess it'll be worth it." He told her she was in their thoughts and they wished her all the best. She said, "Thank you very much. I know that, and I appreciate your concern and caring."

When I got the phone back, I asked De, "How are YOU doing?" He said, "Oh, all right. I'm too mean and stubborn to die." I said, "You are? Mean and stubborn? You sure have ME fooled, then!" He said, "Yes, I do," and chuckled at that. I added, "If there's anything you need, I'm only four miles away, ready, willing and eager!" He said, "No one knows that better than we do." I said, "Good. I'm glad." He said, "Thank you." I then sensed he was getting tired or had run out of topics, so I said, "Thank you for calling! Hug each other for me." He said he would and then added, "Hold on a minute. Carolyn wants to speak with you."

When Carolyn got on the line, she said, "De got up this morning and said, 'I want to call Dorothea today.'" I said, "I'm glad he did. She's grinning ear to ear."

It was a lovely conversation. De's voice sounded better than it had in recent days, but he sounded a bit weak to me.

That week I ordered a sterling silver poesy ring for De for Christmas. Encircled on the outside was a series of raised stars, which reminded me of the Walk of Fame. Best of all, as if it had been written just for that occasion, engraved inside were the words in Olde English "Many are thee starrs I see, yet in my eye no starr like thee." The moment I saw it, I thought, "Boy, this is the perfect ring for a star polisher to give to her favorite star." It would have added significance for De, I knew, because I worked at a studio and saw stars all the time – and NONE had made the impression on me that he had.

On December 18th, I called the Kelleys to thank them for the Christmas tin of popcorn they had sent us. De answered the phone, and he sounded good. I told him we'd enjoy the popcorn while I was on vacation, watching movies at home. De thought my vacation was that week, but I said, "No, it's Christmas week — next week." He asked about my job, and I told him, "I love the people, but the work itself is completely uncreative and really boring. I'm getting antsy to find something a little more compelling at the studio – something that involves some real creativity." He said, "You should be doing something that challenges you in ways you want to be challenged, so that it feels worthwhile, and is fun. You're more valuable to Warners than they know, if they'd use you in the right areas." Then he said, "But who knows? If you stay right there, you might be head of the studio some day; you just never know!" I laughed at that and said, "Right, De! Just what I always wanted! You and Dad! I swear!" He chuckled and then said, "It's strange the way things work. Don't underestimate yourself or what fate has in store for you. It can really surprise you!" I thanked him again and told him I loved him and we hung up.

The poesy ring arrived in the mail the next day, and I delivered it to the Kelley mailbox on Christmas Eve, in the dark, so there was no way De would be able to open it until Christmas morning. On Christmas Day the phone rang. I couldn't wait to pick it up!

Me: Merry Christmas!

De: How art thou? (He had opened the gift, and was trying out his Olde English!)

Me: I art fine.

De: I guess you already know I love that ring. I wish I'd found it first; I'd have given it to YOU!

Me: *awwww*!!! Well, it seemed the perfect thing for me to give to YOU!

De:	Of course, I'm going to love those candy bars, too. Perhaps I can even get Carolyn to give up a few of hers.
Me:	Probably – but that's up to HER!
De:	(chuckle) How's your mom?
Me:	Fine. Real great.
De:	And your father?
Me:	Oh, not so good. He's a sick boy. Coughing all night – aching all over –maybe he has the flu.
De:	Pour down the Nyquil!
Me:	He can't, unfortunately. He's diabetic. He isn't supposed to take that stuff.
De:	Oh. Well, he's in the best of hands – yours.
Me:	IF he'd listen to me!
De:	(chuckle)
Me:	I cam corded some of the package opening last night, so the sisters can share the holiday later – since I get Mom and Dad THIS year!
De:	I'm glad no one's taking pictures of ME today! I surely do love that ring.
Me:	I'm glad. Really glad. I did, too. Duh!
De:	(laugh) Hold on. Here's Carolyn!
Me:	Okay!
Carolyn:	Merry Christmas!
Me:	Merry Christmas!
Carolyn:	I was doing sum'pin' else for a minute there – that's why De got you first.
Me:	Oh, okay.
Carolyn:	Thank you for the candy. De loves his TJ's chocolate bars, too.
Me:	De wants YOURS, too!
Carolyn:	I know he does. I might share – a FEW! Thank you again for everything. We're "sweetly" buried in your kind thoughts.
Me:	I'm glad. Enjoy! Love you!
Carolyn:	Bye-bye.
Me:	Bye!

On January 18, 1998 De and Carolyn called. De thanked me for the birthday goodies (cards and candy) I delivered that day, and especially mentioned the one from the cats as being "the best". He asked me, "Have you seen the article in the TIMES this morning?" I said, "No. What's it about?" He said, "It's about how the entertainment industry is about to boom. I said, "Oh, yeah… while Mom and Dad were here, we watched a lot of TV, and the news mentioned that." De said, "I knew that about six or seven years ago. It's going to be bigger than the defense industry here. Hang in there. You're in a good spot to really climb when it happens." "I'm just very deeply disappointed and distressed that I can't be paid what I'm worth here, because I'd like to stay longer. I love everybody so much where I am; it's a great team." He acknowledged how disappointing it must be "to hear — and to KNOW — how good you are, and then get less than your due for all you do there."

On De's birthday in '98, I called the Kelley household to wish him a happy birthday. Carolyn answered the phone. I said, "Hello, Carolyn! This is Kris. Is the birthday boy there to sing happy birthday to, or do you just want to TELL him happy birthday for me?" She said, "He's sitting right here." To De, she said, "It's Kris, to sing you Happy Birthday." De got on the phone and said, "Okay, let's hear it." I said, "Okay, but plug your ears. You KNOW what a lousy singer I am. Here goes." Then I sang him Happy Birthday and added, in bass, "— and many more!" He thanked me and then said, "I forgot to thank you for the package from Harry and David's when we spoke last. We're enjoying those today." I said, "Good. You're partying hearty, then." He said, "Yes, we are. It seems I can't stop thanking you for things!" Then he joked, "Since you're there at Warners, you might go over to the sound stages and do voice-overs for people who can't sing." I laughed at that and said, "Oh, sure!" Then I added, "I won't quit my day job." He said, "No, I wouldn't."

Some weeks later Carolyn called to thank me for the many Valentine's Day remembrances (two cards, plus an EDIBLE, heart-shaped box of chocolates). She sounded VERY pleased and cheery. She said, "These are the CUTEST cards. De always says, 'Kris always finds the BEST cards!'" She said her favorite, of course, was the one where the cat has brought the dead mouse to the owner's dinner plate. (Inside: "Remember: It's the thought that counts.") She said, "You know MY story about the dead mouse, don't you?" I said, "Yes, I think so. The one where your daddy brought you a dead mouse to pet because he knew you wanted to touch one so badly?" She said, "Yes, that's the one. I thought I had told you that one." We mentioned the weather – black and stormy one minute, blue and calm the next. She said, "De and I knew an old lady, just after we were married, and she would always say, 'Ain't the weather FUNNY?' We always laughed about that – and we still say it. 'Ain't the weather funny?!'" – and she laughed again. I laughed, too, and said, "It sure is. If you don't like it, just wait fifteen minutes – IT'LL CHANGE!"

On March 5th that year, my birthday, I was in the middle of a spring housecleaning when the doorbell rang. It was a courier from CASA DE FLORES in Sherman Oaks, with a basket of four plants and a card from De and Carolyn! The card read: "Happy birthday and all good wishes, De and Carolyn." I about fell over! I called to thank them for their thoughtfulness. Carolyn answered the phone and I blurted my thanks. She said, "Good heavens! Did they get there already?!" I said, "Yes! And they are awesome!" She said, "We like to send plants instead of flowers. They last longer." I told her I was becoming quite the plant fanatic. I told her about the decent news from Mom, but it was now a day-to-day thing. She said, "That's how you have to take it – day by day. We're glad she's well and feeling good. Give her our love."

On March 10th, Carolyn called to ask if I'd heard anything more about Mom and I said, "Oh…yes... It's not good news, though. The tumor is coming back, but not in exactly the same place." I gave her the other details that I had at the moment (which weren't many) and said, "I sent the information to Dr. Black at Cedars-Sinai and Mom and Dad have sent the MRIs to him via Fed Ex overnight, so he can offer his thoughts and suggestions." Carolyn asked, "How's your mom feeling?" and I said, "She's feeling fine. The tougher things get, the better she seems to act." Carolyn said, "She just doesn't want to worry you." I said, "I know." I told her that I'd always thought of Mom as a true pioneer woman – "She'd get across the prairie in a covered wagon, doing whatever it took to make it." Carolyn said, "That's a PERFECT description for your mother. Just perfect." I said, "She keeps telling US, 'Don't worry! It does no good for anybody!'" Carolyn agreed, "That's right!" I said, "As long as she can handle it, WE CAN, TOO! And she's handling it! Is she ever! She's awesome." Carolyn admitted, "She's quite the lady!" Then she said, "Well, I'd better get back to my happy taxes." I said okay and thanked her for calling and we hung up.

CAROLYN BREAKS HER LEG

During an evening hour on April 4th De called and started out by saying, "Thinking this was Friday, I called you at work earlier today and asked you to give me a call. Now I realize it's Saturday, so I'm calling you at home." He continued, "Carolyn fell today and fractured the leg bone just below one hip – the femur." Shocked and saddened, I responded, "Oh, no!" He said, "I was away at the time – I had gone to the nursery for some flowers – and she stumbled and fell, and couldn't get to the phone. I guess she laid there for thirty five or forty minutes before I walked back into the house. I called the paramedics and they came and took her to the hospital. As they wheeled her away, she told me, "Tell anyone you call 'NO FLOWERS!'" Then he chuckled, despite himself. He continued, "It's such a shame, because we have been walking for the past several months, and she was really getting around – walking all over the place." Then he said, "She had surgery and they set the bone. She's out of it right now – I can't even talk to her – but I will get a chance tomorrow again, I'm sure." I was stunned into near silence by his report. I asked him, "How are you?" and he said, "I'm fine." (He sounded fine at that moment, but when I got back to work and heard the message he had left me just AFTER she had fallen, he didn't sound fine THEN. He sounded muffled and a bit choked up, like a man trying to keep his emotions from running away with him.) Then he asked, "How's your mom?" I said, "Oh, she's just awesome. The worse things get for her, the more she gets up on a table and dances a jig so we don't worry about her." He said, "She is an incredible woman, all right." He asked me, "How are you?" I said, "I'm doing all right." I told him I was reading a lot about positive thinking, then added, "Hell, things are bad ENOUGH, aren't they? We don't need our minds MANUFACTURING any MORE!" De chuckled at that and said, "I hope it [positive thinking] works for US!"

I quickly mentioned the present status of our loved ones in as positive a light as I was able. "These are tough times, but we're all still alive – so let's celebrate THAT, shall we?" He said, "Good thinking, Ollie!"

On April 13th, Carolyn was transferred from the local hospital to another long-term care and rehabilitation facility, when it became evident that her recovery period would be lengthy… possibly endless. On April 14th, I called to ask how the transfer went. She said it went beautifully. I told her, "I called the new hospital last night to get your new phone and room numbers, but asked them not to connect me to you, because I knew it had been a busy day for you." She said, "I sure do appreciate you checking up on me. It's very sweet of you...We read your letter about your mother's tumor. How is she doing?" I said, "She's doing just great, emotionally. She called me on Easter from Oregon and you'd never even know there was anything wrong with her. She just isn't letting it get her down. She's going on with her life." Carolyn said, "As we used to say, 'She's some kinda dame.'" I said, "She sure is." She asked, "How's your dad?" I said, "Oh, the same, of course." She asked, "Still nippin'?" I said, "Oh, sure. AND smoking." She said, "Don't'cha just want to kill him sometimes?" I said, "Yeah, but only sometimes. He doesn't have any other coping strategies." She said, "It's good that you can understand that and forgive him."

My own health began to be impacted by the multiple health crises facing family members and loved ones. I began to have dizzy spells and to have occasional numbness and weakness on my left side, including my face, as well as occasional vision problems. These maladies scared me, and sent me straightaway to the emergency room at Saint Joseph's Hospital from work one afternoon. I mentioned the ongoing tests to my family and to the Kelleys. After the tests were completed, the doctor attributed the symptoms to stress and possibly to a rare form of "painless" migraine, which manifests in neurological symptoms rather than as terrible, nauseating headaches. Of course, a "stress" diagnosis made perfect sense. I had plenty of stress! I was being negatively impacted by my sincere and abiding concern over loved ones' health challenges and my inability to do anything about it to help them, other than praying for them and trying to keep their spirits high as much as possible.

Mom's next MRI revealed devastating information. Her tumor was reasserting itself with a vengeance. Her doctors were trying to decide what to do next – if anything – to keep her perking along. She had been their "miracle" up until now, and watching her slip through their skilled fingers was as hard on them as it was on us – if that was possible...

DE DEVOTES TIME TO OUR TROUBLES

On June 10th De called me to get Mom's address in Cle Elum. He said he wanted to send her "a little something" in the mail to cheer her up. A day later, Carolyn called to commiserate over Mom's deteriorating condition. "De told me about it. I was very sorry to hear it." I told her everything I knew about the situation and then repeated Mom's various ways to keep us calm. Carolyn again marveled, "Have you ever known anyone like her?" I said, "No. There's no one else quite like my mommy, when it comes to things like this!" She said, sincerely, "I think you're a little like your mommy." She added, "I think we ALL get scared – even your mother – when it comes to our health. You do, I do, De does… WE certainly don't handle our problems the way she has."

I reported, "Dad is having problems making Mom 'behave' (sit still and stay put) when he goes anywhere. He's doing the shopping and taking the clothes to the laundry now, there in Cle Elum. He tells her to sit down and stay still until he gets back, but she forgets and gets up and sometimes falls down and can't get back up again." Carolyn said, "Oh, dear! Why doesn't he take her WITH him?!" I said, "That's what I suggested. He says it takes too long to get her into and out of the car. She's real weak and his back can't handle it."

I flew up for the 4th of July. It was then, standing together as a family in an examination room in Seattle, when Mom's doctor took her hand and sadly said, "I'm sorry. There is nothing more we can do for you, Mrs. Smith. We've done everything we can." Mom thanked him for all of his efforts and those of his staff, and then told us, "Well, let's go home." As we helped her into the car, her only comment — said wistfully but in no way bitterly — was "Well… It's too bad. I would have liked to have made history [by becoming a cancer-free miracle in a new clinical trial]." I patted her shoulder and said, "You made history, Mom. You made history with all of us." No one at our place slept that night. Our hearts were broken and our tears were relentless.

By the time I left Washington to return to California, Mom needed help getting to the bathroom. Her legs were completely useless and it took my full body strength to lift her from her bed or chair and get her into the bathroom. I would put my upper arms underneath her armpits and lift her, holding her close to my body in a tight, compact embrace, in order to save my back muscles from injury. She still weighed nearly 145 pounds.

Just a few nights before I flew back to California, I had a vivid dream. I was viewing the "lifting of Mom" from a vantage point BEHIND Mom. The person lifting and embracing her (in the way I had been while assisting her) was Jesus. The dream made me realize that at some point I would need to let Him do the lifting and carrying – that I couldn't carry her all the way to her final destination. Instead of feeling saddened by the dream, I felt enormous comfort. She would be in very good hands at the end. I felt it in my bones.

A few days after I got home, I got a card in the mail from Mom. The front showed a sad little bear waving and the words "Bad bye." Inside, the sentiment was, "I'd say good-bye, but what's so good about you leaving?"

On July 21st, De called me to send his and Carolyn's love and best wishes to Mom and Dad. He said, "It's tragic about your mother. I understand very well what you're going through because my mother died of cancer, as you know." He asked how I was, and I said, "I'm fine, but I'm worried about Dad. He's a basket case." De said, "I understand that, too. Your dad is harder on himself and on others than he needs to be, just by the nature of his personality, based on what you've told me and on what I've observed myself."

Responding to a concern I had written about to them, De said, "I want you to know that Carolyn and I aren't upset with you – we never have been. But all hell broke loose with Carolyn at about the time you were writing us all those long letters and we couldn't keep up with them. I'm running my tail off trying to keep everything together right now." I said, "I'm sorry I added to your burden. I didn't know." He said, "I know it." I said, "If there's anything I can do to lighten your load, don't hesitate." He said, "Write shorter, fewer letters. That's all I can think of for right now." I said, "OK. I can do that! But I can do other stuff for you and Carolyn, if you need some extra help – shopping, visiting Carolyn, whatever – to give YOU a break." He said, "If I can think of anything, I'll let you know."

On July 23rd De called just as I was falling asleep. He asked how things were up north and how Mom was, because "Carolyn and I want to do something for her if she's 'with it' enough to notice." I said, "She sleeps a lot of the time, but when she's awake, she is aware and very much 'with it.'" He said, "We discussed flowers and plants and muffins, but all of that gets pretty old after a while, and so I'm calling to ask you what you think she'd enjoy." I immediately said, "Oh, she loves chocolate! Her favorite is See's!" That made him happy!

That's when I let him know that whatever it was he had sent to Mom in Cle Elum the previous month had never arrived: "Dad and I looked for it again both times we were over there, but never found it." I asked what it was he sent her, and he said he had drawn a little dog with a bouquet of flowers, and had included a little note, and I said, "*awwwwwwww!* She woulda LOVED that!" I asked if he'd be willing to do that again and include it with the candy, and he said, "Certainly!" I gave him Jackie's new address so he'd know where to send the goodies.

I asked how Carolyn was, and he said, "She's a little better today, attitude-wise, but the broken bone hasn't knitted well enough to where she can even start physical therapy yet, so she feels almost as if she's in prison!" I commiserated with that, saying, "Well, I guess! It's been three months." I asked him to give her my love, and he said, "I will." He asked if Mom was ambulatory, and I said, "Not at all. Her legs and left side are completely useless." Hearing that upset him, I could tell. Then I told him something humorous about her, to bring his spirits back up: "She's a little dippy at times, but in funny ways." I told him about her methodically polishing the bars of her bed and turning the touch lamp on and off interminably all night long. "So she's staying busy! … Her sense of time is shot to hell — she gave Jackie all of thirty seconds to fetch some maple bars from the donut shop more than a mile away! — but she seems happy and she's not in any pain that Tylenol with codeine can't handle."

It was a terrific call. I thought at the time, "He's just the sweetest guy to think of us when he has so much on his mind already with Carolyn's and his own problems."

During one of my calls with De I asked him to give Carolyn a big hug and kiss for me, and he said he would. I asked if she would ever accept visitors, and he said, "Oh, I doubt it. She hates being in the hospital and isn't in the proper frame of mind for it."

On August 19th Carolyn called me from the hospital for the first time in months to thank me for the gifts I sent to her a few weeks earlier. She was chatty and we talked about a lot of things. She was happy to hear how well Mom was doing again. "I hope this is a miracle in progress and that everyone gets to feeling fine again soon: your dear mother, your dad, me, De…"

I said, "De sounds fine. Is he not feeling well?" She said, "Oh, he's feeling okay. He's just awfully busy these days, doing everything there is to do at home, even the stuff I used to do… and he's doing a wonderful job of it, too. Thanks for checking in on him."

Our calls were spotty, but De and Carolyn were sure to remember Mom. I told them, "She bounced back once again after several days of being really punk. The Hospice people who visit the house say her only current problem is a bit of congestion in her lower lungs, so Jackie and Dennis and Dad have to sit her up more often. When they do THAT, they have to stand and hold her upright, unless they belt her in. Her equilibrium is gone completely, but she's feeling okay again."

On Carolyn's birthday (October 5th) I called and sang Happy Birthday to her. She asked how Mom was and I updated her on that. "Dad doesn't think she'll be around much longer, but she isn't suffering." Carolyn said, "Oh, that's good." I told her, "Dad is handling it okay, although he wants me up there ASAP." She said, "Of course. He'd have you up there all the time if he could get you." I reported, "I told him to hold his horses for just a couple more days; I can't start my Leave of Absence until Jackie's finishes, just in case Mom surprises everyone and lives another 90 days. I may need every day of that leave!"

A few days later, I flew to Washington to spend Mom's final days with her. She was completely bedridden, so I spent the days and many nights sitting and sleeping near her. I gave her bed baths, rubbed oils on her body, and kept her feet well scratched and tickled, which she loved.

About ten days before her death on October 23rd, she refused food and drink altogether. The Hospice people told us the time would probably come when she would do that, so we were advised – but not prepared. The deathwatch had begun. I began to sing "Kumbaya" softly — leaking tears like crazy — almost every time she would look close to dozing off.

Mom and I would sit up late and watch classic movies. One of her favorites came on – THE KING AND I, with Yul Brynner. She fell asleep off and on during it. At one point, she lifted her hand toward the ceiling about ten feet in front of her and gave a cute little wave. I asked her, "Who are you waving at, Mom?" She said, "My little fairy." I asked her what her fairy looked like, and she said, "He's about five inches high, and he has long hair and a face like Jesus'." I remembered my dream from a couple of months earlier – when Jesus had assumed the role of caregiver and bearer. I pondered silently, "Mom, you have always been such a doubting Thomas…"

From that evening on, I would quietly sing or hum "Kumbaya" as Mom slept. My eyes would flood with tears each time I did so, but the song also provided the desperately needed comfort my aching soul needed.

The next night, Mom began to gesture in a way that reminded me of someone plucking feathers, but on a grand scale. The "chicken" would have had to been enormous — on the scale of a human or larger, based on the angle at which her arm was moving. I asked her, "Mom, are you picking feathers?" "Yes," she confirmed. Joking, I continued: "Mother! Are you picking the feathers off your ANGELS?!" NOT joking, she confirmed, "Just the loose ones." Chills went up my spine; my neck hair stood on end. I had expected her to laugh! Finally, I said, "Well, as long as the feathers are LOOSE, I guess it's all right."

Just a few days before she passed away, my no-longer-so-doubting Mom lay in bed as I bathed her. I was bouncing her around a little bit, making her laugh ("You are SO SILLY!" she would proclaim, eyes shining with mirth. "You make me happy!")

A Hospice nurse, Joe, came by and checked her vital signs. He said she was doing okay. Mom said, "Of course I'm doing okay. Kris is doing everything Ben tells her to do."

Ben?!

I asked her, "Mom, who's Ben?"

"Ben!" she said, pointing over against another wall in the room. "The angel who has been telling you what to do the past few days." I looked at the wall. There was no Ben that I could see – but then, I wasn't as close to the door through which she'd soon be passing. I looked at Joe. He smiled and nodded his understanding. I finally looked back at Mom and asked, "Well, am I doing everything right? Am I doing everything the way Ben wants it done?" She smiled and said, "Everything's just perfect."

I believed her. So did Joe. Absolutely.

That night, just before slipping into a coma, Mom gave Dad and me her last instructions for the balance of our lives. The first was, "Don't fight." (In Mom's presence, Dad and I had been discussing *his* health issues and why I felt so strongly that he should curtail drinking and smoking and take better care of himself.) The other instruction was, "Don't be upset [by my death]." I held her hand in mine and started to leak tears. I told her, "Mom, I'm not upset. When I cry, it's just the love leaking out." She nodded and her eyes welled up just a little. I continued, after a long pause, as hard as it was to hear myself say it: "It's okay for you to go whenever you feel ready. I will miss you; I will never forget you. I love you, my mommy."

Within two days, surrounded by her loving family, Dorothea Hope Smith passed away into the loving arms of eternity. Just a few hours before she left, her eyes popped open and she looked up past all of us standing at her bedside, not seeing us but seeing something so far beyond magnificent that we could only marvel at the look of rapture on her face and in her eyes. The brain tumor, which had rendered her mouth smile-less for months, no longer had any hold over her. Her smile was back and her eyes were shining. I marveled, "She has had one foot in heaven already! She knows where she's headed, and boy, is she ever okay with it!"

I will carry the memory of Mom's final expression to the end of my own days.

A large part of my mother's enduring legacy is that she never complained — and the only anguish or angst she ever caused was when she left us.

I called De early the next morning to let him know that Mom had passed away during the night. He was very sweet and sympathetic and sent his and Carolyn's love to the whole family. A few days later I received a letter from De, which I will always treasure.

October 27th 1998

> Dear Kris,
>
> Consider this a note of congratulations for you and your family for the magnificent care and devotion that all of you have given to a terrific lady.
>
> We know and understand your love for her for we could feel the goodness that she reflected in those moments that we knew her.
>
> With deep sympathy,

Love,
De and Carolyn

As soon as the memorial service was completed, two weeks later, I flew back to Burbank. Dad said he'd follow in a month or so, if his doctor would release him, so I wouldn't have to spend the first Christmas holiday alone. Carolyn called to welcome me home and to ask how the memorial service had gone. I told her, "Mom said not to have one unless it could be fun, and funny, so we made it fun and funny. But there were a few tears, too!" I told her, "It was captured on videotape, so the grandkids who are too young to remember her will get a taste of what she was like from folks who DID know and treasure her." Carolyn said, "What a nice idea."

I told her, "All the Hospice people told me I should go into Hospice care, I was so good at it." Carolyn said, "I'll bet you WOULD be good at it. I'll bet you'd be terrific! It would be depressing, though, I think." I said, "I don't know. It was sort of – enchanting, in a way. All the walls fall down, and everyone's love floods out."

Dad drove down in December, but had a terrible time in transit. He ended up in an emergency room in Oregon, suffering from what one doctor diagnosed as congestive heart failure. His legs were swollen like balloons and he was put on water pills. When he got to my home a week or so later, he was still feeling puny, so I took him to a cardiologist, who confirmed the earlier diagnosis, and said he should see an internist and another specialist right away. Dad gave up cigarettes and alcohol until he started feeling better; then went back to them, and started feeling worse. He nearly passed out into my arms twice, yet he absolutely refused to see additional doctors. I was getting frantic. I told him, "Then go back home and see your usual doctors! I'm not going to have you down here falling dead at my feet unless you agree to start fighting for your life!"

Against Mom's final wishes, there we were, fighting again. I didn't know what else to do, short of committing him. He wouldn't respond to reason, to loving suggestion, or to orders. He was simply NOT INTERESTED. It didn't occur to me until later that his reason for living had expired on October 23rd. His race was run, as far as he was concerned. He was depressed and his heart was broken in a way no surgeon would ever be able to fix.

Carolyn called on January 1st, 1999 to wish me a Happy New Year! This was the second call in two weeks! I was surprised, and surmised she must be feeling a lot better. She asked if we watched the Rose Parade. I said, "Dad did. I watched it off and on, but I'm reading THE GREATEST GENERATION by Tom Brokaw, so my attention was divided. It's about – well, it's about YOU GUYS – the World War II generation – THE GREATEST GENERATION!" She joked, "We ARE the greatest! …Tell your dad hello and Happy New Year for me."

On February 19th, De called in the evening at about 9:30! It was so late at night, I was at first concerned that it might be bad news about Carolyn, but basically he was calling to check up on Dad and me. We were both under the weather and I had let De and Carolyn know via a short note. I inquired about Carolyn's chances of recovering. He said, "Very slim. The leg isn't healing. We just don't know what's going to happen." I said, "Boy, that's really rough. I'm really sorry to hear that." Then I inquired, "How are YOU doing?" He said, "Oh —I have good days and bad days." Red flag! De was NOT a complainer.

I hastened to repeat, "De, if there's anything I can do to help you or Carolyn, I'm here for you. Please be sure to call on me." He said, "I've been giving that some thought. I may give you a call one of these days." I said, "Do it. I don't want to impose on your private life, but I DO want to help, if there's any way I can. I love you both so much." He said, "We love you, too, Kris."

Although his voice sounded a little weak, I had no idea that the next call would come close to killing me.

****

PART THREE 1999

Dedicated to the memory of DeForest Kelley…

"and to you, his devoted fans and friends, who so often find ways to keep his memory alive through thoughtful and committed action and compassion"

BEING THERE: DAYS OF DEVOTION

On Sunday, March 14, 1999 A.C. Lyles called and dropped a ton of bricks on me. He said, bluntly, "Kris, I need your help." I said, "Sure, A.C. What is it?" He said, "De is dying." Just like that. I almost died myself! I managed to utter a lifeless, wooden, "Oh." He said, "It wasn't unexpected, was it?" I lied, "No, but it still..." He said, "He has cancer, you know." I again lied, "Yes, I know." He said, "I need you to fax me a copy of De's biography. I don't have one and I have to be ready with information for the media." I told him I didn't think I could readily find the copy I had at home, but that I could drive to WB and access the Internet and get it off the Paramount STAR TREK web site. I asked, "Do you want it today?" He said, "Yes, of course, right away." I said I'd call the Data Center and get someone to let me in. He said, "This is confidential. Don't say anything about it." I said, "I won't."

A.C. gave me his home fax number and said he wouldn't be at home when it came in, as he had to go out right away and do something for De. I said, "Okay." Then he said, "And don't call Carolyn. She's upset right now, as you can well imagine."

I drove to WB half in shock, feeling alternately dazed and sick to my stomach. From my work station I faxed the information to A.C's home. When I got back home, there was a voice mail message on my machine. "Kris, this is A.C. I'm over at the hospital with De in Room 302, and he's doing a lot better today. He's been in the hospital a few days, dear, and he's looking at me now and nodding his head. He's doing better today, and I was talking to Carolyn and to De and we want to ask you a big favor, if we can. I'm sure you'd like to do this because you've told me in the past that you would be happy to do it while Carolyn's in the hospital. While De is here, he'd love for you to have the key to the house... and stop by whenever you can, every day or every other day, whatever. The man next door has been picking up the mail, but they just want to make sure that everything is good at the house, honey, and since you know the house so well and everything, De and Carolyn would be most appreciative if you could do that for them. De has a key here at this room to the house, and if you could come by and get the key, De would appreciate it very much; I know he'd like to say hello to you.... Ask for his nurse and she will take care of you. The key will be waiting for you…So would you – when you get back — I know what you're doing; you're doing something for me, and I appreciate it – when you get back will you call us, please, and De wants to say hello to you. Just a minute."

Maddeningly, the answering machine cut off at that point!

While I was listening to this upsetting voice mail, the phone rang, so I stopped the voice mail and picked it up. It was Carolyn. She said, "Hello, Kris." I said, "Hi, sweetie." She said, "Did A.C. call you?" I said, "Yes." She sighed and said, "Then you know." I said, sadly, "Yes." Then I told her that De and A.C. wanted me to drive out to De's hospital and get De's keys and take care of the house. She said, "Then let's not talk now. You go do that. Call me back later. And thank you." I said, "I will… just as soon as I get back here. I promise."

I called the hospital and spoke with the nurse, who was expecting my call. I asked if I would be able to see De when I came in, and she said, "Oh, yes, of course!"

When I first spotted De, I didn't recognize him. If A.C. hadn't been with him, I'm pretty sure I would have denied that the skeleton occupying the bed was De. He looked no better than a long-term concentration camp survivor – nothing but skin draped over bones. He couldn't have weighed 90 pounds. His complexion was yellow.

I hugged A.C. as he came over to greet me, and then went to De's bedside and took his bony, emaciated hand. He had just eaten a slice of watermelon and was working on a cola, but not very diligently.

De was trying to help us relax and not take his predicament so seriously; he was joking as much as his weakened condition allowed. I told him, "My answering machine shut off just before you came on to tell me what you had to say." De joked, "That's because AC is so long-winded." I asked, "What did you say?" He smiled. "I said, 'I suppose when I get out of here, my car will be gone and my home will be wiped out!'" I responded, feigning serious personal injury, "Well, thank you for the vote of confidence, Mr. Kelley!" He chuckled weakly and said, "Dear girl, if I didn't trust you, you wouldn't be getting the keys!"

His feet and legs were dry, felt like ice and looked nearly lifeless. I asked him if I could put some lotion on them, and he said I could. I did that for a good 90 minutes, being very careful not to hurt him. Eventually, with the lotion and light massaging his circulation improved, so after a while they were pink and warm again. I eventually did his back and left side, too. The nurse came in and gave him whole blood and an IV with lots of nutrition in it. A.C and De joked with the nurse that in three days I'd be ready to join her staff. De decided he and A.C. had a "quorum" now with me there and so could make decisions that would stick.

A.C. left at about 3 o'clock. I walked him to the parking lot, as I wanted to give him the hard copy of De's biography in case the one I faxed over had not been received at his home. AC told me De had rebounded tremendously just in the few hours since we had arrived. I told him, "You scared the living hell out of me with that phone call. I didn't know a thing about De being ill." He said, "You're joking. I thought he told you everything." I said, "I think he was about to, but he hadn't yet." AC said, "So, my call was a shock." I confessed, "It damn' near killed me." He said, "Oh, I'm so sorry." I said, "It's OK. You didn't know."

I went back into the hospital to sit with De for another two hours. He told me his story in harrowing detail: about how he had almost "checked out" at one point. "The room went all white, and it was just like a scene out of ER. I could see two nurses – and then a roomful of people – working over me, trying to bring me back, but I was completely helpless to respond. I thought it was all over with me, for sure, but I just kept thinkin, 'I can't go now. I still have things to do – the taxes, Carolyn…'" He concluded, "What a weird feeling!"

Then he said he had considered asking for my help sooner, "but I was getting along pretty well up until just recently; then everything happened all at once, and here we are." He said he had recently negotiated a bungalow for Carolyn to remain at her facility in the event she was unable to return home. I told him I had three weeks of vacation time coming and that I could probably "fudge" at work and get family leave or – lacking that – a leave of absence to take care of him at home with a Hospice crew, "if need be." He said, "Let's hope the need WON'T be!" I assured him I'd LOVE to help him out, and he said, "There's more to do yet!" I said, "That's fine. That's good! I'm your girl!" He said he needed to write some bills, move some things, check the answering machine. He said I should start the car every few days so the battery wouldn't run down, and to run the sprinklers as needed to keep the lawn and roses looking good.

As he was explaining to me what to do at the house and where to find things, I was concentrating REAL hard, trying to memorize his words and not forget anything. He misinterpreted my gaze as a "worried" look regarding his condition and leaned forward and squeezed my hand, saying, "Don't look so worried. Don't you worry about me, or anything else." I drew back, surprised, and said, "I'm not worrying, sweetie. I'm just concentrating real hard – paying close attention to where you're telling me to find things *so I don't screw up*!" He said, "You CAN'T screw up. Don't even worry about that. Call me if you can't find something." He mentioned what a dear man A.C. is, and what a long-time friend he had been. Then he said, "I'm glad he came over. I love his smile. I love making him laugh." I said, "You did THAT today, all right – several times!" At one point, De grimaced mightily when a nurse pushed a pillow behind him, accusing her of hiding a baseball bat in it. A little later, I was attempting to move his hips underneath him more squarely as he lay in bed, and he grimaced again. I said, "Oh, I'm sorry!" He said, "It's all right. THEY do it, too." I said, "Well, I'LL find a way NOT to!" Then I used the sheet underneath him to move his hips into place; it didn't hurt a bit.

He became weary at close to five and kept nodding off; so I told him I'd let him get some rest and go check out his house. He thanked me for coming by and for my help. When I got to his house, I found out that he had given me one too few keys – I didn't have the key to the dead bolt – so I drove back and walked into his room again to let him know. When I told him my problem, he joked, "I don't like to make it CONVENIENT for you to help me!" I laughed and he told me where to find the missing key.

I went back to his house, got inside, opened the garage door and started the Lexus. I checked on Myrtle, still hibernating in a cardboard box in the garage, and studied the sprinkler system, which was almost Greek to me, but I finally figured it out. Then I checked the lawn for wetness, cleaned the fridge out and kept what I wanted in it, as De instructed. I got the messages off the answering machine and checked out all the rooms, to be sure everything looked okay. I lowered the thermostat to 65 degrees, threw out the junk mail, and then called De's hospital. He was asleep, but his nurse assured me that he was improving hourly. I called Carolyn from their home and let her know what had transpired and that De was doing a lot better. She thanked me several times for "coming to our aid" and I told her how MUCH I loved doing it. She told me, "I'll probably never return home; I have a place here now." I told her I'd come visit and she said, "I'll enjoy that." I told her I'd fix up her legs, as I had De's, and she said, "My LEG, you mean!" She was still in a cast from ankle to hip, after almost a year!

After I hung up with her, I tried calling the Kelley's neighbor. I intended to introduce myself and to see if he had any mail for them, but his line was busy, so I hung around a little while longer, familiarizing myself with the house. On a credenza in the workroom, I spotted a list of "Things To Do" which De had written. On the list, noted twice (once on the front and once on the back) was the notation, "Ask David about a fee for Kris." It was confirmation that De had indeed been seriously thinking about bringing me in to help him BEFORE he was hospitalized. I felt sad that he hadn't. My guess is that he just couldn't admit to himself that he was desperately ill. When I again received a busy signal at the neighbor's phone number, I drove home and put some of De's groceries into my fridge and then nuked a dinner.

I discovered a voice mail message from Carolyn. "Kris, this is Carolyn. Will you please give me a call when you can?"

I called her. She wanted my take on how De was. I told her he was MUCH better and that she should relax now and get some rest. She thanked me again for my help. She mentioned A.C. and I said, "That man sure has a way with words. He scared the stuffing out of me when he called this morning." She said, "I know. He doesn't mince words, does he?"

Almost as soon as I hung up from chatting with Carolyn and reassuring her, the phone rang. It was De. He asked if he was interrupting anything, and I said, "Absolutely NOT." He said, "I want to tell you, you did a good day's work. Thank you." I said, "I loved doing it. I should be thanking YOU for allowing me to be there… and for trusting and relying on me." I added, "You get a good night's sleep and don't HESITATE to call me, day or night, if you want to talk or feel you need me to come over." He said, "Okay." I said, "Goodnight. I love you," and he said, "I love you, too, Kris. Goodnight."

I called the nurse back in ICU and gave her my home and work numbers, asking her to call me, any time day or night, if there was a frightening change, as I wanted to get in there and be with him if he went critical again. She promised me she would call.

The next day, I called Dan Kronstadt, my boss at WARNER BROS., and let him know I'd be late to work; that I was going to a hospital to be with a friend for a while and that I'd fill him in on details later.

I was with De four or five hours. The nurse and I gave him a bath. I was going to leave during his bath, but the nurse asked if I'd stay and help, so I asked De if that would be all right, and he said, "Certainly."

Afterwards, I went to their house and met the neighbor, Don, a lovely man just a day away from turning 85. He gave me their stacks of mail and we chatted for about 10 minutes. Then I went into the Kelley's house and did some chores. I made a pile of the important mail, including wills and hospital documents found on the table in the dining room, and put it in a box to take to De. I listened to and wrote down 15+ voicemails. Then I reported to work at Warner Bros. and confidentially told my boss the situation, asking him what my options were for helping De. Dan was a big STAR TREK fan growing up and the news that De was dying upset him. He told me I had carte blanche to do whatever I needed for De for as long as he needed me; that he'd do his best to hold my job for me until I got back. I told him I didn't think I'd be out very long, and that I wouldn't actually take the allowed one-month personal leave of absence until it became absolutely necessary. "If De gets out of the hospital, I will probably have to stay at his house with him, but he won't be getting out for a while, so I'll just work here and do for De at lunch time, evenings and weekends." Dan said that would work; then, with genuine sadness in his voice, he added, "I wish there was something I could do for De." Surprised and touched by the sentiment, I told him, "Dear man, you just *did*!"

Back at the hospital, the care giving to De began. He was an ideal patient and a good storyteller. He recounted times he and Carolyn had parakeets and what naughty things they had said. "A friend of ours had taught one of them to say, 'F— Hollywood!' while we were in New York…" He frowned, remembering, then added, "This little bit of information made its way into one of the Hollywood gossip columns!" I said, "I'll bet THAT made your return to Hollywood problematic!" He said, "It sure did!" and he scowled.

He was real tired, as they'd moved him from the ICU to the 4th floor that afternoon, so we wrote out only four checks and I outlined the next day's plan of attack for the rest of the bills, which he approved. Knowing he was exhausted, I left him as soon as he seemed ready to let me go and had run out of things to relate. I returned to his house to look for his missing wallet because we couldn't find it in his pocket when we tried to locate it to get his Medicare card and supplemental insurance card to photocopy. The nursing staff said they didn't have it and that it wasn't locked up, so I was getting a little frantic. Then De recalled that his friend John might have it. "John is the one who drove me in the night I came in, and I seem to recall that he may have taken it home with him." That relieved me somewhat, but I wasn't totally appeased, since De also said, "I was so 'out of it' with the pain when I got here to emergency that I couldn't even remember my home address when they asked me." By the time I got to his house, there was a message from him saying he had recalled John's phone number and called him, and that John had the wallet. Whew! What a relief!

When I got home there was a wistful voicemail from Carolyn. "Hello, Kris, this is Carolyn. I'm just calling to ask how you're doing and how De was doing. He sounded pretty good to me. Give me a call, please, when you have time. I know you're a busy girl. Bye-bye." I called and gave her a full report.

On March 17th I went straight to De's hospital and received instructions on what to take out to the accountant so that he could begin working on De and Carolyn's taxes. I went to the house, gathered the documents and drove them out to the gentleman, then stopped by their bank to deposit checks for De before returning to work at WB.

The next day I went to De's house to check on things, then to the hospital to find De sitting in a chair while 6 or 7 nurses scurried around trying to get things done for him. Then we set to work on his affairs.

We discussed my offer to become his full-time, around-the-clock assistant when he got out of the hospital. I told him I had cleared it with Dan, who said I could take a Leave of Absence, and that he had said he would try to hold my job for me. De listened carefully as I explained all the benefits: "I can drive you to your doctor appointments; take you to visit with Carolyn; do your shopping; work with your energy level whenever you want to work – even in the middle of the night, since we both have a tendency to get up and rattle around our respective places from 2 AM to 4 AM. Then when you get tired and want to rest, I'll be able to keep going and finishing whatever tasks you want done." He said, "That sure would be a wonderful thing; very helpful." He nodded his agreement and then said, "Would you call and tell Carolyn about this idea? You explain it so much better than I ever could." I said, "Sure, I will." He said, "Then tell her about it again when you go to visit her on Saturday, because she forgets things and needs to be reminded a lot." I said, "I certainly will."

De's friend John arrived just as we were finishing up. He had De's wallet. After just a few minutes of conversation, a nurse entered and ushered John and me out of De's room and pulled the "privacy" curtain, but then six nurses went in! Two said they wanted to help him change his hospital gown. De said he didn't need six nurses in attendance to change his gown, but not one of the nurses took the hint and left. Having been directed out of the room, I was in no position to protest the nurses' refusal to take the hint and step out. I felt acutely embarrassed for De's discomfort.

Eventually John and I got back into the room and I learned by listening to them, while putting lotion on De's legs, that on an earlier date, De had been separated from his car by policemen. He was on heavy pain medication and still trying to function without help – go places and do things by himself — and he was moving too slowly in traffic, so the officers stopped him and took him to the hospital when they determined he was ill. John and the next door neighbor went to the police station and claimed his car for him. THAT made me realize that he had NEEDED help for quite some time, but was just refusing to ask for it…

Not long after, De became weary again, so I kissed him and said, "You get some rest soon, okay?"

I called Carolyn and told her about the plan to become De's live-in assistant. "Oh, that would be terrific! Just wonderful! It would be such a help, and I wouldn't have to worry about him being there at home all alone." Then she worried, "But where can we put you? It's such a small place. There isn't any room for another bed…" Then she said, "Oh, we have a king size bed! You can sleep with De! You have my permission!" I laughed and said, "Carolyn, that's YOUR job. We'll find or make space for another bed." She said, "I know you will. You're a smart girl."

When I got back to work, I remembered my concern about De's "nursing fans" and called Carolyn to report to her about De's gawkers and asked her permission to "raise humane hell" at the nurse's station to be sure a repeat performance of the morning's antics would not be forthcoming. She agreed emphatically that I should do whatever was necessary to protect De's privacy, time and rest. I told her I'd go back that night, in person, and be sure I'd spoken to the head nurse. About an hour later, De called. He sounded pretty good, except at one point he got a bad twinge of pain. He told me to "take the night off and find out what REAL life is all about." I told him I had planned to come out to speak to the nurses about his need for rest, privacy, efficiency and solitude so he could recover and go home. He said he had already done that and that it was taken care of. I said, "Okay, but if it happens more, let me know and I'll be sure someone gets a report." He thanked me and then said, "But I really don't think it'll be necessary. They're leaving me alone pretty well this afternoon." I was glad to hear that.

I told him I wouldn't call that night because I didn't want to risk waking him, and he thanked me for the thoughtfulness. Then he said, "You have to decide what we should pay you for your help." I said, "De, I don't want you to pay me. As long as I remain employed at Warner Bros., there's no need. I'm just fine, unless we decide I need to take that Leave of Absence. THAT'S unpaid, and I'd need something then, just enough to meet my obligations." He said, "No, we want to pay you something. You decide what it should be, and write the check, and I'll sign it next time you come out." I sighed and said, "I don't have a blue clue." He said, "It's all new to me, too." I told him I loved him. He said, "I love you, too. See you later."

Toward the middle of the afternoon, De called again. His news was NOT good. He said, "This afternoon there has been a dramatic turn of events. The CT scan came back, and I have four new spots on my liver." I was devastated and said, "Oh, I'm so sorry." He said, "That makes two of us." Then he said, "In light of this new development, I think the smart thing for me to do would be to move out to Carolyn's facility. What's your opinion on that? I want to know." I was numb with grief over his announcement of the liver involvement, but managed to say, "Yes, I suppose that's best." I asked if he still wanted me to take a Leave of Absence so I could help him full-time, and he said, "Oh, yes, there's a lot to do and to think about… but I just won't be there at the house with you." I said, "That's okay. You're a good director. I can take instruction over the phone." He said, "Let's plan on that, then, okay?" I said, "You got it."

Carolyn called a little bit later to see if I'd heard the bad news about De. I said sadly, "Yes. I took a long walk after that here at work, you may be sure." She said, "Yes, I'll bet you did." I said, "Would you like me to come out to see you TONIGHT?" She said, "Do you want to?" I said, "Sure! I think we could BOTH use a hug." She said, "I guess so – but I have to tell you, I'm all cried out. I don't have a single tear left." I said, "That's okay." She said, "Okay, I'll see you tonight, then. I'm looking forward to it."

Before we hung up, Carolyn wanted a full report on how De was doing. I told her, "He's doing well. We got all the chores finished in real short order, so he could catch as much rest as possible." She said, "He told me how efficient you were last night, getting everything ready so that all he had to do was sign, sign, sign. You're a smart, sweet girl. We sure appreciate you. Thank you." I said, "It is I who want to thank YOU, for taking such a leap of faith and putting your trust in me." She said, "It wasn't much of a leap: We have known you for a long time and we know how much you love De—" I interrupted and said, "De and you BOTH!"

I prayed mightily over the situation – to be wise, swift and competent. I felt I could do a good job; I did for Mom. De wouldn't stop complimenting me on all I'd done so far, and on how smart I was.

I left work at about four and drove out to see Carolyn. I visited for about two hours. I said, "The best way I can describe how I feel about this is… I just hope that 30 or 40 years from now, when I'm in your shoes, there will be someone who loves me as much as I love the two of you, so that I won't even HESITATE asking them to lend a hand, because I'll know what a joy and pleasure it will be for them TO help, as it is for ME to help in this situation." She said, "I hope you get your wish and that someone is there for you when you need it."

When we finished visiting, at about 7:15 p.m., I called De at his hospital to let him know I was leaving. I asked if he wanted me to stop by on my way home. He was feeling violently ill and said, "No. I'm throwing up. You just go on home tonight. Next time you stop by, though, bring me about three pairs of socks, will you?" I said, "Sure." He said, "Thank you," and hung up fast; I could tell he was very uncomfortable and close to retching again.

On the way home, as I neared his hospital, I just felt, intuitively, that I should stop by anyway, even though I fretted that it might make De angry for having disobeyed. I went to his house and got the socks and drove them to the hospital. As I went up in the elevator, I started to get "cold feet" about disobeying his request to leave him alone, and instead decided just to drop the socks at the nurses' station. When I got to the nurses' station, there wasn't a single nurse on the floor, nor could I spot one in either of the two hallways. Then I noticed that De's call light was on. I hesitated only an instant before going in, as I knew he wouldn't be calling for help unless he needed it, and there was no nurse in sight to provide it.

I went into his room, and found him looking real nauseous. The head of his bed was elevated, but not enough: he was leaning too far back to be able to lean forward and grab the plastic pan someone had placed near his ankles, nor could he lean forward enough to expel any vomit that might be forthcoming. I said, "Hi, De. Can I help? There isn't a nurse on the floor at the moment." He said, "I feel lousy. I'm going to be sick, I think."

I went to his bedside and grabbed the plastic pan, placing it in his lap, at which time he began to retch. I put my arm behind him and pulled him forward so that when he vomited, it would be expelled readily. He was violently ill several times. As soon as I knew he was finishing, I grabbed a Kleenex and wiped his mouth and face, then handed him a new one so he could blow his nose. I commiserated, "The GOOD thing about throwing up is that you feel a lot better afterward!" He leaned back, relaxed a bit, and said, "That's right."

He still felt pretty lousy, so I started to press reflexology points in his hands, hoping to relieve the nausea. I heard several nurses at the nurses' station, so I asked De if he was all right for a minute while I went out to speak with them. He said he was.

I went out and told them what had happened and indicated that if I hadn't been there, he may well have aspirated the vomit and choked to death. They looked a bit unsettled by that. I went on to say that he still felt nauseous and I asked if they had something they could give him for it. One of the nurses said, "Yes, we were just talking about that." I said, "Will it be soon?" She said, "It will take a little while." I said, "In the meantime, do any of you know about the reflexology point for nausea, so I can help him in that way until the medicine is ready?" They hemmed and hawed and guessed for about fifteen seconds, and then I said, "Do you have a reflexology manual?" "No." "Do you have access to the Internet?" "Downstairs on the first floor." "Well, can someone go down there and look up reflexology points?" One said she could, and I said, "Thank you."

I went back into De's room and related to him that the nurses were working on getting him something for the nausea. He said feebly, "Good." I said, "In the meantime, I'm going to rub and press some reflex points on your feet and see if I can help limit the uncomfortable feeling you're having. Is that okay, or do you think it might make you feel worse?" He said, "No, I think it will be okay. It might make me feel better. I hope so." I re-positioned myself near his feet and started to deeply massage and press on areas on the underside of his foot, hoping to find the right spot. Sure enough (thank you, God!), I found the spot pretty quickly, and within a couple of minutes, I could see his rigid, uncomfortable body relax and his breathing become more normal.

"Go ahead and fall asleep if you can, sweetie. I'm right here. If you need help again, I can help. So don't worry." He said, "OK. Thanks." A few seconds later, he said, "I hated to put you through that [the vomiting]." I said, "You didn't put me though anything. I volunteered. You told me not to come by, remember?" He said, "I'm glad you did." I said, "So am I." (Amen, Lord!) Within a few minutes he had relaxed enough to fall into a light doze. About ten minutes later, two nurses came in and said they had IV medication that would help with the nausea. De roused at that time and said, "Good." I asked how long it would be before it would take effect, and they said, "Ten to fifteen minutes." I said, "The reflex points are working well, so he'll be okay until that stuff kicks in, I think."

At last he was truly asleep – so at close to 11, I decided I could risk going home, as long as I got a vow from a ward nurse that she would plant herself at the nurses' station just outside his room and watch him closely. I said, "Mr. Kelley is a very sweet man, and he won't even call for help unless he really needs it, because he hates to inconvenience anyone— so IF he calls for help, please consider it a real emergency and get right in there." She said, "I will. I promise." I said, "If you're short staffed tonight and can't be sure you'll be here to help, I will stay here in his room all night. I DON'T want him to be alone while he feels so lousy and is so dependent on someone to support him if he becomes ill again." She said, "I will watch him. There's no need for you to stay." I said, "Okay, thank you. I'll be back first thing in the morning." Just before leaving the hospital I whispered into De's room while he slept: "Goodnight, sweet prince." It made me cry, but it seemed a good way to ask the angels to keep a close eye on him.

The next morning, I got to De's hospital at 8 a.m. When I walked in, I heard him on the phone calling me rather urgently: "It's not terribly important. I'll get in touch with you a little bit later. Thank you." I immediately poked my head in and announced, "You rang?!" He laughed and said, "My God! Now, THAT'S service! You beamed right in!"

We discussed errands and chores, "Plus, there's the bedding, if you want to go to that trouble." I said, "Sure, no problem." He said, "You'll have to make the bed again." I said, "I think I can manage that!" He joked, "Good dog!" He mentioned he'd like me to find and buy him a new pair of thongs for the shower, as the ones he had at home were ratty.

On Friday I stopped by to see the Kelley's neighbor and pick up any mail. The moment Don opened the door, I asked, "Did you hear the news about De's new tumors?" He said, sadly, "Yes. I didn't sleep much last night." At that point, I got all teary-eyed. As he let me in the door, I embraced him and cried a little. I said, "It just tears me up!" He said, "It sure does. Me, too, doll."

We went in and sat down; he got me a tissue and I poured out all the now-defunct plans about De returning home and directing my steps so that he could have everything taken care of. Don spoke sweet thoughts and comforted me, saying he was so glad I was a friend of De's because he knew I'd handle anything De needed to have done so that he wouldn't feel so out of control. It made me feel better to realize I COULD still help tremendously as far as De's peace of mind went.

With errands run and De on his way to Carolyn's hospital I went back to work at Warner Bros. until 5:30 and then went home and called A.C., to give him an update on De. We spoke for a long time, and he expressed how happy and grateful he was that I was able to help, "because I know it will take a tremendous load off De's mind."

Carolyn called to say that De had a good afternoon after arriving and that he was very happy. I said, "Well, of course he is. He's back near his lady for the first time in what probably felt like forever." She said, "For him and me both." I said, "I know. I'm real happy for you. I'm a hopeless romantic when it comes to the two of you; you might as well know it, if you don't already!"

She said she wanted me to mail a new outfit of hers to her best friend, Florene, sometime when I got a chance. She gave me Florene's phone number and said that she and Florene were classmates and best friends in Seattle "all those years ago" and that they are very close to this day.

Some days later, De asked if I got the sheets done, and I said, "Yes!" and he chuckled. He said, "Carolyn tells me you decided what we'd pay you." I told him what we had discussed ($100 a week) and he approved it wholeheartedly. Then I said, "By the way, this first week is a freebie." He protested, "It was the worst week!" I said, "And you couldn't have kept me away with a team of horses. WB paid me all week and I don't need the money ... I can start the Leave Of Absence any time you say, but in the meantime I'll just report back to work and continue to help you part time until you tell me to go fulltime. How's that?" He said, "That sounds terrific. And listen: please tell Dan thank you for me. You've always told me what a great guy he is, but now I KNOW! I'm very touched by his generosity" — he began to choke up — "so you tell him for me, will you?" I said, "Sure."

At 9:30 that evening De called. He told me that A.C. had called from Santa Barbara to find out how he was doing. I said, "You're up late!" He said, "Yes, I am. I was asleep, but then the phone rang and then the nurse came in and woke me for something." I joked, "Oh, that's right. You can't get any sleep in a hospital!" He said, "Isn't THAT the truth?" He added, "But it's better here than it was at the other hospital."

My next mission was a new bathrobe. He said, "There's a store at Macy's – just outside Macy's – they had robes on sale when I was out there. I nearly bought one then. Take a look out there and see what you can find." I said, "Okay." He said, "Go ahead and write a check." I said, "I can't. I'm not a signer on your account. I'll put it on my debit card and then you can write me a check to reimburse me." He said, "Okay. That'll work." I said, "OR I can use the money in the money clip at your house. There's $101 in it." He said, "No, I want to keep some cash in the house." I said, "Okay. I'll do it the other way, then. No biggy." He said, "Thank you." I said, "On the off chance that I can't FIND a white robe, what color do you want?" He said, "I saw white ones there." I said, "I know, but things change and I'm trying to think of all contingencies so I know what to do in case. How about blue?" He said, "That's what I was going to say." I said, "To match your blue eyes, right?" He said, "You got it!" There was a big smile in his voice.

Carolyn called a few minutes later, wondering why I couldn't write a check for De's robe right out of their account. I explained to her that I'm not a signer on the account, and that if I could do such a thing, ANYBODY could. She said, "Oh, I guess that's right. You'll have to do it the other way, then." I said, "It's no problem. I have $800 in my savings account. I can 'float you a loan' for a day or so'!"

I went to Macy's on the 22nd and walked into the place I thought De was talking about in the mall. The least expensive white robe they had there was $99; the one I liked best – and thought De would like best – was $139! I asked the store manager if I could use the phone for a local call, and then called De. I told him, "I think I'm in the store where you saw the white robe." He said, "You are? Good." I said, "The thing is... what were you expecting to pay for this robe? I want to be sure we're on the same page, here!" He said, "It really doesn't matter." I hesitated and said slowly, "Okay – but the lowest price here is $99 and the one I think you'd like best is $139." He said, "Lord!" I said, "That's what I thought. I was thinking maybe $50 for a robe when I walked in here." He said, "That's what I had in mind, too." I said, "Okay, then, I'll go to Macy's and see what I can come up with that's closer to our plan." He said, "Do that. I hate to run you around." I said, "Don't worry about it." I asked if I should bring him some T-shirts and he said, "No, not at this time. Perhaps later." I went to Macy's and found a single white terry cloth robe there for $65, so I snared it.

The "things to do" list became poignant when De called again and asked if I would e-mail Mary Jensen and ask her to remove his addresses from her web site, as he was getting a lot of fan mail and wasn't going to be answering it much anymore. I said I'd be happy to do that. Then he asked me to write down the web site address because a nurse there wanted to access it from her computer. I said I'd print it out and bring it in. He said, "This morning when Carolyn was here for a visit, I pulled out that sweet angel pin card and poem you gave us. It touched us both deeply. We wanted you to know. You've almost got us believing in angels!" I said, "Almost?! I'd better try a little harder, then!" and he chuckled.

Tuesday March 23rd I saw De and Carolyn again for the first time in four days. De looked a lot better; he was gaining weight like gangbusters. I drove over in the Kelley's car and their neighbor Don rode along. He bragged to De upon arrival, "Not only is she a great gal and a hard worker, but she's a good driver, too!"

Don and De yakked a lot; Carolyn and I mostly just listened. Carolyn seemed rather depressed. With good reason, poor gal! I showed De the e-mail I had sent Mary asking her to take his addresses off her web site. He read it and proclaimed it "a beautiful letter; just right." He asked me to keep it for him. Carolyn read it and nodded her approval of its content.

De and I did the business stuff and he checked out and approved the robe I got him as well as the thongs. I joked, "You'd better like the thongs, or Don gets them!" De said, "They're MINE!" Don said, "Okay!"

After the visit, which lasted about 90 minutes, I dropped Don back at his house and went back to work after depositing the checks that De had signed. There were calls at work awaiting me from De's insurance agency and from his oncologist, asking for clarification on different issues.

On March 24th I called De early. He sounded half-asleep, so I asked if I had awakened him. He said, "Almost." I said, "Sorry, but this is important." He said, "I know it is." I told him that Allison at his insurance agency needed a retrofit inspection on the foundation of his house and said she knew someone who would do it for $75. I asked if I should have her go ahead, or if he knew someone who could do it. He said, "No, I don't know anyone. Tell her to go ahead and do it."

At noon I drove the retrofit check out for De to sign. I stopped first to visit with Carolyn. She was at the vanity in the bathroom applying face cream. She said she was in a lousy mood and didn't feel like visiting. I said OK and helped her back to her place near the bed, then got her a footstool and covered her legs and feet with a lap afghan a sweet nurse had made for her. I told her I'd go see De now, and she said, "Stop back by on your way out."

I went to De's room and found him asleep. I planned to let him sleep while I made out the check that he had to sign, but a nurse came in for some blood and woke him almost immediately. He spotted me in the chair and said, "Kris! I didn't know you were here!" I said, "I wasn't until about 20 seconds ago – just got my butt into the chair." He said, "Oh, that's good."

I got the signature. He asked the nurse for a pain pill. I could tell he was hurting even while he had been sleeping. He told me, "I had a shower, a walk and too much other stuff going on all morning. It wiped me out!" I told him I'd leave him alone and let him go back to sleep. He said, "No, sit here for a little while." So I sat where he could see me.

He asked if I'd bring his bottle of Clear Eyes and his hair spray next time I came out; he told me where to find them. I said, "Sure." He told me to toss the ratty old robe at home, now that he had a new one. I said OK.

I asked if he'd seen any of the Oscar telecast, and he said he'd caught parts of it. I mentioned Roberto Benigni's acceptance speech and how he COULD'VE fallen on Steven Spielberg when he balanced on the backs of chairs in his exuberance over winning.

That reminded De of the "biggest mistake I ever made in my career." Steven Spielberg had asked De to appear in a court scene early in his (Spielberg's) career. "Although it was a WONDERFUL scene, I turned it down. I regret it to this day. I didn't know who he was at the time; he didn't have much of a career yet, and it was such a small scene that I just felt it wasn't going to help much. What a mistake!"

De asked me to call and introduce myself to his attorney and give him my phone numbers. He asked me to be sure his accountant had my phone numbers, too. I said I would.

De's arms and legs looked rehydrated, and his weight was coming back. At about that time Dr. Kaaren Douglas, a visiting doctor and personal friend, came in and they visited for about 5 minutes. By then, De was visibly exhausted, so when the doctor left I kissed him and told him I'd leave so he could sleep.

I went back to Carolyn's room. She was in better spirits. She had me wheel her to the bathroom and after that we visited for quite a while. I did little things for her — adjusting a curtain and putting lotion on her exposed leg. She seemed hesitant to let me go, but she realized I had to get back to work. But I did NOT hurry out, telling her I had as much time as we needed for a good visit. So we talked about 15 minutes more and then lunch was served, so I took my leave.

I called the attorney and the accountant and left my phone numbers with them, as De instructed. The attorney and a consultant for the hospital were planning to take a trip out to see De the following Tuesday at 9:30 a.m. to get some paperwork signed. I told the attorney that De had a doctor appointment outside the hospital that week and that I'd call over to be sure their appointment times didn't conflict. He asked me to get back to him after I'd spoken with De.

A large part of my responsibilities entailed scheduling and cross-referencing the enormous number of things De needed to deal with. It quickly became apparent why the list of tasks had been a burden and a source of stress for him.

At one point Don wanted to know if Carolyn was provided for in case De didn't survive, and I assured him she was. He said, "Oh, that's good."

I got home after work and found a voice mail message from someone who wanted to interview me for being De's star polisher. I called and bowed out, politely. I didn't know what my schedule would be. If De planned to go home soon, I wouldn't have been able to get away, so I didn't want to make a commitment I might have to renege on later.

De was planning and wanting to get out of the hospital and go home, and every nerve and fiber of my being wanted it to work out that way for him eventually. Intuitively, however, I felt it was wishful thinking, unless he went home under Hospice care, with me as the live-in, around the clock assistant. I ordered a few reflexology manuals, in case he was able to go home, so I could keep him feeling well without drugs… or with as few drugs as possible.

I knew if he went home, I'd have to get some nutrition training from an expert at the hospital, to be sure he got enough supplementation (either by eating or via IV drip) to keep on keepin' on and to maintain his nice weight gain. On March 25th during a phone call, we celebrated his six pound jump to 104. "You're on the mend, boy!" I cheered.

He asked how the family was up north; had I heard from them? I said, "Not real recently." He said, "How the hell COULD you?! You've been out and about non-stop workin' for ME!" Then he said, "I thought you'd take today off and rest." I said, "No. I don't need to. I'm feeling good." I told him I got the hair spray and the eye drops. I asked if he wanted me to drop them by at noon the next day, and he said it wasn't necessary. He didn't want to run me around unnecessarily. "Just come out when you have more to do." I said, "Okay." Then I said, "You look wonderful with or without hair spray." He said, "You're prejudiced." I joked, "You think so?" He joked back, "You've got good taste, though!" I replied, "Damn' straight, I do!"

Then he said, "You sure have a wonderful boss." I said, "The best! He's at his desk right now. Would you like to speak with him?" De jumped at the chance and said, "Yes! I would!" So I told him to hold on while I transferred his call to Dan's line.

I ran in to Dan and announced, "Dan, pick up the phone! It's DeForest! He wants to talk to you!" Dan's eyes got real wide and he took a measured breath before he picked up.

Dan was tickled by the call. I closed his door more than halfway, so he wouldn't be interrupted, but listened to their conversation from just outside. De thanked Dan for the loan of his secretary and they discussed me briefly. I heard Dan say, "Yes, she IS wonderful." De said something else, and then Dan said, "Well, I'm happy to do it. And if there's anything else we can do – anything at all – just let me know. You've got it."

De was overcome by Dan's comments, so Dan put him on hold and had me pick up the line. De told me, "I have to hang up now. You two have me crying." I said, "*awwwww* Okay, sweetie. Talk to you later."

I went in and spoke with Dan right away. While he wasn't near tears, I could tell he was deeply touched and visibly moved. He said, "I felt like I was talking to a legend! I WAS – and it felt like it!" He said he was saddened to hear how weak De's voice sounded, and I told him, "It's worlds better than it HAS been – and, incidentally, just so you don't worry too much, his actual voice is very quiet and reserved normally, even when he's WELL. His stage-screen voice is projected a lot more than his normal voice."

Dan said he wished the whole world could know De's precarious health, "so he'd get the outpouring of love and affection that so many millions of people have for him." I told him I understood and concurred, but explained, "De's the kind of guy who would feel he should respond to each and every card, and he just doesn't have the time or the energy left; he has too much other stuff that NEEDS doing." I assured Dan, "De knows he's loved – he doesn't have a blue clue how MUCH, but he isn't exactly suffering from a lack of love or acknowledgment, either." Dan still felt it was sad that he wouldn't be shown. I offered, "Feeling the way you do, and being in on the fact that he's sick, it's okay for YOU to write him a note and TELL him what you think he needs to know about how well loved and respected he is." Dan said, "I think I'll do that this weekend."

After work I called De again to tell him he had affected Dan as much as Dan affected him. De said, "I didn't want to do that [cry], but he's such a lovely man, and said such lovely things, that I couldn't help it." I said, "Don't worry about it. It was terrific, and the feeling was mutual."

He told me his IV bottle of blood leaked while he was reading the newspaper and he looked down and saw the bed awash in blood! "My first thought was, 'Sweet Jesus! I'm bleeding to death!' I called for help, and the attendant came in and assured me it was BOTTLED blood, not my own! Boy, was I relieved!" I said, "I guess!" He said, "I was going to call and tell Carolyn, but she's so upset these days I'm afraid she'd get it wrong and start to panic. So I'm not going to tell her, and don't YOU tell her, either, okay?" I said, "Okay."

I called Carolyn after that and we chatted for about 20 minutes. She asked me to buy her a new bottle of DIORESSENCE at Macy's the next time I was out and about and had a chance. I said I would.

On March 26th I went to visit De to take him the eye drops and hair spray he had been waiting for. I put lotion on his arms in profusion; had to wipe some off afterwards (got a little carried away, as his skin wasn't absorbing it the way it was earlier in his convalescence).

De mentioned my boss again – or tried to – and then said, "This is crazy! Every time I mention your boss, I start to cry!"

I said, "It's okay. You affected him, too!"

He said, "It's getting really awful! (tears were brimming, but he was grinning) "I cry every day over something!"

I said, "That's wonderful – good and sweet and decent and perfectly okay! Don't worry about it. You have a lot of love inside and it's okay when it leaks out!"

He handed me the piece of cake from his lunch tray and said, "Eat this. I saved it for you." I asked, "Share your fork?" He said, "Sure." I put two bites into my mouth and then he asked me, "Are you gaining weight, or losing it?" I said, "I'm LOSING it – and THIS isn't helping!" He grinned.

He mentioned a new drug the doctors were thinking of using on him – to starve the tumors of blood so they couldn't grow anymore. He said he had a doctor appointment on Monday to discuss it.

A volunteer came in then and mentioned that De had requested a milk shake earlier. De said, "Yes." I amended, "He'd prefer a MALT, if you have that instead." She said, "I don't have malts, I'm afraid." De said, "A milk shake is FINE, dear. My assistant should sit idly by and be still!" I flinched (for comic effect) and said, "Yes, sir!" De looked at me, wondering if he had hurt my feelings, and said, "I was joking, Kris. You know that, don't you?" I assured him, "Yes, De, I do." The volunteer said, "The milk shake will be my own concoction, but I think you'll like it." De said, "I'm sure I will."

He mentioned that he hoped he wasn't appearing cranky as a result of all that had been happening to him. I said, "Not at all." He said, "I hope not. Sometimes it's hard, you know?" I said, "If you want to be cranky, do it. I won't take it the wrong way. It's real normal to feel like throwing things when stuff like this happens." He said, "I don't want to do that." I said, "But if you DO, it's okay. It helps you deal with it. You can't hold it all inside. That's no good for you at all." He pondered that but didn't say anything more about it. He was never short or snappish in my presence, not once.

He was getting tired, so he asked me to tell Carolyn he was going to write a letter and then he'd be over afterward. I said, "Okay, sweets. You have a great day and I hope you get some rest." I mentioned that I had written him a little book and that I was leaving it on the tray for him, "For when you feel up to reading it." He said, "Okay, honey. Thanks."

On March 26th De called at 7:30 in the evening and momentarily scared the stuffing out of me! He said, "I don't want to alarm you, but do you have Dr. Shaw's phone number there with you?" My heart went into Red Alert, but I tried to remain calm in my voice. I said, "Yes, I do. It's out in the car." He said, "Oh, I don't want to make you do that." I said, "It's only a few steps out and back, De." He said, "Well, okay." I said, "I'll go get the address book and call you right back."

I flew to the car, got the address book, and returned his call. He said, "I just want to call him and see what time he's coming out today." I queried, "Today? You mean Saturday?" He said, "No, I mean today… this morning." I said, "It's night time, De." De said, incredulously, "It is?! Oh, my God, it is! I wonder if Carolyn knows that? We were wondering what time her doctor would be here to visit with us! We thought it was MORNING!" He chuckled. I reassured him, "Being in the hospital can do that to a person's time sense, for sure. It happened to me and it happened to Mom. It's real normal." He laughed heartily and said, "Wait until I tell Carolyn!" Then he said, "YOU probably think I've lost my ever-lovin' MIND!" I said, "Nope. Not at all. I've been with you, so I know your mind is just FINE. And as I say, it's real normal when you've been confined in a hospital to lose track of days and nights. I'm just relieved you aren't calling him TONIGHT, in an EMERGENCY. That was my FIRST thought!" He said, "We're fine." Then he chuckled. "I'm sorry for the call." I said, "Don't be. It gives me a chance to tell you goodnight and I love you." He said, "Goodnight to you," and we hung up.

On my next visit De was in a VERY chatty mood. I was there with him for over three hours. We talked about A.C's bluntness. I told him what A.C. had told me the morning he called to tell me about him: "De's dying." De said, "He has always been that way. When I fell off a horse, he'd come rushing over in a sweat and ask me a dozen times, 'Are you all right? Are you SURE you're all right!?' I'd say, 'Yes, A.C. I've fallen off horses before; I'll fall off them again. I know what OK is, and I'm OK.' He'd say, 'I'm worried about you, De.' I'd say, "Then go somewhere else and worry about me, will you?""

He told me the history of his tumors. I put the Internet articles re new tumor therapies into his shirt pocket after he got a look at them and decided he did want to share them with his off-site oncologist. I asked him to find out the name of the new drug so I could research it on the Internet when I was at work. He said he would.

We talked about his important meeting on Tuesday with his attorney, accountant, and consultant. He decided I should drive over and sit in on that. I said, "If there are things you want to discuss privately with them, you can kick me out and I'll go visit with Carolyn until you want me back."

He said, "I trust you completely, and I have told David [the attorney] I do, but he had three clients who were burned by people who had access to their accounts, and I pay him to protect me, so I'd better do as he says." He added, joking, "I told him that you might hurt somebody ELSE, but you certainly wouldn't hurt ME!" I assured him, "I think anyone who would do anything like that should be strung up by whatever part of their anatomy would hurt the worst." He said, "I agree."

He talked about all the gifts and stuff in the garage. "A LOT of it is from you. Every other box says 'gift from Kris,' I think!" I told him he had another box from Viacom, too. He said, "Yes, I know. Unopened." I said, "It's open NOW. I looked in it." He said, "Find anything worth looking at?" I said, "There's a McCoy doll in there I wouldn't mind adopting." He said, "You got it."

At one point he drank some water and then told ME to have some: "Hydrate your ovaries!" he joked. I looked at him, incredulous, as he laughed and then he asked, "Do you still have your ovaries?" I said, "Unfortunately, yes, and they're a damned nuisance! I'm not using the parts, so I don't know why I have to pack them around!" He chuckled at that.

When he asked me again about my weight (for the second time in as many days), I reminded him that I'd had intestinal bypass surgery and STILL am packing too much weight around, although I eat normal or sub-normal portions. He said, "Oh, that's right. I'm sorry. Here I am questioning you about your weight, and you have done absolutely everything you can about it. It isn't fair." I said, "I have the reverse problem that you have. You can't keep it on; I can't get rid of it. Either way, it's a struggle." He said, "It sure is." I said, "Now I just exercise to stay fit. If I manage to lose some weight, it's just cream on the coffee. That isn't my aim, and when it happens, it's always a surprise." He said I should write a book about my intestinal bypass experience. "I think a lot of people would be interested in the story regionally. And if it goes, you can write others." I said, "It would be quite a story, all right." He said, "It sure would." He told me he had read my little book (the one I left for him and Carolyn recently) and was very touched by it. "It's very sweet." I didn't respond to that, except to nod.

He mentioned two doctors who had written him recently, asking him to attend important events in their lives, where they would be receiving awards. They wanted him to be there because his portrayal of Dr. McCoy had inspired them to enter the profession. De said, "One of them is a gastroenterologist! Naturally I had to turn them down, but when I told MY gastroenterology doctor about the invitation, he recognized the name of the doctor who was being honored and about flipped! He said, 'Here I am taking care of you, and one of your biggest fans is FAMOUS at what I do for a living!" De laughed, and I said, "You should call him back and tell him to get his butt out here and take care of you!" De grinned and said, "I should! But it would hurt my present doctor's feelings. I can't do that. He's wonderful, too."

When he started to look a bit weary and the topics were pretty well exhausted, I said, "Before I let you go for the day, you left me a voice mail earlier today asking me to put lotion on your upper legs and inner thighs." "Oh, yes!" he recalled. "I need it. I called to remind you to do that, because I keep forgetting to ask when you're here."

I got out the lotion and first put it on the usual areas — his arms and lower legs and feet; then I did his upper legs and inner thighs. While it soaked in, we talked a little more – about his love for Carolyn, my folks' marriage, my reason for never marrying... As I applied lotion and massaged it in, he mentioned how comfortable he felt with me doing that. I said, "Oh, good. I feel comfortable about it, too. I should have done this as a career." He said, "Yes, you should. I've always wondered how people can do something like this day after day." I said, "I'm sure it has to be a calling more than a career. People who are attracted to this kind of service are nurturers, pure and simple." He said, "Yes, I have come to that conclusion, too."

After I had him well "lubed," I bid him adieu and went over to see Carolyn again. She said I looked flushed, and I said, "I am. It's HOT over there!" She said, "It is?" I said, "Well, it's WARM, and I was massaging lotion into De for about ten minutes, so THAT added to the energy expenditure – which always shows on my face!"

I didn't stay long there, as I had additional "chores" to accomplish before six and I had to go by the house and switch cars before I did that. I told her, "I love you," and she said, "Well, that's nice. I LIKE you." She thought about that and said, "I can't say love." I said, "You only love De, right?" She said emotionally, "That's right." I said, "I understand. When you love the very best, all there is, is all the rest." She said, "Right. I'm glad you understand." I said, "I do." Once again, I felt a twinge. The impending loss would be hardest on Carolyn. She had given her heart exclusively to De. Life would never resume its normal shape again for her, if she lived to be 110.

I drove to the Kelley's house and switched cars, then realized I had left the checks that De had signed back at the hospital, so I drove back and walked into De's room looking "guilty." There were no checks there on the table, but he knew what I was looking for and said, "The checks are with

Carolyn. You left them there." I joked, "One little mistake!" Then I remembered something I'd been thinking about in the car. I turned back to De and said: "Oh! About your attorney and his concern regarding my integrity or intentions: I'll willingly submit to a polygraph test every week or month, since he's worried about it, if it'll ease his mind." De said, "Oh, no, no… If that comes up, I will handle it. Don't even mention it." I latched onto De's blanket-covered feet for emphasis and reiterated my feelings: "De, he's a great lawyer. I love him four times as much as I ever thought to before, to know he's protecting you. I'd much rather have him NOT trust someone who's trustworthy than to trust someone who isn't, and really – he doesn't know me from Adam. He's doing ABSOLUTELY the right thing for you." He said, "I know."

On March 28th, De called to ask me, "When will you be out again?" I said, "I guess Tuesday, unless you have something for me to do before then. I don't want to just drive out and visit. I figure you need rest more than you need visitors." He said, "I don't consider you a visitor." I guessed that meant he wanted me out there, so I asked, "Do you want me to come out today, or tomorrow at lunch time?" He said, "Why don't you come out today?" I said, "I'd love to." He said, "How soon will you be here?" I said, "About an hour and fifteen minutes. Have a nap until then." He said, "I will." I said, "I'll give your back a loofah scrub when I get out there." He said, "Okay." I said, "I look like a street urchin at the moment. I just walked with my next door neighbor and am in jogging pants and a ratty shirt. I'd better change before I drive out." He said, "I don't care how you look." I said, "Maybe YOU don't, but they might not let me in the door when they got a look at me, so I'm going to play it safe and change." He said, "I guess you're right. SHOW A LITTLE RESPECT AROUND HERE." I said, "Yes, sir. See you in about an hour."

I took a quick shower and then drove out. I got there thirty minutes early, so stopped at Carolyn's room. She was in a great mood and wanted to visit, so I stayed for forty minutes. Then she said I'd better go over and see what De wanted, so I told her I'd be back afterwards.

I went over to De. He was still asleep. I woke him and it took a while for him to "get with it." I got a warm cloth and he washed his face with it. I pulled out the loofah scrub and wash and also the aromatherapy spray I had bought and sprayed that into the middle of the room.

He reiterated that he wanted me to attend Tuesday's meeting. I assured him I would. We discussed his upcoming doctor appointment outside the hospital and I asked if he'd like me to fax the Internet information over that he was going to hand carry to the doctor. De said, "That's a great idea. Then he'll have it ahead of time and be able to look at it before we get there." I asked, "Do you want me to go with you to your doctor appointment?" He said, "Why not?" I said, "Okay. I can help you remember what was said; take notes, ask questions." He said, "That's right. Yes, we can meet there." I said, "Be sure and let me know the exact time and address ahead of time." He said, "I will."

He got nostalgic and started to tell me about a number of people who had been pressuring him to let them write his biography. He said, "I know you wanted to do it, too." Then he said, "I'm going to tell you where, in the garage, my history IS. I'm going to let you know where EVERYTHING is, in case something happens to me." He said he kept letters from Jake Ehrlich, the lawyer he portrayed in 333 Montgomery Street, and that there were scrapbooks starting in 1945, perhaps even earlier, which would chronicle his career. He said, "I graduated from high school at 16." I said, "I know, De." He said, "Oh, that's right. You do! So, enough about me; what do *you* think of my career?!" He laughed at his own joke, and so did I. He said, "There are important papers – not many – in a safe deposit box at the bank." I asked, "Does your will detail who gets this stuff?" He said, "Not much of it." He said, "You can have the historical stuff regarding my career." I protested, "Not NOW!" He said, "No, not yet. I just want you to know where it is, in case I get incoherent later and can't tell you. There's a lot of private, personal, sentimental stuff in there…" I said, "I'll bet." He sighed. "You can use it however you choose. I never agreed to let anyone else do a book because I felt I couldn't contribute to it…"

He got up at one point, saying he had to use the bathroom. I stood very near him in case he became weak and needed an assist as he used the walker to get into the bathroom, then I went out to the nurses' station to let them know he was in the bathroom and would be there for a while. I asked if they'd change his bedding since he was up. They said okay and the head nurse came in and we changed it. Once during the process, the nurse called in to De, "De, how you doing?" He said, "I'm doing wonderfully. How YOU doing?" She went in to assist him toward the end and stood by as he got himself back out to the bed. I said, "Before you get back into bed, De, will you just sit at the edge of it for a few minutes, so I can get your back washed and oiled." He said, "Certainly." The nurse started to leave and De joked, "I don't know if I can trust this girl! Perhaps you'd better stand by here and keep an eye on her!!" I heaved a fake sigh of exasperation, and he chuckled.

As I cleansed and then oiled and massaged his back, he continued joking in the vein started with the nurse. "Carolyn would say this was improper activity for you to be doing, you know." I dead-panned, very nurse-like, "*Please* be sure and let her know I am not a sexual predator and that I respect your marriage." He joked, "I will have to!"

I helped him back into bed by lifting him, and he mentioned how strong I was. I said, "I lifted Mom completely, and she weighed 145." He said, "My God, you ARE a strong little shit!" Then he practically did a soliloquy on my wonderful mother. He said, "I knew the minute I laid eyes on her that she was a beautiful woman. She was a wonderful, wonderful soul." He asked where she's buried, and I said, "She isn't. She was cremated, at her request. She said if there was such a thing as reincarnation, she wanted to come back as one of my pets! She also said that she didn't care what we decided to do with her ashes, but that she wanted PART of them to be next to Deaken's in my bedroom, so I did that." I paused and then went on, "I didn't know if I'd like it, but it's okay with me… doesn't bother me… because I know it's what she wanted, so her spirit can keep a close eye on me." He said, "She was pure love, wasn't she?" I said, "Yes, and I always marveled at it. She did NOT have an easy life or an easy life partner, but by golly she understood him and stayed by his side from beginning to end. They were beautiful together at the end. I understood THEN – and ONLY then – what they had going. It never looked like much until Mom got sick."

De became weary and I said I'd go back and visit with Carolyn for a while. He said I should go in and joke to her, "Sorry I can't stay, Carolyn; gotta run!" I said I could NEVER joke with her like that: it might hurt her feelings. He said, "If she said, 'Goodbye!' you'd know she wanted you to go!" I said, "And if she DIDN'T, I'd feel like a heel for treating her that way." He smiled and said, "I think you should do it. I think she'll BEG you not to run off." I said, "I'd rather find that out another way, if it's all the same to you." He smiled, "Okay."

Then he said, "Oh, one more thing. This kissing business." He took my hand and said, "I don't want to hurt your feelings, but WE don't kiss anyone on the lips except each other, and she got into a tizzy because you kissed her on the lips." I said, "Okay, I won't." He said, "Kissing cheeks is fine, though." I said, "I'm surprised, though. I leaned over her chair to kiss her on the lips, and she leaned forward with a big grin and kissed me right back!" He said, "She DID?!" I said, "She did! Twice!" We kissed each other simultaneously on the cheek and I sprayed the aromatherapy into the air and told him to enjoy his nap. Then I went back over to Carolyn's and sat with her for almost two hours. She was in the mood for a chat and for a companion while she watched a special on Carole Lombard.

Soon after the show finished, De came ambling over, rejuvenated and in fine spirits, and started to pretend he was perturbed by absolutely everything – his nurse, Carolyn, me. He sounded like McCoy quarreling with Spock! It was VERY cute and very entertaining! His nurse said, "If you're going to start arguing, I'm leaving!" Carolyn said, "I don't argue with De!" I said, "Neither do I! I'm outta here!" De said, "It's about time! Gawd Awmighty, I thought you'd NEVER leave!"

I drove to their house, got the account information and picked two lemons from their tree to take to De on Tuesday. Then I visited with Don for nearly an hour, until it was pitch black outside and I was very weary and hungry. I excused myself and drove home.

On March 29th I was at work. At close to 11:30 I called De to see how he was doing. He said he'd had a bad night and a pretty lousy morning again – "I threw up a few times." I said, "Oh, I'm sorry to hear that." He said, "I'm feeling better now, though, thankfully." I said, "I'm calling to ask if you're okay there until the meeting tomorrow, or if I should drive over." He said, "Why don't you drive over – unless it's a real drag." I said, "It's never a drag. It's a delight. I'll get in the car right now and be there in – oh, about 40 minutes, unless the traffic is bad." He said, "If the traffic is bad, just forget it." I said, "It should be fine – it's still early."

I arrived wearing a copper penny shirt and brown slacks, and he commented on how nice I looked in it. Then he said, "You HAVE been losing weight. When you walked in just now, I could see it." I said, "It's about time. Over the winter, no matter how active I stay, the weight just stays on." He said, "I know all about that. People become bears – really pile on the grub for their hibernation." I said, "Then springtime comes along and the weight starts to drop off – thank God!"

I told De how good he looked with his weight coming back and his skin re-hydrated and glowing. I asked if he wanted me to wash his back again, and he said he did. "I'll sit up straight in a little while, and you can do that."

It was such a beautiful day that I asked De if he'd like me to throw the door open for a while. He said, "Yes, let's get some fresh air in here. I love fresh air." I opened the door.

The nutritionist came in and surveyed De on his meal plans. He said he'd had a rough night, throwing up, and couldn't even THINK about eating yet. He also mentioned to her that he had asked for two soft-boiled eggs that morning and a blueberry muffin, but all that had been delivered was the muffin "and there was no one nearby to ask about it". The nutritionist said, "I need to know when things like that happen, De." I reminded De, "That's what your call button is for." De said, "Everyone here is so busy, I hate to stop them for something so small." The nutritionist said, "That's NOT small. Call."

De said he thought the supplemental nutritional drink was too rich and that's what made him ill, "possibly." The woman asked if he'd had other bouts of nausea, and he said, "I did once, at the other hospital. I don't think they ever decided what caused it." I reminded him, "Yes, they did, De. They had found your potassium level real high and had given you something to bring it down. They SAID it might make you sick to your stomach, and sure enough!" De said, "That's right. I remember that now. It's a good thing you were along for the ride, Kris! I don't know my own story well enough to relate it!"

The nutritionist asked how often I was at the hospital visiting De, and I said, "Oh, every day or every other day, usually." She said, "That's good." De said, "It sure IS! She has all the information you need stored in that computer brain of hers!"

I asked her if De could have Sustacal or Boost if I went out and bought it for him. She said, "Certainly." De said, "No. You have enough on your plate already. You don't need to be driving around doing that." I said, "De… there's a Sav-On right across the street from here. It'll take ten minutes, max." He said, "It really isn't necessary." I said, "If it'll keep you from getting sick, it IS necessary… and I'm going to do it." De then mentioned he'd like to have a mixed fruit plate. "They have wonderful ones at Ralph's or Gelson's." The woman said that would be fine.

At one point, the nutritionist was quizzing him on what he wanted as far as palatable meals – what sounded GOOD to him. De responded, "FREEDOM sounds good to me! I want FREEDOM!" The woman said, "You and me, both!" De joked, "When I get out of here, we'll go lay on the beach together!" and grinned. She said, "You bet we will."

After the woman left, I told De I'd run over and get the drinks at Sav-On and be right back. He said, "Okay." I went over to Carolyn's room momentarily and told her I was on a mission to get Sustacal and Boost for De across the street, and asked her if she wanted anything. She said, "No, but would you open the door to the outside before you leave?" I said, "Sure!" I did that and then drove over to Sav-On.

When I got back to De's room, I cleared off the table. He again mentioned the book I had written him and Carolyn and said he'd read most of it.

Carolyn called and asked De if he'd send me over to wheel her over to his room for a visit. He said, "Certainly. Kris, please go yonder and bring my lovely here." I said, "Yes, sir!" and walked over and fetched Carolyn. When I got her to the room, she stood and leaned over and kissed De, then settled down and put her foot on his bed to elevate it.

De was confused as to what day it was. He thought it was still Sunday, so he was surprised when I said, "I'd better head back to work." He said, "You didn't tell me you were at work when you called." I joked, "Do I have to tell you EVERYTHING?!" He said, "I guess not!" I said, "I only work for YOU part-time at the moment, remember?" He said, "Yes, I do." I said, "A new employee is starting today, so I need to be there this afternoon to show him the ropes and get him settled in." De said, "You'd better go do that, then." I said, "Yep… much as I'd rather be here, duty calls." I kissed them both and left.

On March 30th I got to De's room at 8:45 a.m. in case I needed to "rouse" him before the attorney and consultant arrived. I DIDN'T; he was wide awake and in his white robe, having just finished breakfast. He said he'd had the best night's sleep since this whole ordeal began.

I cleared off his tray table so there was room for paperwork, then put lotion on his arms and legs since I had skipped doing them the day before. While I was applying lotion to his legs and massaging it in, De pondered with a fond smile, "I wonder if your dear mother is sitting somewhere right now watching these goings-on and saying, 'Never, in a hundred years, would I have imagined Kris one day putting lotion on DeForest's feet and legs!'" I laughed and said, "Probably!" De chuckled. He added, "I'm not a praying man normally, but I sure did pray for your mother." I said, "It worked! Thank you!"

When the associates arrived, the three of us (without De) went to Carolyn's room with her will and power of attorney papers so she could sign them. The attorney had added several items to Carolyn's will because she had hand-written in several items she wanted to give to long-time friends. De saw the additions and figured she wanted them added. The Durable Power of Attorney threw her for a loop. She asked if she could be wheeled over to De's room and be with him while she signed it. We said, "Certainly!"

I wheeled her over to De's room and propped her broken leg on his bed. The gentlemen explained the document carefully… At one point, De told them, "Wherever Bette or Anne have rights or responsibilities in the documents, I want Kris to be listed, too." At first the attorney objected, thinking the situation would very likely become unmanageable with three people in the decision-making process. De said, "No, I just want them to be successive choices; if Bette can't serve, and Anne can't serve, then Kris can." The attorney asked me if I was all right with that, and I said, "Yes. Whatever De wants is fine with me."

At that point De made it a point to tell the attorney and the consultant, "I want you both to know that I trust this woman (indicating me) completely. She is completely honest and straightforward. If you have anything to tell me, you can tell me through her and I will know I got the message exactly as you intended it. She's a gem, and I trust her with all my affairs." The men nodded in my direction and I nodded back silently.

Carolyn was confused and a bit upset by the news that De might get well enough to return home. She thought he was a permanent resident now, in the same way she was. The men didn't seem to be able to explain this to her, so I tried, and succeeded. I told her, "At the moment, the doctors don't know if De will get well enough to go home, but if he DOES get that much better, he can't stay here under Medicare coverage, which is paying for him now; he'll have to go. If he stayed, the costs of his remaining here as a resident would fall to you two, the way the costs of your residency are being charged to you NOW."

Understandably, she wanted him to stay near her so she remained silent and I knew she was upset. De assured her, "I'll always be stopping by, the same as I always have." She didn't say anything. It was heartbreaking. I knew EXACTLY where she was coming from. She was caught in a no-win situation. If he was able to go home it would mean she would see him less; if he stayed at the hospital, it would mean he was dying – but at least she would be at his side as she had for half a century. My heart went out to her.

I kissed De and Carolyn goodbye and went to their house, made a few phone calls on Kelley-related business, and then went back to work. De phoned me at work and asked me to help him recall what had transpired during the signing earlier in the day. I repeated the MAJOR points, refreshing his memory, and then I said, "Gee, I went from just being an assistant and a temporary helpmate to having some responsibility for you and your estate, if the other two ladies can't serve." He said, "Yes, you did." I said, "I'm not particularly AFRAID of the responsibility, and am happy to do it; I DO wonder how we let the banks know about your decision to let Bette, Anne or me write checks on your accounts if you can't or aren't here to do it. Is that something the attorney does, or do we?" De said, "I think the Durable Power of Attorney takes care of that, but remind me in the morning again, and I'll call David to find out for sure. It's a good question — and one that requires an answer." I asked if he had eaten and he said, "Nothing tonight, but I ate breakfast and a good lunch." I said, "Oh, that's good. You can 'eat' via the drip for dinner!" I wished him another restful night and told him, "I love you." He said, "I love you, too, Kris."

On March 31st Carolyn called later in the morning while I was away from my desk and left a voice mail message saying that De didn't sound or feel well. She asked me to call her back, so I did. As soon as she picked up the phone and said, "Hello," a nurse came into her room with a message from De. I said, "Go ahead and get the message. I'll wait."

I heard the nurse telling her that De was about to have a blood transfusion, so not to call him; that he'd call her back when it was over and he felt better. She said okay.

I told her I had heard the message and that I wouldn't call or visit that day unless De called later to tell me to come in, as I wanted him to be able to rest as much as he wanted. We talked about the previous day's events. Carolyn said, "It was tiring for him and emotional for me." I said, "I think it was BOTH for ALL of us — emotional and tiring. Emotion IS tiring!" I added, "I have Friday off – Good Friday," and she said, "Oh, good, you can rest. You need it: you've been SO busy!" I said, "But it's been a GOOD busy, and I'm loving it, so don't give it another thought. I can come visit or work any day you want over this long weekend, for as LONG as you want me there." She said, "That's up to De. You need to relax some, too."

She mentioned being anxious about De. When she said, "He's getting a blood transfusion now," I said, "He gets those occasionally." She said, "He does? I didn't know that. Why?" I said, "I'm not really sure. I didn't ask. But YOU can ask his nurse." She said, "They won't tell me anything." I said, "Sure they will."

She was feeling frantic about De. I said gently, "Sweetie, that doesn't help and it HARMS you. Try to occupy your mind with pleasant thoughts instead of imagining those damned worst case scenarios." She said, "Easier said than done." I said, "I know. It happens to me, too, but then I remind myself I'm IMAGINING things, and that things are certainly a lot better at the moment than I've been fearing for him all along. I think of my own downer thoughts as an unhappy nuisance that will pass if I'll just allow it. I'm sure you'll relax and enjoy the thoughts that he's doing okay – BETTER than okay, in fact. He's even having some FUN! You should visit more often, and see."

That night in my journal, I wrote, "When De's feeling really lousy, I don't know whether to go out and hold his hand and rub his feet or to leave him alone. I'll ask him, so I KNOW. He liked it when I rubbed his feet at the other hospital when he was sick. (It helped him relax and fall asleep.)"

At nearly 5 p.m., De called. He said, "I'm calling to check up on you." I said, "I'm glad you did, because that way I can check up on YOU!" He said, "I'm doing better. I got a blood transfusion today. I had a couple of bad nights there. I'm going to call Carolyn in a minute and see if she wants you to bring her anything from home." I said, "I ask her that almost every time I'm out there, and she always says, 'No'." He said, "When I was visiting, she always said that, too. She'd say, 'No, I have everything I need right here, thank you.'" Then he told me, "If you ever feel the need, fall into bed at our house and sleep there, rather than driving home tired after a busy day." I said, "I haven't been there enough yet to feel the need, but if I do, it's good to know. Thank you."

I asked him if I should drive out the next day or give him another day off, and he said, "No, I think you should work out there for Dan tomorrow. I don't want to take advantage of his generosity." I said, "Tomorrow is my last day of work there for three days. Friday is a holiday – Good Friday." He said, "Oh, in that case, for SURE go to work tomorrow. We can catch up on Friday and through the weekend." I said, "Okay, but IF you need anything tomorrow, or just want a visit, don't hesitate to let me know. It's only a short distance, and I can come out during my lunch break without any problem at all." He said, "Okay, I'll remember that."

When I got to work, De called me again. He asked if I'd bring in four more photos, plus his white pen and two more manila envelopes when I returned. I said, "Sure. Which photos do you want?" He said, "Two cowboys and two straight." I was confused by the terminology and inquired, "Two cowboys and two – McCoys?" He said, "No, two cowboys and… two straight." I said, "Straight. I don't get it… OH! You mean two DE's – studio shots of you as YOU!" He said, "That's right. You got it." I said, "I'm learning new terminology, here!" He chuckled at that. I added, "Okay! I'll bring them!"

I asked him, "When I come by tomorrow at close to noon, do you want me to bring you a fruit plate from Ralph's?" He said, "It sounds good NOW!" I said, "But it may not sound as good tomorrow. I'll call just before I drive out from your house and see if it still sounds good, because as you know, it won't LAST if you don't eat it right away." He said, "You're right! Good thinking, Ollie!"

On April 2nd I called De at about 9 to let him know I was on my way out the door on the way to his place. I asked how his night had gone, and he said, "Pretty well!" I said, "You sure SOUND good!" He said, "This sounds silly – they'll think I'm about to go out over the wall! – but will you bring me the new green corduroy trousers that are in my bathroom closet?" I said, "Sure! How are you feeling about a fruit plate this morning? Still interested?" He said, "Yes. Get a little one, though. You know my appetite." I said, "I'll get the smallest one that has a good variety." He confirmed, "Yes, do that."

I drove to their house and looked for the photos I thought De wanted. Problem was, when I surveyed the selection, I noticed there were very few non-McCoys left, so I grabbed some of them, plus a few of De with motion picture information printed on them, hoping they were in line with what he wanted. Then I drove to Ralph's for the fruit plate.

When I got to De's room, I called out, "Knock knock!" He responded enthusiastically, "Come in! Come in!" I stepped into the room. He was lying in bed with his hospital gown draped solely over his midsection! Surprised but grinning, I exclaimed, "Well, hello there, gorgeous!" He laughed. He said he'd just been up visiting Carolyn and when he got back he felt something warm and looked down and found himself covered with blood again! I said, "That damned bottle!" He said, "Yes." I said, "Well, just be glad it's the bottle and not YOU!" He said, "I certainly am!"

Then I noticed spots of blood on one of his suede moccasins from the earlier incident with the leaking bottle. We had asked the nurse if it could be laundered (as his robe was being laundered that morning). She said she didn't know how, so De suggested I take it to a shoe shop and see what they could do with it. I said I would, and asked if there was anything else he could think of for me to do at their house. He said, "Would you vacuum the carpets in each of the closets?" I said, "Sure, I'd be happy to." He said, "There are shoes and other things on the floor in the closets; you'll have to pull them out first." I said, "That's no problem."

A nurse came in and said she was sorry I had walked in on a "naked" man; she hadn't known anyone was on the way in. I said, "Well, I SAID 'Knock knock', and he SAID 'Come on in!' so in I came! What the hell!" She joked, "Typical of ANY man!" De laughed.

She said she was going to find him a gown that snapped, and took off. I said, "Before she comes back, and while you're totally exposed, I should put lotion on you!" He said, "Yes, go ahead."

His skin was very dry again. His chest had never been done and it was caked with the iodine solution they'd been putting on parts of it, so I worked a lot on that area until it was saturated, then worked on his legs, feet and arms. At one point, as I was helping lift him to a sitting position, he asked if the exertion would give me cramps or anything else adverse. I said, "No." He said, "Are you sure?" I said, "I'm sure. I lifted Mom, and I've baled hay. I'm one strong woman!" He said, "You sure are."

He mentioned how well Mom's neck pillow was working for him. "I don't know what I did without it. I hope dear Dorothea doesn't mind me using her neck pillow!" I said, "Not a chance. She's loving it."

When De was positioned comfortably, sitting at the side of the bed, I gave him his fruit plate, which he ate with great relish. I was surprised when he ate more than a third of it, and when lunch arrived only about 40 minutes later, he also ate half of a large cup of tomato soup with crackers and some ice cream and drank some coffee. De said he'd like to stop by the house after his doctor appointment to check things out. I said, "I hope the transportation people who bring you out will let you do that."

I showed De the photos I had found, but said there were so FEW of them at his house that I thought they were the wrong ones. He confirmed that. I said, "I don't see many other straight ones. There's one of you with Fancy, but that's just about it." He said, "I have a lot of them in the costume." I queried, "The costume? Oh! You mean the Starfleet uniform?" "Yes," he said. "Oh! I was calling those McCoys, and you told me you didn't want McCoys, I thought." He said, "I'm sorry I confused you." I said, "That's okay, as long as we're on the same page now. I'll bring them in tomorrow." He said, "You may as well bring 12 or 15. If I have to sign more than THAT at once, I'll croak!"

At one point, I went over and got Carolyn and she came over and sat with us for a while. When De told HER about the "blood-soaking" incident, he expressed to her that at first he thought it was HIM bleeding, and his eyes got misty. I could tell it had really scared him.

Later, when we were alone again, De said, "Every time I look at Carolyn, she seems to be looking at me as if she's thinking that perhaps she's seeing me for the last time." I spoke softly then: "I know. I wish there was some way to help her NOT think like that, but I don't know what to say or do that would—" He interrupted, "There's nothing you CAN say or do. It's just the way it is. She's very dependent in some ways and yet very independent and stubborn in others. She is going to think whatever she thinks to think, and no one is going to talk her out of it." I said, "I just wish we could." He said, "So do I."

At about three I thought he was beginning to look as if he could use a nap – he said he wouldn't sleep, though — "but you can go if you want to or need to." I said, "If you want me to get to the bank today, I'd better leave here pretty soon, or it'll be closed." He said, "Oh, that's right. You go ahead!"

At 8:15 that evening De called. When I answered the phone, he asked, "What are you watching?" I said, "I'm not watching anything." I was in bed, close to falling asleep. He said, "When you come out tomorrow, I'd like you to take some of this miscellaneous out of here – letters, cards, notes, one thing and another. I keep trying to clear off my tray table and it just gets piled higher and higher!" I said, "I almost mentioned that today, and then promptly forgot when we got going on something else." He said, "I've read MOST of your angel book, but you know, around here, and with my mind the way it is right now, I can't stay with any reading for very long." I said, "I know how that goes. I hope you read the LAST half, more than the first part. The first part is just quotes from other folks. The LAST part is from ME!" He said, "Yes, I know. You're becoming quite the philosopher!" I said, "I've been working at it for a lot of years." He said, "Well, you've made the grade, girl!"

He continued, "Don called me about thirty minutes ago. He just went on and on about how impressed he is with you! I told him, 'Yes, Don, we've been impressed with Kris for years – over her diligence, smarts, what-have-you, but on and on he went!" I said, "Well, I'm impressed with him, too. You've said for years what a sweet and helpful guy he is to have nearby, and it has been borne out. We've had a number of great visits together." De said, "His reaction to you put me in mind of that movie with Nicolas Cage and Cher, where Cage says, 'I think I'm falling in love with you,' and Cher slaps him and says, 'Snap out of it!'" I laughed heartily at that!

He asked, "When will you be out tomorrow?" I said, "I don't know. When do you WANT me out?" He said, "I don't want to rush you." I joked, "So… 8 AM, right?" He said, "Right!"

I asked if the air mattress we were trying for his comfort was working well for him. He said, "It's better than the other one." I asked if he could feel the air going in and out of it. He said, "No. When I sit on the edge of the bed I can – but not just lying here, I can't. I can HEAR it, though. Psshhhh… pssshhhh." I said, "That'll help keep you from getting bed sores." De said, "Yes, that's why they said they were putting it here."

He again asked when I'd be out the next day, and I said, "I'm really not sure. I should vacuum those closets. I didn't get to them this afternoon, as I figured the bank deposit was the priority and I was getting weary. I got up at 4 AM today for some ungodly reason, so it was a long day." De said, "Just forget about those closets." I said, "I don't mind doing them, De. I'll get to them sometime this weekend. I hope you have a good night and get lots of good rest." He said, "I hope you do, too. We'll see you tomorrow." I said, "I love you," and he said, "I love you, too, Kris…"

On April 3rd I got to the Kelley's house at about 9 intending to call De to let him know what was happening and where I was, in case he wanted to reach me. Indeed he did: I arrived to find a voice mail message for me waiting on his answering machine! Part of it was, "Remember to look for the pen I told you about." The other part was about whether he was bothering me too much, calling me at home late at night and so forth. I called him right away and told him, "Absolutely NOT, you're not bothering me. I'm LOVING it! It gives me a chance to find out how you're doing. I feel uncomfortable calling you, as I'm afraid I'll catch you when you're trying to rest, so when you call ME often, my mind gets its report and I can relax." He said, "Oh, good. I have to call when I'm thinking about something, or it leaves me and then I may not think to remember it again – and that could be dangerous, if it's something important." I said, "You call ANYTIME. I don't care when, or for what." I let him know I'd be at their house for at least an hour, and while there, I'd clean the closets. He said, "Bless your heart." I asked him how his night went and he said, "Very well. I finally got to sleep at about 3 or 3:30; I managed to read everything I wanted to read last night." Then he reported, "I got up twice to use the bathroom and fell both times." I said, "Oh, no! You were doing so great in the hallways yesterday! I'm surprised." He said, "I was, too." I asked, "Was anyone there to catch you?" He said, "Yes. The first time it was a gal. The next time it was a male nurse. They had to dig me out of my walker." I commiserated over that, but he didn't seem unduly disturbed by it, so I joked, "Well, in a little over an hour, I'll be out there and I'll hold you up!" He said, "You may have to!"

I cleaned all three closets and then set the clocks ahead one hour in the house — a day early, but since no one was living there, I knew it wouldn't cause a problem. Then I drove to the hospital and first stopped in with Carolyn to show her the checks that De would be signing for deposit that day. I offered to take her over for a visit, but she was still ensconced in bed and said, "Oh, no. I heard that De had a bad night and I'm not sure he wants me or anyone over there right now." I said, "Well, if he DOESN'T, I'll be right back for a nice long visit, if that's okay with you!" She said, "That's fine with me." I said, "Okay… I'll be back… sooner or later… depending on whether we can get our work done quickly, or if he'll even SEE me right now!" She said, "Okay. When you get back, will you give me a report on how he is?" I said, "Certainly." She asked, "An HONEST report?" I assured her, "Of course, Carolyn… an honest report."

I walked over and De was asleep, leaning way over to the right side. I got his neck pillow and another pillow and said, "Here, sweetie, let me get you straightened up a little so you can be more comfortable." He continued to sleep and I propped him up straight and got the neck pillow behind his neck.

In just a couple of minutes, he realized who it was that had helped him, and he awoke with, "Oh, that's YOU, Kris…" He tried to chat, but he was still very doze-y so I just waited while his mind cleared. At one point he realized he wasn't making a whole lot of sense, and he joked about it. "Am I around the bend yet, do you think?" I assured him, "You're just fine, De. As soon as your brain gets the picture that you want to wake up now, you're going to be just fine!" Very shortly thereafter, it did. I put lotion all over him except for his back, asking if he ever slept on his stomach. He said, "No, I never have." I said, "It's too bad you can't sleep on your tummy. It'd be good to get you off your back for a while – but the air mattress is probably doing all right for you, anyway."

He again recounted falling in the bathroom, as he showed off his new gauze bandages. I just kept applying lotion, not reacting much, as I didn't want to seem overly concerned or anxious about his occasional weakness. He said, "I knew I was going to go down, but not soon enough to let anyone know." I asked, "Did you pass out?" He said, "No, it was weird. I just—" Words failed him so I guessed, "You just got weak suddenly?" He said, "Rather like that, I guess. I'm not sure what happened."

I showed him the color McCoy photos I'd brought in. He said he preferred to give out black and whites rather than the color ones. I said, "Oh, okay. I'll get THOSE, then, and bring them to you tomorrow." He said, "I send the color ones to people like you, people I know, or to sick people. There isn't a difference in the quality between the color and black and whites, but in the price, there's a big jump… so I don't use those except for very special occasions." I said, "I can understand that, after seeing the amount of fan mail you get!"

I started to clear off his tray table and put stuff in my bag that he wanted taken home, and followed that by making a list of all his pertinent, oft-used numbers so he would have only one piece of paper to refer to. He told me he had re-read parts of my angel book, and he wanted me to take it home because he was afraid he might get blood or water or something on it, "and I don't want it ruined. It's very special." I said, "Well, I'm glad you like it." I admitted, "I cried while writing parts of it." He said, "And I cried reading parts of it. It's very sweet and I appreciate it more than you can know."

He told me he'd eaten every last bite of his breakfast, and at close to noon (just before lunch) he started on the second fruit plate I'd purchased for them the day before. I said, "If you get started on this, when the heavier meal comes along, the juices from the fruits and your stomach will help the heavier stuff process and digest more easily." He said, "You're right about that. I've noticed that I don't have any nauseous inclinations when I eat this way. Haven't for a few days, anyway. Let's knock on wood!" I said, "You won't. Not the way you're enjoying it today!" He advised himself, "Stay positive, DeForest!"

He was relishing his fruit plate like gangbusters when Carolyn called. De said, "I'm eating your fruit plate. Do you want to come over here and help me finish it?" Carolyn said, "No, my lunch is about to be served." De said, "Okay, I'll see you later, then." He hung up and a nurse brought in his tray of lunch. I took the uneaten balance of his fruit tray and placed the lunch tray in front of him, to see if any of it intrigued him. It ALL did – he was ready for MORE food. He sliced everything in half, right down the middle except for the half peach, and said, "Get a plate. You're going to help me eat this." I took half and two crackers and we went to town on those.

Just as he was finishing and grabbing the ice cream and coffee, John and his pal came in for a visit. The phone rang, too; it was Carolyn. De said to me, "Let's get Carolyn over here and have a visit all together!" I went over and wheeled her over.

They visited quite a bit, reminiscing about old times, old movies, how good De looked… I kept taking stuff from De as he'd finish it to get it off the tray and near the door to be picked up, and finally Carolyn joked, "Have you been working here long?" I joked back, "Not long, but I'm getting the hang of it, huh?!" Then she said, perfunctorily, "I've been replaced." De and I both protested that statement. Carolyn was the love of De's life; we didn't want her feeling she had become less necessary to him.

After that brief moment of discomfort over Carolyn's proclamation, De lightened up and told John and his friend how one of his nurses had built up his appetite by saying, "You don't have to eat everything. Just have a leetle bit of this, and a leetle bit of that…" De told them, "He was right! Leetle by leetle, my appetite came back!"

John and his friend didn't stay for more than about 40 minutes, and shortly thereafter I left, too, as I had to stop by Don's house for the day's mail and also stop at the Kelley's again to get the black and white McCoy photos.

I went to Don's and picked up more mail. Don was chatty and cheerful and friendly as usual… talking a lot about his wife and son, both of whom have been dead for many years.

On the way home that night, tears welled up in my eyes; for many blocks, I was engaged in sad thoughts. "If I consider who I'm about to lose from my life, it more than half KILLS me! But then I think of poor Carolyn and I realize, 'SHE'S losing even MORE! How will she ever survive this?' I feel SOOOO sorry for her! MY loss and pain – it will be immense (the worst loss I will EVER have to endure) – but it has to be a fraction of what SHE will be losing. She has had him in her life on a daily basis for over 55 years! I've had him in mine as a constant for only a few weeks! IT BREAKS MY HEART! I know that's what De is fighting so hard for – he doesn't want to break our hearts! It ISN'T his fault; he can't help it. He wants to PREVENT heartaches, not CAUSE them! He and Mom are much the same in that way. He is just SO wonderful. I wish everyone could have met and known him in the way I have. I am so fortunate!"

On Easter 1999 I went star polishing and to the grocery store, then out to the Kelley's house to enter into their "black book" the various residual payments De had received since I began keeping his books. As I was doing that, I called him to see how he had passed the night. He said he'd had a good night. I told him where I was and what I was doing and he joked, "Good dog." I asked if he'd like another fruit dish before lunch, and he said he would. "Just get a little one, though – or you can eat half." He said, "Oh, here's a little bit of good news! They weighed me yesterday, and I'm up to 112 pounds!" I practically shouted, "Jesus, De! That's FANTASTIC!"

I drove to Gelson's. They had a plate with a large variety of fruit in it, so I got one of those. It was a larger size, but I figured the nurse could refrigerate it and De would have some the next day.

I got to the hospital at about 11:30. De looked good, well rested. I gave him the fruit dish right away, since I knew lunch would be along shortly and that he'd have time to process the fruit before it arrived. As he ate, we discussed some of the items I'd been dealing with – checks and insurance primarily. He was very chatty and told a few stories about his acting days.

At one point, I wanted to clarify whether or not he had given me permission to write his biography, and he said, "That is such a big topic, I can't even THINK about it right now. I have so many other things occupying my mind. I feel as though I have limited time left, suddenly, and there are so many other things I need to think about." I said, "That's fine. I understand." He said, "A lot of people want to write it. I haven't given any of them much hope, as I don't have the time to involve myself in the effort. You know, time gets away from you before you know it and suddenly, you have to make choices." I said, "Yes, I know." He pondered, "Even if I get OUT of here and go home, a biography won't be a likely part of my agenda." I said, "That's okay." I added, "I just want to say, I wasn't planning to involve you in it. You had given me verbal access to your personal history, out in the garage, and so I was wondering if that implied that I could use it to write your story." He said, "After I'm gone, it won't matter to me one way or the other, of course…" Finally he said, "I just feel – and God knows, I may be wrong – that this is all premature!" and laughed. I quickly agreed, "Of course it's premature! With all the strides you've been making recently, I think you're getting out of here and going home and having more life and times ahead of you!" At that point, we both got pretty misty! We were discussing his legacy and trying to NOT talk about his dying – and our aversion was staring us BOTH in the face! I said, "I hate even TALKING about this." De said, "It isn't my favorite topic, either." So we dropped it.

His nurse came in packing a lunch plate and told me that not only had De's weight been improving like gangbusters, but his blood sugar level was rising as well. It had gone from 93 to 123. After the nurse left, De said, "That's good news. When he told ME – he doesn't mince words, that one — he said 'Only DEAD people have a blood sugar level of 93!'" I laughed and said, "He was exaggerating by quite a lot, De!" My Dad was a diabetic, and so I was pretty familiar with blood sugar levels. De ate a few bites of the ham and perhaps one bite of the au gratin potatoes, then shoved the plate across the table to me. He ate about a quarter cup of the cream of potato soup, then passed IT to me. I joked, "I WAS losing weight!" as I swallowed his abundant leftovers.

Then I "lathered him up" with the new skin lotion I'd bought. I got his back this time, too. It looked very good. He said it itched, so I massaged it until he said it was okay and that the lotion would take care of the rest.

De went into his most recent call from Don. AGAIN, Don had regaled De with statements such as, "Do you KNOW what you have in that girl?!" "Yes, we do, Don." "Do you see what she drives?" "Yes, I know – a little red jewel." Don shot back to De: "SHE'S the jewel!"

I was laughing and feeling acutely embarrassed as well! De just would not stop – he was on a roll, telling me "Don said this, Don said that… Don asked, 'How long have you known her?'" … I said, "About twelve or fourteen years WELL…" "Well, you just don't know what you have there. She's just amazing!"

Excruciatingly embarrassed, I finally joked, "To quote Mark Twain: I can live for a week on a compliment!" Then I got a little philosophical: "I'm awful lucky in that way: I get compliments a lot at work – two or three times a week – and I think poor Dan gets SICK of hearing it from his vendors and work associates." De said, "Well, I guess you know it all, then. We talk ABOUT you all the time in glowing terms, but we forget to tell YOU about it!" I said, "That's okay. It embarrasses the hell out of me, anyway — but it IS great to think BACK on — later!" He said, "You know, we all tend to think we have all the time in the world to tell people what they mean to us, and then one day we find out we don't." I said, "I know. I'm only 48, and I'm beginning to get that message loud and clear already." He said, "You're way ahead of me, then!"

About half an hour after he finished his meal, I said I'd go visit Carolyn until she got tired of me. "Shall I stop back by afterward, or just go home after that?" He said, "Oh, stop back by. I'll be here!"

I went over to Carolyn and we began to chat. She wanted to know what De and I had talked about, and I gave her a report on that. At about that time, Dr.Kaaren Douglas, a frequest guest, came by with her dog Sammy for a visit with Carolyn.

Then Kaaren went over with Sammy to visit with De. I spoke with Carolyn for a few more minutes, then asked if she had seen De yet today. She said, "No… and it's getting kind of late for that today, anyway." I said, "No way! You gotta SEE him – he's looking SO good! Want me to wheel you over there?" She said, "Why not?"

I wheeled her over. She and I basically listened while Kaaren and De chatted. De recounted a few stories about his career. A particularly funny anecdote involved Christopher Plummer in Star Trek VI and the fact that both he and Plummer had worked with Burt Lancaster and Kirk Douglas in different pictures, and what "selfish" actors they were, wanting the best lines, the best angles, what-have-you. Then Plummer and De got into doing shtick the next day on the set of TREK VI along those lines – with Plummer calling De "Burt" and De calling Plummer "Kirk"! It was hysterical!

At about four, Kaaren sighed and said, "Well, I have to get home and get dinner going." She kissed us all and took her leave. Not long thereafter, I put lotion on De's legs again — little areas needed it, so I did their entire length again, just for good measure – and Carolyn said, "THIS will be an interesting part of your book!" We all laughed.

Wrapping up, I said to De, "I'll see you tomorrow at your doctor appointment. Call me if there's a change and you don't go." De said, "I will." Carolyn asked, "Why wouldn't he go?" I said, "I don't know. I'm just covering all the bases." I added, "At one point, the doctors were thinking of coming out HERE." Carolyn said, "That's before, when he wasn't feeling well." Taking the lead, De said, "I'll be there. Park in the parking structure there and give me your ticket. I'll pay it on the way out." I said, "I'll see if I can park on the street or in the hospital lot next door and save you the fee."

The next morning I called De at about 9:30 to see how he had passed the night. He reported, "Very well." He said, "I'm putting on my pants now for the doctor appointment." I said, "You're being awfully pre-punctual, aren't you?" He said, "These things take a while. And I had a problem. You know those new green trousers I had you bring out to me? What a difference six or eight pounds make: I can't get them on this morning!" I laughed and said, "That's WONDERFUL! Getting too big for your britches, eh?!" He said, "I guess so!" I said, "That's okay. You still have the other pair you wore the night you came to the hospital. You can wear those." He said, "Yes, I can, but the green ones would be warmer." I said, "Just throw the white robe in the vehicle with you, to have it along in case you're not dressed warmly enough."

At 10:15 I drove to De's house to pick up his sweater and to turn up the heat in the house so it would be warm inside when he visited after his doctor appointment. Then I watered the roses for about ten minutes and drove to the clinic.

I met up with De at about 11:35 in the lobby (along with the transportation coordinator, who was stationed with us so she could call for the vehicle when we again needed it – but we didn't know this at the time). We went up to the oncologist's office. Several cheery nurses started bantering with De right away. There was a long form to fill out, so I did that while a technician drew blood from De's arm. Then we went into a room and waited for the doctor to arrive.

It wasn't long before the doctor entered and performed a cursory check of De's lungs and then his leg edema, which was slight but getting worse as the day progressed, due to the fact that his feet weren't elevated for hours. Then they launched into a discussion of De's current status. De handed the doctor the two articles I had found on the Internet re ways to try to thwart liver cancer. The doctor said one wouldn't work at all, as De's cancer has spread beyond the liver and colon, and there was just no way to pinpoint and attack all the spots that would need to be addressed. The other idea was a viable option. I asked about drug therapies that cut off the blood supply to tumors, and he said there are 16 or 17 drugs that do that; plus other clinical trials for other things they could try. The doctor listed De's three options:

Do nothing at all – De's current election – no chemotherapy, radiation… just keep him comfortable and perking for as long as possible.

Chemotherapy — there were several options here, with a 1 in 3 chance of shrinking the tumors 20 to 30% and giving De a better quality of life and greater longevity. "If it works for you, you'll FEEL better." I asked about the side effect of nausea, and the response was, "He's ALREADY nauseous. We can limit nausea significantly with drugs." De said, "The stuff I'm on now does wonders in that way."

Clinical trials — the doctor knew about two trials just off-hand that offered some promise – one at UCLA and one in Houston. He had called the facility in Houston and said he'd follow up on that call. I was put in charge of calling UCLA and getting an appointment for De as soon as possible. 60 Minutes had just run a segment on the trial the previous evening and good results had been seen there. So I said I'd call first thing in the morning, from work.

The doctor said to make another appointment with him in two weeks and said also to call him back on Thursday to see what he had found out, or to report any changes. We were then directed to get De's monthly Sandostatin shot. There was a slip up there, because the chart didn't get in the nurse's "to do" slot, so everyone went off to lunch! De and I were planning to drive to his house anyway – where he had some of the drug in the fridge – so a nurse told him, "Go ahead, and call us from there to be sure the drug is the right dosage. If it isn't, come back here after you've been to the house and we'll give you the shot then."

We went downstairs and the transportation coordinator then advised us that the driver had gone on another call and wouldn't be back for 45 minutes to an hour! We were chagrined, to say the least.

About 45 minutes later, De's doctor came back into the building and we mentioned that De hadn't received his shot – so we went back up. The doctor said he couldn't give the shot – it was a specialty shot – and we'd have to wait for the return of a nurse. So we sat and waited and chatted with the insurance coordinator for the facility. She offered to help me pick my secondary plan when I went on Medicare to be sure I received good coverage and wouldn't be "surprised" by costs later on for things we never think we'll need – until we do.

By this time, 30 minutes more had passed, and a nurse popped her head in and said she could give him the shot. Then she said, "I'm so sorry! I've been back here for a good twenty minutes, but no one let me know you were in here waiting." De said, "Nothing surprises me TODAY. It's Murphy's Law, right and left!" The shot was a real ow-ee, but he did fine with it.

Then we went back downstairs — to find that the driver had AGAIN been called away and would not be back for an hour! We were sitting in the chilly lobby, and De was beginning to get weary and deeply frustrated! I said, "I'll take you over in my car, and the driver can come there to pick you up." De said, "Good idea. Let's go." The transportation coordinator said, "No, no, you cannot do that! I must call my supervisor!"" I said, "Okay." She called the supervisor, who at first denied the request for me to take De to his house. Furthermore, she denied the request to have the driver take De to his house afterwards! "We are supposed to deliver patients only to their doctors, and then back to the hospital."

I asked De, "What do you want to do? You're my boss." He said, "I want to go to my house." I felt that if I violated the hospital's transportation rules and just took off with their patient without permission, I could get into a lot of trouble. So I was quite hesitant to do as De wanted. On the other hand, I knew it was the fondest wish in his universe at the moment to see his home again, and I was willing to risk ALL to fulfill it. So I tried again with the transportation coordinator: "I have my orders. I'm taking him to his house." She was pretty frantic, and asked, "Will you speak to my supervisor, please?" I said, "Certainly, I will. I'd be happy to." So the supervisor was dialed up again.

I got on the line and said, "Mr. Kelley is six blocks from his home. His doctor appointment has been over for more than 30 minutes, and transportation took off to get another patient, so we are pretty much stuck here in a cold lobby for the next 45 minutes to an hour. This is no good for Mr. Kelley, and he wants to go home for a brief look-see before he returns to the hospital. Can I get your approval to drive him the six blocks to his house? We can wait for the driver there." The supervisor said, "Certainly." I gave De a thumb's up! We couldn't leave the transportation coordinator stranded, so I asked her, "Would you like to come along?" She nodded, "Yes!" So I told her supervisor, "She'll come with us." The supervisor said that would be fine.

We piled into my little Mazda, wheelchair and all, and drove to De's home. I wheeled him into the house. The transportation coordinator called the driver and gave him the address, so he'd know where to come to pick De and herself up when he got around to it.

By the time we got to the house De had to use the bathroom, so I decided to wheel him into Carolyn's bathroom because the wheelchair access was slightly better. As we passed the bed, I said, "Here's the bed. How'd I do [in the bed-making department]?" He inspected and then reported, "Not bad." I said, "Not exactly military…" He said, "Well, nobody's perfect."

I lifted him out of the wheelchair and was figuring out how best to support him as he headed into the bathroom. We were standing face-to-face, so I tapped my shoulder with one hand and said, "Here, grab on here." He grinned and joked, "That isn't what I had in mind to grab on to." I gave him a look and said, "You flirtin' with me, boy?! BEHAVE YO'SELF!" and we laughed.

After I got De back into the wheelchair, we passed the bed again. He studied my bed-making once again and then joked, "Have you had a sex party on my bed?!" I laughed like crazy and then feigned weariness. I said, "No, De. I haven't even been staying here. But I'm guessing, now, that you think I did a really lousy job of bed-making, by that remark!" He chuckled and said, "No."

I pushed his wheelchair slowly around the house, so he could check everything out. He asked me to turn more water on the roses, so I did that. He dialed Carolyn and told her, "Here we are, looking out the window into the backyard." They spoke for a few moments about the crazy, time-consuming day, then hung up.

At about that time, the driver showed up — too soon, as De had wanted to stay a while and savor the ambience of his home — so I told him and the coordinator that they could leave and I would drive De back to the hospital in his Lexus. I said, "Your supervisor gave me permission to drive him. So you're in no bind in going on ahead without us." So they left.

De was emotional in his home. He told me twice that he had hoped to spend time there ALONE that afternoon. "You could go out and have a bite to eat or do the banking or something." I told him that, as much as I'd LOVE to respect that wish, I felt COMPLETELY responsible for him now and would worry my fool head off if I left him there alone. He said, "I understand completely. You don't have to explain. It's all right. You're doing the right thing. Stay put." I went out into the yard to put water in the birdbath and do some other miscellaneous chores so he'd have a few minutes in the house alone. I could keep an eye on him through the window, so he wasn't "unattended" – we were just separated by glass.

When I got back inside, he said he was ready to head back. I wheeled him to the car and put him in it, then loaded the wheelchair. I drove to the hospital and helped him back into the chair, then wheeled him to Carolyn's room. They spoke for about fifteen minutes. De reported on the doctor's appointment, and then mentioned what a "strong champion" I had been all day: keeping at the issue of getting him to their house against the protestations of the transportation folks until they finally relented.

Carolyn asked what it was like to go back to the house. De got emotional and said, "It felt like our house… but it was… odd. It was a weird feeling." I said, "You probably felt like an exiled visitor, since you weren't able to stay." He teared up at that. I wanted to say, "Don't worry, you'll be back," but I didn't want to say it in Carolyn's presence, as I was aware that her return home was highly questionable.

After just a few more minutes, I wheeled De back into his room. He was extremely weary by then. I helped him into bed and propped him up with pillows, and then did his legs.

His feet and lower legs were puffy. Two nurses came in and took his vital signs and asked how the day went and what had transpired at the doctor's office. De told them part of it; I told them part as he began to run out of steam.

I stayed for about 90 minutes and massaged his feet and legs until the edema started to resolve itself. Just as I had kissed him good-bye and was about to leave, the dinner tray came in. He felt a little nauseous and didn't want to eat anything. I reminded him he hadn't had any lunch, and he said he hadn't had much breakfast either: "They forgot my eggs this morning."

I exposed the dish of food and asked him to have "just a leetle bit of this and a leetle bit of that" – which he did. He had one bite of fish and one bite of rice and then about half of the green beans and about half of the ice cream cup. That was plenty for him; he told me to eat the rest.

He again thanked me sweetly for all my help. I reiterated how much I enjoyed doing it. Since I had already kissed him goodbye prior to the arrival of dinner, I said, "No more kisses." He joked, "I've had four from you today already." I protested, "You have not! I met you in the lobby —!" He held up his hand and smiled, "I'm just joking!" I said, "Okay. Sheesh!"

I went over to Carolyn's and visited for a little while. She said how glad she was that I was willing to go through everything with De. I told her it was a big thing to me to be able to SHOW how much I love and appreciate them. "You have been so kind to ME for so many years." She said, "We have known you for a long time, haven't we?" I said, "Yes… and every day has been a big blessing for me."

I left there at about 6:30 and took the Lexus to the gas station near De's. They happily agreed to fill it for me, after I said, "I know you recognize this car, but not me." They did. The station manager said, "Give Mr. Kelley our hellos and love." I said I would.

On April 6, I called UCLA Medical Center and left voice mail messages at two numbers. I gave a brief history of De's situation and asked someone to call me back as soon as possible. Within a half hour a doctor's secretary called back and told me the doctor would accommodate De's schedule; that he would make himself available to see De. I called De's room twice, but there was no answer, so I called Carolyn to see if he was with her. He wasn't, and she hadn't seen or talked to him all day. So I called the nurse's station and gave the nurse the information. I asked how De was, and she said, "He's a little out of it today; he tried to reach for the phone when it rang but he didn't get to it in time." She added, "He's getting better as the day goes along. I think they gave him a sleeping pill last night, or else he's just still wiped out from yesterday." I said, "I won't call him again. Will you pass along the message?" She said she would.

De's physician in residence called me at about 4:30 that evening to get more information than the nurse had taken down as to what I'd learned and arranged for when I called UCLA that morning. He wanted to know my relationship to the Kelleys, and I said, "Long-time friend and presently assistant." I asked him how De was doing this afternoon and he said, "He's improving." I said I'd heard earlier that he was pretty low this morning, and he confirmed that, saying "He was awful this morning, but as the day goes along, he's coming back." I told him that De had a very long, rough day yesterday due to transportation glitches and he said he had heard about that.

At about 5, I gave De a quick call, based on his doctor's indication that he was bouncing back. De answered the phone slowly after several rings. He spoke slowly and without much energy. I said, "Hi, De. This is Kris." He said, "Hello, Kris." I said, "I heard you had a bad day." He confirmed that. "Did you sleep last night?" He said, "Not much. Oh, I did get a little sleep, I guess. What's new out there?" I asked, "Did your nurse tell you I called UCLA and opened the door for you to see the doctor at your convenience, any time, whenever you're feeling up to a drive again?" He said, "She told me something. I don't think I'm going to be going to UCLA for any seminars, though." I could tell he wasn't getting the picture – still a bit dazed – so I said, "That's OK. We'll talk more about this on a better day." He said, "OK, honey. I love you. Have a good night tonight."

De called me at ten and asked if he had awakened me. I said, "No." He said, "Oh, good. I thought twice about calling you at this late hour –" I said, "Don't *ever* think twice. Don't hesitate: If you want to call, call."

He said, "I was wondering if you have any extra photos of me at your place." I said, "Not many." He said, "Oh." I said, "I did get 12 or 15 of the black and whites you want, but in all the craziness yesterday, I forgot to drop them off with you when I took you back to the hospital." He said, "Oh, for heaven's sake. Well, remind me next time you come out to get them. I have two here to sign, but I need some more." I said, "They're here, and you'll have them soon." He said, "That's good."

I asked De if he remembered me telling him about his invitation to meet and speak with the UCLA doctor about what they may be able to do for him. De said, "With the energy I have right now, I don't think it will ever happen. But I may feel differently about it later." I said, "Perhaps he can come to you." De said, "I just don't know if I want to get involved in anything like that. I haven't up until now." I said, "I understand that, and it's totally your decision and we honor that." He said, "A number of times, they've told me they can't help because of what has already been done to me." I said, "Well, your oncologist and the UCLA doctor are discussing your history, so they'll reach some sort of consensus before they'd think to involve you in a trip down there, so that it won't be a waste of your energy or time." "That's good," he said. Then he reported, "I've had a bad day. I'll just get to sleep and someone will come in and awaken me. It just happened again, and I thought, 'Well, I think I'll wake KRIS now!'" I laughed and said, "Any time, De. Any time at all." He concluded with, "So I'll let you go now." I said, "Okay. Night-night. I love you," and we hung up.

On April 7th I drove to the Kelley's house, arriving at about 10:40 after having deposited checks at the bank. Then I called De. He picked up the receiver after about six rings and answered sleepily, "Hello?" I said, "Hi, De. This is Kris. Did I wake you?" He said, "Almost." I said, "I'm sorry." He said, "Well, it's time to wake up." I said, "I'm here at your house. I'm planning to drive over and see you in a few minutes and bring you the photos you've been waiting for." He said, "Oh, good." I asked, "Is there anything else here at the house you want me to bring along?" He said, "Let me think…. No, I don't think so." I said, "Okay. I went over to Don's for the mail, but he isn't there, so I'll stop back by this afternoon and get whatever he has gathered." He said, "That's fine." Then he said, "When will you be here?" I said, "Oh, about twenty minutes, I guess." He said, "That's good. I look forward to seeing you again." I said, "Take a nap until I get there." He said, "I will."

I walked into De's room and found him groggy. He said, "Hello, Kris," and I said, "Hello, De!" I pulled out the envelope of photos and showed him that I had them and would leave them. Then I checked out his feet and legs and said his edema was all gone. I asked if he'd like lotion and a massage, and he said, "Oh, yes. I'd like that." So I put lotion on his feet, legs, arms, back, chest and neck. I told him his skin was looking great, and he said, "Thanks to you, it is. You really stay on top of it, and it shows."

About that time the head nurse on shift could hear us conversing, and she came in saying to De, "Well, you're awake NOW, so let's get your blood pressure and other vitals checked out." De joked, "We have to stop talking about her while she's here," and I said, "Oh, that's right. Too bad." The nurse laughed, knowing we were pulling her leg. She said to De, "Lunch will be along soon, so I'm glad you're with us again."

Scarcely a minute later, the nurse returned bearing a large pill. She said, "Here's a new pill for you. Bactrim. You have a little bit of a urinary tract infection this morning." De said, "Yes, I noticed that the tip of my penis is a little puffy this morning." I was embarrassed to be an ear-witness to this conversation, but there I was, and so the situation seemed right for an injection of humor. I piped up, "*I've* had that before – a URINARY TRACT INFECTION, not a puffed penis!" De commented ruefully, "In THIS town, NOTHING would surprise me!" The nurse laughed and said, "Well, swallow the pill and I'll leave you two alone with your urinary tract infection and your puffed penis!" De looked at the pill and said to me, "Good Lord. Look at the SIZE of this thing, will you?" The nurse said, "Let me break it in half for you." She did that, and the pill went down easily.

I asked De if he'd like me to raise the head of his bed a little more, since lunch was due shortly and he wasn't elevated enough to partake safely. He said yes, so I did that – then noticed that his body was so far down in the bed, it looked as if the bed was trying to fold him at his chest instead of at his hips! So I smiled and said, "I think perhaps we need to find you a new POSITION in the bed, as well!" He looked up at me and shot back, joking, "THIS certainly isn't it!" That cracked me up, so – laughing – I headed around the end of the bed to get into a position to push him UPWARD when he lifted his upper body off the bed using the "monkey bars" they had recently set up for him. I took hold under his legs and behind his back and said, "Okay – on three! 1, 2, 3!" and I hurled him upward toward the head of the bed. His body weight was so negligible that he practically SAILED into position. The neck pillow shot right off the bed, and I said, "Wait! Your pillow just developed legs and walked! It's gone AWOL!" He said, "How did that happen?" I said, "Danged if I know! We are awesome powerful, we are!"

Another sweet nurse came in and asked if De's menu for the next day had been filled out, and he said, "Not completely." She said, "That's okay. You two can work on it together. I'll come back in twenty minutes to get it." I said, "Okay, it'll be ready."

As soon as she left, a volunteer came in with her "companion animal dog" Mitzi and De was one happy camper. Mitzi and De visited for a good twenty minutes, with Mitzi sharing his bed and giving him a few kisses on the hand and chin.

Just as Mitzi and the volunteer left, lunch arrived… and so did the nurse, hoping for the menu. I apologized, saying we were interrupted by a doggie visitor, and she was very understanding and patient. She said to De, "You have a good friend, here." Then she said to me, "You're here every day, aren't you?" I said, "Just about! As often as I can be, I am." She said, "That's important." De said, "It sure is." The nurse said, "I'm happy to see it. Jackson, you're a fortunate fellow." I said, "He's a wonderful fellow. I think you should call him DeForest, though. Nobody calls him Jackson." At the mention of the name DeForest, her eyes opened wide, and I think that's the first moment she realized "who" this Mr. Kelley WAS! I thought she was going to drop her teeth! I continued, "He didn't know his first name was Jackson until he was in the Army Air Corps and saw his birth certificate for the first time. His family always called him DeForest." That led De into, "I can STILL hear my mother calling to me from the front porch: 'De For est!!'" His eyes filled with tears at the reminiscence. He said, "I could hear her down in the school yard: 'De For est'!!!"

He said, "I had a little brown dog named Sandy. At 3 every day, I would go near the window to sharpen my pencil, MOSTLY to let Sandy know I was nearly ready to leave school for the day. That little dog's tail would raise up, and off he'd go, down the street, in through the window without the screen, and all around the house; then he'd come back and lead me home." The nurse tapped me on the shoulder, and I stood up and hugged her. She said, "I'll be back in a little while for the menu." I said, "It'll be ready." She said, "I'm really in no big hurry. He's my last patient, and I'm patient!"

I mentioned to De that his painter had called the house and left a voicemail message. De said, "Please return his call. Tell him I'm in the hospital, but when I get out, I'll want him to come over and do some painting at the house. I have a short list of things that need doing, but I want to look around some more. He'll do everything you tell him, but it has to be on that list." Then he laughed, "It's amazing what pops into my mind! I just thought of that funny little box you sent to Carolyn because she had been confined to the hospital for so long. The box that looks like someone's in a crate and it yells, 'Get me out of here!'" I said, "Oh, yes!" He said, "I could sure use it right now!" He continued, "When I get out of here and we get to the house, I'm going to show you how to make a bed." I scowled, "Are we back on that friggin' BED, again?!" He said, "You need a lesson." I said, "Geez! Okay. All right, boss! But my FIRST question is: Do I have to be able to bounce an egg off it, the way they insist on in the military?!" He said, "No, I hated that. We ALL did." I insisted, "I *don't* make that lousy a bed. If it had wrinkles on it, it's because I SAT on it on both sides to set the clocks ahead one hour for Daylight Saving Time." He joked, "Oh, sure." I then said, "And who the hell is going to SEE your bed, may I ask? And what's it going to look like the second you get IN it?! I don't understand the rationale behind having a PERFECTLY made bed." De smiled and said, "Well, you'll learn how to MAKE a perfect bed, ANYWAY!" I gave a world-weary sigh. "Okay, okay. Jeez!"

We again talked about the possibility of bringing Carolyn home when or if De came home, since I would be there to assist them. I told him that one time a doctor had asked Carolyn about getting an assistant and going home. "Carolyn had said then that you wouldn't want an assistant at home if you were both there. Then she said that if she went home she knew she would just have to come back someday, so it would be too sad to go back." De pondered that. I told him, "As long as you're there, I don't see why she'd be unhappier being there than being here this far away from you. At home, you'd be together. But I can see why she'd be unhappy to go back to the hospital if you WEREN'T here anymore." De didn't say anything, and looked sad, so I said, "But you know, if she WANTED to stay there – at your house — for the rest of her life, I'd stay there with her and take good care of her." His head came up; that seemed to make him feel a LOT better. He said, "It's a lot to think about – and I don't even know if I'M getting out of here… so at the moment, it's just something to think about."

I remembered to tell him that his "Decision" episode was going to air on BONANZA the next day. He said, "Is that the one where I poisoned a bunch of Indians?" I said, "No, that was HONOR OF COCHISE." He said, "You have an amazing mind for stuff like that." I gave him an outline of the episode and said it was a GREAT portrayal and asked if he wanted to catch it. He said, "Yes, I might do that." I said, "You might have company – a whole roomful of nursing fans – if you let them know it's coming on." He smiled, "Yes, I might." I told him I'd put a note on his bulletin board to remind him when it would air and on what channel. "A nurse will spot it and be sure you tune in, I imagine. And I'll try to remember to call you just before it comes on, to be sure you're awake and aware, IF I don't get swamped at work and forget to look at the clock. I'm recording it at home, so if you don't see it, you can see it later." During lunch De was having trouble cutting the crust of the pizza because it was so tough, so I cut it for him. Then I cut the cherry pie into a few small bites for him so he could concentrate on eating instead of dissecting food. He said, "If I let you keep doing this, you're going to spoil me." I said, "If I thought you'd LET me spoil you, I'd do it!" He asked, "What would you do to spoil me?" I said, "Well… I'd cut up your food…" He said, "You're already doing THAT!" I said, "Once! I've done it exactly once! I'd do it all the time! And I'd massage you… Hey, I guess I AM spoiling you!" He said, "Yes, you are!" I said, "Good! You deserve it!" De said, "I wish Carolyn would take advantage of the massages, too." I said, "So do I. I did it once, and she really liked it, but then she never let me do it again. She told me, 'It doesn't turn me on.' I told her if it turned her on, I'd get pret-ty nervous!'" De threw his head back and laughed.

While he was eating the last few bites of his meal, the phone rang. De said, "That sounds like Carolyn's ring." I said (because his hands were occupied by a soup cup), "Do you want me to get it?" He said, "Yes. Tell her I'm finishing lunch and will call her back in five minutes." I picked up the receiver and gave her the message. She said, "Oh, okay," and asked how long I'd been there. I guessed, "Oh, about an hour, I guess." She said, "Okay," and hung up, but fewer than two minutes later she called again, telling me, "I'm sorry to call again, but I'm very anxious about De." I said, "Oh! Then by all means, here he is, sweetie!"

I handed the phone to De, who told her he was fine – that he'd had a couple of rough days, but that he felt better and would see her again soon. I motioned to him to let me speak to her as he was finishing up, so I could calm her fears by telling her, "The nurses gave him sleeping pills real early yesterday morning and this morning; that's the reason he's lethargic. The pills allowed him to get some really good rest. There's nothing to worry about going on over here, sweetie. He's doing fine." She said, "All right. I was just concerned." I told her I'd be over in just a few minutes to visit, and she said, "Okay, then," and we hung up.

In a few minutes, I left De and went to Carolyn's room. She seemed happy to see me. She said she was sure glad I could help De; he sure appreciated it. I said, "I enjoy helping the two of you. It's a pleasure." She said, "You're not helping ME." I said, "Well, I certainly WOULD, if you'd LET me!" She said, "What do I need?" I said, "It isn't a matter of need. It's a matter of – whatever. I love putting lotion on your legs. I'd love putting it on your back and giving you a back massage. I'd love to bring you something from home or something from a store. ANYTHING that will make you FEEL better would be a nice thing for me to do – and I'd love it." She said, "I don't need you to do anything nice for me." I said, "You don't have to need it. Would you like lotion on your legs?" She said, "Yes, that would be nice." I put lotion on her legs, and while I did, she asked how Dad was, so I gave her the run-down on that. She asked if I had put lotion on Mom's legs, and I said, "Oh, yes. You bet. She loved it. She'd say, 'I'll give you two hours to stop that.'" Carolyn laughed and said, "I'll bet!"

Her nurse came in to take her for a walk, so I bid her farewell, and then remembered to tell HER about De's BONANZA episode. Then I remembered that I hadn't left De the note about the episode, so I told her I had to stop back by and pin it on his board. I said, "He'll probably be asleep, so it will just take a second. I won't wake him."

I went back over to De's room, intending to sneak quietly in and pin the message on the bulletin board. To my surprise, he was sitting on the edge of the bed thinking about getting himself to the portable toilet next to his bed. I said, "You're not supposed to be getting out of bed alone..." He said, "It's not far." I said, "Never mind how far. You're supposed to ask for help." He said, "Yes, nurse."

A male nurse came in and helped him onto the commode, so I wrote the note about the BONANZA episode and taped it below his TV set, where he or a nurse would be sure to spot it.

When he was finished using the commode, I helped him back into bed and gave him eyewash for his eyes. After he finished using that, De told me, "The last time I saw your dear mother was the first time I realized I was probably doomed." That brought me up short, and I said sadly, "Really?" He said, "Yes. No one had TOLD me yet – but I just FELT it." I said, "Intuitively?" He said, "Yes." I almost cried. He added, "I will tell you more about it when I think I can get through it without crying." I said, "Okay."

After a time, he said, "We thought long and hard about who we should involve in our troubles." I said, "You PROTECTED me for the longest time." He said, "Yes. Perhaps we should have been honest with you from the outset, though." I only half-joked, "It DID come as quite a shock a few weeks ago, the way A.C. brought it to my attention! I was hearing about conventions you were attending, and I was figuring you must be all right. But the calls were fewer and shorter and I began to get a feeling that all was NOT as rosy as you had been telling me, so I started to ask you again if there was anything I could do. You kept saying NO, so I finally figured – just to keep myself from going crazy – that you probably had somebody else lined up and just didn't want to risk hurting my feelings." De said, "No, we didn't have anyone else lined up… I was handling everything pretty well up until relatively recently. I regret keeping you in the dark for so long, though. I guess it's always better to know what's going on than to have to wonder and worry about it." He seemed genuinely remorseful for having left me uninformed for so long, so I finally assured him, "De, you made the right decisions for yourself and Carolyn all along the way. Don't try to second-guess yourself now. Don't even WORRY about it anymore. I'm not upset. I love you for having protected me for so long. I know you did it out of concern for me." He knew I had been dealing my mom's terminal illness. "I completely understand." He said, "I'm glad you do."

He then asked me, "If you could start over, become anything in the world you wanted to be, do anything you wanted to do, what would it be?" I laughed and said, "De, I have been a VERY lucky person. I have pretty much DONE all I ever wanted to do in my life. I worked on a horse ranch when I was crazy about horses; I worked at a wildcat sanctuary and other places when I was hot on wild animals; I worked at API when I wanted to make a difference for animals; I came down here and got into the entertainment industry because I wanted to. There really isn't anything I haven't done up to this point that wasn't a real passion of mine. I think if I have a goal now, it's to help people in crisis, and also to write about it in ways that show other people how to help and how to give the type of loving service that is required and so much appreciated." I paused and then said with utmost sincerity, "Right NOW, I'm living the epitome of my life's dreams – doing something meaningful to help YOU, because you have done so much to help ME all these years." I gave his hand a quick kiss. I paused again, then continued: "I feel, now, that my life is pre-destined, like the course of a river, and if I'll just jump in and go with the flow, I will be carried to the spots where the greatest contributions can be made. I trust the process. I'm spiritual in that way. God knows what He's doing, even though *I* don't always know what He's doing. I'm just – I don't know – I feel lucky and happy! I'm DOING exactly what I WANT to be doing." He said, "I'm very glad about that."

As I was getting ready to leave for the day, De asked if I had tried to get his car filled with gas yet. I said, "Oh, yes! I've been meaning to tell you about that!" I told him the story, and gave him the love and prayers of the man at the station. He was touched by it.

On April 8th De called me at 7:15 a.m. and asked, "Were you in the shower?" I said, "No." "I didn't wake you, did I?" "Nope." "I'm wondering when you'll be by today." "Noon-ish – or do you want me sooner?" He said, "I'm going to have a shower at 8 this morning, and then you could put lotion on me. I need to get my butt out of bed and get going today!" He sounded so strong, with it and energetic, I said, "So! When do you want me? 9:00? 9:30?" He said, "Either of those are fine." I said, "Okay, I'll be there!"

I drove by Don's place to get the mail he had gathered the past few days, as he thought there were important things in one or more of the envelopes. We chatted for just a few minutes about De's amazing progress. Don said, "I'm hoping, now, that De WILL be home soon." I regaled him with some of De's funny stuff while he was at the house the other day ("Did you have a sex party on my bed?!") and Don ROARED! I told him that De didn't like my bed-making much and that he said he was going to TEACH me how to make it when he got home. Don said, "I'm persnickety that way, too." I told him how funny I thought that was, seeing as how no one ever sees their beds and when they get into it, it immediately becomes a shambles, anyway! "But, whatever!"

After we chatted for a few minutes, I traded cars and drove De's Lexus to the hospital. He sounded so wired, I thought he might want me to drive him somewhere!

When I got there, he looked fantastic. He was hooked to the nutrition bottle again, as the thought of food made him feel ill. He was otherwise just fine – chatty, funny, with it.

He asked me to take an envelope and letter over to Carolyn and then come back. I did that. I asked Carolyn if she wanted to go over and visit with us while I was there, and she said, "Sure, why not? Do you think De will mind?" I said, "Heavens, no!" I put her brace on her leg and wheeled her over. De was happy to see her. Carolyn got up and kissed him, then sat down in the wheelchair and put her leg on his bed next to him, so he could pat it.

He asked the nurse for a pain pill, saying his lower back ached. She went to get the pill for him. I asked if he'd like me to put lotion on his lower back and rub the achy part. He said, "Yes. I think that would help." So I put lotion on him and rubbed the areas he specified. It took about four minutes, and then he leaned back on the pillow and said, "Wow! What a difference!" I said, "Sitting all the time, you probably just needed some circulation there."

The nurse brought the pill then, and he took that, too.

We began to talk about me, for some reason. We were talking about sex-linked roles, and I said I was lucky in that I never felt constrained by society's ideas of what girls should be. "Until I was ten or eleven, I was going to be a cowgirl!" I told them that Mom was a tomboy and I was a tomboy. Carolyn said, "You're an interesting girl. You don't act particularly feminine." De added, "But you don't act masculine or butch, either." I said, "I think I act pretty androgynous." He said, "That's it exactly." I said, "I LOVE the name Kristine but never felt it really fit me – too feminine – although KRIS fits me perfectly." Carolyn said, "You look so much younger than your years. It's hard to think of you as 48."

At about that time, one of De's doctors came by. We had spoken on the phone before, but this is the first time we had met. I remembered to tell him that De had his monthly Sandostatin shot. He said it was good that I told him, as it hadn't been listed in the treatments De had received. De mentioned that he used to have to inject himself twice a day. I told him, "It's a recent development that it can be given on a monthly basis now." Carolyn said, "That's a good thing." De said, "It sure is. I was running out of places on my legs to put it!"

The doctor said he'd been in touch with De's other doctors and with the doctor at UCLA and that they were putting their heads together to see if there was anything in clinical trials that would be of significant benefit to De. De said, "I don't think I'll be taking in any seminars down there." I clarified, "These aren't seminars. They're clinical trials. They have drugs there that haven't made it to market yet. No one here has access to it until it's tested. If there's something there that's a wave of the future, state-of-the-art drug to help you, they'll look it over and let you know, so you won't be wasting your time going down there." De said, "Oh." Then he sighed. "I'm just not sure I want to involve myself in that." The doctor said he wasn't pushing the idea, nor discounting it, and he would honor De's wishes. De said, "Well, I feel confident with the treatment I'm receiving NOW, so I'll respect your judgment as to whether I should give the trial thing a shot."

Not long after, he confided to me, "I got in so easily at UCLA that I'm a little afraid it'll just become a celebrity thing; that I'll be making an

APPEARANCE whether or not they have anything for me there." I nodded my awareness regarding that possibility. He said, "Isn't that awful? I shouldn't be pessimistic like that—" I said, "Well, it's certainly understandable!" He said, "I've had only a very slight taste of what Elvis or Michael Jackson had to deal with; it's really a double-edged sword. On the one hand, it's flattering and can be a lot of fun, but on the other hand..." I concluded for him, "It's invasive and un-fun." He said, "It can be. MOST people are very nice and perhaps once or twice per trip to the market, I'll be stopped, which I don't mind. But when you're rushed, or don't feel well...." He didn't finish the sentence. I again nodded my understanding.

Carolyn said to me, "YOU'LL probably be a celebrity one of these days, with your little books, and THEN you'll know all about it." I told them then that I had been called to do another Walk of Fame interview re being De's star polisher next week, "but I didn't know what we'll be doing next week, and if we're doing NOTHING, I should be at work WORKING! I can't think how to ask Dan for MORE time off to do an INTERVIEW!" De said, "No, I wouldn't push my luck. He's done an awful lot for you – for US ALL – recently!"

De said, "Of your five days at work, which are the busiest?" I said, "I used to make them ALL as busy as could be. I'd look around like a maniac for extra stuff to do when things got quiet – almost to the point of dusting and washing the windows! – but then I realized I wasn't being paid any more for those efforts *and* was wearing myself to a frazzle, so I just slowed down. I told myself, 'It's going to take you eighty years to get to age 80 whether you walk or whether you run, so you may as well SLOW DOWN and enjoy the trip before it's all over." Carolyn (who considered me hyperactive) joked, "You told yourself that? When?" De guessed, "When Dorothea got sick, I'll bet." I said, "Yeah. Right around that time."

De then said, "I keep coming up with springtime things that need doing, a whole list of things, and then a doctor comes by and reminds me that my time is so short. It kind of takes the wind out of my sails." I said, "I'll bet. But don't let the doctors tell you what to think or do. They aren't God. Live your life exactly the way you want to; don't limit yourself to the prognostications of others." De said, "Good advice."

As De became wearier, Carolyn and I decided we should leave and let him nap. I took her back to her room, and then went back and put extra pillows underneath him so he'd be comfortable. I gave him a warm cloth to wash his face and cleaned his glasses for him. Then two nurses and I exchanged the "monkey bars" above his bed so they wouldn't dangle so close above his head. It was a much better arrangement, although by the time we finished, he was nodding like crazy, about to fall asleep and wishing mightily we'd get lost!

I finally said, "Okay, I'm outta here!" and he said, "It's about time! Get going!" I said, "Yes, sir!" and he chuckled.

De called me at work later in the afternoon and we had a few moments of banter. Then he said, "I awoke and remembered the BONANZA episode. I only caught the last twenty minutes, but it was a good one. I called Carolyn and she tuned in and enjoyed it, too." I said, "I wish you had seen it all. You seemed to be such a SNAKE in the beginning, sitting in jail... but as the episode progresses, you find out why. It was a terrific portrayal." De said, "Let me tell you a little secret about actors. Sometimes we get a chance to experiment. This episode was just such an experiment." I said, "Well, it was sensational. Whenever people say they haven't seen you in anything besides TREK, I always recommend that they catch two of your BONANZAS – the one you saw today plus HONOR OF COCHISE – and then APACHE UPRISING, and THE LAW AND JAKE WADE." He chuckled. "Awww... APACHE is one of my favorites." I said, "Mine, too. I even had a dream about you one night as the guy in that portrayal! I wouldn't want to meet THAT guy in a dark alley!" He chuckled and said, "We may have to try that – resurrect that hombre!" I said, "What?! And ruin your reputation?!" He said, "I guess I can't do *that* – ruin my reputation!" and laughed.

We exchanged a few more pleasantries and then he said, "I'll see you tomorrow. When will you be out?"

On April 8th I drove out to the hospital to get a check for $450 from De to give to his accountant for the tax services. De was waiting to have his shower – impatiently. He said he had to wait until an IV drip finished before they'd take him in – "and I've been waiting since 7:30."

He was sweetly frustrated by the long wait for a bath. When a male nurse came in, De inquired as to when he might get his shower, and was told the bather was bathing folks who were going to be released that day. De joked, "So since I'm STUCK here, I can wait all f——' day, right?"

I could tell De was really frustrated, but he was being philosophical about it. His predicament reminded him of the six-hour, transportation-plagued day he'd had on Monday and he groused about that again. I just listened and nodded, since I couldn't do a darn thing about either situation and figured he just needed to vent.

I reported, "It's COLD outside this morning. If you could see a little farther northeast than your viewpoint allows you'd see that the entire mountain range is white with snow." He said that had happened a time or two the past year when he drove out to visit with Carolyn, and it was always a glorious sight.

I didn't stay long, as I was due at the accountant's at 11:30. I told him I'd go get gas in my car, then go by the accountant for the paperwork and then come back for him to sign it. He said, "Okay." I asked if he'd like a fruit dish when I got back, and he said that sounded good: "But just a little one."

I drove out and did the tax stuff, grabbed a quick hamburger at a drive-through, then went to VON'S for a fruit dish. I got a medium size one because it had the most variety in it.

I drove back to the hospital. De was now sitting in a chair, having just finished his shower. He was cold, but looked fresh and DRY! I put lotion on his legs and arms. He said he had edema in his legs and in a spot below his navel. He said, "It has not been a good day."

We got started on the IRS paperwork. Just after De signed and was about to get back into bed, Carolyn came over. She took the paperwork and proclaimed she didn't understand it, but wanted to look it over anyway before she signed it. De said, conversationally, to both of us, "Who DOES get this tax stuff? Our accountant is the only one who has to know what it all *means*." I chuckled and agreed.

Leaving Carolyn to her long-term tax return pondering, I diverted the conversation to another topic and explained to De why I had brought him some green tea. I told him that drinking it was good for his health since it limits blood vessel growth to tumors. Carolyn looked up from the paperwork and interjected that she didn't know anything about green tea, but if we'd talk about dogs, she'd join in. I said, "Talk about dogs, and sex, and anything else that brings your spirits up. THAT improves your immune systems! Happy thoughts! Happy thoughts!" They both laughed and their eyes sparkled – at least for a few brief moments.

On April 10th De called me at close to nine a.m. and said he had tried to reach Don, but got no answer. I told him Don was at the market. He asked if I'd keep trying to reach Don until I had luck. "Please tell him to call me. I want you to bring him out here this morning. I want to have a personal, private talk with him." I said, "Sure! I'll keep calling until he answers and will have him call you right away." He said, "Thank you."

I called every fifteen minutes or so, but De was the one who managed to reach Don first. Then De called me and said he'd reached him. I said, "Gads! He must have just walked in the door, then! I've been trying!" De said, "Don said you were planning to wait until the mail comes this afternoon to come out." I said, "No, those were YESTERDAY'S tentative plans. I told them they could change at the drop of a hat if you wanted something else." De said, "Yes, that's too late. I want to see you this morning." I said, "I'll call Don right now and tell him I'm on my way to pick him up. We'll be there within the hour."

I drove to Don's, picked him up, and we drove to the hospital. We were both pretty nervous! This sounded real serious/almost urgent!

I led Don to De's room, kissed De hello, and then said, "I'll be over with Carolyn. Give me a buzz when you want me to come over." Don said, "I will."

After ninety minutes or so Don came over to get us. We went back to De's room with him. Don and I both mentioned how great De looks. I said, "Every DAY, I can see an improvement!" De joked wryly, "That's why I called you out here, so I could hear that!"

I put lotion on De's arms, feet and legs and told him the new mail could wait until tomorrow; there was nothing in it that was a show-stopper.

Don, Carolyn and De talked about old movies and other times gone by. Then Don said he'd like to get back home soon, so I asked De if he wanted me to take Don home and come back, or just plan to come back the next day. De said, "Do we have any work today?" I said, "Nope. Nothing that can't wait." He said, "I hate to have you come all the way back here if there's nothing to accomplish." I said, "It's not far. It's just up to you." He said, "Let's just do it tomorrow." I said, "Okey dokey!" I kissed them both and we left.

As we drove back to the house Don said there were only a few minutes of confidential talk; the rest was just guy stuff. "It sure felt good to have a good old-fashioned chat with De again," he said. "He's looking so good and acting so well, I'm beginning to have hope again!" I said, "Me, too! I wish the doctors would stop reminding him how sick he is and let him feel as good as he feels while he's feeling it!" Don said, "I do, too. He doesn't need to be reminded."

I did about an hour's work at the Kelley's house. At about the time I was going to head out for the day, Don came over with the new mail. I put it with the other mail I'd be taking out the next day. Then Don said, "When we spoke today, De told me he thinks the world of you." I said, "He thinks the world of YOU, too. It's just one huge Mutual Admiration Society, isn't it?!" Don said, "Yes – and isn't it wonderful?" I said, "It sure is." He said, "Bye, doll." I said, "Bye, Don."

De called at about 7 that evening and asked, "How's the Number One Girl?" I wasn't sure I'd heard him correctly (if at all) and I said, "Excuse me? What did you say?" He said, "How's the Number One Girl?" I said, "Oh! I'm fine."

I told him I had called his painter and given him the message. De said of his painter, "Joe is very religious." I nodded and added, "He was sure relieved to hear an update on you. I guess he stopped by a couple of weeks ago, planning to see you before you took off to visit Carolyn, and found you weren't at home, so he called, and when he didn't get an answer, he began to worry. He said my call was an answer to his prayers."

I asked if he had any naps that afternoon, and he said he didn't. "I don't really want to. I'll sleep better at night if I don't." After a pause, he said, "I hope I get to feeling better. I'd like to have one day – better, two – at home." I said, "I think you WILL feel better SOON. You're looking great and you have more vim and vigor daily — perhaps you can't notice it, but I sure can see a daily improvement. Your energy is a lot better recently." He said, "Energy! YOU'VE got energy!" I said, "Good thing, huh?!" and he said, "Yes! Good thing! But I wish you'd SIT DOWN once in a while!" I said, "I AM – right NOW!"

He asked when I'd be out the next day, and I said, "I thought I'd leave that up to you." He said, "Don't leave it up to me. Come out whenever you want. Tomorrow morning is star polishing day, isn't it?" I said, "Yes, but I'll do that real early, IF it isn't raining." He said, "It's so cold right now, why don't you just skip it tomorrow?" I said, "Not unless it rains." He said, "I don't want you going out there and getting stove up." I said, "I won't. I dress warmly, and it only takes five minutes." Then I said, "Besides, if I shiver, just think of all the extra calories I'll burn!" He said, "Just keep doing what you're doing; it'll happen."

I told him I had watered the plants indoors and under the eaves at his house; checked in on Myrtle (who was still lethargic) and aired out the house while I was there. He said, "Good dog!" I said, "Well, that's MY update." De said, "And I can't think of anything else." I said, "Okay. I'll see you tomorrow," then added sincerely, "I love you." He said, "I love you, too. Have a good night. Bye-bye."

On April 11th after star polishing, I carried a vase of De's home-grown roses to his room. He was still asleep when I arrived at 8:20 A.M. so I sat them and the other materials down in his room and went back out into the lobby. The head nurse was working at her station, so I went over and patted her on the back to tell her, "De is crazy about you." Then I asked her to put me down as the person to contact in an emergency. I said, "He listed me as the emergency person at his regular doctor's on Monday, so I thought I should be listed here that way, as well. After all, he's HERE, not THERE!" She agreed, and let me fill in the information.

At about 8:50, the nurse decided she'd better rouse him "before his breakfast gets too cold." She went in and jostled him awake. He looked so cute and unstressed asleep, I wished she could leave him alone longer.

He awoke and we raised the head of his bed. He said, "Kris, you're here early. What time is it?" Then he looked at the clock and said, "Good Lord. You're not early; I'm LATE!"

I got him a warm wash cloth for his face. The nurse brought in the tray and it just about turned his stomach. He told her, "I can't eat just after I've come awake." She said, "I can't either. Don't worry about it. It's here for when you want it." I asked if a little of the fruit from the fridge sounded manageable, and he said, "Yes, it does!" so I got that out and he had a few bites of that. I hoped it would whet his appetite for something a bit later – and it did.

I showed him roses I'd picked at his house, and he just about flipped, saying they were the most beautiful things he had ever seen. At almost that exact moment, Carolyn called. He picked up the phone and told her good morning; said he'd just been roused, and "Kris is here and has a vase full of flowers from our garden." He asked me to carry them over to her to see. I did so while they continued to chat on the line. She loved them, and I said I'd bring her some too if she'd let me (a week earlier she had declined the offer), and she said, "If you'll take care of them, I'll take some."

I took the roses back to De's room. He was still on the phone with Carolyn, saying that he had called A.C. the night before at about 10:15 and chatted for over an hour, "All about the night I almost died." De started to get teary-eyed and said, "He said he was there holding my hand. He said they thought they were losing me… I remember seeing A.C. as if from a distance, across the room, dressed so well, the way he always is. The room was all white. It was not peaceful or placid at all. It was very scary. It scared me." Then De told her, "A.C. and I also were talking about how fortunate we are to have Kris…"Again De started to get choked up and was unable to continue, so I responded, loudly enough so Carolyn could hear me at her end, "No! It is how fortunate *I* am to have *you two*!" That made the tears spill down De's cheeks and I grabbed his hand, nearly in tears myself, and kissed it and rubbed my cheek on it. He put the phone down, and I picked it up and said, "Carolyn?" She said, "Kris, I want to tell you, too, how lucky we feel to have you in our lives at a time like this, so willing to help with everything." I looked up at teary De, and repeated, "I'm happy to be here, and happy you allowed me." De took the phone back, and sniffled, "I'll come over and get you later, after I've tried to choke down some breakfast."

He turned his attention to me. "After A.C.'s call last night, I didn't get to sleep until about 2 or 2:30. I just kept thinking about that night when I almost died." His eyes were far away, thinking about that awful night. Then he said, "I'm sure glad we're HERE now, and not there anymore!" I said, "Me, too!" He said, "It was scary and awful." I said, "That's because it wasn't your time to go. When it IS, it won't be like that. It wasn't for Mom. You had a bad reaction to a drug then, I'm guessing – they may have given you too much pain medication. It wasn't a normal situation. That *isn't* the way it happens, De." He said, "I sure hope not." He was still haunted by the memory.

I told him, "I had a similar experience that time I developed bronchitis. I couldn't even stand up without the room becoming black; it felt as though I didn't have enough breath in me to stay alive. I was going to call 911, but Emese said she'd come and get me. It seemed to take forever for her to get to me, but it was probably only about thirty minutes. I was SO scared. When your body betrays you, it's a terrible feeling." He emphatically nodded his complete agreement. Then I added, "We think EARTHQUAKES are scary! They're NOTHING compared to a feeling like THIS!" De said, "You have it exactly right. There's nothing scarier."

Carolyn called and said she had to go to the bathroom and no one had come in to help her. So De said, "Go help her. I can wait." I jogged over to Carolyn's and "spotted" her while she got into the room; after she finished, I piloted her back and asked if she'd like lotion on her legs before I put on the brace. She said yes. Then she told me that one area on her leg had recently gone numb, so I massaged it and said I would tell the nurse or doctor about it. Then I remembered that De had been thinking about getting into the bathroom, and said I'd go help De to the john and back and be right back to put her brace on. I went over to De and helped him into the bathroom. The phone rang, and I picked it up. It was Carolyn, saying she had to go again! So I told De to stay put – "PROMISE ME!" – until I got back. He said he would. I ran to Carolyn and helped her back to the bathroom. She had more success, so I helped her back into the bed and then went and got De back into bed. Then I went back and put Carolyn's leg brace on.

As I was heading back to De's room, the head nurse said, "WHAT are you DOING?!" I said, "I'm running a bathroom relay between these two!"

She said, "You don't have to do that!" I said, "I'm loving it!" She said, "Then carry on!"

After that, he was going to shave, but suddenly decided, "YOU shave me!" I said, "Ho boy! THIS is a first! THIS makes me nervous!" I shaved his sideburns with the trimmer and then ran the electric razor over his face and neck. After I'd had a shot at it, he took the razor and got the nooks and crannies I had missed (for fear of injuring him). I said, "I think I'd have done better with a razor than with the electric," and he said, "So would I."

While he was shaving, I asked him if he wanted a mirror; after a little bit he said he did, so I handed him the small compact Carolyn had loaned him when he was admitted. He affected a gay blade lisp and said, "I feel a bit femme using thissss compact." I laughed and said, "De is getting in touch with his feminine side – with the softer side of De!" De said, "Yesssss, I am." He was so GOOD when he assumed a role – ANY role!

He mentioned that Mom's neck pillow had been a real blessing and then said he'd appreciate it if I'd take it home and wash it. I said I would. I said I'd wash his two pairs of dirty socks at the same time. He said his socks were too tight. I told him about diabetic socks, which are loose and expand as needed, and asked if he'd like me to get him a pair to try. He said, "Yes, I would. They sound like just what I need." I told him I'd get a pair on the way home. He said, "Good dog." I said, "That's the height for a compliment – to be considered as good as a dog!" ('Cause De LOVED dogs!) He said, "It sure is, Ollie!!

He said his edema had put a few pounds on him. I said he didn't seem to have much in his legs, and he said, "Up here high I do, they tell me. They're going to start me on something today to relieve it, I think. I'll probably be peeing my brains out once I get going on that."

We talked about Carolyn and about how insecure she seemed to have become. De then informed me, "She can be a difficult person. She'd be tough to work for." I said, "She's hard to READ. It's hard to know where I stand with her. For a year I asked permission to go visit her, and never got a YES, so I figured I'd be imposing if I just showed up – then when I showed up here to help YOU, she said SHE'D never had visitors in a YEAR!! It was pretty exasperating! I guess with her you just have to assume she wants what everyone else would want, whether or not she'll admit it or say it, and then be prepared to get kicked out if she really DOESN'T want what you think she wants!" De said, "That's it, exactly! You're reading her perfectly! That's good!" I said, "It's so much easier when people tell you what they want!" He nodded, "I know it." He again said, "It's difficult." I said, "I know – but it's okay, because I think I understand it and because I love her." THAT statement made him almost tearfully happy.

We discussed two convention offers he had received. He dictated to me how to respond, and asked me to call Joe Motes and get more information on an upcoming convention because he wanted to make an appearance at it if he felt up to it.

As he was reading an invitation from actor John Hertzler about appearing at a Berlin, Germany convention, he looked at me and said, "See? If I was feeling up to it, we could be traveling all over the place!" I said, "Keep the faith, boy! Perhaps you will, yet!"

De got ready to go for a walk. We walked around the "block" and ended up in Carolyn's room for a rest, at which time De said he'd love a donut. I said I'd run across the street and get him some, and some black coffee, and he said okay. I did that.

When I returned, he was in his own room, and ate a few bites of the donut and then drank some of the coffee. Then he wanted to get back into bed.

He confided, "I'm almost afraid – as is Carolyn – to ASK what her status is on her leg. I'm afraid of their answer. I'm afraid they're going to tell me she'll never walk again on that leg." He looked as if he might cry when he made that confession. I said, "De, as she told ME about six months into this, someone told her that this kind of thing could take up to two years." He frowned. I continued, "So yes, it's a long haul, but that DOESN'T mean it's a hopeless cause." I think that gave him some hope that he was beginning to lose.

Later on, with Carolyn over for a visit, we talked about our upbringings, and Carolyn said she was spoiled by her dad; "All little girls are spoiled by their dads." She asked De if he was spoiled by his dad. De said, very seriously "No. Never! He was very strict with me." I said, "Boys are different. Their dads expect BIG things from their sons." De said, "Mine sure did!" Then he mused, "When I told him I had decided to become an actor, he was sure my soul was lost forever. I was going straight to hell!"

The nurse came in at one point and De asked when the doctor would be in that day, as he had a couple of things to ask him. She said she wasn't sure. De said he wanted to ask about Carolyn's new numbness in her leg. The nurse found out where the numb spot was and said it was a good idea to tell the doctor about anything new that occurred. Then De said he was curious as to what was going on with Carolyn's leg. The nurse explained that Carolyn's type of arthritis was causing her bones to mend very slowly. "It's a long process and she's still very fragile."

De began to look a bit tired, so Carolyn said she'd go back to her room. I wheeled her back and got her long sock (so I could wash it), then went back and straightened De's tray table so everything he needed was easily within reach and the garbage was tossed away. Then I kissed him goodbye.

He looked good. He was talking about wanting to go home and getting some stuff done (even if it was just in a series of drives whenever he felt up to going out). I thought he'd be able to do that – and possibly more. Only time would tell, though…

On April 12th I called De at about 11 to see if he wanted or needed me to come out. "Yes, by all means, come out." I said, "Okay. I'll be there in – oh, about 40 minutes if the traffic is moving." Then I said, "I washed the pillow and Carolyn's sock, plus your socks, but I think the neck pillow is still a wee bit damp." He said, "That's all right. It can finish drying here." I said, "Oh, okay! I'll bring it along then."

He asked me if there was any money in his dresser at home, and I said, "No, but there's $101 in your money clip over at Don's. I can get that, if you want it." De said, "Yes, bring me at least half." I said, "Okay, I will. I'll call Don to be sure he's home. See you soon."

I called Don and let him know I had Ted's check and that I needed to get $50 out of the money clip for De. I said, "He wants it in small bills, so I'll have to get one of the fifties broken somewhere." Don said, "I can do that for you, doll." I said, "Cool!"

I drove to Don's and got the cash, then went into the Kelley's house just momentarily to be sure everything inside was good and that there were no important phone calls.

I drove to the hospital and walked in. De was in bed, with his gown hanging down from his chest. He was still pretty prone, so I asked if he wanted to sit up more, and he said he did. I raised the head of his bed.

He then said, "I called you twice, but you were already on your way here, I guess! I wanted you to bring Bill Shatner's phone number with you." I said, "I always have your personal phone book with me, so I have it, if it's in there." He said, "It is." He asked me to dial "Willie Boy's" home number for him. "Say it's DeForest Kelley calling."

I called Shatner's house and a housekeeper answered the phone. She said he wasn't there, so I asked for his work phone number. She got it for me and recited it. I called THAT number and reached his assistant Stephanie. I said, "Hi, this is Kris Smith calling for DeForest Kelley. Is Mr. Shatner there?"

She said, "No, he isn't. He's out of town until Wednesday night. This is Stephanie." I said, "Oh. De, do you want to speak with Stephanie?" De said, "Sure." I handed him the phone and he said, "Hi, Stephanie. I wanted to speak with Bill, but I guess he's out of town. Would you have him call me back when he gets back? I'm here in the hospital, just where nobody likes to be." She asked what for, and he said, "Oh, I've been fighting this cancer thing for over a year now." It was news to HER, and when he hung up, he mused, "Bill didn't tell Stephanie anything about my cancer." I said, "Well, maybe he thought that the fewer people who knew about it, the better the chances it would remain a secret." He said, "Perhaps. But Bill is strange – he can't talk about cancer or death or dying." I said, "Neither can A.C. He gets real squeamish." De said, "Yes, he does."

He asked, "Where's Dorothea's pillow?" I grabbed it for him and said, "Right here. Do you think it's still wet, or just cold?" He felt it and said, "It's a little damp, but it will dry in no time." Then he said, "I wonder what Dorothea thinks of this." I smiled and said, "I'm sure she's happy to share her pillow with you." He smiled and nodded, then said, "I hope so."

He started to tell me something about the last time he saw Mom, which brought tears to his eyes even before he spoke the words, but the phone rang. It was Carolyn. De told her I had just arrived and that I'd be over soon to give her leg a massage.

Then he said to me, "Carolyn is anxious to see you this morning. She called me and asked, 'When will Kris be out this morning? I'd like her to massage my leg again.'" I said, "Awright!" happily. De said, "I was happy to hear it, too. It's a breakthrough. She really likes you and it's beginning to show." I sighed a happy sigh. "I'd better go right over!" He said, "Yes, you'd better."

I went over and gave her a good morning kiss. She was already sitting in her chair and had her brace on. I said, "I'd like to do your legs, if I can take the brace off." She said, "Oh, we'd better wait now. Lunch will be delivered at any moment." As if on cue, the nurse came by with her tray. I said, "Okay, but as soon as you finish and want me back, you give me a call, okay?" She said cheerily, "Okay!" I asked, "Where's your vase?" "In the bathroom." I said, "I'll get it and go get you some roses." She said, "Where are they?" I said, "In De's room." She said, "Oh, you mean those roses from yesterday?" I said, "Yes, he has lots more than he needs, and I didn't stop by long enough to get more – plus the buds are still too tight." She said, "It can wait. I don't need the ones that are already here. Let De have them all."

I went back to De's room and told him lunch had arrived and that she would call me when she was ready for the leg massage. De discussed how insecure Carolyn had become since her leg break. "She seems to have lost most of her self confidence. Age and infirmity can do that to people."

At about that time, De's lunch was delivered. He said he wanted a cola to go with the ham sandwich, so I went to the cafeteria and bought one for him. He ate more than he had in days and really enjoyed it, and said that late the night before he'd had some more of the fruit. Then he talked about the places we could go for his favorite foods after he got out of the hospital. These cues to his renewing health were music to my ears. Chili cheese dogs, pastrami sandwiches... A week earlier, if he'd have mentioned them he probably would have become sick to his stomach. He seemed to be on the mend.

I ate half of his sandwich and some of his soup. Then I ate his ice cream and the balance of his cola.

De said, "Oh, by the way, before I forget again...I was going to say – I'll never get through this — I was going to say that the last time I saw your dear mother, and I embraced her... twice... I somehow felt a COMMUNION with her... as if we were going to be sharing the same fate. I just felt – even though no one had told me yet; I hadn't been diagnosed yet – that I had the same prognosis as she did. And it seemed almost as if SHE knew it, too! It was just – very weird, and just — very much like a communion, of sorts." I said, "You know... my Mom and you would have gotten along like gangbusters had you known each other better." He said, "I know that. I felt it then and I know it now." I added, "I have to say this... of all the people I have ever known in my life, there have been only three – Mom, you and my Grandma – who seemed to me to be God's prototypes for what He had in mind for us as a species. You three have always epitomized to me what it means to be truly and wholly wonderful." He got a little teary all over again! I continued, "I don't think ANY of you had it easy – far from it, in fact – and yet you managed to keep your love flowing through it all." De said, "My mother was like that, too. She had a tough, tough life as the wife of a poor preacher. She never got the chance to see me make it big – she saw the start of it, but she wasn't here for STAR TREK." I quickly said, "She was looking down – she still is — and she knows." He joked, "She's probably yelling, '*Where's the money, De For est*!'" He and I both laughed, then he added wistfully, "I wish I could have made her life a little easier..." I told him, "Although I really feel that Mom is looking down on me and is happy for me, the past month or so I have wanted in the worst way to just pick up a phone and CALL her and talk to her." De said, "I know exactly what you mean. I felt the same way about my mother. Still do, at times." I said, "It's nice to know they don't need phones now to hear us." He said, "Yes, but I wish there was some way they could let US know that they know!" I nodded in total agreement…

We were both in tears before the conversation ended.

Carolyn called and said she wanted some more ones, so I took ten more over to her. Then she dug $14 out of her vanity and pondered long and hard as to why she needed so many ONES. I told her I'd take any she didn't want back to De, and she said, "Just a minute… Let me count what I have here… I can't think and listen and talk all at the same time." I said, "Okay," and waited… and waited… and waited. She kept counting it wrong, so I'd correct her, and she'd count it again… wrong. This went on for about fifteen minutes. Finally, I suggested, "Why don't you just keep five fives and five ones. If you need more, you can call and ask De for it. He'll send over anything you want." She said, "All right," and I carried the extra nine back to De, and collapsed in the chair. He laughed, understanding that I'd just been through the ringer in some way.

I said, "I got so CONFUSED over there, trying to straighten out her confusion!" De said, "I know exactly what you mean. I've been dealing with it for a few years now. She was always nervous and frantic about some things, but now it's more prevalent and more intense." I said, "At one point, I almost got to wondering if she thought I was trying to pull a fast one on her with your money! She thinks she's a dollar short, but she only had fourteen to start with in her drawer, not fifteen." De reached out and took my hand and said, "Don't you EVER worry about us not trusting you!" I half-laughed and said, "As long a SHE feels that way, too!" He said, "She does. She just gets confused. When she is, even *I'M* suspect!" and he laughed, then continued, "She'll tell me, 'Don't look at me while I'm trying to think!' – so I look the other way!" We both laughed – I think to keep from crying! He said, "Two hours from now she'll call over here and ask me, 'Do you think I hurt Kris's feelings today?' and I'll tell her, 'No, honey, you didn't.'" I said, "She DIDN'T hurt my feelings. I just felt… embarrassed to be the apparent cause of her nervousness, but she wouldn't let me go. She said, 'You stay right there until I have this figured out!' So I stayed!" He said, "Getting old is a real pain, in so many ways. For everyone involved."

De was much stronger and his weight was steadily increasing. The doctors were considering giving him Lasix for a mild edema he still had, but they were waiting as it seemed to be resolving itself.

On April 13th I drove to the hospital, arriving at about 11:25. De and Carolyn were in De's room, as were two doctors. De's usual physician motioned me into the room when he spotted me and I shook hands with both of the doctors and then said hello to De and Carolyn. The doctors said a few more things and shortly thereafter, they left. I walked around the end of the bed and kissed Carolyn. I walked back and got busy with something, and Carolyn said, "You didn't kiss De." I said, "I didn't?" De said, "Yes, she did." Carolyn said, "No – she didn't." I joked, "De would say I kissed him whether I did or not."

I asked him if he wanted the head of his bed raised "now that the doctors have finished mauling you," and he said he did. I started to raise the head of the bed and Carolyn said to De, "Why can't you do that yourself?" He said, "I can," and I joked, "I got to the button first!"

De mentioned, "This is a work day, isn't it?" I said, "Yes, but I escaped." He said to Carolyn, "Wouldn't it be a hell of a thing if she lost her job over helping us?" Carolyn said, "I somehow doubt that will happen."

Following a short visit, I wheeled Carolyn back to her room. When I returned to De's room, he told me that Carolyn had again asked when I'd be out today. That cheered me, to know she was asking for me. I said, "I didn't even know if you WANTED me out here again today, but I figured I'd drive out anyway and if you were sick of me, you could send me home!" He said, "I could never get sick of you. I'm glad you came out." Then he added, "As a matter of fact, just this morning Carolyn said to me, 'You miss Kris when she isn't here, don't you?' and I said, 'Yes, I do.'" I said, "*awwww* That's so nice to hear! Thank you!" He said, "Well, it's true." I added, "I miss you when I can't be here, too."

I pulled out an e-mail response I had received from actor John Hertzler, who had recently invited De to Germany for a convention, because it was such a great note. In it, he revealed that Bones was his favorite TREK character of all time and that he hoped he would be able to work with De sometime in the future. De read it and said, "Isn't that something? That's a wonderful little letter." He was deeply affected by it. I said, "This letter is a keeper!" He said, "It sure is."

The lunch arrived not long after and De couldn't eat much of it, since he'd just eaten berries, so he pushed the plate to me and said, "Eat." As I ate, we filled out his menu for the next day and he joked, "So! What do you want for lunch tomorrow? Circle it!" I laughed and said he'd better pick the stuff HE liked, in case his appetite kicked in full force. He said, "I ate every bite of my breakfast this morning, and every bite of those berries. That's all I'm going to ask of Jesus today!" He talked about going to one of his favorite haunts for lunch or an early dinner after his doctor appointment on Monday. He also said he wanted to go by the house again for a while. I said, "Cool." (I thought immediately, "I'll have Don help me make De's bed so De has nothing to grouse about next time he gets a look at it!") I said, "I'll get permission to drive you around in your Lexus from now on, so there won't be any more transportation headaches." He said, "Good thinking, Ollie."

I put lotion on De's legs and feet. His physical therapist came in to walk with him. We walked around the "circle" and ended up in Carolyn's room. There I put lotion on her legs, then massaged her legs and feet until she said, "That's enough. That's fine, Kris. Thank you very much."

We went back to De's room and I helped him into bed. He looked a bit troubled momentarily as a memory crossed his mind, and then he confided, "This morning I almost lost my cool with one of the nurses. I feel badly about it now, but at the time, I was really fried. I didn't get to sleep until about 2:30 – the sleeping pill didn't kick in until then – and then she came in at 8:00 a.m. I was dead asleep, really sawing them off, and she woke me out of a sound sleep and said, 'I have to weigh you now.'" He frowned and continued the story, "I said, 'This is unbelievable. I cannot believe it. You woke me to WEIGH me?' She said, 'I have your breakfast, too.' I said, 'I haven't washed, I haven't brushed my teeth, I haven't washed my face… I don't even want to be awake!' She said, 'It's my job to do this now.' At that point, I was just fit to be tied, but I thought, what the hell… just get up and get weighed and go back to sleep. So I got up and waited while she weighed me, then got back into bed – and she walks in with the tray and puts it in front of me! I didn't know whether to laugh or cry. I told her, 'You know, I can get nasty if I have to!' That scared her, she backed off a little, and then I felt remorse and started to cry a little! I think that was probably good, because she apologized and said it was just her job to get the food to everyone while it's hot, and she was sorry that it was upsetting me."

I said, "I wish I could be here 24 hours a day, but unfortunately, I can't." He said, "No, of course you can't. Please don't feel that way. That isn't what I intended in telling you this." I said, "I know, but I say that because IF I could be here all the time, I'd know when you had gotten to sleep and I'd let you sleep as long as you needed before waking you. I'd go GET you breakfast when you were ready… stuff like that." He said, "You know, as it is now, I think the nurses are a little jealous that you're here, and that you do everything for me that needs doing while you ARE here." I looked at him, incredulous, and said, "Really?" He said, "I sometimes get that feeling." I said, "I'd think it would *relieve* them, having an extra pair of hands and legs for a few hours; give them some breathing space." He said, "I would, too." (Then I reminded myself silently, "He's such a pleasure to help – such a light in everyone's life — that they MAY be jealous when I show up and take over their duties!")

He said, "But back to my nurse this morning. I apologized to her as soon as I could when I saw her again." I said, "I don't see where you needed to – you were just assertive, not nasty." He said, "No, I wasn't – but I let her know I COULD be. I'm sure THAT had an effect on her that I didn't want to linger." I said, "Well, as much as we hate it, sometimes it's just plain necessary, unfortunately, to let people know where the cat crapped in the buckwheat. Sometimes they don't hear it unless it's in terse terms." He said, "I think you're right about that." I said, "I think that's how Dad became a bully early in life. No one listened to him if he wasn't demanding or commanding, and it became a pattern in his life that existed up until recently."

Then he said, "That's how I got the role as Jake Ehrlich, you know. I was doing the test with a fellow actor. In the scene, he turns away, not looking at me, and I grab his shirt and pull him back [he almost did it to ME; if I had been closer, he would have!] and say, 'You LOOK AT ME when I'm talking to you!' Jake Ehrlich chose me himself after he saw that. He said, 'THAT'S the guy I want portraying me! That's exactly who I am!'" Then De said, "Jake was a hard man – a hard man." I said, "I could tell in the pilot [333 Montgomery Street]. I think you HAVE to be hard as nails to be a criminal defense attorney." He nodded, "I think so, too." I said, "You stayed with him for a while, researching the role, didn't you?" He said, "Yes, I did. We went to a different restaurant every night, Gene Roddenberry, Jake and I. It was an intense period of time."

I stood up, and he said, "Sit down for a while and relax, will you?" I said, "I'd love to, but I can't stay long today. I don't want Dan getting the idea I'm abusing the privilege." De said, "Oh, that's right. You're right. He has been so good to let you get away like this. Go on back." I said, "I have to go by Carolyn's again and sit with her for a while, too. I don't want her to feel left out – so I'd better go right now." He agreed, and thanked me for coming out. I said, "I wish I could stay." He said, "I do, too, but get going before you lose your job!"

I walked over to Carolyn's. At that very moment, her walker came by to walk with her. I frowned. The walker quickly put Carolyn's sock and brace on, then her shoes, and I said, "I don't suppose you'd walk someone else first, and then come back for Carolyn?" She said, "Yes, I would. It will be a half hour." I said, "Perfect – if that's all right with YOU, Carolyn." Carolyn said, "That would be just fine!" So we sat down and spent another forty minutes together.

I wandered back over to say a final good-bye to De for the day, but he was asleep, so I walked back and told Carolyn he was. I dropped a card on Carolyn's desk as I left. It was a sweet card about not having to be brave all the time… knowing that she was facing challenges… but that I'd always be there for her.

Just as soon as I got back to work, the phone rang. Carolyn said, "I won't keep you long, but I just wanted to say how much I loved the card you left for me." I said, "Oh, I'm glad." She said, "Thank you very much. You didn't sign it, though…" I said, "You're JOKING!" She said, "No." I said, "What a dippy I am! You knew it was from me, though, because of the sentiment on the envelope, right? (To Carolyn, with love ever-lasting.)" She said, "Yes." I said, "Well, I love you… and I'll sign it when I get out there next time." She said, "All right." I said, "I meant to tell you something when I was out there, too, but there was so much going on that it totally slipped my mind." She asked, "What is it?" I said, "If you'd like me to go get Florene this weekend or some other weekend – I know she can't travel herself — I'd be happy to do that." She said, "You don't know where she lives." I said, "I have her address, and you can give me directions easily enough." She said, "Let me think about that. It would be fun." I said, "I could do it this weekend, if you ask her and she can come out then." She said, "No, I think Bette and Anne are coming out this weekend." I said, "That's why I mentioned it. Perhaps you'd like them all at once, like a big party." She said, "No, I would like them spaced out." I said, "Okay. Whatever. Do they know each other?" Carolyn said, "I don't think so. I'm not even sure Bette and Anne know each other. They're an entirely different set of friends." I said, "Oh, okay. I thought maybe you hung out together, playing cards or whatever, and it would be a treat for everyone to get together again." She said, "No, I don't think so. I'd like to see them individually." I said, "That's cool." I could hear the smile in her voice as she said, "I'm glad."

On April 14th De called at 6:30 a.m. I was in the bathtub but had taken the phone into the bathroom "just in case" he called, luckily! I jumped out of the tub, picked up the receiver and said, "Good morning." He said, "Is this – Kris or her answering machine?" I said, "It's me, in the flesh." (He had no idea how accurate a statement THAT was!) "Oh, good. Good morning, Kris. Did I get you out of bed?" I said, "No." He said, "You weren't asleep?"

"No." He said, "Say, can you find me a larger calendar? The ones out here are too small to see from the bed." I said, "Sure." He added, "Also, will you bring out those size 32 trousers when you come out today? The ones I told you about, that are in the closet?" I said, "Sure. No problem." He said, "They're the beige ones. I have two pairs in that size, I think – a beige pair and a dark pair – almost black, if not black." "How soon do you need the pants?" He said, "Oh, I don't need them. I just want them here so they'll be available for the doctor appointment next Monday. No hurry." I said, "Okay. I'll be out at around noon." He said, "Okay, honey."

I went to Don's for the mail, clipped four rose buds for the Kelleys, and then drove out to the hospital. De was sitting in a chair in his room, looking good. He said, "Good morning, Kris. You'll have to unload the wheelchair in order to sit down this morning, it looks like." I said, "No problem." I showed him the trousers. Then I showed him the wildcat calendar I had brought from my home. He said he had one larger than that at his home. I said, "I don't think so. I think you brought that one in for Carolyn." He said, "Oh, that's right. This one is fine – it's larger than the one I have." I showed him the large photo of serval kittens on one of the pages, and he said, "That's perfect." I said, "I guess you KNOW why I chose this calendar!" He said, "I do, indeed...Oh! I straightened the thing out about you." I queried, "The thing?" He said, "I spoke to the head nurse this morning about your visits here. I didn't want there to be any animosity about your being here among the nurses." I said, "Oh." De said, "There's no problem with you being here. She said it's a big help." I said, "Oh, good." I added, "I wondered why it would be considered anything OTHER than helpful, but then I remembered WHO you are and also how much FUN you are to help, and then I really did begin to wonder if you were right about there being some jealousy." De said, "I did, too. I wondered if they wanted to keep me all to themselves. But that isn't the case. I like to clear the air if I feel there is a problem." That led me to ask, "Are you psychic at all?" He said, "Sometimes I think I am. I know my mother was as least a little psychic. She would call me from Georgia and tell me things I was doing in California, and there was no WAY she could have known." I said, "I think that's pretty common between parents and children who are really tight with each other. I know I was psychic when I was a child. Mom and Dad would go off on a vacation for a week or two, and I'd tell our sitter, 'Mommy and daddy are coming home today!' – even if it was DAYS early. She always told me, 'You just miss your mommy and daddy; they won't be home this soon.' I said, 'Yes, they will. They're coming home TODAY!' And they did!" He said, "You have it, then." I also told him the dream I had about Robert Kennedy the night he died – in all its details – and that REALLY sealed my "psychic" abilities for him. He said, "You ARE psychic, girl!"

I tried the diabetic socks on him; he swam in them! I said I'd get a smaller size for him to try.

As we went through the mail, the phone rang. It was Carolyn. De said I'd just arrived and that we were going through mail. She said her knee and leg were hurting her and that the nurse said she had to keep it down. She told him, "I don't want to live like this."

The phone rang again. Stephanie had Bill Shatner on the line, so I gave the phone to De. De spoke with him and found out that he was calling from the airport in Atlanta and that he'd be out to visit with De on Friday. De said, "That would be great. I love you, Bill." He hung up and gave me that news. I said, "Okay. I won't be out on Friday, then, so you two guys can talk." De thought about that for a moment and then decided, "Yes, I guess that would be best."

It was a warm, beautiful day, so I threw the door wide open. De could hear the birds and was loving it. Overcome by the juxtaposition between the beauty of the day and the tragedy of the situation at hand, I said to De, "I wish I could take on your cancer and Carolyn's broken leg so you two could go home and have more time together." He quickly responded, "Oh, don't say that; you'll make me cry – because I know you mean it." I assured him emphatically, "I DO mean it!" He said, "I know you do. Bless your heart." He grabbed a Kleenex and we sat there, sniffling.

After a few more minutes, I told him I should see if Carolyn wanted to visit (since she was hurting and depressed, I figured she might not). He said, "Just go on over and ask her." I said, "It'll be easier for her to tell me no if she doesn't feel up to it, if I CALL her from here." He said, "Okay, call her." I did so and asked, "Do you want me to visit you today?" She said emphatically, "Yes!" I said, "Okay! I'll be right over!" I gave De the thumbs up – he grinned – and I announced, "She wants me!" He said, "Good. Go see her."

I left and went over to Carolyn's. I rubbed her knee and she told me how much it hurt whenever she had to move it. I told her that it was probably going to hurt for a little while, since it had been held immobile for so long. "But each day, I think it will feel a little bit better. Your knee has to learn how tough it was before, and work to get that way again."

I gave her two rose buds and she put them into the bud vase and admired them. I told her that De had told me she was having a bad day, and so that's why I called first, to be sure she wanted a visitor. She said, "What did De tell you I said?" I said, "He said you're having a bad day and that your knee is hurting and you're tired of it." I signed the card I'd left her the day before.

She said she wanted to go over and see De, so I wheeled her over. Not long after, the nurse came by to walk her, and I said, "Can you come back in a half hour, so we can visit for a while longer?" She said, "Yes," so I put Carolyn's brace on, then her shoes and socks.

De told us a funny story about sitting in the lobby that morning and having two girls stare at him for at least ten minutes. Carolyn said, "You should be used to that after about 50 years of it." De said, "No, that wasn't it. Let me finish the story." He said they stared and stared at him, and then his nurse said something fast in Spanish to the other nurse, and De, who could understand a respectable amount of Spanish, told the nurse, "That one went too fast. It got by me. What did you say?" And the nurse admitted, "Those girls are staring at your balls!" "I guess I had my gown hiked up enough and my legs open enough that everything was in full view!" I cracked up; De chuckled, thinking it was plenty funny. I think Carolyn was just mortified.

After a co-piloted trip to the bathroom, De washed his hands and then uncapped the toothpaste tube to brush his teeth. I stood there as a spotter, of course. He observed as he brushed, "When you're in the hospital, so much for privacy!" I said, "I'd leave, but they want you to have a co-pilot!" He said, "I know. I'm not complaining – just mentioning how different life is once you become ill!" I "spotted" him back to bed and asked if he wanted a back and kidney massage before he laid back down. He said, "Yes." As I massaged his back, I asked, "Feel good?" and he said, "Wonderful…" I said, "I don't get it with Carolyn. I did her back a couple of times, and it didn't even seem to be much of a pleasure for her. It's heaven for me." De said, "Me, too. But she has always been that way."

On April 15th De called everywhere he could think to reach me, but I was already on my way to his house. When I got there, there were two messages from him asking me to call. "It's nothing terribly important, but if you get this message, please call me before you come out."

I called from his house and he said, "Something very funny happened this morning; I have to tell you about it. I called your house – or THOUGHT I did – and someone answered the phone who sounded just like you! So I started out joking, 'You know, this has happened once before, and if you're late reporting to work one more time, I'm going to have to fire you!'

The gal said, 'I know, but….' I figured you were just playing along, so I said, 'No excuses, now. I have to be able to rely on you, or I have to let you go.'" He chuckled. "I went on like that with her – I thought it was you – trying to defend yourself. Finally, about a minute or more into the conversation, the girl asked me, 'Who IS this? and I said, "Well, I don't know who this is, but I hope you're Kris Smith!' and she said, 'No, I'm not!' We both hung up! I probably gave her a heart attack!" I was loving it. I laughed my head off and then said, "So, am I fired?" He said, "No!" I said, "That's good!" Then I told him I was walking into his garage to look for the archiving box we'd be using to file the necessary paperwork that Carolyn had saved for years in envelopes. "I'm also going to look for the tennis balls for her walker that are out there somewhere." De said, "I can describe which cabinet they're in." I said, "OK, I'm taking you with me. I'm using your new cordless phone. I'm walking out into the garage now." He said, "You can put the phone down and come back to me if you can't find them." I said, "No, I'll just take you along, and we'll find them together!" He chuckled and said, "All right." I reported as I advanced, "O.K. I'm entering the garage now, opening a cupboard drawer on my left. Here is fertilizer and garden food." He said, "It's the next cabinet over, to your right." I opened it and said, "Aha! Here's the archiving box – cool – and here are the tennis balls! I got 'em!" He said, "That was fast!" I said, "Shall I bring two balls for you, too?" He joked, "If I have FOUR balls to look at, I'll NEVER get out of here [I'll be such a curiosity]!" I laughed. So did he.

I walked back into the house, and said, "I'll go to Don's and get the mail, then come out. It'll probably be about a half hour." He said, "Okay, honey. I'm looking forward to it."

I visited with Don for about fifteen minutes – he wouldn't let me "desert" him any sooner than that – and then headed for the hospital. There was a slight traffic snarl on the way in, so there was a delay getting there.

I walked into his room and said, "I probably really AM fired, now!" He said, "Not a chance." I gave him a hello kiss and then he noticed the TOUCHED BY AN ANGEL T-shirt I had on. He commented, "Boy, THAT'S appropriate for you to wear! You ARE an angel!" I looked at it and then at him and said, "Well, thank you! I'm an angel in training." He said, "You're an angel in FACT!" I said, "Well, it takes one to know one. Anyone who ISN'T a fellow angel would probably say I'm just a goody two shoes!" He chuckled at that and said, "You're probably right!"

He said, "I haven't told Carolyn yet that I'm thinking about staying overnight on Monday night. I'm a little hesitant." (He hadn't confirmed that with ME, either. I was nervous about taking complete responsibility for him for 24 or more hours.) I said, "You can't just disappear!" He said, "I know. I'll have to tell her." I said, "Have you asked the doctor if it's all right to do that?" He said, "No, I haven't yet. I have to do that, too." I said, "You might want to get HIS approval before you mention it to Carolyn." He nodded. I joked, "I think I'm going to have Don help me make your bed before you get home, so you don't do any grousing about it when you get there!" He said, "No, I'M going to show you how to make the bed."

Then I showed him the newest pair of diabetic socks, which he tried on and flipped over. "I have to show these to Carolyn. I've been looking for socks like these for years!" I told him I'd wheel him over. At the last moment before I wheeled him out the door with one hand while dragging the medicine rack behind me with the other, I placed two of the tennis balls into his lap to carry, joking, "There! NOW you have four balls." He joked, "Christ, I'll NEVER get out of this place now!"

I wheeled him over to Carolyn's room. He got up and gave her a kiss and I gave her the tennis balls and the two black clips she had requested. She, too, mentioned the TOUCHED BY AN ANGEL T-shirt and said, "That certainly is a good shirt for YOU to wear! You ARE an angel!" De grinned, "I just told her the same thing!" I said, "Stop, now! Or I'll get a big head."

De remembered to tell me at that point that he had lost two pounds, but it was water weight pounds, not actual fat or muscle. He weighed in at 114. That was a tremendous gain from when he was in the ICU in the other hospital not long before. The added pounds really showed. He looked, acted and felt so much better. It seemed to be a miraculous, wonderful recovery. I thought hopefully, "There's plenty of life in the old boy yet" – and no one was any happier than I was about it. Carolyn was too nervous or superstitious – or realistic, perhaps – to dare to hope.

John called and told De that his nasal cancer had completely disappeared following radiation and chemotherapy treatments. De was very happy. When he got off the phone, he related to me what John had said, then said, "Hand me a Kleenex. I'm going to cry!" and he did! He was so happy for John. Just then the phone rang; it was Carolyn. I gave HER the good news, and then handed the phone to De. He cried again telling her how happy he was to hear John's great news. He told her, "See? It can happen! YOU can get better and I can get better."

After he hung up, I asked, "Have you pursued the UCLA thing any farther?" He said, "No, the doctor and I pretty much decided against it." I said, "But your oncologist said they might have something there that can

HELP you. If he calls there and feels confident about something, don't you want to TRY it? No one would think to drag you down there and put you through it if there wasn't a real chance that it will make you feel better and perhaps even stop the spread of the tumors." De said, "The oncologist is the one researching it. I will abide by what he suggests."

Not long after, De's physical therapist came by to take De on his walk. De looked so sturdy that I mentioned, "I don't think he even NEEDS a walker today." The therapist said, "I agree. Do you want to try it without the walker, De?" De said, "Sure." The therapist dragged the walker along behind, in case De got tired, and I dragged the bottle rack. De didn't tire at all. We wound up back in Carolyn's room, and chatted a bit. Carolyn said De looked good, strong and sturdy again.

Not long after that, Carolyn's physical therapist came by! De and his P.T. headed out so I could prepare Carolyn's leg for her walk. I did that, and then Carolyn, Carolyn's walker and I went over to De's room. De was sitting in the lobby in an easy chair, so we sat with him for about four or five minutes. De was sure to keep his gown down so he wouldn't cause a riot again with the family jewels. I joked, "Girls learn early on to keep their legs together and their skirts over their knees, but it isn't exactly second nature to GUYS who wear gowns LATE in life!" and we all laughed.

Carolyn got up to walk some more. I asked De if he wanted me to stay and help him into his room, and he said, "No, I'll sit out here for a while longer." I got up and walked with Carolyn back to her room, commenting on how well she was doing and how strong and normal her stride was suddenly. Her P.T. said, "It's a big improvement."

Not long after, I went back to De's room. He was almost back in bed, but was standing next to it without a "spotter." I cautioned him, "De… you aren't supposed to be moving around on your own." He looked real tired and said, "Someone helped me come in." I said, "OK, then, I won't swat you. But, get into bed. No traipsing."

A nurse trainee came in and told us that she was going to disconnect De from the bottles. He said, "Hallelujah!" She said she was going to give him his meds, too, and De said, "Yes, I thought it was about time." They discussed the fact that she was just about to graduate from nursing school. She was eager and De told her she was very good and would be a wonderful nurse. He signed a photo for her. She was delighted. After she left, he commented on the edema in his feet and legs, and wondered if it would be more effective for him or me to call his doctor in to check on it. I said, "I don't know." He said, "Why don't you go ahead and call?" So I did. The doctor said he'd come by at around four.

While we waited for his arrival, De mentioned, "I think we [the original STAR TREK cast] still have another movie in us. I have a couple of ideas for a movie involving us. I've told Bill about them, but nothing has come of it yet." He added, "I've told you about one of them, I think." I said, "Oh, yes! The one where Uhura gets kidnapped." He smiled and said, "Yes." Then he said, "I have another one, too…" I didn't hear his other story line other than a mention that it had a post-retirement theme.

Not long after, I told De, "I'd better get going pretty soon and make another appearance at WB today." He said, "Oh, yes. Before you go, will you straighten my tray table – throw out anything that isn't absolutely essential… and that list of phone numbers looks terrible now, too." I said, "I'll re-write it for you, and then I'll computer-generate it at work, and bring you a GREAT one when I come in on Saturday." He said, "What day is this?" I said, "Thursday." He looked a bit perplexed by that, and I figured it was because he was wondering why I wouldn't be back before Saturday, so I reminded him, "Remember, Bill is coming out to see you tomorrow." He said, "Oh, yes!" I said, "There isn't much point in me coming out if he's going to be here at one – unless you want me early in the morning or after work tomorrow night." He said, "No, that isn't necessary. Take the day off and have your lunch time at Warners tomorrow – but we'll be in touch tomorrow, probably more than once." I said, "I hope so, or I'll have withdrawal symptoms!"

Not long after that I gave him a kiss and told him I loved him. He thanked me for coming and said, "I love you, too, Kris."

At 10:40 P.M. De called. He asked, "Did I wake you?" (Strangely enough, he hadn't.) I said, "No." He said, "Oh, good. Will you remind me on Saturday to call a hospital authority about our plan to stay at the house overnight following my doctor appointment on Monday? I mentioned it to a nurse and she says if I do that, Medicare can decide that if I'm well enough to be home one night, I'm well enough to be released, and my Medicare coverage could end. I can't risk that! Someone told me earlier that I could do that, I think – unless he was just talking about Carolyn, who's a resident out here. Perhaps we're under different rules. Anyway, I need to clarify that." Then he said, "Rather than Saturday, I'd better do it tomorrow, in case he leaves town for the weekend. Or perhaps *you'll* call him *for* me tomorrow, early? I'd rather have my angel do it, if you will." I said, "*awwwww* Sure, I will!" He said, "Thank you. I'll try not to call you again tonight." I said, "Don't worry about that. Goodnight."

He called back at 11:15 and said, "Last call of the night! I just called Carolyn and she asked if I'd ask you to bring her a pair of scuffs next time you come out on Saturday?" I queried, "Scuffs? Are those slippers without heels?" De said, "Yes. She said she doesn't remember where they are, but I do. They're in her bathroom closet on the south side of the closet." I said, "Okay. Sure. I'll bring 'em."

De said, "I hope we get the go ahead to stay at the house Monday night. I want to be there early in the morning in case I need to call Joe [the painter] in from outside the house. I don't want to mess around." Then he chuckled and joked, "*You* won't let me mess around, will you?" I laughed and then joked back, "Well, let's see, now… Carolyn DID give me permission to sleep with you — but we'd just screw up your precious, neat-and-tidy bed, and we can't have THAT!" He guffawed as loudly as he was able.

Then I said, "I'm glad you called back, actually. I wanted to ask you what the doctor said about your edema." He said, "Oh, he didn't seem at all concerned by the edema; in fact, he says it's less than it has been." I said, "Great! Did he think some of it was weather-related, because it has been so warm?" De said, "He didn't say. They don't give you a lot of information, do they? He says mine is a result of my albumin levels, which they're working on. But he didn't seem at all alarmed. Perhaps he's just staying calm to keep from alarming me." I said, "I don't think so, De. It probably IS nothing to worry about. I think they're being straight with you."

Then I said, "Regarding Medicare rules. When Mom had that infection in her brain…" De said, "Yes, I remember that time very clearly." I said, "Medicare wouldn't let a nurse come into the home to treat her. They wouldn't pay for it. Dad wouldn't let Jackie do the treatments – which the doctors said they could show her how to do – so Mom had to go to a nursing home during that time in order for Medicare to pay for it. So Medicare ended up paying a whopping bill where they COULD have saved money just paying for a nurse to come in once a day and give Mom the treatments. So they have some pretty unfathomable rules." De said, "That's why I want to be sure we don't mess up and get into trouble with Medicare. We have to find out." I agreed. Then I asked, "If you end up being released and getting back home, and Carolyn wants to come out with you, will she in any way jeopardize her ability to go back to the hospital or lodge you have established for her out there?" De said, "I don't think so. But these are things we need to speak to the hospital consultant about, definitely. We need to get the answers to these questions."

I said, "Oh! I also found out about the upcoming local convention. It'll be July 30, 31 and August 1st." De said, "If I'm feeling up to it, I want to go out there. I need to tell the hospital consultant about that, too. See if that will cause any problems." Then he said, "I'll try not to call you any more tonight." I said, "PLEASE don't worry about that, De. It's OK to call me anytime." He added, as an afterthought, "If I go to the convention, you have to go along, too." I said, "Sure. No problem." He said, "You will have to wheel me into the bathroom, like you do when we go to the oncologist. You'll have to stay in there with me, so I don't fall on my face." I said, "Yep. I know that. You might have some splainin' to do to the men standing at urinals, though!"

On April 16th I called De at about 10 to let him know I had a call in to the hospital consultant. He said, "Oh, thank you very much." I said, "He's already out of town for the weekend, but his assistant said she would page him, and she's sure he'll return the call." He said, "Oh, good." I wished him a good visit with Bill Shatner.

I said, "I'll go get two more pairs of diabetic socks for you at lunch time today." He said, "You can bring them by, even if Bill is here. We'll probably be out on the patio; it won't interfere." I said, "If it doesn't matter to you, I'd prefer to bring them out tomorrow when I come. The socks are in Glendale – in an entirely different direction from where you are. And you have a pair there for today that you can wear." He said, "That's fine. Do that."

Since I had received no return call from the hospital consultant by 3:30, despite the fact that he had been paged again by his secretary, I called Social Services at the hospital to see if they would have an answer as to whether or not De would be allowed by Medicare to stay overnight at his house. A representative from Social Services returned my call shortly thereafter and said that if De's doctor would certify that the trip home was a pilot attempt at re-entry into the community, Medicare would probably approve it. I said, "Thank you. That's good news. I'll get the message to Mr. Kelley right away, because he's going to talk to his doctor about it this afternoon."

I called De and told him what the representative had said. He said, "Oh, I'm not going to mess with that. I don't want to take any chances. We'll just plan to go out there after the doctor appointment for a little while, so I can talk to Joe." I said, "Okay." He said, "But thank you for all your efforts on my behalf today." I said, "No problem. My pleasure. Always."

On April 17th I got to the Kelleys early and watered the roses, put Miracle Grow on the indoor plants and put the archive box together with the files I'd made earlier. When it was time to leave, the Lexus wouldn't start! I had left a door slightly ajar and the battery had run down. I called De to let him know I'd be in as soon as I could get the Auto Club to give me a jump.

More than an hour later than originally planned, I walked into De's room joking, "Well, I guess I really AM fired NOW!" He shook his head, "No." I could tell he'd had a bad night. He didn't look like a happy camper at all. He told me he was having breathing problems; it was making him anxious. I said, "I know this sounds nutty as hell, like the OPPOSITE of what you WANT to do, but if you will just breathe more SLOWLY, and take deeper breaths from the abdomen, you'll feel better and your breaths will do more for you." He nodded and tried that for a moment, but soon reverted back to the earlier, less effective breathing pattern. I let him know that his color was good and that even though he felt he wasn't getting enough air, he was. I pressed the tip of one of his middle fingers, to determine how much time it took for the blood to return underneath the fingernail; that little test was normal. I assured him he was all right. He still didn't look convinced, so I told him I'd tell the nurse, and he nodded that he'd appreciate that. I went out and told the nurse, and she said she'd be in to give him something to help him breathe better. I went back and told De. The nurse came in real soon and told him exactly what I had, about how he should breathe more slowly, deeply and from the abdomen. He looked at ME as if to acknowledge, "You were right!" and adopted the new breathing rate more religiously than he had previously.

When he had a handle on his breathing and felt better, he told me he had been sick to his stomach again the night before. I sympathized mightily. He said he had called for a nurse when he felt the sickness coming on, telling her he was feeling nauseous, but no one responded soon enough, and so he got sick twice into the little emesis basin before anyone arrived. "I rang again, telling them I was throwing up, and THEN someone came in, right away. Good thing, because there was no room for anything more in the basin." I said, "NEXT time, be sure to tell them you're about to throw up. Saying you're nauseous doesn't necessarily mean you're about to vomit. They need to know. I'm sure they would have come right in HAD they known you were that close." He nodded.

I told him I could stay all day and also overnight on weekends to be sure he got the assistance he needed whenever he needed it. He said, "I appreciate that, because I know you mean it. But you do enough with all you do already.

I just have to let you know I was never so happy to see anyone walk in that door as I was YOU this morning." I almost cried, and so did he!

De told me about the visit with Shatner. Then he said, "It's sure nice having you around, someone I can discuss dying with. I can't do that with Shatner or with many other people; it upsets them so. They'll talk about ANYTHING else, but not dying!" I said, "Well, I used to be the same way." De said, "So did I. I understand it completely. Still, it's good to have someone I CAN talk to about it."

On April 18 I got there at 9:15 A.M. De had breathing problems again. I told the nurse. She gave him more Lasix and we added oxygen to his medical repertoire.

He ate melon and berries and for lunch had almost half of a grilled ham and cheese sandwich. He drank ½ to 2/3 of a soda.

De mentioned that the yard and roses probably could use a good dousing of water again. I said I'd get it done in the next day or so. He said, "No hurry — just whenever you happen to be out there. It doesn't have to all be done in one day."

Nichelle Nichols came for a visit at about 2:45. De, Carolyn and I waited in De's room for her to arrive. When she was overdue by almost twenty minutes, De said he hoped they wouldn't be waiting much longer. He was beginning to feel and to look tired. Luckily, just moments later Nichelle arrived, and she stayed only about an hour. Her visit perked him up considerably.

Not long after Nichelle left, De said he was beginning to feel a little nauseous, so I told the nurse and then went back to press the reflexology points in his hands until the anti-nausea drug could take effect. A male nurse came in and asked what I was doing. I told him. De told him, "I thought she was making this stuff up, until another nurse knew exactly what she was talking about!" The nurse nodded and said that acupuncture works wonders, too, when all else fails.

I left the hospital as soon as De felt comfortable again, to let him sleep, but by the time I got home, De called and asked me to remind him to call the doctor in the morning. I said, "I'm going to be on the road very early in the morning, on the way to you; I won't be able to call and remind you, I don't think." He said, "Okay, I'll remember to call." He asked, "Can you get here by 8 tomorrow?" I said, "Sure, I can get there any time you want me there." He said, "I think the earlier, the better. If I can have your help to get ready, things will go more smoothly. I won't have to wait on the nurses to help me dress, or to shave." I said, "No problem. I'll do everything so you can conserve your energy and save it for the doctor appointment and the stuff at home afterward." He said, "Yes, that's the best plan." I said, "I'll be there," and we hung up.

About five minutes later, I called him back and said, "Since you want me there so early in the morning, I think I'll drive to your house and stay the night, to be past the 405 rush hour crush in the morning." He agreed, saying, "Good idea." I said, "So… if you need me again tonight, I'll be at your place." He said, "Okay."

I got some stuff together and drove to the Kelley house, arriving at about 8:15 P.M. I managed to get too close to a chair that was sitting against a sheet-rocked wall, and the front end of the car bumped it hard enough to put a hole in the sheet-rock. I was mortified! I called my dad in Washington, panicked, to see what it would cost to fix, planning to pay for it myself. Dad said, "Hell, it's nothing. It's easy to fix." I was glad to hear that!

I decided to water the lawns and work in the office on filing. I worked from 8:30 to 11:45 and then fell into bed and slept like the dead until 6:30 A.M.

On April 19th I drove out to get De, arriving at about 7:40. I was amazed to find him awake already. He had already shaved, but that had taken most of the starch out of him. He was moving very slowly. I helped him into the bathroom for a bath and washed his armpits and upper body. As I washed him, I recognized he was very weak and I let him know we didn't HAVE to go anywhere but to the doctor, if the trip home afterward seemed to be too much for him. He said, "No, I really want to get home today. I need to talk to Joe about what needs to be done." I said, "You can tell him over the phone." He said, "No, I have to walk around and show him." I said, "Okay, but just remember, this doesn't HAVE TO be done today. We have permission to take you out again any time you need to go." He nodded. I mentioned to him that I felt a little nervous, taking him out when he was feeling so low-energy, then said I figured the nurse wouldn't LET me take him if it was dangerous for him. De agreed with that assessment, but then added, "Listen, I want you to know something: If ever I should happen to die while I'm at the house with you, I don't want you to feel guilty about it. That's where I'd prefer to die, anyway." I took a quiet, deep breath at THAT, and then said, "Okay, I won't feel guilty – but if it DID happen, I think we'd ALL have some mighty tall 'splaining to do!"

I got him back out near the bed and helped put his clothes on, then got him into the wheelchair. We were ready very early, but the IV drip had to be slowly shut down, so we sat and he ate some breakfast while we waited to be cut loose for the trip.

I called the painter to confirm that he'd meet us at the house after De's doctor appointment. His wife answered and De talked to her. She told him they were very sorry, but that Joe wouldn't be able to meet with him that day. De was horrendously disappointed, and let her know that getting out to the house was a tremendous effort and that he didn't know when or if he'd be able to do it again. She said she'd try to reach her husband and let him know how important it was. De said, "Please do, and call us back to let us know." She said she would. When she didn't call back, I called again and only got voice mail. I left a message saying that we were leaving for the doctor appointment and that I hoped Joe would be able to make it out, but if NOT, to please call De's house and leave a message letting us know. I finished with, "We'll be there at noon. We very much hope Joe will be, too."

When De was finally cut loose, we went to Carolyn to tell her good-bye for the day. De looked like a whipped puppy; he didn't feel well. When Carolyn bid him farewell, he cried, and she wondered why. He said, "I'm just emotional today." She said, "You're stealing my stuff!" I said, "That's okay. It's okay to cry." Carolyn said, "It sure is. Have a wonderful day, honey."

I wheeled him out of there and got the car. After I got De into the car, and while the door was still open (to let heat out) a reed-thin, frail young man approached the car. He, too, was quite obviously a patient. He apologized for imposing – "I would normally NEVER do anything like this" – then told De how much joy De's career had brought him and how important he was to him as a human being. De asked him what his malady was, and they spoke for a minute or two. De became teary-eyed again and told the young man that his kind words meant a lot to him. He wished the young man well and thanked him for stopping by. As we drove out, De said, "I wish I could have thought of something more helpful to say to that young man." I assured him, "Just spending the time with him was helpful, De. It made his day." He said, "I hope so. He sure made mine."

We drove to the oncologist's office and waited 90 minutes to see him. De and I tried to leave twice, but received assurances that the doctor would be right with him, so we waited. We were told that the doctor had some hopeful news for De, and that it would be a productive meeting. When we finally got in, the doctor mentioned a few more things he had tracked down – other options to consider – and said he'd research them and get back to us. He asked De to return and see him again in a week, so we scheduled another appointment.

As we drove to the house, I confessed to De that I had punched a hole in his drywall in the garage. I told him I'd pay Joe whatever it would cost to fix it. De chuckled and said not to worry about it.

We got to De's house at 12:45. I showed him where I had punched a hole in the drywall. He didn't seem upset or concerned about it in the least.

When we got inside, we discovered that Joe's wife had called and left a message, saying that they were very sorry, but that Joe was unable to meet with him that day. De was very disappointed, but there was nothing we could do about it. He decided to call his friend John, who was a retired hairdresser, and let him know he was at home for a while. John offered to come out and cut his hair, and De jumped at the chance.

I went back to the garage and heard Myrtle rattling around in her box. I lifted her out and set her down on the patio, then reported to De that Myrtle had emerged from hibernation to welcome him home. He mentioned what a dear thing she was and said he wondered if there was anything in the fridge to feed her. I said, "I have cantaloupe and honeydew in there." He exclaimed, "Those are her favorites!" I pulled them out and took them to her. She started right in eating. We watched her for a while.

While we waited for John to arrive, De wandered around the house using a cane, and I cooked two small pizzas. It was a horrendously hot day, but De wanted the doors and windows thrown open, so I did that. It quickly became even warmer in the house. I was sweltering. De was happy as a clam.

He talked about the possibility of Carolyn and himself eventually coming home, if they got better. I said that would be terrific. He said, "We'd have to get you a bed." I said, "Yep, I guess so. Or I could stay with Myrtle – most of the year, except during the rainy season!" He laughed at that. I said, "I stayed in a tent in the back yard with Deaken a LOT in Encino." He said, "Yes, I remember you did that."

He called a couple of neighbors and chatted with them. Soon thereafter John arrived and De sipped on half a beer while John and I ate berries and melon. Then we went outside so John could cut De's hair.

After the haircut, John said his goodbye and De decided he wanted to have a shower in his very own shower! I told him that after he got out of the shower I wanted to put lotion on his back and neck and upper arms, because they were so dry and two nurses had mentioned it that morning. He said, "Okay, when I get out I'll let you know."

He got into the shower and bathed for such a long time that I began to get a little nervous about his status, so I called in, "De? Are you okay?" Absolute silence! I almost panicked and tried again, "De?!" He heard me the second time and said, "Yes?" I said, "You okay?" He said, "Yes. I'll be out in a minute." I said, "Okay!"

He came out and called me in to put lotion on him. It was sweltering in the house already, but the second I walked into the bathroom, he asked me to turn on the wall heater! I did so, and immediately began to baste in a veritable torrent of perspiration. I very quickly doused him with lotion and then asked him, facetiously, "Are you warm enough?" He sighed, "Yeah, it feels good." I said, "Well, before *I* die of heat stroke, I'm getting the hell out of here, boss!" He said, "Go!" I escaped to a cooler (98 degree) part of the house and waited for him to emerge, but pretty soon he said, "You can come in and turn off the heater now. I'm not strong enough to do it anymore." I said, "Okay. You've finally come to your senses, I see! You sure are a hot house plant!" He didn't respond to that.

He came out and put on underwear and then flaked out on the bed. Within a minute, he was fast asleep! I worked in the office for close to an hour, cleaning it up after my night of activity, figuring he needed the rest. At 5:20 I tapped him on the shoulder and roused him a little. I said, "I'll let you sleep longer if you want, but if we don't get going pretty soon, you'll miss dinner back at the hospital." He sat up and said, "How long have I been asleep?" I looked at my watch and said, "Almost an hour." He said, "That's the best sleep I've had in a month!" I put his clothes on him as he sat looking out the bedroom door, marveling, "This is a beautiful, beautiful place." I said, "It sure is."

De walked into the workroom again, marveling at how much I'd done already. I told him, "I did MOST of it just last night, and that's why the room looked pretty disorganized just BEFORE you fell asleep. But now it looks better because I took out the trash just now while you were sacked out." He said, "My little angel deserves a big hug for all the work she has done for me recently." I said, "Awright!" and collected the sweetest hug, right there on the spot.

Just as we were about to leave, two of De's neighbors came over to tell him they missed him and Carolyn and to chat about the young man's college choices. They visited for about five minutes, with De leaning half on the cane and half on the wall in the main hallway.

We went back to the car. We drove to the hospital and I wheeled him most of the way in and then asked him if he wanted to walk into Carolyn's room and make her day. He said he did, so I helped him stand and he sauntered into her room, newly groomed and looking dapper. He told her about the wonderful, productive day and she just beamed at how happy he looked and acted.

After a few minutes of reporting to Carolyn all that had gone on, De and I went back to his room. He looked at the bed, NOT wanting to commit himself to a HOSPITAL again after the wonderful afternoon at home. He mentioned the air mattress and how he hated it, so I went out and asked the nurse to remove it. "If his skin begins to look ratty, it can go back on, but for now, please let him have the bed the way he wants it." She said, "Of course!" and soon came to take the mattress off.

We were both tired and I was a little silly with fatigue. De sat in the wheelchair as we ate dinner and we chatted and joked. At one point, De meant to say something to me but mis-spoke and what came out was: "Before you go, I want you to get into bed with me." I laughed as he figured out what he had just said and reacted to it! I quickly commented, "Gee, that's the best offer I've had—" De laughed and finished, "— all day!" I said, "No, in my entire lifetime!" He joked dryly, "Well, I suppose you *could* get into bed with me, but nothing would happen!" I laughed it off and assured him, "That's okay!"

The nurse came in to take off the air mattress. After she left, I helped him get undressed and into the gown and then helped him into bed.

As I got ready to leave at about 8:15 P.M., he seemed hesitant to let me go. He kept asking me to do last minute things for him. I was so sweaty from the hot, busy activities all afternoon that I hated to get very near him to help him undress, go to the bathroom, get into bed, and the like. He said he didn't care about my perspiration – it had all been for HIM – and that I could take a nice long bath when I got home. I said, "You can BET I will!"

As I was leaving, he got all teary-eyed. He said, "I just can't begin to express to you how wonderful it is having you so willing to help do anything we need." I said, "You don't have to, De." He finally said, "You're the best." I countered with, "No, YOU'RE the best!" THAT blew him away! He lost it entirely! I rushed over to him, took his hand, and said, "Oh, sweety, don't cry!" Then I said, "Oh, go ahead. It's okay! It's okay to cry." I kissed his hand, cried a little with him, and left shortly thereafter.

On April 20th I got to the hospital at about 11:30 and stayed until 2:10. De told me, "I slept great last night." He wasn't as full of energy as he had been the day before, but I could tell it was a happy, comfortable tired, not a sick kind of tired. He mentioned what a great day it had been, and I agreed. He asked if I'd had my bath, and I assured him, "God, yes!" He chuckled and said, "I thought about you last night!" I joked, "Why didn't you call?" He said, "I didn't want to electrocute you! That's ALL we'd need now!" I laughed.

He told me that Shatner wanted to read one of his poems at the Pasadena convention that weekend, "but I'm not at home to find one for him." I told him, "I have copies at my house of all of your TREK-related poems," and he joked, "Boy, I hired the right girl, didn't I?" I told him I'd get them to Shatner via fax. I called Stephanie and got the fax number, so I could do that. De wondered how, exactly, Bill planned to use the poem, and so we put in another call to Stephanie. Bill called back not much later and they discussed the plan. De told Bill I'd fax the poems to him the next day so he could choose which one he would read on the weekend...

Carolyn called and I went over and brought her to De's room. We discussed De's effect on fans. Carolyn sometimes thought it was a little silly, and I said, "USUALLY it's a really heartfelt, wonderful thing. That's why I love going to conventions when De appears. I love how the audience loves and interacts with him." We discussed the number of doctors and nurses that De's career spawned, and Carolyn mentioned how wonderful he was with the fans, saying, "De is a sweet man. A GOOD BOY!" De got tears in his eyes over that... I agreed wholeheartedly! De again mentioned the sick fan he'd met outside the hospital the day before, saying he wished he could have done more.

On April 21st I faxed the three STAR TREK-related poems to Shatner's secretary, then received a voice mail message saying that the poems were too long, and that they wanted something shorter, if De had something. I called De and gave him the scoop, and he said, "Well, I'm stuck here and can't get to the shorter ones." I told him I could get them and bring them to him, and he told me where they were in the house. He asked how soon Shatner needed the poem, and I said, "This weekend." He said, "It would be good if I could get them early this afternoon," and I reminded him that my gang at Warner Bros. was taking me to lunch for Secretary's Day. He said, "Oh, forget it, then. It's really not all that important." I told him I could bring them out that evening when I planned to visit again, and he said, "It really isn't necessary to visit at all today." I told him I'd call Stephanie back and let her know we'd look for a shorter poem, and that if we found one, I'd fax it to her no later than Friday. He said, "Okay."

I went off to lunch and when I got back, there was a voice mail message from a social worker at the hospital asking me to call her back, "since you're a longtime friend and know so much about Mr. Kelley." Just as I was retrieving her message she called back and related that Mr. Kelley wasn't forthcoming with her on some issues. "Different people feel differently about social workers, and I honor that, but just as a precaution, I wanted to know if you know if there have been any final arrangements made in the event he should pass away while he's here at the hospital." I said, "Oh, yes. He has that all arranged and paid for. He's to be cremated and his ashes scattered at sea by the Neptune Society." She said, "Can I get copies of those instructions?" I said, "Not unless he releases me to give them to you. But I know right where they are and can put my hand on them if it becomes necessary." She said, "Oh, okay. That's good enough. That's all I need." I said, "Incidentally, his doctor recently gave him some hopeful news, so all of this is premature." She said, "I hope I haven't misled you. The information I'm gathering has NOTHING to do with any thought that he is close to death. It's just preliminary in CASE something unforeseen would happen." I said, "I see. And I understand." She said, "Thank you very much for your help. Since Mr. Kelley was so hesitant to speak with me about less grave issues, I certainly didn't want to address THIS one with him." I said, "I understand. If I can help in some other way, please give me a call."

De called in the evening at 9:00. The first words out of his mouth were, "I missed you today." I said, "I missed you, too!" He said, "I'm having a procedure done next week at another hospital." I said, "Is it the liver embolism procedure?" He said, "Yes, I think it is." "Is your oncologist doing it?" De said, "Yes. I will be there for a while – probably a week." I said, "Oh, really? He said it wasn't really very invasive." De said, "There will be some pain." I said, "He mentioned that – a degree of discomfort for a few days." De said ruefully, "I love that term – 'discomfort.'"

I told him there was a phone call from Bob Justman on his answering machine at home and said, "I'll bring his phone number with me when I come in tomorrow. I don't know if you want to call him back, or not." He said, "Yes, I do."

I told him I tried to feed Myrtle some more melon, but she walked away. He said, "She usually just eats grass the first few days. Don't worry about her. I suppose we're going to fall in love with her again and want to keep her instead of giving her to the neighbor across the street." I said, "Nothing wrong with that!"

I asked if he'd had a good day, and he said, "I can't remember." Then he said, "I'm trying to decide if there's anything else I wanted to tell you... Let me think... I guess not." I said, "If you think of it later, you can call back." He asked, "What time do you go to bed?" I said, "It depends on what I have to do. Tonight I had mail to go through – yours and mine – and some of mine to answer – so I just got into bed about twenty minutes ago. Some nights I'm up until midnight. It just depends." De said, "That's what I do, too."

He said, "Well, I'll let you go. I'm going to call Big Mouth now." I queried, "Big Mouth?" De said, "A.C." I chuckled and said, "Oh! Big Mouth!" He said, "I'll try not to call you again tonight." I said, "Call any time you want, De. It's fine. Bye bye, I love you."

He said, "I love you, too, Kris. Goodnight."

On April 22nd I drove to the hospital, arriving at about 11:30. I arrived with perfect roses from their garden. De marveled at them and then said I would have to take them to Carolyn later for her to choose which ones to keep; he had so many plants and flower arrangements in his room at that time that he couldn't handle any more.

He told me about the following week's surgical plan. I showed him the liver embolization paper I had written up; he thought it was amazing that I had remembered so much of what we were told. I asked if I should give his doctor a copy of it, and he said I should, so I carried him a copy and handed it to him. He started to read it and I said, "I heard the information twice, and then wrote down what I remembered of it that night." The doctor was reading it and said, "This is very good." I said, "If there's anything I got wrong in it, please let me know, so I can correct it." He had no corrections to recommend after finishing it.

I pulled out the poems I had collected from De's house, and while he went through them, I went to Carolyn's room for a visit; ended up staying more than an hour. I massaged lotion into her legs. We chatted for quite a while, then I wheeled her over to be with De.

The Kelleys were affectionate, lovey dovey. De's hands were cold, Carolyn noticed, and he said, "I don't have my body warmer in bed with me the way I used to." She took his hand in hers.

De was very emotional again that day, becoming teary-eyed whenever anything was said that would touch the heart. Carolyn and I both told him it was all right to be emotional; "we are too." He said, "Then why do I always seem to be the only one crying? No one else is crying." Carolyn said, "I used to be just like that. Hated it." I said, "There's nothing at all to hate about it – it means you feel things, which is wonderful." Then I reminded De that I had cried with him a time or two last week, and he nodded, remembering. I told them I cried at night. Carolyn said she did, too, sometimes…

De read some of the poems I had brought him, and picked one of them, "THE YELLOW BALLOON," for me to fax to Shatner for the convention. He said, "When I wrote these, they didn't seem to me to be depressing, but now that I read them again, most of them are!" I asked if he wanted me to fax the poem to Bill in its original hand-written form, or to fax it after I had typed it. He said, "Type it first." I said, "Okay."

I had a terrible time faxing De's "Yellow Balloon" to Shatner. It was a nightmare of redundancy. Time after time it kept stalling. It took over an hour for the transmission to finally succeed. De's "angel Kris" was issuing a variety of colorful metaphors inside her brain, although I made sure the words didn't actually issue from my lips. I thought, "I will never, ever forget De's #%!%# 'Yellow Balloon'!"

After that Hurculean effort, I returned to De's room and asked him where he wanted me to put the extra copies of the liver embolization paper, and he told me. Carolyn said, "What's that?" I said, "It's my report of what we heard in the oncologist's office the other day, about the procedure De is having done." She asked, "May I read it?" I said, "Sure. You can have your own copy, if you want." De quickly told her, "It's my fault you don't have one already. I told Kris I didn't think you'd be that interested in the documentation." She said, "Well, let me see it…" and read it. Then she said, "I would like to keep this copy, if I may." I said, "You bet."

Just before 3:30, Carolyn decided to go back to her room. As soon as she left, De reported that he was beginning to feel nauseous, so I informed a nurse and then went in and pressed the reflexology points until the shot was administered. It hurt this time. He was also feeling chilly, so I covered him well.

He fell asleep for 90 minutes soon afterwards, and when he awoke, he ate a few bites of dinner. He was still tired. We watched the news about the Littleton Colorado shootings and we both cried. Then he said he was still very tired, so I kissed him and went over to sit with Carolyn for another 40 minutes or so. We watched WHEEL OF FORTUNE together and I explained the following week's liver embolization procedure further, so she'd fully understand the benefits he should reap from it. She said wistfully, "Perhaps he'll outlive us all, then."

On April 23rd I called De at 10 a.m. He told me he'd had a helluva morning. When I got to his room, I showed him his computer-generated poems and let him know I could re-do them in script font or any other font or size he wanted in a jiffy. I showed him where a couple of the poems didn't look finished, and he said he'd work on them.

He told me about his morning of showering and medical treatment. I called John for him and they chatted for a while, then I went over and got Carolyn to come over for a visit. De didn't want lunch, so I had a few bites of his. After that I excused myself to go back to work. De thanked me for everything and I told him, "You're welcome. See you tomorrow."

On April 24th I polished De's and A.C.'s stars and then went to the Kelleys' house. I started the bedding and towels in the washer and then went to Don's for the mail. I updated him on the liver embolization procedure De's oncologist had told us about. I told him De had decided to have it done at UCLA rather than in Tarzana, because UCLA had the most experienced doctor doing the procedure, but that the procedure wouldn't take place until a few weeks later. After I got back to De's house, I called De to let him know where I was and that I was washing the towels and bedding.

During our next visit De showed real signs of weakness. I told De I'd call the oncologist's office first thing on Monday and schedule a Tuesday or Thursday appointment. He said, "Okay." His eyes were getting droopy, so I said I'd let him sleep. He nodded and went off to dream land.

While De slept, I went over to Carolyn's and sat with her and watched television. A couple of hours later, De called over to Carolyn's wondering if I had gone home. Carolyn said I hadn't; I was right here, and that she'd send me over.

I went over to sit with him. He was sick to his stomach in the evening a number of times, and the vomit smelled foul, so the nurse put in a call for the doctor. It took two hours for a doctor to come in, and he ordered an x-ray for first thing in the morning.

As we sat all that time waiting for the doctor, he mentioned to me, "I'm sure glad you're here. Sometimes I think you're here too late at night, but when things like this start to happen to me, I'm so glad you're right here! It's a comfort to know I have help." I said, "You bet you do."

De began to look more comfortable and unlikely to vomit again at around eleven, but I offered, "I'll stay all night if you want." He said, "No, you go home now and get some sleep."

On April 25th I got to the hospital at about 9 A.M. De still felt puny and asked me to call a long-time friend of theirs, and cancel the visit they had planned for that day. I did that. I didn't stay on long and was speaking quietly, as De's eyes were closed and I didn't want to disturb him much. After canceling the visit, I told her I was very much looking forward to meeting her, but guessed it would have to be on another day now. The woman cheerfully stated that she was looking forward to meeting me, too, but that it could happen on another day. With that, we signed off. I looked at De and he opened his eyes long enough to comment, "Good dog. That's all we can do about that today."

When Carolyn found out that the visit had been cancelled, she was very upset and let me know it, in no uncertain terms. She told me I had upset her friend terribly by speaking to her so abruptly; that she had called Carolyn back in tears! Based on Carolyn's recounting of the conversation, it was as if two separate phone conversations with the woman had taken place. I didn't believe I had handled the call at all inappropriately. Certainly De hadn't objected to what I had said – and he had heard every word.

Seeing how angry Carolyn was over the matter, I offered to call the friend and apologize, but she vetoed that idea. I apologized for the change in plans, then let her know the reason for the cancellation: De's condition that day was terrible; he felt lousy and didn't want anyone to see him that way. Still visibly angry by De's decision to cancel the visit, she told me to go back to De's room and attend him. "Nothing good is happening here today." Rattled beyond speech, I left.

De slept away most of that day trying to escape his discomfort. During his waking moments that evening we talked, and I let him know how livid Carolyn had been with me over canceling their friend's visit with him. It upset him. "You were just doing what I asked you to do." I sighed and said, "It's all right. She's just having a helluva time dealing with all of this. The anger has to go somewhere, and I'm safe. She knows I'll always love her."

Thereafter, he did a lot of appreciating! We had been watching Touched By An Angel in his room for several weeks running by this time, and both of us had been brought to tears by each of the episodes. Because I had just been through the ringer emotionally with Carolyn and had managed to transcend the hurt I felt in order to hold on to my love for her, De became curious, and then asked – very sincerely, truly questioning me – "*Are* you an angel?" His question touched me deeply, and had I been able to somehow manufacture a halo, a la Roma Downey, I may well have succumbed to the enourmous temptation to say, "yes," so great was my desire to reassure him at the moment that he was indeed, surrounded by angels. I took his hand and said, "No, but I'm trying to be." He nodded and said, "I think you are." I said, "From what I've read about angels, they're an entirely different species. We never become angels and our guardian angels aren't people who have passed away before us. But one quote I just LOVE, by Og Mandino, goes something like this: "The trouble with full-time angels is that they are completely unpredictable and you cannot just send out for one. That is why part time angels are so important. Part-time angels are you and me." He liked the quote so much that he asked me to repeat it.

Not long after, Carolyn called De and told him she wanted to see me soon. More than a bit apprehensive, I took a deep breath, walked over and sat down near her. She said, "I hope you're not upset with me." I couldn't help but get teary-eyed as I said, "I just don't know where I stand with you anymore. I'm doing everything I can to make things as easy for you and De as I possibly can, and it just doesn't seem to have any effect at all." She said, "I don't know if I can explain it. I'm just depressed and I feel slighted. De never seems to want to see me anymore."

I told her that she was welcome to come over and sit with us any time she wanted and watch De sleep – "which is pretty much all he's doing because he's going end-stage." She said, "End-stage? What's that?" I said, "His body is slowly shutting down. He has very limited energy reserves left. Do you want to come over and sit through that with us? You're welcome!" She said, "No, I don't want to do that." I asked, "Then... please tell me... What DO you want? I can't figure it out, and if you don't tell me, I won't know." She said, "Kris, I don't even KNOW what I want." I nodded at that, understanding her degree of distress. She said, "I used to do everything for De, and now I can't do anything." I said, "You do it all. You love him with every ounce of your being, and he knows it. That's the most important thing you can do for him, and it always has been. The stuff I'M doing for him now is just STUFF. Please try not to feel as if you're no longer necessary just because you can't schlep stuff around. That's never been what's important between you. What's been important is what's still important."

She said, "I just want to say I apologize for making you cry. I didn't mean to upset you in any way. You've been very helpful and I appreciate all you do very much." I said, "I love you. I always have, and I always will. I understand, to the degree I can what you're going through, although I'm sure I can't understand fully what you're going through. I just want us to get through this together, you and me. I don't want to lose your friendship over this. It would kill me." She said, "Thank you for all you do. I mean that." I said, "Thank YOU for allowing me to do it."

She asked if I had told De about their friend being upset with my phone call. I said, "Yes, I did. I told him the effect it had, and he was as stunned as I was. He said, 'I heard every word you said, and I thought you handled it beautifully.'" Carolyn said, "Well, different people hear things differently." I said, "Boy, is THAT the truth! I'll be afraid to use the phone ever again, after THIS experience!"" She said, "Oh, don't feel THAT way."

I sat with her for about two hours and then, as I left for De's room, she again said, "I want to say again how sorry I am that I upset you this morning." I said, "It's over and done. Let's just forget it and get back to where we were before that, okay?" She said, "All right."

I went over to De's room. I could tell by the look on his face that he was curious as hell over how it had gone. I gave him a thumbs-up and said, "Everything is fine. We talked and she told me what's been eating her." He asked me what it was, so I told him.

Not long after, Carolyn came over for a short visit. De was sweet to her, and explained carefully that his pain, discomfort and reduced energy level were what was keeping him from wanting to visit. She understood and was real sweet in reply to him.

At nearly midnight, I decided to go home. I told De, "Since your doctor appointment has been re-scheduled, I'll plan to report to work tomorrow and then take the day off when your appointment is set." He said, "Okay, honey." I said, "So, I'll see you at noon." He said, "I'm going to make this up to you. I don't know how I'm going to do it, but I am." I said VERY sincerely, "De, forget it. You made it up to me LONG before I even started doing it. I love you. Have a good night."

The next day I got to work at about 7:50 and at 8:10 De called and said he'd had a terrible night and that he was going to have a terrible day. I asked, "Do you want me to come out?" He said, "Yes, if you can." I said, "I'll be there in 40 minutes. Sooner, if the traffic allows." He said, "Okay, honey. See you then. I appreciate it."

When I got there, De told me about how nauseated and uncomfortable he had been all night. They had given him the routine treatment for the situation, but it hadn't done anything to solve his problem.

De's male nurse described a procedure – brief but painful — that would result in swift relief. De agreed to it. As the nurse prepared the way to do the procedure I asked De if he wanted me to step out of the room while it was done. He said, "No. You've been through the rest of it; you may as well be though the worst of it."

Mercifully, the procedure lasted only brief seconds. De swore mightily, "God damn!" then quickly apologized, saying, "I almost never swear using those words. I just couldn't help it. I have been through a lot of pain, but that was the worst ever." Not long after, his system began to respond. He was comfortable again and soon enjoyed a restful nap.

On April 27th when I got to the hospital, De's first words were, "You've received a lot of compliments." I said, "I have? From whom?" He said, "From the staff here." I said, "Oh, that's nice."

The head nurse came in, checked De's lungs, and told him he had some lung involvement, and De agreed, saying, "I can feel it." She said, "You were lying down most of the weekend because of your discomfort. Try sitting up straighter today, and when you're out. That will clear your lungs." De said he would.

De and I got to the doctor's office and had to wait a good ninety minutes again. De was a bit miffed and said, "He's always overbooked. This happens every time." His strength was waning and waiting in the office always wore him out, so he hated it. Toward the end of the wait, De decided, "Let's just go. We have people waiting for us at the house, and I don't want to tie them up." I started to push him out of the office. The doctor noticed us leaving and entreated us to come back, saying it would be only five more minutes.

When we finally got into the office, the doctor again explained the liver embolization procedure. He did it in such an unattractive way this time that De decided against the procedure. The doctor said, "I don't even know what decision I'd make for MYSELF if I were in your shoes, so I honor your decision." De asked how he would die, and the doctor said, "You're dying already. Your energy is becoming less and less, as you know. You will begin to sleep more often day and night. Eventually you will slip into a coma, and you will pass away from there." De said, "That sounds good. That's the way I want it. No pain." The doctor said, "We will do absolutely everything possible to be sure you don't experience any pain." De nodded and said, "That's good." Then he looked at me, teared up, and said, "You'll take good care of Carolyn, won't you?" I said, "Absolutely, De. You have no worries there. Relax on that one."

The doctor shook our hands and said, "I'll see you again in a week or two." De said, "I hope." The doctor said, "If you can't get here, I'll come out there and visit you. I don't have privileges at your facility, but I will come out just as a friend, to visit." De said, "All right."

As we left the exam room, De said he wanted to stop by the nurse's station and thank the nurses "and say good-bye. Then I want you to take me to another office in this building, to Dr. Shaw's office, so I can tell him and the nurses there good-bye. Everyone has been so good to me." I said, "Okay," and we did that. Dr. Shaw wasn't in, so De said he'd call him later from the house to say his good-byes.

I was very upset that De had decided against the liver embolization procedure, but tried not to show it. I was nearly in tears. By the time we got to the car, I could no longer hide my emotions. I blurted out, hugging him, "Oh, De, I just love you so much!"

I helped him into the car and we drove to his bank for some cash and then to his house. He gave me $100 of the cash (against my protestations), saying, "I'm not paying you enough for all you do for me." I said, "You're paying me enough to pay my bills. That's all I need." He said, "But it's not all you deserve. Take this. Don't upset me." So I took it.

Not long after we arrived at the house, the painter Joe arrived and De showed him what needed to be done to the house. Then Tony Kirk, the mailman, stopped by. It was at this point I learned, from listening to De on the phone to Dr. Shaw, that he thought his oncologist had told him he had only a week or two left to live! My head came up in a hurry and I quickly whispered to Joe and Tony, assuring them that De was mistaken. As soon as De hung up, I told him, "De, your oncologist didn't tell you that you only had a week or two to live!" He looked at me and said, "I heard what he said." I said, "Sweetie, he didn't say that. I promise." De said, "I heard what I heard." I said, "Will you let me call him right now, so I can find out which of us is right?" De said, "Okay."

I called the oncologist from another room and told him that De had misinterpreted his comments and thought he had only two weeks to live. The doctor said, "Oh, for heaven's sake. Let me speak to him." Before I carried the phone to De, though, I asked him, "Do you KNOW how long he has left?" The response was, "I can never be sure about these things, but based on what I'm seeing, I'd say he has another 1 ½ to three months." I said, "Okay. Thanks. I don't think De wants to know how long he has, unless he asks you, but I need to know." He said, "I understand."

I carried the phone to De and the doctor straightened him out promptly, telling him that he would never be able to say when. "It depends on so many factors."

De hung up, relieved, and told the guys he was mistaken. Then he looked at me and said, "Why do I ever argue with you? You're always right. I won't argue with you again." I asked, "When have you argued with me BEFORE?" He said, "Not much, because you always end up being right!" I said, "I'm sure glad I was right about THIS!" He said, "So am I! Don't tell Carolyn what I thought I heard!" I said, "I won't, believe me!"

Greatly relieved, De's mood lightened up and he told the men a story about his role in the pilot of Steve McQueen's television show, saying that when he walked in for the audition, McQueen looked at him and said, "You're not what I have in mind for the heavy." De said, "Well, perhaps I can convince you I *am*." He threw McQueen around a bit, snarled, and McQueen quickly agreed, saying, "Okay, I was wrong! You're just right for the part!" The guys got a big kick out of their vision of gentlemanly De throwing his weight around and punching McQueen out!

When we got back to the hospital, we went to Carolyn's room and reported on the day's events. De told her he had decided against the liver embolization procedure, and she didn't argue with him over it.

I took De back to his room and he said he wanted to do something for my boss, Dan. He asked what Dan would like. I said, "I don't think he wants anything." De said, "I want to sign a photo to him, at least." I said, "Okay." He said, "Please get me a color photo." I got one out of his photo envelope and handed it to him. He signed it, 'To Dan, With deep gratitude for you know what! DeForest."" I told him Dan would love it.

I went over to see Carolyn after leaving De for the evening. She was having a lot of angst about De's decision. She wanted to know how long De would last without the procedure, and I said I didn't know for certain, but that I guessed he'd probably pass away in under three months. Then she began to grouse, "And I don't have any say in the matter as to whether or not he has the procedure." I said, "You have EVERY say in the matter. You need to tell him how you feel, if you feel differently; if you want him to undergo the procedure and be with you longer." She said, "I can't do that. I can't make that decision for him." I said, "Okay, then. That's the way it will be, then – the way he wants it." She said, "I want what he wants." I said, "You're a brave little soldier, sweetie." She said, "I'm not brave. I'm just realistic."

On Wednesday April 28th I went for a visit at noon to let De know how much Dan loved the signed photo. De was happy about that. He dictated a few letters that were intended for friends, as he didn't feel up to writing them himself and yet felt he owed them a letter. He said, "Before I do this, I want to tell you I'm not a good dictator." He did a FINE job of dictating the letters.

De was very tired. We didn't talk much. At one point, he asked me, "Do you think you're fired yet, at Warner Bros.?" I smiled, "No, De." Then I added, "Even if I was, it would be the most honorable firing ever!" De agreed, saying, "I guess it would! Fired for helping a dying friend during his last days!" I said, "THAT'S a firing that could go on a résumé!" De laughed and nodded over that statement!

On Friday April 30th I took the afternoon off at work and went out to be with De. I was telling him that I had read a book on being an executor, and it was quite involved. I told him I could loan the book to Bette, his executor, if she hadn't done anything like it before. He didn't say anything except, "No, hang onto it."

He told me he'd like to give me Power of Attorney for Health Care Decisions and also Durable Power of Attorney, so I could carry out business dealings for him if/when he became incapacitated and couldn't decide things for himself. I said I'd be happy to. I added, "You have to tell me what you want as far as health care decisions, though. Don't make me guess." He said, "Oh, it's all in the paperwork. My wishes are spelled out. You just need to be sure they're carried out." I said, "Oh, sure. Okay." He said, "Then, you'll do it?" I took his hand and said, "I'd be honored." He teared up and said, "You're a wonderful friend." I said, "Takes one to know one, sweetie."

On May 1st when Carolyn came over to see De, he advised her that he had decided to make ME the executor of his will! I about fainted! I said, "You HAVE?!" He said, "Yes. That's all we talked about yesterday." [It was news to me!] I said, "I thought I'd have power of attorney over your business affairs and your health care, but I wasn't aware I'd have any responsibilities over your will!" He said, "Well, I want you to have that, too. Do you want to do it?" I hesitated briefly and then said, "If it's what you want – but I'm a babe in the woods on this one!" He said, "I know you'll do a good job." I said, "Okay." He told me to call his attorney on Monday and let him know there would be some changes to his will and powers of attorney.

After Carolyn left, De said, "I really hate being in the hospital, even though it's a wonderful hospital with good people. I miss being at home." I discussed with De the possibility that he could return home under Hospice care for the duration of his life. He said, "I know. Carolyn was home under that for a while." I said, "No, she wasn't. She was home under Home Health Care. Hospice is strictly for terminally ill patients. She wouldn't have qualified for it." He said, "Oh." Then he said, "Carolyn would hate it if I went home. She wants me here, near her." I said, "You could still visit her, while you're able. And she could come home on three day leaves, and be there with you, watching the birds and squirrels in the back yard." De said, "Oh, you couldn't take care of TWO of us. It would kill you." I said, "It would not. She's pretty self-sufficient." He said, "She'd be directing you how to do everything. She rules the roost there." I said, "Well, I'm willing to give it a try, if you are." He said, "I don't know if I am! I know what it would entail." I said, "Okay," and let it drop.

A little while later, De confessed, "I hesitate about visiting with Carolyn anymore. Every time we visit, she looks at me as if thinking it's the last time she's going to see me. The way she looks at me makes me feel sicker than I do at any other time. It just ties me up in knots."

De was upset almost all day. He did some crying. When he cried in front of Carolyn, she consoled him with, "You cry, I cry!" He said, "Everything makes me cry now." I said, "Don't worry about it. I cry, too. So does Carolyn." De said, "How come I'm the only one I ever see crying, then?" I said, "I sneak it in when no one's looking!" Then he said, "I just can't believe this is happening to me. Whenever we talk about Hospice, about terminal illness, I can't believe we're talkin' about ME! Most of the time I seem to forget." I said, "That's good. Keep on forgetting and keep on living."

On May 2nd I was with the Kelleys twelve hours. We watched the Kentucky Derby. Carolyn was in a low mood, agitated. At one point, De said to her, "I can't seem to say or do anything right today. All we seem to be doing is upsetting each other."

Carolyn hadn't been in the room enough in recent days to see how De was fading. She didn't realize how hard it was for him to talk, visit, or carry out social amenities. Her feelings were hurt because he couldn't carry a normal conversation. I had tried previously to explain to her that De was working with fewer energy reserves than we had and that he had to save his energy to get out of bed, eat, tell me what needed doing to get his affairs in order, etc. My explanations didn't satisfy her, and she continued to act as though he was intentionally snubbing her. It drove me nearly to tears to watch, but I couldn't do anything about it. It was probably a full-blown case of denial causing her to believe he could do better than he was, if only he'd try harder.

On May 3rd, De and I were at his house, shredding unnecessary, obsolete documents and ages old receipts. He took a shower, saying that the shower at the hospital ran hot and cold, so he wanted to come home for his showers. I said, "That's fine." He said, "I can sleep at my own house like the dead, but I don't sleep well at the hospital. I'm being interrupted all the time for blood work, weigh-ins, meals." I again mentioned the possibility of Hospice. I could tell it intrigued him. He would be at home living life as he wanted to live it until he passed away. But he knew it would upset Carolyn terribly if he were to leave the hospital, so I knew he wouldn't do it. His love for her had shaped his life, and now it was shaping the manner of his death.

Friends Tony Kirk and Allen Knighton, jack of all trades, came by. De told them stories about his Army Air Corps days in New Mexico, the control tower days, and tears came to his eyes as he recounted one horrifying incident when he came close to landing one plane atop another.

That afternoon when we got back to the hospital, De and Carolyn ended up having their walks at the same time. Using their walkers, De joked, "And here they go, like a herd of turtles!" I chimed in, "It's been quite a while since you walked down the aisle together!" and De joked, "Yes, it has. We were moving quite a lot FASTER that first time!" As we rounded one corner, one of the nurses noticed De, Carolyn, HER assistant and De's two assistants; I was pulling the TPN cart along; another nurse was assisting De. She said, "Here comes the Kelley entourage! Make way!"

On May 4th I worked one half day at Warner Bros. and then began my one month personal Leave Of Absence to work for De full time. The doctors estimated he had about a month of life left. Ironically, this particular May 4th (1999) was the 31st anniversary of the day we had first met in Wenatchee at the Apple Blossom Festival Parade. I thought sadly as I drove out to the hospital, "There will be no more anniversaries like this one, with De in them." Then I prayed silently, "But thank you, God, for making it possible for me to be here now, doing what I'm doing to re-pay him for all he has done for me and for so many other people."

On May 5th we met with the attorney at De's house and had a good talk. I left and dead-headed roses while they chatted about something confidentially, and then I called David out into the garden and let him know how scared I was about taking on the executorship of De's will. David reassured me I could do a marvelous job of it, and that he would help me in any way I needed. He confessed that he had started out wary of me, but that now he knew De had made a great choice. I was happy to hear that. I told him I'd do the executorship thing if David could PROMISE me I'd do it adequately. I told him, "I DON'T want to take on any responsibilities for the Kelley estate or financial affairs that I feel I won't be able to handle magnificently." He told me I would do fine and that I'd have all the help I needed whenever I needed it to be sure the management of their affairs was handled well.

On May 7th De and I returned to his house. Merry Maids came in to clean. De's gardener Ted Naruo picked oranges and said hello to De. I was developing a bad cold and washed meticulously before helping him or serving him.

We discussed buying office chairs for the house, but realizing that De wouldn't be around much longer I talked him out of the idea, saying that what they had in their little office was just fine. "I can lift you out of them. No biggy."

De signed some photos for the Merry Maids workers. He had a one-hour nap, but no shower, as he was too weary and weak.

On the way back to the hospital, De again talked about wanting to attend a local convention in July, then stopped mid-thought as he acknowledged to himself aloud, "Gosh, I might not even be here in July." I reached over and playfully slapped his left hand, saying, "Oh, now THERE'S a positive attitude, DeForest." He paused for a long time and then said, "Tell me again about that liver embolization procedure." I again explained the procedure, and told him that it would pretty much ensure survival past the rapidly-approaching convention. He said, "***People*** wants to do an interview with me, and Bill Campbell wants me to receive a couple awards this year…" I said, "Well, if you still want to do those things, you need to get going on the liver embolization option, sweetie." He said, "I'm going to think about that again." I was jubilant!

We drove to Solley's for deli sandwiches to take back to the hospital for Carolyn and us. On the way there, De kept giving me directions, so I finally reminded him that I knew the way. He "locked" his lips with a key, motioning the way he and Carolyn did to one another whenever one told the other something they already knew.

As we were driving back toward the hospital, De mentioned how emotionally satisfying and significant hand-holding was to him. I told him I liked it, too – that it nearly always made me want to cry. Then I recounted that I would occasionally reach over and take my Dad's hand in the car when we drove places and then tell him I loved him. Then I confessed, "I have felt very much like doing that with *you* a few times, when we've been en route to some place or other, but then I thought twice about it, because you're a married man, NOT my Dad, and I thought it might be misinterpreted." De said, "Oh, don't worry about that, at all. It's all right." I said, "Good." But I never could bring myself to do it, even after he gave me the go-ahead… except in the hospital, if he'd take my hand first. Then I'd kiss his hand and tell him, "I love you, De," with tears nearly always threatening to flood my eyes.

As we were approaching the hospital, the song FOR ONCE IN MY LIFE, hauntingly rendered by Robert Goulet, came on the radio. I was LIVING every word of it, silently, very near tears, thinking about how caring for De these past weeks had been my opportunity to pay him back for all the times he had been there for me. The lyrics hit me hard. I had no idea they were affecting De as well. As I was steering the Lexus to the hospital entrance and braking to a stop, the final line ("I have someone who needs me") rang out. De reached over, patted my hand sincerely and said, "I need you, dear girl." Tears flooded my eyes and I cried out, "Oh, God, De!' I exited the door, walked to the trunk, lifted the wheelchair out, unfolded it and then pushed it to the passenger's side of the car. As I lifted De out of the car, I sniffled, "You have perfect timing, Mr. Kelley!" We were both in tears. He said, "You're terrific," and I said, "You're pretty terrific yourself, you know!" We cried all the way to Carolyn's room.

That evening, back in his room, De asked me, "Do you believe in angels?" I told him, "I most certainly do." He said, "You're an intelligent woman, so I respect that. And you know? I'm beginning to believe in them, too. So many times in our lives, when we needed that extra boost or bit of help or piece of the puzzle, it always came through." I reminded him of Mom's experiences as she approached death, and about "Ben," the angel Mom had told me about. He nodded and took it all in. He said, "I don't know if Ben is your angel or your mother's angel, but I hope he's my angel, too." I told him, "I think he is. ONE of them, at least!"

Later in the evening De began to cry, saying, "I feel so sorry for Carolyn — and for you…" I think he felt he was betraying us by dying. I told him we'd be okay. I thought I might be lying, but knew he needed to hear some sort of reassurance along those lines.

I stayed overnight at the Kelley's, shredding stuff and doing other necessary tasks. I also cried. I thought about the millions of fans who were going to get a big shock in the near future. I could feel their grief already – their shock, denial, anger…

On May 9th De asked how my cold was, and I told him, "I'm a little bit compromised, but feeling fine." We took roses and cards to Carolyn for Mother's Day, which she enjoyed, although she again reminded us both that she's NOT a mother.

De slept most of the day. This was becoming more common as the days passed. At one point, though, he said, "When I get out of here and am back at home, I'm going to have to go star polishing with you when you go." I queried, "Really?! Are you serious?" He said, "Yes." I said happily, "Okay! That would be terrific! But WHY?!" He said, "I don't know. I just feel I want to do that – see the old star again – watch how you care for it." I said, "Okay! Cool!"

I visited Carolyn many times while De slept. She sighed at one point, "Wouldn't a miracle be wonderful?" I agreed it would.

On May 10th De mentioned, "I've been thinking about all that unused Sandostatin that's in the refrigerator at home. That stuff is expensive, and I'm not going to be taking it anymore. At some point – no hurry – you should call the doctor's office and see if they can take it back and give it to someone else who needs it and can't afford it." I told him I would do that, and also mentioned that it was a very thoughtful idea. It astounded me that he could still be thinking about others at a time like this!

On May 11th, actor Bill Campbell came in for a visit and regaled De and Carolyn with some terrific and enjoyable stories. He gave De and Carolyn little rocket clocks, which they very much enjoyed. Bill and his wife Tereza became frequent visitors thereafter. De always enjoyed them.

De again asked me about the liver embolization procedure. I let him know that if he was considering it again, he'd better get a move on, as his condition was deteriorating and at some point he would no longer be considered a candidate. I called his oncologist and he said he'd call UCLA to arrange a consultation. De was in an up, positive mood after deciding on the liver embolization procedure.

On May 12th De received a large stack of autographs from a vendor on the east coast. He had agreed to sign 350, but became too weak and ill to keep the commitment. He ended up signing a bit more than half of them over the course of the next two weeks.

On May 13th a new cadre of nursing trainees walked into De's room, giving him an unintended and unexpected anxiety attack. He asked me to ask the head nurse not to allow new people into his room. He had begun to look bad and, as his appearance was important to him, he didn't want strangers looking him over and bending his ear when he had no energy to respond.

We were watching TV together. At this point, De rarely had enough energy to do anything else, other than sleep. Unexpectedly, he reached out and held my hand. I thought it was very poignant, and I picked it up and kissed it and told him, "I love you." He said, "I love you, too, Kris."

On Friday May 14th I became more involved in concentrated personal care and hygiene matters, since De was becoming too weak to do it without exhausting himself. At one point, just after mentioning how comfortable he was with me doing such intimate, personal things for him, he joked, "THIS will look good in your book!" I assured him, "No, De. This won't go into any book. It's personal and confidential. I'm a nurse now!" He said, "Hell, at this point, I don't even CARE what goes into that book. Go ahead and tell it all! You just CAN'T stay modest in a hospital environment. It's impossible..."

He continued, "It's so good to have someone you can talk to about dying. Most people can't deal with it. Everyone else acts as though there's nothing much going on; it's just another day, as far as their conversations with me go."

On Saturday May 15th I shaved De with a real razor for the first time. I told him how nervous I was about it. "This is the worst task I've ever been asked to do for you. I'm afraid I'll cut you!" He told me not to worry about it. I worried, anyway, working up a nervous sweat before I was even halfway finished. I held up the mirror to ask how I did, and he said, "Not bad." Then he took a moment to catch the few areas beneath the jaw and under the chin I had missed or been too afraid to attempt.

Sunday, May 16th would have been Deaken's 20th birthday. We did a lot of Deaken reminiscing that day. That led to reminiscences about our mothers, his and mine; then to more thoughts about his dear Carolyn. It was a poignant day.

Monday, May 17th was the date of my second attempt at shaving De with a blade. After I finished, he looked into the compact mirror and proclaimed, "Not bad. You're getting better already!" Then, out of the blue, he said, "You've come a long way since you left Washington all those years ago." I said, "I sure have — with your help and your faith in me. Thank you."

Tuesday May 18th. In the room next to De's Romaine Hoscik, a stroke patient, was staying. She hadn't been there long, but her indomitable spirit captured both De and me. She was completely paralyzed except for her left arm and leg, unable to speak, yet she exuded the type of strength and love that was impossible to ignore. She waved at everyone with her good arm, and motioned them over for a hug. She could utter happy sounds, but no actual words. De and I fell for her within days, long before we actually introduced ourselves. De would watch her from his room as she pulled herself forward in her wheelchair, heading out and down the hall. He'd proclaim, "Isn't she sum'pin'? I admire her. She is an inspiration to me."

On Wednesday, May 19th De took a shower at home. He needed my help this time, and had to sit on a medical stool halfway through. I felt a poignancy that nearly overwhelmed me. I remembered Mom getting to this stage, and knew the day was coming soon when De would be helpless.

On Thursday May 20th the attorney returned with more legal matters. When I shaved De that day, just before the attorney arrived, he raved,

"Perfect! You're hired!" I said, "I'm less nervous now about cutting your handsome face! THAT helps!"

On Saturday May 22nd we talked again about Romaine in the next room. De said, "She makes me cry, she's so courageous and sweet." He asked me to take him out into the hallway in his wheelchair. When I did that, he gave the dear woman's hand a kiss. She uttered a happy sound and laid her head on his shoulder in gratitude and love.

On Sunday May 23rd De reiterated, "You can write whatever you want when this is all over. The bio, a personal memoir." I said, "I thought we had decided that WEEKS ago. You and Carolyn keep saying, 'THIS will look good in your book!'" De laughed and said, "Oh, good. But I just want you to know, you have my permission." I said, "Thanks, De."

On Monday May 24th De tried to sign a few hundred photos for an east coast vendor. Bill Campbell visited and De told him what a terrible time he was having trying to get through them all. Bill said, "De, forget about those damned photos. Just forget them. You don't need that."

On Tuesday May 25th De was weak and very weary. He insisted on going home, though, where the showers didn't run hot and cold. I helped him with the shower, helped him dress, and then he slept. De called John later that day and told him next time he was out, he'd have John and his friend come over and they'd all eat the lobsters that I had purchased on sale a few days earlier for De. John eagerly agreed.

De had me call a doctor on the east coast for him. I dialed, established contact with the doctor, and then handed De the receiver. De thanked him for the information he had sent on his disease and asked his opinion on the liver embolization procedure. The doctor agreed that it was a perfectly viable option, if he was well enough to undergo it, and that it had the potential to extend De's life and make it of better quality. The doctor was quite familiar with the procedure and had actually recommended it to a number of patients.

On Wednesday May 26th De signed a few more vendor photos, then said he could do no more. I could tell he was losing strength rapidly, and that it was both frustrating and anxiety-provoking for him, so I felt the sooner the photos were out of there, the better. Bill Campbell came by that day, fortunately, and collected the photos, saying he would send them back to the vendor for us.

On Thursday May 27th De went out into the hallway and spoke briefly to a fellow actor he had worked with in a couple of television series episodes. The other man had suffered a stroke and was unable to speak. De told him, "You'll be out of here in no time. We'll get you some fresh squeezed orange juice from my trees next time we're out." The actor nodded a voiceless, "Yes – thank you" and looked pleased to see De.

On Sunday May 30th De and I drove to Westwood to pick up Carolyn's long-time friend, Florene. Carolyn wanted to visit with her. Before driving to the hospital to see Carolyn, the three of us stopped by the Kelley's house so Florene could get a look at it and pick up a coat Carolyn wanted her to have. Florene was using a walker, as was De, but she was in much better shape and went right in without any trouble at all, whereas I had to co-pilot De and help him up small steps, and help him into and out of his chair.

We then drove Florene to the hospital where she visited with Carolyn for a couple of hours, and then I drove her back alone. De was chagrined and mentioned several times during the next few hours and days, "Florene is in better shape than I am!" Only when comparing himself to others did he truly recognize the precariousness of his own health and physical condition. He just couldn't believe that he was failing so badly.

On Monday May 31st De mentioned my 25-pound weight loss in glowing terms. "Kris, you're losing so much weight. You look great. Can you wear any of my shirts or sweaters?" I countered, "Oh, I doubt it." He said, "Well, if you can, be sure and pick your favorites and keep them." I said, "Okay. Thanks!"

Sometime during the course of the day, De asked me if I'd ever been really angry. I told him, "Oh, yes, I have. *Murderously* angry once, with a sister, when I was a teenager." I told him when it was, and how badly it scared me afterwards to realize what I would have done had I not been thwarted by my sister's evasion tactics and by her eventual laughter, which had a calming effect on me. He said, "I've been that angry a time or two myself." I said, "It SCARED me – afterwards. I made it a policy never, EVER to allow myself to get that angry again." De said, "I did, too." He never did divulge to me what had made HIM that angry, or when it had been.

Tuesday June 1st De managed to have a shower at home, but became completely helpless during the first minute in the shower stall. He was weary to the core, and thereafter resigned to accepting total assistance. When I got him back to the hospital the head nurse noticed how wiped out he was and mandated: "No more outings, De. You're missing too much TPN. You *need* that nutrition." De sadly concurred and nodded his agreement, even though it meant he'd never go home again.

I told him during the course of that afternoon that "Please" and "Thank you" were extraneous effort and he didn't have to say them every time he asked for something; I understood his energy level and he could leave off stuff like that. He said, "Then it sounds as though I'm ordering you around." I said, "No, it doesn't. Your voice is sweet and appreciative all on its own." He said, "Okay, then," but still often took the extra effort to say please and thank you upon occasion – if he felt or imagined I was expending significant effort on his behalf – lifting him, repositioning him, taking care of his bodily functions.

Wednesday, June 2nd. In the hospital for keeps, De was weary, sad, and resigned to the inevitability of his fate, realizing the end was drawing near. We asked for thyroid function tests, but the results came back several days later indicating "negative." His thyroid was functioning fine. It was the rest of his body that was shutting down. The doctor told him there was nothing more that could be done to improve the quality of his life. This was it.

De switched to using the urine bottle at this point, rather than having me help him out of bed each time he felt the urge. He kept saying, "I don't want to hurt your back, lifting me," since he was by now too weak to assist as I got him out of bed. I told him, "It's okay – I'm strong and lifted my 150 pound Mom [when she was completely incapacitated]" – but he preferred staying in bed unless he needed to get out. I think he was really just too weary and end-stage to want to be hauled out of bed.

David Grant, one of the pastors at the hospital, brought De a couple of books, one of which he had written, hoping they might help him. De told me after David left that he didn't think he'd be able to get through them, so I told him I'd look through them for him and mark any passages I think he might like to read or may benefit from. He nodded his weary approval.

De watched TV a little and slept most of the time, so I began to go through the books – first the one the pastor himself had written, then one by Bernie Siegel. At one point as I was going through the books De asked me, "Are you becoming bored with me?" I looked up, startled, and said, "Absolutely NOT! Why do you ask that?" He says, "Ever since you got into those books, I've felt lonely. I know how Carolyn feels, now, with no one in her room." I put the book down and said, "Well, for heaven's sake. I won't look at them any more, then." He said, "Oh, I don't want you to do that. Forget I said anything." I said, "I was only looking at them to mark passages for you, and then only when you were watching TV or sleeping, I thought." He said, "It's okay." I said, "No, it isn't. I won't do it anymore." And I didn't.

Beginning that night and during ensuing afternoons and evenings, I would help De turn onto his right side. Then I would place a pillow between his bent knees and massage his back, kidney areas and buttocks, to keep the blood circulating properly and to keep those areas from aching. Occasionally I would massage his tummy gently. He would often fall asleep for fifteen or twenty minutes at a time while I was doing this. I was always glad because, in sleep, he looked completely relaxed, untroubled, and comfortable.

Thursday, June 3rd was another long day of sitting by De's bedside while he slept most of the day, gathering a bit of end-stage strength. Late that night, De asked me to try to find something on TV that he was in. I searched, but could find nothing. It broke my heart because on any other night the request could have been met with just a few clicks of the remote, but not that night. When nothing came of the search, he said, "That's okay. Forget it." I turned to massaging lotion into his feet, legs, arms and hands until he closed his eyes and got a few winks.

On Friday, June 4th, the attorney came by for the last time, and De signed his final will and testament. That evening, De again implored of me, this time with slightly different wording, "Please take as good care of Carolyn as you have of me." I took his hand and said, "I will, De... You got it, sweetie."

On Saturday, June 5th, I gave De a bed bath and shaved him. I stayed overnight, lying on the floor in a corner near the patio door. I helped him in and out of bed as necessary so he could use the portable toilet next to the bed. He was extremely weak, and sat on the commode with his head and shoulders hunched over, as though nearly asleep or unconscious. Then I would help him back into bed, lifting his legs and slowly lowering his back to the bed at the same time.

On Sunday June 6th he seemed a wee bit better, although his energy level was very low. The extensive rest, the day before, did him some good. I gave him a back and kidney massage and rubbed lotion into his skin, chest to toes.

The nurse told me De's eyes were becoming yellow from jaundice, indicating that the liver involvement was now extensive and end-stage. She confided to me, "If there is anyone else he wants to see, now is the time." I asked De if there was anyone he wanted to see that hadn't been in to see him? He said, "No." He didn't want to see anyone. He didn't have the energy any more, and I suspect his appearance upset him. He stopped looking into the compact Carolyn had given him to use. Instead, he asked me to brush his hair for him. His arms felt like lead weights to him. The phone receiver was "heavy," and he had a hard time lifting it to his ear, so I sometimes held it for him if he had to talk on it for long. Most conversations lasted less than 45 seconds.

I went to VON'S for some watermelon for him at one point and when I got back, De said he had just hung up from talking with A.C. "I had to cut him off. The receiver is just too heavy anymore. They wanted to come over for a visit, but I told them no. Not after the day we've had. I just couldn't do it." I said, "I'm sure he understands, De. It's okay."

I was beyond weary and told De I needed to take the next day off. It would be only my third day off since leaving Warner Bros. on May 4th. Fourteen-hour days had become the SHORT ones, seven days a week. My body was screaming for a break. De said it was okay to take the day off, as he was just resting and sleeping anyway. I told him, "I really don't WANT to do it, but if I don't, I might become ill and unable to help you more. I can feel my body telling me to knock off for a day." He nodded his approval but said, "I will miss you." I said, "I will miss you, too. I hate taking days off."

On Monday June 7th I called De in the evening to see how the day had gone without me. He said, "Miserable. Nothing went right, and I missed you. But you have been so sweet to me, I should give you another day off." I immediately responded, "DON'T YOU DARE!" knowing that I could no more stay away another day than fly to the moon. He loved my response and said, "OKAY, GET YOUR BUTT BACK IN HERE TOMORROW MORNING!" I promised, "I WILL!" "GOOD!" he said.

He told me his TV had gone out and no one brought a new one in until late afternoon, so he was stuck looking at four walls and there wasn't even anyone to look at. I said, "Go ahead, make me feel even guiltier!" He said, "Don't feel guilty." He asked how my day went, and I told him I rested. He said, "That's good."

He said, "I've said more to you right now than I have to anyone else all day long." I said, "I know it wears you out, so stop talking now and rest. You have a good night's sleep and I'll see you first thing in the morning. I love you, and I'm here at your house if you need me tonight." He said, "I love you, too."

On June 8th De's first words to me were short and to the point, "Missed you." I said, "I missed you, too, sweetie."

Sometime during the day I shaved him. I was aware that it might be for the last time. He nearly slept through the process. I put lotion on his legs and massaged his feet and legs. He had very little energy. We watched television or he slept. He didn't touch a bite of food, but had about four ounces of beer all day long, late in the afternoon.

The discomfort was becoming more than he wanted to deal with, so he asked a nurse for some help. She applied a medium-strength morphine patch to his chest. That took care of it nicely. The next day I asked him if the patch was too strong; he seemed groggier than he had ever been. He said, "No, I think it's fine. I can still think – I think!"

I could sense that his days were numbered, and asked him if he'd like me to stay overnight again. He said, "Oh, yes, I would." I asked the nurses to order me a rollaway bed so I wouldn't have to be on the floor and so De could see me from his bed and remember I was there in case he needed me in the middle of the night.

Sometime during the course of the evening I was surprised to hear him say, "It's finished." I wasn't looking at him at the moment he said it, but was aware that he hadn't been working on anything – a snack, a beverage, a note, so I looked up then, wondering what he meant. He looked calm, resigned, spent. It was only then that I recognized the comment as among the last words Jesus spoke before He died. I managed to choke back a sob, took his hand and kissed it. He said, "You'll take good care of Carolyn." I said, "I will." He said, "You're terrific." And tears came to him again. He didn't cry them alone.

From that moment on I began to quietly sing "Kumbaya" whenever he dozed. The words, as always, made me cry, but they also were the prayer I most needed to express.

On Wednesday June 9th De's doctor came in to evaluate him. De's chest hurt and we took him down to X-ray. Nothing ill showed, but the doctor deemed him too ill to travel to UCLA for the consultation. I called to cancel the appointment, which was scheduled for the next day. The person who took my call indicated that their office had been in contact with De's resident physician and that De's rapidly-failing condition would have disallowed him as a candidate for the procedure anyway. Needless to say, it was a heartbreaking thing to hear. I kept the comment to myself (feeling pretty certain De knew the score without my verbalizing it) and cried later that night when alone at home, knowing what it meant for De's longevity.

David Grant, the hospital chaplain, came by and chatted with him for a while. De said his father had been a minister. David asked De if he'd like him to say The Lord's Prayer for him. De said, "I would love it." As David did so, I began to cry silently, as I had been reciting it all day in silence, thinking De probably WOULDN'T want to hear it, as it made everything seem so final. Later, after David had left, De pondered aloud, "I wonder if that's the same version I learned…" I said, "It's the version I learned. Do you want me to repeat it? He said, "Yes. Please." I recited the prayer again and he agreed, "Yes, that's the same version I was taught as a boy."

There wasn't much additional discussion that day. That night, I put my bed right next to De's, as he was too weak and disoriented to find and push the call button for the nurse. I lay down on my much-lower bed with my arm and hand held upward and extended onto his bed, so he could grasp it and squeeze it if he needed assistance.

A few times during the night he just reached over to hold my hand. I squeezed his hand lightly and ran my fingers along the back of his hand, as if rubbing lotion onto them. He always relished that type of massage on the back of his hands.

At about 4 a.m., he grabbed my hand and said he had to get up to use the bedside commode. I got up and helped him onto it, but he became so limp and weak that I had to completely lift him back into bed afterwards. I told the nurse about that, and she came in and checked his legs, finding them mottled. She said, "No more getting out of bed, De. You have to stay in bed from now on. I'll put a chuck [disposable pad] under you." De nodded and fell asleep.

His body was shutting down. He was dying. When he again awoke he wanted to get out of bed again, for the same reason, but I told him not to worry about a thing; I would take care of it. He implored, "Oh, please, Kris. Help me get up." I couldn't pacify him – he kept asking – so I finally decided that if he was willing to risk death to preserve his dignity, I'd assist him. So I quickly called to the nurse to help me get him up. We helped him reach his destination and the nurse left. IMMEDIATELY, De collapsed forward into my arms and torso. I called for the nurse; called again. "This is an EMERGENCY, nurse! Get in here!"

The nurse came in, checked him and said, "Oh, my God! He's passed [away]!" She started to call out to him and shake and pound on him a little, looking for some response. He took a few no-breath breaths, and she again said, "He's passed." She literally lifted him and then threw him onto the bed, calling out an emergency code. Then she started to call to De and do a little CPR pumping on his chest. I said, "I'm his medical power of attorney. He has a DNR ("Do Not Resuscitate" order)."

By now half a dozen nurses and technicians had responded to the code call, and the nurse said, "Check his code, check his code." Someone studied De's records at the nursing station while the nurse continued to try to call De back from wherever he was. They found that he had a limited code, and were trying to decide what to do; MORE intervention might bring him back, but less might allow him to die.

I was shuttled out into the hall to make room for more emergency personnel. One of the nurses came out to the lobby where I was sitting and told me, "This is a grave situation. It's very touch and go. It can go either way. Are you prepared?" I said, "Yes," but I felt numb and queasy. I second-guessed myself as to whether I should have helped him out of bed when he insisted; then decided I had done the right thing, as I couldn't deny his wishes; that's why I was there.

The supervisor for the crisis was looking at De's book and saying, "I wish I knew what he wanted." I went over to him and introduced myself, saying, "I have his Power of Attorney for health care decisions." The man looked at me and said, "What do you want to do?" I said, "He said to let him go if there's no reasonable expectation of his return to a quality of life." The man said, "As you know, his quality of life right now is just awful, and will only get worse." I said, "Then let's just stand by and see what happens. If he comes around naturally, okay. If he doesn't, let him go."

It was a terrible thing I was hearing myself say, but it was what De wanted, and I felt inextricably bound by it. I didn't want to betray his trust in me.

It was a long time, probably only three or four minutes, an eternity, as we waited to see what would happen. The nurse continued to speak to him: "Mr. Kelley, can you hear me? Come on back, De. Come on back. Where are you? Can you find your way back?"

Suddenly – music to my ears and everyone else's — I heard De's voice, loud and clear, even as far away as I was in the lobby. He asked, "Kris? Where's Kris?!" The nurses motioned me in and I flew to his side and grabbed his hand. I said, "I'm right here, sweetie." He asked me, "What happened?" I said, "You passed out — WAAAY out!" The nurse reported to all in attendance, "He's responding! He's talking with Kris!"

His voice was very quiet and hoarse again, suddenly, and so I put my ear close to his face. He said, "Don't get too close to me, Kris." I said, "Honey, what you got, I can't catch!" He nodded, closed his eyes, and said, "All right, then."

His blood pressure was so low all the rest of the day that he slept most of the last day away. Late in the afternoon he rebounded a bit and asked to sit up, so the head nurse elevated his head some. I asked if he was thirsty and if he'd like some ice chips, and he said he would. I gave him some and put Chap Stick on his lips. All TPN, foods and medications were discontinued, except for the morphine patch.

I again slept by his bed the night before he died. He slept quite soundly until about 2 a.m. and then grasped my hand and started trying to sit up. I had learned my lesson, and quickly sat up myself and told him he couldn't sit up. He said, "I have to get up. We have to go." I asked, "Go where?" He answered, "We have to go home, Kris." Sadly, I said, "De, you can't go home now – not until you get to feeling better." He still tried to sit up, so I said, "If I sit you up, will you promise not to try and get out of bed?" He said, "I will, I promise." So I helped him to a sitting position and allowed his legs and feet to go over the side onto my bed. I sat in my bed and held his body forward so he could sit without effort.

Subsequently, he seemed to go into a flashback. His voice was strong and sounded very young. He said, "I have to find a bug." I queried, "A bug?" He said, "Yes, a bug." I asked, "You mean, like a butterfly?" He said, "Yes, but an ant would work just as well." I finally discerned he might be having a flashback and asked him, "Is this for a science project?" He confirmed that it was. I said, "Well, De, I don't think you're going to find any bugs in HERE. This is a very clean place!"

That seemed to snap him out of it. He looked at me, a portrait of embarrassment, thinking I might be considering him "over the edge" now! I smiled and said, "Don't worry about it. It happens a lot when people are sick. You haven't gone nuts." He nodded, relieved that I hadn't been surprised by what he'd said.

He said he was thirsty and I made him promise to sit there while I ran out to get him some ice chips. He promised me he wouldn't move, so I ran out — scaring the nurse on duty half to death. I told her, "Not to worry – he just wants ice chips, but he's sitting on the side of the bed with his feet on MY bed, and I want to get back to him quickly." Then I told her, "He was working on a Science Project a minute ago, wanting to find a bug." That piqued her interest and we went back inside together.

I gave him the ice chips and the nurse interviewed him. "Hi, De." "Hi." "Do you know who I am?" "Yes." "Who am I?" De stated her name. "Do you know where you are?" "Yes." "Where are you?" "I'm in the hospital." "Do you know you're not supposed to be sitting up?" "Yes, I know that." "Are you going to lie down now so you don't make me mad at you?" "Yes," he said, and obligingly leaned back against the pillow.

That is the last anecdote I can really tell about De. He slept the rest of the night, but by morning he was just this side of comatose. I could tell he didn't have long to live, but truly DIDN'T think he would pass away that day.

THE ONLY THINGS CERTAIN ARE DEATH… AND TAXES

I had to go to De's bank first thing Friday morning, June 11th, to get his estimated tax checks mailed to the IRS that day, but I dreaded having to leave him, as I didn't know if he'd be alive when I got back. A nurse assured me that if he passed away while I was out, it might well be because he wanted to: "Often it's easier to let go when there is no one else in the room. A loved one's presence can sometimes hold them here when they'd prefer to go." I said, "Okay," then went back into the room and told De where I was going.

"De, I have to go to your bank and to the post office to get your estimated taxes out. Is that okay?"

He nodded yes.

"Will you be okay while I'm gone? Can I leave you for a little while?"

He nodded yes.

I then asked, "Shall I stay here with you a while longer instead?"

He nodded an emphatic no, and then whispered almost inaudibly, "I can't talk."

I said, "Okay, then. I'll be back as soon as I can. You just rest; a nurse will be with you all the time, so don't worry."

He nodded and shut his eyes, so I'd go.

I said, "I love you. I'll be back soon."

I drove to the bank, where I got two checks for estimated tax payments. I drove from there to the post office and mailed the checks, then drove back to the hospital.

I had no more than started down the long hallway to De's room when the nurse I had spoken to earlier came rushing out and said, "Oh, Kris, thank God you're here. I think he's waiting for you. Hurry." I started to run toward his room. "Don't run," she cautioned me. "Don't run." I ran anyway.

When I got into the room at close to 11 A.M., I spotted Carolyn and Chaplain David Grant at De's bedside. Carolyn said, "Oh, thank God, you're back!" I set my stuff down and took a seat next to Carolyn and David, close to De's head. I took Carolyn's right hand (she had De's hand in her left hand) and David's right hand.

De was lying on his left side. I had read that hearing is the last sense to go and that comatose people can hear, so I told him, "Hi, sweetie. I'm back.

I got your taxes all taken care of. Everything is taken care of and WILL be taken care of, De, so you can relax. We'll take good care of Carolyn, so don't worry about a thing."

Carolyn said she'd had about 25 minutes alone with him and had said all she wanted to say to him. "I told him he could go; I told him I love him."

The chaplain asked Carolyn to recount some of their life and times together as we waited and the minutes ticked by, so Carolyn told a few cute stories. Occasionally she would laugh or giggle at the remembrance. Each time she did, I would look over at De. I could see the pulse in his neck becoming less and less pronounced and the breaths coming less frequently. I prayed that he was hearing her laughter and feeling that she would be okay, if she was okay at a time like this.

As the time drew very near, I told David, "De loved hearing the Lord's Prayer the other day. I even repeated it to him again later that same day." David said, "Oh, really? Shall I offer it again?" I said, "I think so." Carolyn said, "That would be nice." So David stood and placed his hand on De's forehead and recited the Lord's Prayer and then the 23rd Psalm, finishing with Numbers 6:24. It was poignant, almost beyond endurance. With tears threatening to flood my eyes, I said, "Go with God, De, whenever you feel ready. It's okay, sweetie."

I believe these were the last words De ever heard. He slipped away at 12:15 P.M. June 11th Pacific Daylight Time — peacefully, never regaining consciousness.

****

Epilogue

The Long Year After – Learning How To Live Again

"When he shall die

Take him and cut him out in little stars
And he will make the face of heaven so fine
That all the world will be in love with night
And pay no worship to the garish sun."
-Kris Smith, speaking at De's memorial service
at Paramount, June 22, 1999,
quoting lines from William Shakespeare's
Romeo and Juliet

The year that followed De's death began as a time of unmitigated turmoil for me. Because I was wrapped up in continuous care-giving to Carolyn for an additional seven months, I denied myself the right to truly grieve. I knew Carolyn had the greater "right" to grief and that I should remain strong for her and just "gut" my way through.

As any of you know who have tried it, "gutting" one's way through grief is counterproductive. I became angry that I was denied the ability to gather with other fans who were experiencing my loss in a way *I*, too, wanted to be feeling it. I would be able to CRY with them without feeling any embarrassment or any degree of comparison.

Carolyn seemed to be in a kind of competition with me, as to who was most entitled to miss De. She had lived with him for nearly 55 years; I had died with him for "only" three months. The stakes seemed very high to her for a while. I HAD to lose! So I lost – over and over again. And this is how I foolishly allowed *my* grief to remain tightly bottled.

Carolyn was angry, as well. She felt she had been denied De's last months of life; that I had taken over to provide the care he needed. She became insecure and wondered whether more was going on than I was reporting. Against all assurances that my care giving had been platonic and honorable, she fretted that De had perhaps transferred his affection to me in those final days. It was excruciating for me to undergo these "inquisitions," repeated almost daily because her failing short-term memory denied her the ability to retain what we shared in conversation from day to day.

This issue comes up in many instances where a loved one is dying. It is not at all uncommon for a surviving spouse to convert his or her pervasive sadness regarding the loss into vitriolic anger or distrust toward the care-giver or other loved ones who assisted during the final days and hours. It will half-kill you when it happens, especially if you love the survivor as much as you loved the one who perished, as in this case.

Because I was also a fan of De's, the issue of trust probably seemed much more valid to Carolyn than it might have otherwise. I couldn't get across to her that it had been years since I regarded De as anyone other than a good friend or (fancifully) "my California Pop." That's part of the reason I attended the later conventions featuring De: I could re-capture, albeit briefly by watching the fan reaction to him, what it had been like when I first became "DE-lighted, DE-mented, DE-voted." To my mind, by the time I was called in to assist De, my favorite actor "DeForest Kelley" and my friend "De" were two different people. And I believe De felt the same way about me – I wasn't a fan, I was a good friend – someone he could trust to behave! Had that not been the case, I never would have been called in.

Take heart and try to be patient if a similar period of distrust or attack happens to you during a care-giving situation with a friend, relative or other loved one. With any luck at all, eventually the pendulum will swing back and the anger will dissipate to a point where the survivor can acknowledge the loss without placing blame onto someone else. The day THOSE clouds part is a happy, happy day. Sometimes it takes a period of actual physical separation for this to occur, as it did with Carolyn and me; in other cases, time or introspection alone salves the wound and allows healing to occur.

It is also common for the dying to gather around them only those people with whom they feel COMFORTABLE while undergoing the deterioration of their bodies and abilities. They may separate themselves from loved ones who are enormously dear to them because of reactions or anxious glances that remind them too strongly or too poignantly of their declining condition, causing anxiety and distress. In other cases, they may separate themselves from loved ones who seem unable to accept their slide toward death and who refuse to speak with them about it when they want to address it. It is important to try NOT to feel "abandoned" or "betrayed" if you are not among the ones "chosen" to sit at a bedside. At the end of your own life, if in a similar situation, you will adequately understand this. The wishes of the dying should be honored; it's their last chance on earth to get what they feel is right for them. Dying people have nearly all the rights, in my book.

Caregivers need to understand THEIR few basic rights, too. Your bodies, minds, lives and needs are important. When your body and spirit tell you to take a day off, do it! Regard your body's messages as direct orders, not as suggestions to be considered if you can manage to find some time. You will otherwise be taking a victim to a rescue – and that places additional risk on a situation that is already on quaky ground. Ask for help when you need it. If your own family or friends cannot provide it, an agency can. If funds are low or non-existent, check with a church or synagogue (your own or a friend's). Loving, concerned, compassionate volunteers can be found there. Don't feel you are "stuck" in a hopeless situation. You aren't.

Check your bookstore or library for excellent references on care giving. Locally, you can join a caregivers support group and exchange strategies, hopes, fears and tears without worrying about consequences. The participants in these groups are all going through a similar ordeal; they all understand. You can get all the hugs you need there.

Following De's death, I would find myself wanting– in the worst way— to pick up a phone or take a drive and FIND HIM, speak with him again. That's probably the most frustrating part of being left behind. A person you trust and love beyond expression has vanished – and it seems IMPOSSIBLE. Poet Merritt Malloy's line, paraphrased, comes back to me, "How could you just go and leave me like that — here in a world full of strangers?"

Seek out others who have had a loss similar to yours. Believe me, they are everywhere. Just open your mouth and express yourself, and you will find them. You can join a bereavement group, if that idea resonates with you.

Another way works for me, as well. Since I'm not gregarious, and sadness and loss are things I usually try to keep hidden from others, I write letters to De frequently. I wrote him and Carolyn all the time while he was alive, and I write him occasionally still. (I wrote him a lot during the course of writing this book!) Write and tell the one you're missing what you're feeling. Let him or her know what has been happening with you; let them know of the times you most wanted them with you – or the times when you felt their presence (spirit) with you as you leaped a new hurdle or experienced a particular joy or success. They ARE with you – as near as your heart. That's why you continue to feel the way you do about them. Your soul can connect with theirs. Allow it to do that. Tell them hello and ask God to allow their spirit to reach you regularly to renew the connection you have with each other. As the old adage says, "To live in hearts we leave behind is not to die."

I find that community involvement and activity helps me to "give a little more of De" back to the world. His compassion and concern for others was legendary – HE was one of the greatest caregivers of all time! I rescued an abandoned poodle recently and named her Angel. Angel is a goodwill ambassador to all humankind, with the personality of a Golden Retriever, but perkier. She and I take trips to hospitals on a regular basis to give smiles and a few hours of our time to let shut-ins know that they are not forgotten and that someone cares about them other than their families. You can devise something that resonates within you as a "De-thing" and do it. Whatever your heart wants to do, take a few minutes and do it. Write a letter, tell someone what they mean to you, and do it without expectation. Giving is truly its own reward.

"Prayer Should Be Our First Resource, Not Our Last Resort"

— bumper sticker

Early one morning two or three days after De passed away, emotionally distraught and exhausted beyond belief, having nowhere to turn even for a hug, I knelt beside my bed and prayed (an exceedingly rare occurrence at that point in my spiritual evolution).

Tearfully, I choked, "I don't know which of you can help me with this – God or De – but I hope one of you will give me a sign – a recognizable sign of some kind – that De is all right now... That he's happy and comfortable. I would just like to know. It would mean the world to me. Thank You. In Jesus' name, amen." I stood up and got dressed, still crying but beginning to recover emotionally after having "spilled my guts to God."

Less than fifteen minutes later, I was driving west through the Sherman Oaks area to be with Carolyn again at the hospital. I had recovered emotionally and had forgotten completely about the earlier prayer. Suddenly, over the freeway directly ahead of me, thirty feet in the air, with a long string attached, floated A YELLOW BALLOON! A yellow balloon, after all the hassle and struggle I'd had trying to get De's poem by that name faxed over to Shatner a few weeks earlier! This was a recognizable sign, identifiable DIRECTLY and SPECIFICALLY to De. Only an Enterprise fly-by could have been more convincing!

The hair on the back of my neck stood up and I thrust my thumb to the heavens, again in tears. "AWRIGHT!" I yelled. I had to pull off the freeway briefly to pray, "Thank You, Jesus" — and to drown in a flood of relieved tears.

So... where from here? Those of us who love De can extend ourselves to others, De-fashion, if it's within our personalities and characters to reach out and touch others in ways that heal. If that path doesn't resonate within us, surely it's enough just to remember the Physician's Oath: "Do no harm."

ABOUT THE AUTHOR

Author Kristine Smith has been a fan of DeForest Kelley for three and a half decades. She has also meandered among his fans at numerous conventions and at individual and collective ceremonies honoring him and STAR TREK. She writes: "I have witnessed first-hand the enormous love and the respect people have for De. And I continue to see, almost daily, how people have remained enchanted with him, even following his passing in 1999. Millions of people were immediately and acutely affected by his unanticipated death. Tens of thousands of them expressed outright anguish – feelings akin to losing one's best friend or a family member. A single, cursory visit to just one of numerous DeForest Kelley websites (national and international) proves the veracity of this declaration.

"Categorically and undeniably, De became — and will endure as — one of the most-loved and best-remembered personalities in the world. His Dr. McCoy is at the heart of STAR TREK's mythology, and TREK is a tenacious mythology which will last, in all likelihood, until the day humans forget how to aspire to a higher standard for themselves and their progeny.

"De was my friend, but he was also my hero — one of very few heroes whose durability was sorely tested, yet found to be utterly reliable. I wrote this book to show how deeply De influenced my life – and to remind you, his fans and friends, how seamlessly and comfortably he fit into yours.

"I undertook this endeavor for the millions of fans who never had the pleasure of meeting De 'up close and personal.' My sincerest goal for this book is that it will validate every intuition you ever had about DeForest Kelley being one of Hollywood's 'good guys.'"

Smith is a member of First Presbyterian Chruch of Hollywood. She is owned by three cats and is (seasonally) a foster "mom" to myriad other creatures (furred, feathered and finned) who somehow manage to find their way to her door. Smith has been an animal welfare advocate and humane education staff worker and executive director, a wild and domestic animal caretaker, an animal rescue worker, a construction laborer, and the office manager of a continuing education school. Presently she is a freelance executive secretary working at major motion picture and television studios.

"THANK YOU, DEAR READER, FOR BEING THERE!

Thank you for allowing me to massage your memories
-- and your heart --
with these very personal recollections of DeForest Kelley –
a man so many millions of people will always love beyond words."
-- Kris Smith --

Printed in the United States
118629LV00012B/235/A

9 780759 653085